# The Weaving of Words
## Approaches to Classical Arabic Prose

# BEIRUTER TEXTE UND STUDIEN

HERAUSGEGEBEN VOM
ORIENT-INSTITUT BEIRUT

BAND 112

# The Weaving of Words
# Approaches to Classical Arabic Prose

Edited by

Lale Behzadi
Vahid Behmardi

BEIRUT 2009

---

ERGON VERLAG WÜRZBURG
IN KOMMISSION

Umschlaggestaltung: Taline Yozgatian
Druckbetreuung: Sara Binay

Coverbild unter Verwendung von:
Unvollständiges Lehrgedicht über Rhetorik (incomplete poem on rhetoric)
8° Cod. Ms. arab. 59 (unidentified manuscript, approximately 16. century, incomplete: 1056 verses)
Verzeichnis der Handschriften im Preussischen Staate Hannover/Göttingen, hrsg. v. Wilhelm Mayer, Berlin: Verlag von A. Bath 1893.
Mit freundlicher Genehmigung der Staats- und Universitätsbibliothek Göttingen.

Bibliografische Information der Deutschen Nationalbibliothek
Die Deutsche Nationalbibliothek verzeichnet diese Publikation in der Deutschen Nationalbibliografie; detaillierte bibliografische Daten sind im Internet über http://dnb.d-nb.de abrufbar.

Bibliographic information published by the Deutsche Nationalbibliothek
The Deutsche Nationalbibliothek lists this publication in the Deutsche Nationalbibliografie; detailed bibliographic data are available in the Internet at http://dnb.d-nb.de.

ISBN 978-3-89913-678-4
ISSN 0067-4931

 Gedruckt mit Unterstützung des Orient-Instituts Beirut, gegründet von der Deutschen Morgenländischen Gesellschaft, aus Mitteln des Bundesministeriums für Bildung und Forschung.

Ergon-Verlag GmbH
Keesburgstr. 11, D-97074 Würzburg

Druck: PBtisk, Pribram
Gedruckt auf alterungsbeständigem Papier

*Table of Contents*

# Introduction

Since the beginning of literature and the start of literary analysis, there has been an ongoing debate about what literature is and how we can distinguish literature from other texts. Uttering words or writing down a text immediately causes a change in meaning by initiating a process of interaction with the (implied) receiver of the communication and thus creating something new and variable. In all cultures and at all times we can find attempts to use language as an instrument and to develop certain skills in this field. The "literariness" of texts, however, is defined by a set of ideas and concepts that differ from one time to another and from one culture to another.[1]

In this volume, we have assembled articles about artistically produced language, i.e. products that are purposefully meant to shape language in order to achieve a specific aim. In these collections, the art of writing manifests itself through linguistic refinement, rhetorical skills, compositional strategies, and political circumstances. Since these articles focus on classical Arabic literature, the texts are distinguished by two characteristics that influence our way of reading: they are Arabic texts and they are from a former period of history, i.e. the first centuries after the *hijra* ($2^{nd}/8^{th}$ until the end of $4^{th}/10^{th}$ century).

There are many ways of reading historical literature. It is a literature which has been written in another time and therefore reveals information about a particular period in history. It sometimes claims to report about a certain situation and reveals information between the lines and pages. Historical literature tells stories and recounts events from a bygone time. The text still exists but the circumstances under which it evolved are no longer existent and often hard to reestablish.

There are similarly many ways to read Arabic literature. It is a literature of a specific geographical and cultural area. It is written in Arabic, a fact which causes numerous further associations such as: the divine role of Arabic as the language of the final revelation for Muslims, Arabic as the language of the Bedouin poetry, the assumption that Arabic is especially eligible for rhetorical and poetical aesthetic perfection, and various statements and stereotypes that exist in other cultures, too, from within and are marked on it from without.

Since readers and audiences vary, social conditions change, every epoch finds a new approach to former texts. Experts in classical Arabic literature, who read

---

1 Searle pointed to the fact that there are no features that are common to all literary works, hence it is up to the reader to decide whether he calls a text a literary text or not (whereas it is up to the author to decide whether something is fiction or not). See John R. Searle, *Expression and Meaning. Studies in the Theory of Speech Acts*, Cambridge: University Press 1979, chapter 3, here quoting from the translated version *Ausdruck und Bedeutung: Untersuchungen zur Sprechakttheorie*, übers. V. Andreas Kemmerling $1990^3$, Kapitel 3, 81f.

Arabic, who know the historical background and think about mechanisms of literature, have an exciting and challenging task: they try to do the texts justice by working them up for an interested audience without closing the hermeneutic door. It remains open for every single reader, dead ends and detours included.

More importantly, our authors show the diverse ways of looking at a text, reading and understanding it. They put their knowledge about poetics, criticism, poetry, history and Arabic language at our disposal. This rich variety of tools enables us to follow the unexpected turns a story can take, the contrasting directions of statements given in a plot and the subtle meanings hidden in a text or in fragments of text. Where is that supposed to get us? First, it is entertaining, the foremost reason to read literature. It keeps our brain busy with a lot of information and emotions. It enables us to do something that we normally are denied: to know what others think (or what they want us to believe they think), the classical authors as well as their literary personnel. And last but not least we learn – to a certain extent – how the producers of literature and literary pieces worked in those days, the means and instruments the writers used, the turns and tricks their texts take (with their knowledge or without), how they create illusion and at the same time reality, whatever the difference might be.[2]

While looking at the textual setup, we learn furthermore how literary strategies and language shaping methods form texts alongside the primary literary sources. We also learn how the knowledge and the skills concerning language help in introducing aesthetic categories in fields where those categories are not expected. Our authors show how this knowledge became a powerful apparatus, which reveals a lot more than it actually says in the fabric of the words. The task here is not merely to discover something to be literature, to decipher the hidden meaning and to unfold the historical procedure of writing; rather the whole richness of hermeneutic and semiotic work is spread out in front of the interested reader in order to let him take part in the never-ending process of understanding a construction that is rooted in another brain and in a distant and different time.

Arabic literature in the first Islamic centuries consists of a number of very different manifestations and serves very different purposes. It includes the rich poetical heritage and the oral tradition as well as the Qur'anic revelation, the court conversation and entertaining education as well as the collection of valuable information and scholarly dispute. The presentation of anecdotes required performing and compositional skills that were also necessary in political contexts. To master rhetoric refinement not only secured intellectual praise but established significant influence on matters of importance – to be heard and noticed (if consulting a higher authority) and to gain respect amongst equals and subjects (the authority itself).

---

2 A valuable collection of articles on the relationship between the "real", the "fictive" and the "imaginative" in Arabic literature is given in *Story-telling in the framework of non-fictional Arabic literature*, ed. Stefan Leder, Wiesbaden: Harrassowitz 1998.

In all these fields we find authors of literary pieces – be it a story, an anecdote, a critical remark, a compilation, a verdict or a speech – who were aware of the potential impact of their composition. The lyrical subject proves to be an active designer of its fortune; at the same time, it is bound to a network of relations that are situated inside and outside the text. The following contributions try to access these complex pictures of perception; they consider the cultural and historical peculiarities without letting them overshadow the theoretical potential of the texts. In the end, what matters is the fact that along with every single text or fragment of text we witness a "production", a "staging", and that it is worth looking closer at this act of presentation and self-interpretation while being aware that text analysis means walking on slippery grounds.[3]

We are glad and grateful to have found experts in the field who were willing and interested in exploring the nature of very different texts with various theoretical equipment and in considering the tools then used by the authors of the investigated texts. It is our aim as contributors and editors to demonstrate both the craft of classical Arabic writing and the possibilities of getting access to it, thus promoting an art that affected and still affects many aspects of human life.

We would like to thank both Prof. Dr. Stefan Leder, the current director of the Orient-Institut Beirut, and Prof. Dr. Manfred Kropp, director in Beirut from 1999 to 2007, for accepting this book in the series *Beiruter Texte und Studien*. This publication is, after surviving difficult times in Beirut, also the result of a fruitful cooperation between the Orient-Institut Beirut and the Lebanese American University in Beirut.

Our sincere gratitude goes to Dr. Sara Binay who has guaranteed the production of this book as Publication Manager of the Orient-Institut, and, last but not least, to Ms. Lana Shehadeh, our English editor, for her patience and support.

Lale Behzadi
Vahid Behmardi

Göttingen/Beirut
September 2008

[3] The „staging" – Wolfgang Iser calls it „Inszenierung" – would be the never-ending human attempt to come to himself; it is the institution of human self-interpretation. Thus, by creating *simulacra* we can catch a glimpse of the endless number of possibilities, temporarily escaping the feeling of powerlessness. See Wolfgang Iser, *Das Fiktive und das Imaginäre. Perspektiven literarischer Anthropologie*, Frankfurt/M.: Suhrkamp 1993, 508-515.

# Ibn al-Muqaffaᶜ's *Kalīla wa-Dimna* and Boccaccio's *On Poetry*: A Hybrid Poetics and Avant-garde Hermeneutics

*Marianne Marroum (Lebanese American University)*

> Perhaps as you read, you will wonder to see the meaning that was lately hidden under a rough shell brought forth now into light…
> Giovanni Boccaccio[1]

> Interpretation is not the art of construing but the art of constructing. Interpreters do not decode poems: they make them.
> Stanley Fish[2]

Horace's *Ars Poetica* (19 BC), ᶜAbdullāh Ibn al-Muqaffaᶜ's *Kalīla wa-Dimna* (750/132), and Boccaccio's *On Poetry: Being the Preface and Fourteenth and Fifteenth Books of Boccaccio's Genealogia Deorum Gentilium* (1350-62/750-763) are the object of this study in comparative poetics. It may come as a surprise to some to juxtapose *Kalīla wa-Dimna* to works written at disparate times, in different languages, for different purposes by authors belonging to divergent cultures. It might even seem problematic to establish similarities between the works at hand as one may immediately think of dissimilarities rather than a correspondence between them, bringing to mind a clash of cultures rather than a confluence. Some may also question the validity and the meaningfulness of such a comparative endeavor. To that query, one may respond that such a comparison will lead to a further understanding of some crucial aspects of critical thought in their intricate convolutions, diachronically and synchronically, and to an understanding and valorization of literature, not only as a discipline but also as a tool of cross-cultural encounter.

Who are the authors whose work is under study, and what kind of literature did they produce? All three of Horace, Ibn al-Muqaffaᶜ and Boccaccio occupy a central position in the annals of world literature. Horace (Quintus, Horatius Flaccus) (65-68 B.C.) is a Roman poet who wrote in Latin. His main works are

1 Giovanni Boccaccio, *Boccaccio on Poetry: Being the Preface and the Fourteenth and Fifteenth Books of Boccaccio's Genealogia Deorum Gentilium* [1350-62]. Charles S. Osgood, trans., Indianapolis and New York: The Bobbs-Merril Company, inc. 1956, 16. All quotations hereafter are from Osgood's translation.

2 Stanley Fish, *Is There a Text in this Class? The Authority of Interpretive Communities*, Cambridge: Harvard University Press, 1980, 327.

the *Satires* (*Sermones*), the *Odes*, the *Epistles* and *The Art of Poetry (Ars Poetica).* The eighteen satires, published early in the poet's career, are written in hexameter verse. Enlivened by anecdote, dialogue and fable, they thematize human folly, especially the insatiable desire for wealth. His *Odes*, the works of his middle period, written in old Greek lyric meter, imitate those of the Greek poets Alcaeus and Sappho. They contain comments on wise conduct. They deal with the brevity and uncertainty of life and put forth a hedonistic philosophy. Love songs and songs in praise of wine and the gods are also prominent among his *Odes*. In his later life, he wrote twenty two *Epistles* or Letters in verse. His latest work, *The Art of Poetry (Ars Poetica)*, is a collection of statements on poetry and the training of the poet addressed to a young friend interested in producing tragedies.[3]

Ibn al-Muqaffaᶜ[4] is an author of Persian origin. He was born in Furizabad in the year 102/720 of a noble Iranian family and was murdered in 139/736 at the age of 36. He was educated in Middle Persian as well as in Arabic. His surviving work in Arabic include *Adab al-Ṣaghīr* (*The Lesser Book of Conduct*) to distinguish it from *Adab al-Kābīr* (*The Comprehensive Book of the Rules of Conduct*). The first, of disputed attribution to him, is a collection of aphorisms. It is a book of advice for the growing class of gentry laying the principles of good conduct and illustrating its application. It is partly culled from his *Kalīla wa-Dimna.* As to *Adab al-Kabīr*, it offers practical advice to princes, to their courtiers and to men of fashion who aspire to a career in government. His third work, *Risālat al-Ṣaḥāba*, (*Epistle on Caliphal Companions*) is an administrative document and a treatise on political and social issues in a clearly identifiable historical context, addressed to the second ᶜAbbasid Caliph Abū Jaᶜfar al-Manṣūr.

Ibn al-Muqaffaᶜ was also known as a translator. Employed as a secretary by the Arabic rulers of South East Asia, he dedicated himself to the translation of Pahlavi works such as *Khudāynāma* (*Book of Kings*), *Āʾīn Nāma* (*The Book of Proper Conduct*), *Kitāb Mazdak* (The *Book of Mazdak*), *Kitāb al-Tāj* (*The Book of the Crown*), *Letter of Tansar* and *Siyar Mulūk al-ᶜAjam* (*The Histories of the Persian Kings*). His most famous translation, one that singled him out as a brilliant translator, was *Kalīla wa-Dimna.* His original text was lost as were many of his other translations. The earliest manuscript available, that of Aya Sofia of the 7th/13th century, reproduced by the The ᶜAzzām edition, and the Syrian of the 8th/14th century, fol-

---

3 "Horace," in: *The Reader's Companion to World Literature*, second ed., Calvin S. Brown, ed., New York: A Mentor Book 1984, 249-252.

4 See J.D. Latham, "Ibn al-Muqaffaᶜ and early Abbasid Prose," in: *ᶜAbbasid Belles-Lettres*, Julia Ashtiany, T.M. Johnstone, J.D. Latham, R.B. Serjeant and G. Rex Smith, eds., New York: Cambridge University Press, 1990, 48-77; F. Gabrieli, "Ibn al-Mukaffaᶜ," in: *Encyclopedia of Islam*, new ed., vol. 3, Leiden: Brill 1971, 883-885; C. Brockelmann, "Kalila wa-Dimna," in: *Encyclopedia of Islam*, new ed., vol. 4, Leiden: Brill 1978; Michael Cooperson, "Ibn al-Mukaffaᶜ," in *Dictionary of Literary Biography: Arabic Literary Culture*, 500-925, vol. 311 Los Angeles: University of California. Gale 2005, 150-163. 24 August 2005 <http://galenet.galegroup.com>

lowed by Cheikho, vary in regard to form and substance, that there is perhaps not a single page where one may be certain of finding the original version in its entirety.[5]

*Kalīla wa-Dimna* has been hailed as one of the masterpieces of Arabic literature. Its stories originated in India from the Sanskrit classics *Pañcatantra* and *Mahābhārāta*. The book is also known as the *Fables of Bīdpāi* (or *Baydabā*) after a legendary Indian sage. Each fable is narrated by Bidpai or Baydabā at the request of his king Dabishlīm. The book is a mirror for princes, intended to instruct them in the laws of polity.[6] From Sanskrit, the fables were rendered into Pahlavi, a Middle Iranian language, at the request of the Sasanian king Khusraw Anūshirwān by his physician Burzūya. About two hundred years later, Ibn al-Muqaffaᶜ translated Burzūya's version, which was in Pahlavī, and prefaced it with a fourth introduction, as the first chapter is preceded by three introductions that have their roots in the Indian and Persian traditions.

Critics laud Ibn al-Muqaffaᶜ for having introduced literary prose narrative to Arabic literature at a time when lyric poetry as a genre was highly regarded. J.D. Latham notes that *Kalīla wa-Dimna* "illumined the path along which others would move and served as a stimulus to the development of a style suited to the needs of a creative prose literature."[7] In his view, Ibn al-Muqaffaᶜ's translation of the Indian fables from Middle Persian forged an "effective and pleasing" prose style, one that is "plain, and free and distinguished as much as by the ease and straightforwardness of its syntactical structures as by its clarity of expression and simplicity of diction."[8]

While some critics praise Ibn al-Muqaffaᶜ for promoting Arabic prose as a means of literary expression on par with poetry, others go on to say that he was one of the most prominent exponents of the intellectual awakening and literary development enjoyed by Arabic prose in the period between the 8th and the 11th centuries.[9] F. Gabrieli is one of the critics who highlights Ibn al-Muqaffaᶜ's "unrivalled cultural achievement in having been the first to present this literary jewel from India to Arabo-Islamic civilization, and through it to Byzantine and Latin West."[10] One should keep in mind, as Saleh Sa'adeh Jallad notes, that every facet of the economic, social, political and religious life during the first half of the Abbasid rule, around 850 AD was influenced by the appropriation and translation into Arabic of works of Hellenistic, Persian and Indian civilization origin.[11]

---

5 Gabrieli, "Ibn al-Mukaffaᶜ," 883.
6 Brockelmann, "Kalila wa-Dimna," 503.
7 Latham, "Ibn al-Muqaffaᶜ and early Abbasid Prose," 53.
8 Ibid., 52.
9 Saleh Sa'adeh Jallad, "Translator's Forward," in: *The Fables of Kalilah and Dimnah*, Saleh Sa'adeh Jallad, trans., London: Melisende 2002, 14.
10 Gabrielli, "Ibn al-Mukaffaᶜ," 884.
11 Jallad, "Translator's Forward," 14.

Ibn al-Muqaffaᶜ's translation spread rapidly to other cultures and served as a basis for many others into Syriac, Greek, Hebrew, New Persian, Latin and Castilian, to name a few. A cross-cultural encounter ensued from his translation.

Giovanni Boccaccio[12] (1313-75) is an Italian storyteller and poet distinguished in world literature for being the first biographer of Dante, *Life of Dante,* and for his story telling in *The Decameron*, written during the ravaging plague at the time of the Black Death and over a period of ten years. Boccaccio was, along with Dante and Petrarch, a pioneer of Italian vernacular literature and of humanism that characterize the European Renaissance. Boccaccio was a narrative and a love poet in addition to being a scholarly critic. His first literary works, written in Italian, comprised allegorical poems and two romances: *Filostrato*, a version of the story of Troilus and Criseida and *Teseida*, a source of Chaucer's *Knight's Tale.* Under Petrarch's urging, Boccaccio abandoned composition in the vernacular and under his guidance wrote exclusively in Latin. The fruit of his labor was four learned treatises, among which is *Genealogia Deorum Gentilium* (*The Genealogy of the Gentile Gods*). This work is an encyclopedic compendium in Latin of Pagan mythology designed as a guide to the ancient poets, culminating with a defense of poetry against the criticisms of it that reach back to Plato's Republic. In the Preface, Books 14 and 15, Boccaccio stands in a long line of practicing poets who have written in defense of their art from Antiquity to the Romantic period.

This synopsis of the authors' lives and their works reveals a certain confluence between Horace and Boccaccio. Both lay out important critical theories about poetry, its nature and function. Both deal with poetics in its narrow sense defined as a system or body of theory about poetry and the principles or rules of composition, and in its broader sense, as a descriptive or normative theory of literature. Where would one place *Kalīla wa-Dimna* in this binary relation? The answer lies in the preface written by Ibn al-Muqaffaᶜ. A close reading of the preface reveals a poetics conceived cross-culturally. He, like Boccaccio, espouses concepts harking back to Horace as to the dual function of poetry, to teach and to please. He also meets with Boccaccio in expounding an allegorical theory of literature, that of compositional allegory, as well as a hermeneutics consisting of an allegorical reading and interpretation of texts, or allegoresis. In addition, one can argue that both Ibn al-Muqaffaᶜ and Boccaccio are precursors of the concept of "interpretive communities" put forth by Stanley Fish in his modern reader-response theory.[13] According to Fish, interpretive communities are "made up of those who share interpretative

---

12 See "Boccaccio, Giovanni," in: *The Reader's Companion to World Literature*, second ed., Calvin S. Brown, ed., New York: A Mentor Book 1984, 67-70; Vincent B. Leitch, "Giovanni Boccaccio 1313-1375," *The Norton Anthology of Theory and Criticism*, Vincent B. Leitch, ed., New York: W.W. Norton & Company 2001, 253-255.

13 Stanley Fish, *Is There a Text in this Class? The Authority of Interpretive Communities*, Cambridge: Harvard University Press, 1980.

strategies not for reading in the conventional sense but for writing texts and constituting their properties…"[14] Hence, the aim of this study is to bring to light this trans-cultural encounter of poetics, one that I propose to call a triangulation of poetics, (be it between Horace, Ibn al-Muqaffaᶜ and Boccaccio, or al-Muqaffaᶜ, Boccaccio and Fish) despite the cultural, literary and linguistic disparity between Ibn al Muqaffaᶜ's *Kalīla wa-Dimna* and the other authors' respective works. This will show how the literary performance of Ibn al-Muqaffaᶜ is a presentation of literary theories espoused by critics who preceded him and succeeded him, elevating him to the rank of prominent literary critics and theorists.

## *I. Context*

In the first lines of his Introduction, in a declarative and emphatic statement, Ibn al-Muqaffaᶜ introduces *Kalīla wa-Dimna*. He then sheds some light on its etiology and nature, as well as its authors and their intentions:

> This is the book of *Kalīla wa-Dimna*. It is composed by the scholars of India. It consists of maxims and fables by means of which they aspired to put forth their most eloquent thoughts in a manner of their choice. The men of wisdom of every sect have always sought to have their aim understood, and thought of contrivances to bring to light the knowledge they had acquired. Hence, they thought of placing these doctrines in the mouths of birds and beasts and deemed it beneficial to have found a way of expression, and a form to adopt.[15]

Ibn al-Muqaffaᶜ chooses to call attention to the wisdom and knowledge of its authors in order to introduce an alien literary genre, and to lessen the incongruity between the adopted form and its content. Gholam-Ali Karimi in "Le conte animalier dans la littérature Arabe avant la traduction de *Kalīla wa-Dimna*" states that *Kalīla wa-Dimna* seems to have inaugurated the tradition of fable and bestiaries in Arabic literature. Acknowledging that there are some tales that give importance to animals before the fourth century, he yet contends they do not have the characteristics of fables and are classified as anecdotes. He concludes by saying that we cannot talk of fable per say before the infiltration of the Persian cul-

---

14 Quoted in Stephen D. Moore, "Negative Hermeneutics: Stanley Fish and the Biblical Interpreter," *Journal of the American Academy of Religion* 54.4 (Winter 1986), 710.

15 All translations and paraphrasing in this paper are rendered by the author from the Arabic text edited by L. Cheikho. See Ibn al-Muqaffaᶜ *Kalīla wa-Dimna*, 2nd ed., L. Cheikho, ed., Beirut: Catholic Press, 1923, 46.

هذا كتاب كليلة ودمنة وهو ممَّا وضعتهُ علماء الهند من الأمثال والأحاديث التي أُلهموا أن يدخلوا فيها أبلغ ما وجدوا من القول في النحو الذي أرادوهُ ولم تزل العلماء والحكماء من أهل كل ملَّة يلتمسون أن يُعقل عنهم الغرض ويحتالون في ذلك بصنوف الحيل ويجتهدون في إخراج ما عندهم حتى كان من تلك العلل وضعُ هذا الكتاب على لسان البهائم والطيور فاجتمع له بذلك خلالٌ منها أنهم وجدوا منصَرَفاً في القول وشعوباً يأخذون منها.

ture under the ʿAbbasid period.[16] Robert Irwin in "The Arabic Beast Fable" explains that though a large corpus of beast fables in the Middle Ages were produced in Arabic or translated into that language, there was no word or phrase that corresponds closely to the term fable or beast fable. In his view, this absence of nomenclature corroborates the novelty of fables and the lack of classification of such stories as a distinctive literary genre.[17] Even in one of the prefaces of *Kalīla wa-Dimna,* the one entitled "Dabshalim the King and Baydaba the Philosopher" written by ʿAlī Ibn al-Shāh al-Fārisī, we learn that "animal roles were an amusing novelty, however, what they uttered was wisdom appropriate to the highest levels of the sciences, arts and letters".[18] Hence, since readers would be estranged from such a novel genre and may deem its use inappropriate, Ibn al-Muqaffaʿ sets out to justify it and to explain its modalities.

In the "Preface" of his work, Boccaccio refers to the occasion that prompted him to write his encyclopedic work. When he was a young man, King Hugo IV, the king of Cyprus and Jerusalem from 1324 to 1358, asked him to write a work on the mythology of Antiquity, to compile a Genealogy of the Gentile Gods and on the heroes who sprang from them. Donino of Parma, one of the king's distinguished soldiers transmitted the king's request, along with a justification for it:

> You added a further request, that I explain the meaning which wise men had hidden under this cover of absurd tales, on the ground that his renowned Majesty thought it a stupid notion for men learned nearly in every doctrine to spend time and labor merely telling stories which are untrue and have only a literal meaning.[19]

This request reveals an incongruity similar to the one encountered in Ibn al Muqaffaʿ' s introduction between the form adopted by the learned men of Antiquity and the content this form embodies, one that Boccaccio will move to defend. It also reveals, as in the former work, that the authors of the tales are men of great learning contrary to what some may think.

One may presume that the king's request was instigated by the cultural and religious setting of the Christian era. In "Medieval and Humanistic Perspectives in Boccaccio's Concept and Defense of Poetry," Giovanni Gullace explains that Plato's condemnation of poetry had never before the Christian era found such a receptive audience. Plato had lambasted poetry for containing no true knowledge but simply appearances which are the sources of falsehood. He also found poetry misleading and dangerous to society as the words and actions it portrays might be immoral or emotional. Gullace adds that with the advent of Christianity, and

---

16 Gholam-Ali Karimi "Le conte animalier dans la littérature Arabe avant la traduction de *Kalila wa-Dimna,*" *Bulletin D'études Orientales* 28 (1975), 51.

17 Robert Irwin, "The Arabic Beast Fable," *Journal of the Warburg and Courtauld Institutes* 55(1992), 36.

18 Jallad, *The Fables of Kalilah and Dimnah*, 55.

19 Boccaccio, *Boccaccio on Poetry*, 6.

throughout the medieval period, poetry lost favor with a public dominated by religious preoccupations alien to the poetic world. The early Christian conception of life leaned heavily towards asceticism and thought to obliterate whatever appealed to sense enjoyment. Churchmen leveled frequent attacks against poetry and likened it to sinful pleasure. Since poetry was a tradition of the pagan world, they rejected it altogether.[20]

Boccaccio's task was rendered more difficult because of the number of specific charges against poets and their poetry. A mere compilation and explanation of the tales of the ancients would not suffice and would lose its validity without a defense of poets and their works. Charles G. Osgood, the translator of Boccaccio's preface, as well as of the fourteenth and fifteenth books of the *Genealogia Deorum Gentilium*, asserts that "to explore and defend antiquity or mythology is to explore and defend the art of poetry."[21] As described in books IV and V of the *Genealogia*, maligners claim that poets are tale-mongers or in lower terms liars, tellers of untrue stories. They are accused of being seducers to evil, and the seducers of the mind in addition to being philosophers' apes. As to their poetry, it is a useless, futile and absurd craft; poems are false, obscure, lewd, and replete with false, absurd and silly tales of pagan gods. Plato banished them from the state; Boethius called them the muses' drabs. Hence, it is a crime to read them.[22]

Boccaccio vindicates a literary form that has been denigrated, while Ibn al-Muqaffaᶜ defends a work prior to its denigration, as if anticipating one. Despite the positive reception of *Kalīla wa-Dimna* in modern times, its reception in the Middle Ages was somehow negative. As Irwin points out, Ibn al-Nadīm in the tenth century catalogues in his *Fihrist* all the known literature of his century; though he devotes special attention to *Kalīla wa-Dimna*, he classifies the fables as part of the larger category of miscellaneous prose such as treatises on farriery, on smells, on coming across objects unexpectedly. In his view, they fall randomly into his broader category of secular entertainment and instruction. Since fable is something which is not true, he lists them as *khurāfāt*: stories that are deemed to be both pretty and fictitious, and therefore most suitable to be told in the evenings after work, if they must be told at all. Al-Tawḥīdī, a late tenth century author, suggested that such *khurāfāt* were more suitable for women and children. In the category of such fiction, he included *Kalila wa-Dimna*.[23]

---

20 Giovanni Gullace, "Medieval and Humanistic Perspectives in Boccaccio's Concept and Defense of Poetry," *Mediaevalia* 12 (1989), 227.

21 Charles S. Osgood, "Introduction" in: *Boccaccio on Poetry: Being the Preface and the Fourteenth and Fifteenth Books of Boccaccio's Genealogia Deorum Gentilium* [1350-62] Charles S. Osgood, trans., Indianapolis and New York: The Bobbs-Merril Company, inc. 1956, xxix.

22 Boccaccio, *Boccaccio on Poetry*, 35; Osgood, "Notes", 154.

23 Irwin, "The Arabic Beast Fable," 36-37.

## *II. Authors*

Both Ibn al-Muqaffaᶜ and Boccaccio deal with authorial intentions. Boccaccio, the critic, dwells on the nature of the task at hand, cognizant of the difficulty of unveiling authorial intentions and textual significations:

> I must proceed to tear the hidden significations from their tough sheathing, and I promise to do so, though not to the last detail of the author's original intentions. Who in our day can penetrate the hearts of the Ancients? Who can bring to light and life again minds long since removed in death? Who can elicit their meaning? A divine task that - not human! ...[24]

This statement brings to mind what W. K Wimsatt and Monroe C. Beardsley refer to as "the intentional fallacy."[25] They coined this phrase in 1942 to describe critical methods that seek to interpret a literary work by reference to the author's intention. They declare that the author's intentions are not available for study and could never satisfactorily be recovered; the work could only be read and judged in its own terms, without reference to extratextual information. Yet, Boccaccio does not go as far as saying that the authors' intentions are not desirable as a standard for analyzing the given tales. He does not proclaim "the death of the author,"[26] an expression that came to mean the resistance to using information derived from the writer's life or known authorial intentions as part of the process of interpretation since this presumes that the author imposes the final limit on meaning and attributes to him (or her) self a godlike status."[27] To the contrary, he invokes the ancients and states that he plans first to write what he learns from them, and then will try to discover the truth by the aid of many commentators and authorities, ancient and modern, at his disposal. Where they fail to inform him and when he finds them inexplicit, he will set down his own opinion,[28] relying upon what Osgood calls his poetic insight.[29]

Unlike Boccaccio, Ibn al-Muqaffaᶜ is not estranged from authorial intentions which consist of transmitting their wisdom. He even urges the readers of this book "to know the facets it embodies, and the author's purpose for using proverbs, parables, and analogies in addition to animals and non-speaking creatures."[30] He implores them not to be oblivious of the purpose of the Indian

---

24 Boccaccio, *Boccaccio on Poetry*, 11.

25 See W. K Wimsatt and Monroe C. Beardsley, "The Intentional Fallacy," in *20th Century Criticism: A Reader*, David Lodge, ed., London: Longman 1972, 344-345.

26 See Roland Barthes, "The Death of the Author," in: *Image, Music Text*, Peter Heath, trans., London: Fontana Press 1977, 142-148.

27 "Death of the Author," in: *The Continuum Encyclopedia of Modern Criticism and Theory*, Julian Wolfreys, ed., New York: Continuum 2002, 842.

28 Boccaccio, *Boccaccio on Poetry*, 12.

29 Osgood, "Introduction," xv.

30 Ibn al-Muqaffaᶜ, *Kalīla wa-Dimna*, 47.

scholars and not to think that the aim of the book is to tell stories about animals.

Both Ibn al-Muqaffaᶜ and Boccaccio portray their respective authors as men of great learning, distinguished by their wisdom or *sapientia*. Perhaps Ibn al-Muqaffaᶜ did not feel the need to dwell on the wisdom of the authors of the book, as their knowledge had already been highlighted in the introductions that narrate the history of the work, from its transmission from the time of its supposed composition by the Indian sage Bidpai until his translation from Pahlavi into Arabic. Unlike him, Boccaccio chose to put forth a lengthy defense of the poets of Antiquity as a response to their denigration. Despite his lack of knowledge regarding authorial intentions, he is able to shed some light on the qualities of the Ancient authors or poets. He describes them as "great men, nursed with the milk of the Muses, brought up in the very home of philosophy, and disciplined in sacred studies."[31] For them to become poets, it is necessary to master "the precepts of grammar and rhetoric" and "to know the principles of the other Liberal Arts, both moral and natural, to possess a strong and abundant vocabulary, to behold the monuments and relics of the Ancients, to have in one's memory the history of the nations, and to be familiar with the geography of various lands, of seas, rivers and mountains."[32] The poets under study are the privileged few who receive this gift of "poetic fervor" from heaven. He attributes their poetic invention to divine power, "springing from God's bosom,"[33] rather than to human talent. Their words are "the words of Holy Writ, clear, definite, charged with unalterable truth though often thinly veiled in figurative language."[34] He asserts that poets are beholders of a theological physical and moral truth: "Physical theology is found in the great poets since they clothe many a physical and moral truth in their inventions, including within their scope not only the deeds of great men, but matters related to their gods.[35]

## *III. Allegorical Texts*

Both the learned men of Antiquity and the Indian sages of Bidpai impart their wisdom and knowledge by means of texts displaying allegorical modalities. The former use myths and fables identified by Boccaccio as poetry; the latter opt for maxims, and proverbs in addition to fables, and bestiaries. These modes of writ-

---

وينبغي لمن قرأ هذا الكتاب أن يعرف الوجوهَ التي وُضعت لهُ والى أي غاية جرى مؤلفهُ فيه عندما نسبهُ الى البهائم وأضافهُ الى غير مُفصح وغير ذلك من الأوضاع التي جعلها مثالاً وأمثالاً.

31 Boccaccio, *Boccaccio on Poetry*, 54.
32 Ibid., 40.
33 Ibid., 41.
34 Ibid., 11.
35 Ibid., 122.

ing have traditionally been subsumed by allegory. They may be said to belong to what critics call "compositional allegory, in order to differentiate it from "interpretive allegory" or allegoresis. The former refers to the way a text is composed, namely with meanings of a possible moral, religious, political or personal import embedded, masked, veiled, or concealed under the surface of the story whose elements have various forms and degrees of concealment. Generally, such texts attempt to evoke a dual interest; a secondary one in the events, characters, setting presented, and a primary one in the ideas they are intended to convey or the significance they bear. Hence, these narratives are intended to be read on two (or more) levels: literal and figurative. As to "interpretive Allegory" or allegoresis, it stands for modes of interpretation of given texts. However, the readers' exegesis is not necessarily limited to works that are intended to be allegorized.

*Kalīla wa-Dimna* has been classified by critics as an allegorical text, and rightly so, as it incorporates many of its characteristics. Peter Heath identifies it as prominent landmark of pre-modern Islamic allegory as "it introduces into Islamic literature a genre of beast fable that has attained a high degree of self-consciousness and self reflection." He explains that the prefaces that narrate the history of the work are "replete with directives about how the book was formulated by a philosopher for the benefit of the intellectuals *(ʿuqalâʾ)* who should seek in it the secrets of wisdom (*al-ḥikma*)." In his view, though the book "largely falls into the genre of political and moralistic allegory, it also presents a rationalist tradition of 'double meaning.'"[36] Ibn al-Muqaffaʿ himself highlights this duality a number of times. He explains that the book comprises a surface/literal level and a deeper/figurative one. In many of his injunctions, he urges its readers to be aware of the apparent/exoteric (*ẓāhir*) and the secret/esoteric (*bāṭin*) meanings. He says:

> In a similar manner whoever reads this book and cannot attend to aim, both in its surface and deep levels, and does not reap any profit from its writing is like a man, who when offered a walnut, cannot benefit from it until he cracks its shell.[37]

Boccaccio as well uses the image of the shell and "the outer mythological covering"[38] to draw attention to the allegorical nature of the tales used by the Ancients. In his view, poets express their very deepest meaning in their poems and conceal it beneath their fables. In his address to the king in Book 14, he informs him that perhaps as he reads, the king "will wonder to see the meaning that was lately hidden under a rough shell brought forth now into light – as if one were to see fresh

---

36 Peter Heath, *Allegory and Philosophy in Avicenna (Ibn Sînâ) with a Translation of the Book of the Prophet Muhammad's Ascent to Heaven*, Philadelphia: Philadelphia University Press 1992, 4.

37 Ibn-al-Muqaffaʿ, *Kalīla wa-Dimna*, 47.

وكذلك من يقرأُ هذا الكتاب ولم يعلم غرضهُ ظاهراً وباطناً لم ينتفع بما بدا له من حظ نفسهِ. كما أن رجلاً لو قدَّموا له جوزاً صحيحاً لم ينتفع به ألاَّ أن يكسرهُ وينتفع بما فيهِ.

38 Boccaccio, *Boccaccio on Poetry*, 70.

water gushing from a globe of fire – …"[39] In his *Life of Dante,* he is as explicit about the allegorical nature of the fables. He makes use of the traditional medieval image of the "hidden fruit" in contrast to "the bark and the visible leaves" to point to the presence of a hidden esoteric meaning. He does not distinguish between wisdom concealed, as in pre-Homeric riddles, and disguised wisdom in authors like Homer, which is hence accessible only to those who seek it.[40] He says:

> So, in order that truth acquired by toil should be more pleasing and that it should be better preserved, the poets concealed it under matters that appeared to be wholly contrary to it. They chose fables, rather than any other form of concealment, because their beauty attracts those whom neither philosophic demonstrations nor persuasions could have touched. Was then shall we say of poets? Shall we suppose that they are mad men, like those carping fools, speaking and not knowing what they say? On the contrary, they are profoundly intelligent in their methods, as regards the hidden fruit, and of an excellent and beautiful eloquence as regards the bark and visible leaves.[41]

Boccaccio uses another conventional Medieval image of allegory, that of the "veil." Since poets "are not constrained by this bond to employ literal truth on the surface of their inventions,"[42] they transmit the truth they possess in a veiled manner by means of poetic fiction. As he puts it, poetry "veils the truth in a fair and fitting garment of fiction."[43] In his view, there is no disgrace in using stories and fables for

> the word "fable" (fabula) has an honorable origin in the verb *for, faris,* hence "conversation" (confabulatio), which means only "talking together" (collocutio)… Hence if it is a sin to compose stories, it is a sin to converse, which only the veriest fool would admit. For nature has not granted us the power of speech unless for purposes of conversation, and the exchange of ideas.[44]

However he notes, transmitting and exchanging ideas does not reduce poetry to rhetoric. He contends that poetry is superior to rhetoric, though it was the practice in the Middle Ages to subordinate poetry to grammar and rhetoric and hence, to debase it. He declares that poets know and employ the precepts, rules, and method of rhetoric. Yet, "poetry transcends rhetoric in majesty of style and dignity, and particularly in the freedom and spontaneity of its invention, especially allegorical invention."[45] He retorts: "Who but an ignoramus would dare to say that poets purposely make their inventions void and empty, trusting in the superficial appearance of their tales to show their eloquence?"[46]

---

39 Ibid., 16.
40 Ernst Robert Curtius, *European Literature and the Latin Middle Ages*, Willard R. Trask, trans., Bollingen Series XXXVI, Princeton: Princeton University Press 1990, 205.
41 Boccaccio, *Boccaccio on Poetry*, 52.
42 Ibid., 63.
43 Ibid., 39.
44 Ibid., 47.
45 Osgood, "Notes," 160.
46 Boccaccio, *Boccaccio on Poetry*, 52.

Boccaccio contends that poetry is in harmony with philosophy: "[Poets] never veil with their inventions anything which is not wholly consonant with philosophy as judged by the opinions of the Ancients."[47] The difference between poets and philosophers is that of method. Like philosophy, poetry does arrive at the truth though by different means:

> The philosopher, everyone knows, by a process of syllogizing, disproves what he considers false, and in like manner proves his theory… The poet conceives his thought by contemplation, and, wholly without the help of syllogism, veils it as subtly and skillfully as he can under the outward semblance of his invention .[48]

In addition to being philosophers, poets are craftsmen. Using etymology, Boccaccio proves that poets are not liars as some choose to portray them. Detractors carelessly choose to attribute the origin of poetry to *poio*, *pois*, which is but Latin *fingo*, *fingis*, which is to cheat or deceive by made up stories. In his view, "poetry" is rather derived from a very ancient Greek word *poetes*, which in Latin means exquisite discourse (*exquisita locutio*)."[49] Hence, he defines poetry "as a sort of fervid and exquisite invention, with fervid expression, in speech or writing, of that which the mind has invented."[50] He emphasizes the careful disposition of words on the one hand, and on the other the existence of a hidden meaning, an allegorical significance. Unlike the exponents of formalism, he does not favor the cultivation of an artistic technique at the expense of subject matter. To the contrary, he works a symbiosis of the two. True, his definition of poetry relies on form: "for whatever is composed under a veil, and thus exquisitely wrought, is poetry and poetry alone."[51] Yet, he highlights the allegorical significance of poetry and its content: "Fiction is a form of discourse, which, under guise of invention, illustrates or proves an idea."[52]

Hiding or concealing, or veiling and disguising the truth, leads to the obscurity of poetry, a fact that Ibn al-Muqaffaᶜ acknowledges and Boccaccio defends. Ibn al Muqaffaᶜ brings to notice the obscure information the learned youth finds engraved in his heart, one, however, that turns out to be useful at the opportune time: "They found engraved in their hearts some obscure information, they were cognizant that what is at hand is a written coded text."[53] Boccaccio retorts that obscurity is not confined to poetry; poets are obscure, so too are the philoso-

---

47 Ibid., 79.
48 Ibid., 79.
49 Ibid., 40.
50 Ibid., 39.
51 Ibid., 42.
52 Ibid., 48.
53 Ibid., 46.

واتخذَهُ المتعلمون من الأحداث منشِطاً في حفظ ما صار إليه من أمر. برزويهِ في صدرهِ ولا يدري ما هو بل عرف أنهُ ظفِر من ذلك بمكتوب مرقوم.

phers and the writers of the scriptures. The thoughts proceeding from the Holy Ghost are full of ambiguities, yet critics, for fear of blasphemy, do not accuse them of deliberate obscurity for the sake of appearing clever. If the concealment of the truth is right in the Bible, which is meant for the multitude, it is much more permissible in poetry, which is meant for but the few. As to philosophers, their close reasoning is not always "simple and clear as they say an oration should be."[54] Referring to Plato and Aristotle, he states that they "abound in difficulties so tangled and involved... that they have yielded no clear nor consistent meaning."[55]

The rendering of obscure poetry is for Boccaccio a religious duty. Poetry seeks to protect the truth from the many and it makes it available for the few. The poet thinks himself obliged to keep the multitude from debasing the truth that originates from God: "For we are forbidden by divine command to give that which is holy to dogs, or to cast pearls before swine."[56] Elaborating on such duties, he adds: "Rather where matters truly solemn and memorable are too much exposed, it is his office by every effort to protect as well as he can and removes them from the gaze of the irreverent, that they cheapen not by too common familiarity."[57] As such, "while philosophy is without question the keenest investigator of truth," poetry becomes "its most faithful guardian, protecting it as she does beneath the veil of her art."[58]

In a similar manner, Ibn al-Muqaffaᶜ lays bare the elitist nature of poetry and its philosophical hermeticism. He states that the fourth objective of the book, the most sublime, is addressed specifically to the philosopher. Hence, it is ineluctably addressed to the few, those who are able to dwell on its esoteric meanings and hidden secrets. This aim is at variance with the third objective which draws the curiosity of the many, the kings and the gentry alike, and as such, is comprehensible and attractive to a broad spectrum of readers.

It is worthy to note that Ibn al-Muqaffaᶜ himself employs fables in his introduction as a philosophical vehicle, be it to expound the poetics of *Kalīla wa-Dimna* and the hermeneutics it engenders, or to put forth his own philosophical doctrines. He produces a literary work artistically and didactically on par with the original Pahlavi fables. Nonetheless, in an interesting reversal that reveals his artistry, he uses fables to illustrate his clearly stated philosophical views regarding rationality, knowledge, active engagement, destiny, to name a few. His approach contrasts with the book of fables where meaning is embedded and has to be extracted by the reader. Furthermore, Ibn al-Muqaffaᶜ gives prominence to his philosophy when he places his doctrines at the centre of his introduction as a core,

---

54 Ibid., 58.
55 Ibid., 58.
56 Ibid., 62.
57 Ibid., 59.
58 Ibid., 84.

and frames them with the description of the book, its etiology and aim. In both instances, as with Boccaccio, fiction acquires the characteristics of philosophical reflection.

## *IV. To Teach and to Please*

From Ibn al-Muqaffaᶜ's and Boccaccio's allegorical definition of poetry stems a twofold power that rehearses and reiterates the Horatian dictum "to instruct and delight", binding them into a triangular poetics. Osgood, along with other critics, asserts that Boccaccio owned a copy of Horace's *Ars Poetica* .[59] As to whether Ibn al-Muqaffaᶜ owned or read Horace's work, nothing can be said but one may suggest that he was acquainted with it.

Horace, in his renowned text, views poetry as a craft and sheds some light on the poet's aims, which he views as either "to benefit or amuse, or to utter words at once both pleasing and helpful to life."[60] Likewise, Boccaccio regards poetry as "an art or skill not empty, but full of sap"[61] that provides "profit and pleasure to the reader."[62] In the opening paragraph of his introduction, Ibn al-Muqaffaᶜ describes the book as one that "infuses wisdom and delight."[63]

For Horace, Boccaccio, and Ibn al-Muqaffaᶜ pleasure may be brought by the satisfaction of the canons of art. For Horace, this canon consists of decorum which requires that the poet fit the part to the whole, the subject to the appropriate genre, meter and language to both character and circumstance. For Boccaccio, as stated earlier, the canon consists of a fervid and exquisite invention, which appeals to the delight of taste, and physical enjoyment. For Ibn al-Muqaffaᶜ, this delight of taste is engendered by the ornamentation, engravings, and illustrations that accompany the book and not by any linguistic means.

One facet of this pleasure or the *dulce* resides in the emotional impact poetry has on its readers or hearers. Horace states that "Not enough is it for poems to have beauty: they must have charm, and lead the hearer's soul where they will."[64] Echoing Horace, Boccaccio highlights the pleasure poetic fables produce, attribut-

---

59 Osgood, "Notes," 166.

60 Horace, "Ars Poetica or Epistle to the Pisos," in: *Horace: Satires, Epistles, and Ars Poetica with an English Translation*, H. Rushton Fairclough, transl., Cambridge: The Loeb Classical Library, Harvard University Press, 1999, 478-479.
*Aut prodesse volunt aut delectare poetae/aut simul et iucunda et idonea dicere vitae.* (333-334).

61 Boccaccio, *Boccaccio on Poetry*, 39.

62 Ibid., 105.

63 Ibn al-Muqaffaᶜ, *Kalīla wa-Dimna,* 46.

وأما الكتاب فجمع حكمة ولهوا.

64 Horace, "Ars Poetica," 458-459.
*Non satis est pulchra esse poemata; dulcia sunto/et quocumque volent animum auditoris agunto.* (99-11).

ing it concurrently to form and content, namely to the veiling of the truth in a fair and fitting garment and to the narration of pleasant stories. He gives the example of "princes who have been deeply engaged in important matters, but after the noble and happy disposal of their affairs of state, obey, as it were, the warning of nature, and revive their spent forces by calling about them such men as will renew their weary minds with diverting stories and conversation."[65] Likewise, Ibn al-Muqaffaᶜ declares that one of the aims of the book is to give pleasure to certain groups of people: "The second is to portray animals of various kinds and colors, as a diversion for the kings, instigating them to cherish the book and value it because of its illustrations."[66] In addition to kings, the book is intended to delight the young: "The ministry of animals was intended to entice the shallow youth to acquire the book and read it for entertainment, so to affect their hearts."[67]

Another facet of this *dulce* resides in the alleviation of pain, which stands for the negative definition of pleasure in contrast to the positive one, the presence of pleasure. For both Horace and Boccaccio poetry uplifts dejected spirits and has a rejuvenating power. Horace states that the poet "to the helpless and sick at heart brings comfort."[68] In the same way, Boccaccio points out to the healing power of fiction: "By fiction, too, the strength and spirits of great men worn out in the strain of serious crises have been restored."[69] Elsewhere he adds, "Fiction has, in some cases, sufficed to lift the oppressive weight of adversity and furnish consolation…"[70]

Poetry can perform the function of the *dulce* and *utile* concurrently. Horace commends the poets who are capable of teaching the reader while pleasing him: "He has won every vote who has blended profit and pleasure, at once delighting and instructing the reader."[71] Boccaccio confirms that poetry teaches by the very charm of its beauty and its music and not by precept alone.[72] Quoting Petrarch,

---

65 Boccaccio, *Boccaccio on Poetry*, 50.

66 Ibn al Muqaffaᶜ, *Kalīla wa-Dimna*, 52.

والثاني إظهار خيالات الحيوانات بصنوف الألوان والأصباغ ليكون أُنساً لقلوب الملوك ويكون حرصهم أشد للنزهة في تلك الصور.

67 Ibid., 52.

أحدُها ما قُصد من وضعهِ على ألسن بالبهائم غير الناطقة ليتسارع الى قرائته واقتنائه أهل الهزل من الشبَّان فيستميل به قلوبَهُم.

68 Horace, "To Augustus," in: *Horace: Satires, Epistles, and Ars Poetica with an English Translation*, H. Rushton Fairclough, transl., Cambridge: The Loeb Classical Library, Harvard University Press, 1999, 406-407.
*inopem solatur et aegrum*. (131).

69 Boccaccio, *Boccaccio on Poetry*, 50.

70 Ibid., 50.

71 Horace, "Ars Poetica," 478-479.
*omne tulit punctum qui miscuit utile dulci,/lectorem delectando pariterque monendo*.(343-344).

72 Osgood, "Introduction," XI.

he states: "Such majesty [of style] and dignity are not intended to hinder those who wish to understand, but rather propose a delightful task, and are designed to enhance the reader's pleasure and keep with care and support his memory."[73] That being so, the *dulce* for Boccaccio can paradoxically bring about edification. Correspondingly, Ibn al-Muqaffaᶜ posits a causal relation between pleasure and instruction. He contends that the entertainment the fables offer can coax the young into learning. The learned youth memorize the book at hand and consequently find themselves involuntarily and unknowingly instructed: "They are like a young man who, when reaching manhood suddenly finds that his parents have left him a deed that would spare him the hard work of earning a livelihood and is enriched with a wisdom that relieves him from seeking any further knowledge in other types of letters."[74] Ibn al-Muqaffaᶜ's reference to the involuntarily edified young lads is commensurate with the story of Robert, the son of King Charles, narrated by Boccaccio.

> How as a boy he was so dull that it took the utmost skill and patience of his master to teach him the mere elements of letters. When all his friends were merely in despair of his doing anything, his master, by the most subtle skill, as were, lured his mind with the fables of Aesop into so grand a passion for study and knowledge, that in a brief time he not only learned the Liberal Arts familiar to Italy, but entered with wonderful keenness of mind into the very inner mysteries of sacred philosophy. In short, he made himself a king whose superior in learning men have not seen since Solomon.[75]

In both cases, to use Boccaccio's terms, it is clear that "Through fiction…the mind that is slipping into inactivity is recalled into a state of better and more vigorous fruition."[76] Hence, fables and the outer glitter of poetry, lead to the fashioning of men of superior leaning, comparable to the well-rounded individuals of the subsequent Renaissance period.

Despite the possible concurrence of the two functions of poetry, the *dulce et utile*, for Horace, Ibn al-Muqaffaᶜ, and Boccaccio the useful has prominence over the delightful and is of a greater import. Some critics may think that Horace is more preoccupied with delight and careful craft than with moral edification. In fact, Horace differentiates between various kinds of poets. He believes that while some poets aim at merely giving pleasure (*delectare*), others aim at the improvement of their readers (*prodesse*). Still others aim at combining both. As J. Tate notes, Horace regards the true poet as someone who "ought" to instruct. He adds that the "ought" is that of expediency and not of morality, because the au-

---

73 Boccaccio, *Boccaccio on Poetry*, 61-62.

74 Ibn al-Muqaffaᶜ, *Kalīla wa-Dimna*, 46.

وكان كالرجل الذي لما استكمل الرجولية ووجد أبويه قد كنزا لهُ عقداً استغنى بها عن الكَدْح فيما يستعملهُ من معيشتهِ فأغناهُ ما أشرف عليهِ من الحكمة عن الحاجة الى غيرها من وجوه الأدب.

75 Boccaccio, *Boccaccio on Poetry*, 51.

76 Ibid., 51.

dience, or an important section of the audience desires it and therefore is the best policy.[77]

Ibn al-Muqaffaᶜ emphasizes that *Kalīla wa-Dimna* is not essentially written for delight: "It is imperative for the one who looks at our book, not to set his goal to skim through it to enjoy the engraving and illustrations that often accompany it, but to study its fables up to the last page, and to read closely every single parable and word it incorporates."[78] He reiterates the word profit in the series of normative statements that frame his philosophical message. Nonetheless, he stresses that the wisdom gained from the reading of the fables loses its intrinsic value if it is neither transmitted to others and nor put to practice: "If a sensible man understands this book, assimilates its knowledge, pursues its reading till the end, and knows what it embodies, he should act according to what he has learned from it in order to reap some profit, and should set it as a model to shape his behavior and a path he should not deviate from."[79] He goes on to assert his view using the following maxims: "It has been said that knowledge is deficient without action. Knowledge is like a tree, and action is its fruit. A learned man should put to practice what he acquires in order to benefit from it. Failing to do so, he cannot be called wise.[80] Ibn al-Muqaffaᶜ follows the Greek belief that "poetry contains and must contain not only secret wisdom but also universal practical knowledge."[81]

Turning to Boccaccio, he maintains that the poet is essentially a dispenser of truth and not of pleasure as was believed by the Christian community. He brings to the fore a number of aspects pertaining to the usefulness of poetry in its theoretical and practical aspects. He refutes Plato's classic condemnations that poets are corrupters of morals: "if the reader is prompted by a healthy mind, not a diseased one, they will prove actual stimulators to virtue, either subtle or poignant, as occasion requires."[82] One aspect of the usefulness of poetry consists of moral edification. In Boccaccio's view, poets are useful to the individual as they "rouse

---

77 J. Tate, "Horace and the Moral Function of Poetry," *The Classical Quarterly* 22.2 (1928), 68.

78 Ibn al-Muqaffaᶜ, *Kalīla wa-Dimna*, 51.

وقد ينبغي للناظر في كتابنا هذا أن لا يجعل غايتهُ التصفّح لتَزَاويقهُ بل ليشرف على ما تضمَّن من الأمثال حتى يأتي على آخرهِ ويقف عند كل مثَل وكلمة ويعمل فيها رويَّته.

79 Ibid., 47-48.

ثم أنَّ العاقل إذا فهم هذا الكتاب وعلمه وبلغ نهايتهُ وعلم ما فيه ينبغي لهُ أن يعمل بما علمهُ منهُ لينتفع بهِ ويجعلهُ مثالاً لا نحيد عنهُ.

80 Ibid., 48.

ويقال ان العلم لا يتمَ الاَّ بالعمل وان العلم كالشجرة والعمل فيها كالثمر صاحب العلم يعرض بالعمل لينتفع وان لم يستعمل ما يعلم فلا يسمَّى عالماً.

81 Curtius, *European Literature and the Latin Middle Ages*, 206.

82 Boccaccio, *Boccaccio on Poetry*, 74.

the reader's mind to higher feelings."[83] Their fiction "subdue[s] the senses with the mind"[84] and has been the means "of quelling minds aroused to mad rage, and subduing them to their pristine gentleness."[85] In a lengthy passage he expounds the multifarious effects of poetry:

> It can arm kings, marshal them for war, launch whole fleets from their docks, nay, counterfeit sky, land, sea, adorn young maidens with flowery garlands, portray human character in its various phases, awake the idle, stimulate the dull, restrain the rash, subdue the criminal, and distinguish excellent men with their proper meed of praise…[86]

Likewise, Horace acknowledges and praises the moral edification poetry effectuates. In his epistle "To Augustus" he states, describing the poet:

> Though a poor soldier, and slow in the field, he serves the State, if you grant that even by small things are great ends helped. The poet fashions the tender, lisping lips of childhood; even then he turns the ear from unseemly words; presently too, he moulds the hearts by kindly precepts, correcting roughness and envy and anger. He tells of noble deeds, equips the rising age with famous examples, and to the helpless and sick at heart brings comfort.[87]

Nevertheless, Horace, Ibn al-Muqaffaᶜ and Boccaccio are aware that some of their readers or listeners are not edified by poetry and fables. Horace differentiates between the hearers who merely desire pleasure and those who demand instruction. Boccaccio categorizes people into the learned and the unlearned: "Such then is the power of fiction that it pleases the unlearned by its external appearance, and exercises the minds of the learned with its hidden truth; and thus both are edified and delighted with one and the same perusal."[88] Ibn al-Muqaffaᶜ also distinguishes between those who read the book for edification and those for pleasure: "Wise men choose to read it for instruction and ignorant men for the entertainment it offered."[89]

---

83 Ibid., 105.
84 Ibid., 39.
85 Ibid., 50.
86 Ibid., 39-40.
87 Horace, "To Augustus," 406-407.
*militiae quamquam piger et malus, utilis urbi,*
*si das hoc, parvis quoque rebus magna iuvari.*
*os tenerum pueri balbumque poeta figurat,*
*torquet ab obscenis iam nunc sermonibus aurem,*
*mox etiam pectus praeceptis format amicis,*
*asperitatis et invidiae corrector et irae,*
*recte facta refert, orienta tempora notis*
*instruit exemplis, inopem solatur et aegrum.*
(124-131).
88 Boccaccio, *Boccaccio on Poetry*, 51
89 Ibn al-Muqaffaᶜ, *Kalīla wa-Dimna,* 46.

فاختاره الحكماء لحكمتهِ وجعلتهُ السفهاء لهواً.

## *V. Readers and Interpretive Communities*

Allegory requires not only a particular way of writing narratives but of reading and interpreting. There is in allegory an intrinsic need for allegoresis. Both Ibn al-Muqaffaᶜ and Boccaccio contend that edification requires the unveiling of a hidden and disguised truth as the pedagogic merit lies beyond the literal sense and could only be achieved through interpretation. However, Boccaccio asserts that "it is not one of the poet's various functions to rip up and lay bare that meaning which lies hidden in his inventions."[90] Who then would remove the veil if it is not the author? Clearly, it is the reader. Hence, Boccaccio presents us with a hermeneutics consisting of an interpretive act, or allegoresis that shifts the emphasis from the author and the text to the reader, while still acknowledging that the author is the conveyor of this concealed or veiled signification. So does Ibn al-Muqaffaᶜ with the series of injunctions addressed to the readers to help him break through the hermeticism of the allegorical text. These injunctions, which constitute the bulk of his preface and frame his philosophy, set an appropriate hermeneutical methodology. Consequently, his preface becomes a manifesto of hermeneutics, in addition to being a vehicle for philosophical expression.

As stated earlier, Boccaccio's definition of fiction is allegorical and ineluctably requires the reader's stripping the surface of the poetic cover in order to reach the meaning the author has embedded: "Fiction is a form of discourse, which, under the guise of invention, illustrates or proves an idea; and, as its superficial aspect is removed, the meaning of the author is clear."[91] Boccaccio follows the steps of medieval writers who "commonly refer to the interpretive act as a cracking open of the shell to obtain the nourishing seed, in the context of both biblical exegesis and secular *enarratio*. For example, Dominicus Gundissalinus refers to the author's intention as the 'kernel'; to neglect the intention is to 'leav[e] the kernel intact and to eat the poor shell'. Both the writer who performs allegoresis on a classical text and the reader who interprets an allegorical fiction extract the kernel of the truth from the husk, removing the veil or *integumentum* that conceals the meaning."[92]

Ibn al-Muqaffaᶜ refers to the reader as one who has to extract the meaning the author has concealed, like a walnut from its shell: "Whoever reads this book and cannot attend to aim both, in its surface and deep levels, and does not reap any profit from its writing is like a man, who when offered a walnut, cannot benefit

---

90 Boccaccio, *Boccaccio on Poetry*, 59.
91 Ibid., 48.
92 Suzanne Conklin Akbar, *Seeing through the Veil: Optical Theory and Medieval Allegory*, Toronto: Toronto University Press 2004, 16-17.

from it until he cracks its shell."[93] He then offers the readers directives as to how interpretation should proceed. Such a hermeneutical paradigm consists first of all, to be cognizant that the primary aim of the book is not to tell stories about animals. The reader has to be aware that the fables comprise two levels. Subsequently, s/he has to perform a leap from its surface exoteric level to its deeper esoteric one. Failing to do so is an act of ignorance hindering any kind of edification:

> Similarly, the ignorant who do not think deeply about this book, those who fail to dwell on its secret meanings, and are satisfied with the superficial meanings disregarding the deeper ones are like the man who has the knowledge of philosophy yet spends his time in merriment. He is like the farmer who did not gain any benefit from having spent his time rooting out the thorns out of a field, picking the wild flowers around his plants and neglecting to tend them.[94]

Heath describes such a hermeneutic approach that assumes a semantic bifurcation between exoteric (*ẓāhir*) and esoteric (*bāṭin*) levels of meanings as radical. In his view, it is at variance with the standard approach of traditionalist Qur'anic commentary (*tafsīr*), which assembles materials of a historical and philological nature to help clarify and explain the meaning of the text. However, he notes, the Qur'an provides foundation for this radical stance when it states that its text consists of verses whose meaning is clear and others whose verses are ambiguous.[95]

As to Boccaccio, he chooses his own interpretive tools, rules, and stratagem, by means of which he is able to decipher the allegorical text. Rather than follow to the letter the Medieval traditional fourfold interpretation, consisting of the literal, moral, allegorical and anagogical levels, he opts for a simpler classification. As Osgood explains, Boccaccio was aware that trying to unfold all four traditional meanings in each myth would impede his freedom and pleasure. His favorite interpretations were the deeper ones, the moral and the allegorical, in contrast to the superficial one, the literal.[96] Boccaccio dwells on the difficulty of the

---

93 Ibn al Muqaffaʿ, *Kalīla wa-Dimna*, 47.

وكذلك من يقرأُ هذا الكتاب ولم يعلم غرضهُ ظاهراً وباطناً لم ينتفع بما بدا له من حظ نفسهِ. كما أن رجلاً لو قدَّموا له جوزاً صحيحاً لم ينتفع به ألاَّ أن يكسرهُ وينتفع بما فيهِ.

94 Ibid., 52.

وكذلك الجهّال على إغفال أمر التفكُّر والاغترار في أمر هذا الكتاب وترك الوقوف على أسرار معانيهِ والأخذ بظاهرهِ دون الأخذ بباطنهِ. فقد قالت العلماء: أنَّ مثل هذا الرجل الذي يظفر بعلم الفلسفة فيدعهُ ويصرف همته الى أبواب الهزل كرجل أصاب روضة هواؤها صحيح فزرعها وسقاها حتى إذا قرب خيرها واينعت تشاغل عنها بجمع ما فيها من الزهر وقطع الشوك فأهلك تشاغلُهُ ما كان أحسن فائدة وأجمل عائدة.

95 Heath, *Allegory and Philosophy in Avicenna*, 195.

96 Osgood, "Introduction," xviii.

leap from a surface to a deeper level. He states that in some cases, the nature of the veiling and the language of the author may be a hindrance:

> Some things, though naturally clear perhaps, are so veiled by the artist's skill that scarcely anyone could by mental effort derive sense from them; as the immense body of the sun when hidden in clouds cannot be exactly located by the eye of the most learned astronomer.[97]

At other times, the veil exists in the minds of the audience and not in the language of the poet. Some truths are so profound that, though expressed in the clearest terms, they will appear obscure to most people:

> [These cavillers] should have realized that when things perfectly clear seem obscure, it is the beholder's fault. To a half-blind man, even when the sun is shining its brightest, the sky looks cloudy. Some things are naturally so profound that not without difficulty can the most exceptional keenness in intellect sound their depth...[98]

Though Ibn al-Muqaffaᶜ and Boccaccio uphold a traditional view that meaning is embedded in a text to be extracted, they concurrently expound a more modern position that brings to mind Fish's early reader-response criticism. Such a stance allows the text to retain its manipulative role in relation to the reader, and yet posits meaning "as an experience one has in the course of reading. Literature as a consequence is not regarded as a fixed object of attention but a sequence of events that unfold within the reader's mind."[99] The emergence of meaning resides in the reading process and stems from it. Hence, "the locus of signification" for both Ibn al-Muqaffaᶜ and Boccaccio "comes to be seen in the reading consciousness."[100] As such, both authors offer their readers some guidelines as to the process of approaching their allegorical texts. Ibn al-Muqaffaᶜ states that reading should be characterized by patience, reflection, and scrutiny:

> It is imperative for the one who looks at our book, not to set his goal to skim through it to enjoy the engraving and illustrations that often accompany it, but to study its fables up to the last page, and to read closely every single parable and word it incorporates.[101]

Boccaccio dwells on a process of reading that is congruent with the one dictated by Ibn al-Muqaffaᶜ. In order to "appreciate poetry, and unwind its difficult involutions" the reader has to follow these guidelines: "You must read, you must pre-

---

97 Boccaccio, *Boccaccio on Poetry*, 59.

98 Ibid., 59.

99 Jane P. Tompkins, "An Introduction to Reader-Response Criticism", in: *Reader-Response Criticism: From Formalism to Post-Structuralism,* Jane P. Tompkins, ed., Baltimore:John Hopkins University Press 1980, xvi-xvii.

100 Moore, "Negative Hermeneutics,", 709; See Fish, *Is There a Text in this Class?, 21-67.*

101 Ibn al Muqaffaᶜ, *Kalīla wa-Dimna*, 51-52.
وقد ينبغي للناظر في كتابنا هذا أن لا يجعل غايتهُ التصفّح لتَزاويقهُ بل ليشرف على ما تضمّن من الأمثال حتى يأتي على آخرهِ ويقف عند كل مثَل وكلمة ويعمل فيها رويّته.

serve, you must sit up nights..."[102] The process of reading should not be discursive as it will not enable the reader to derive any profit from the stories and will push him/her to believe that poets invented useless shallow and harmful tales. In addition, the readers of the tales of Antiquity, like those of the Indian Fables, must inquire, and exercise their rational faculties: "Wherefore I again grant that poets are at times obscure, but invariably explicable if approached by a sane mind…"[103] The truth to be discovered is not and should not be easily accessible but should be "the object of strong intellectual effort" challenging the reader not to succumb to sloth and to exert his utmost mental power.

Boccaccio puts forth a second modern view of a reader who succeeds in unveiling not merely a fixed and stable repository of meaning but in engendering one that is in the process of formation. The reader becomes the critic who delivers the pregnant text: "What is more fitting than to unite with such discourse the pregnant meaning of a myth?"[104] Such a text does not embody one meaning but multiple significations construed by multiple potential interpretations:

> Surely no one can believe that poets invidiously veil the truth with fiction, either to deprive the reader of the hidden sense, or to appear the more clever; but rather to make truths which would otherwise cheapen by exposure the object of strong intellectual effort and various interpretation, that in ultimate discovery they shall be more precious.[105]

Clearly, this multiplicity of interpretation owes its existence to the fact that "these myths contain more that one single meaning. They may indeed be called 'polyseme', that is, of multifold sense."[106] In Boccaccio's view, this multiplicity was earlier acknowledged and commended by Saint Augustine in *The City of God*, Book Eleven when he states that the obscurity of the divine word was a source of enrichment as it caused many opinions about the truth to be started and discussed, each reader seeing some fresh meaning in it.[107]

This multiplicity or instability of interpretation brings to the fore another avant-garde hermeneutics whereby the reader for Boccaccio, and as we shall see for Ibn al-Muqaffa$^{c}$ becomes the producer of meaning, dethroning and superseding the author. Boccaccio urges the reader to do the following: "If one way does not lead to the desired meaning, take another; if obstacles arise, then still another; until, if your strength holds out, you will find that clear which at first looked dark."[108] This statement is reminiscent of the distinction E.D. Hirsh Jr. makes between the validity of interpretation, which implies the correspondence

---

102 Boccaccio, *Boccaccio on Poetry*, 62.
103 Ibid., 60.
104 Ibid., 104.
105 Ibid., 60.
106 Osgood, "Introduction," xvii.
107 Boccaccio, *Boccaccio on Poetry*, 60.
108 Ibid., 62.

of an interpretation to a meaning represented by the text and conceived by the author, in contrast to inventiveness of interpretation.[109] Boccaccio tends towards inventiveness in the reading of the pagan myths and fables. One can argue that his exegesis is determined and shaped by a specific explicit belief system, that of the Christian community. He reconciles the pagan and Christian elements in order to salvage the literature of the ancients from religious condemnations and denigration. To use Robert de Beaugrande's phrase, he shifts from "the *ethical* mandate of traditional criticism, ("serving the interest of 'truth' and 'objective knowledge'") to a *political* mandate, ("serving the critic and his or her community").[110] Boccaccio posits himself as a member of a Christian interpretive community when he extracts a Christian structure of meaning or truths that might be at odds with the original authorial intentions and the form that embodies them. The mechanism of this process is described by Fish in his own reading:

> Rather than intention and its formal realization producing interpretation (the "normal" picture), interpretation creates intention and its formal realization by creating the conditions in which it becomes possible to pick them out. In other words, in the analyses of these lines from *Lycidas* I did what critics always do: I "saw" what my interpretive principles permitted or directed me to see and then I turned around and attributed what I had "seen" to a text and an intention.[111]

Hence, Boccaccio's interpretation ceases to be "an art of construing", and becomes as Fish would see it "an art of constructing."[112] Instead of decoding the fables and myths, he makes them.

Ibn al-Muqaffaᶜ, like Boccaccio, puts forth in the opening and closing lines of his preface a hermeneutics that brings to mind Fish's interpretive communities. Despite his fear of not having the authors' intentions understood he, in the opening and closing of this preface, undermines the authors' authority by indirectly foregrounding the readers as members of a variety of interpretive communities. It is true that in a conventional manner he calls for the active engagement of a reading subject to extract the esoteric meanings posited by the wise scholars of India, yet he denotes that this meaning is established as much by the reader as by the author. He abolishes the existence of the text as an entity which always remains the same from one moment to the next. Adopting a modern stance, he views the text as a protean entity dependent on the subjectivity of specific kinds of readers who assign to the text its properties. As such, in their reading, they write it either as philosophical, artistic, entertaining or informative text, or one

---

109 E.D. Hirsh Jr., *Validity in Interpretation*, New Haven and London: Yale University Press 1967, 10.

110 Quoted in Moore, "Negative Hermeneutics", 712; see Robert de Beaugrande, "Surprised by Syncretism: Cognition and Literary Criticism Exemplified by E.D. Hirsh, Stanley Fish, and J. Hillis Miller", *Poetics* 12 (1983), 116.

111 Fish, *Is There a Text in this Class?*, 163.

112 Ibid., 327.

that is a source of employment, depending on the interpretive community they belong to. Paradoxically, their writing of the text is acknowledged and aimed at by the original authors of the fables who favor one interpretive community over the others, namely, that of the philosophers. He says:

> It is essential for the reader of this book to know that this book has four parts and aims. The ministry of animals was intended to entice the shallow youth to acquire the book and read it for entertainment, so to affect their hearts. The second is to portray animals of various kinds and colors, as a diversion for the kings, instigating them to cherish the book and value it because of its illustrations. Third, is to drive the royalty, and the gentry to acquire the book, leading to the proliferation of its copyists, contributing to its lasting preservation, and bringing employment to the copyists and illustrators alike. The fourth, aim, the most sublime, addresses the philosopher.[113]

Hence, a community of interpreters produces the text with their interpretive strategies and would continue to do so as it has happened since *Kalīla wa-Dimna's* inception. The fables have been appropriated by a variety of interpretive communities and were subjected to their rewriting, preempting authorial authority and intentions. H. J. Blackman, in *the Fable as Literature* explains that "the book translated from Sanskrit was thus domesticated in Zoroastrian, Islamic, Christian and Hebrew religious cultures; and the various versions have interpolations and adaptations, suited to the purpose of the translators in his own cultural content."[114] In fact, Ibn al-Muqaffaᶜ himself, as a translator of the text greatly adapted his material to suit his literary objectives, and to make known and appreciated the cultural values of his Persian civilization and that of India.[115] The end result is, with Ibn al-Muqaffaᶜ as with Boccaccio, a cross-cultural encounter, in addition to a hybrid poetics and an avant-garde hermeneutics foreshadowing a modern reader-response Fishian theory.

---

113 Ibn al Muqaffaᶜ, *Kalīla wa-Dimna*, 52.

وينبغي للناظر في هذا الكتاب ومقتنيهِ أن يعلم أنَّهُ ينقسم الى أربعة أقسام وأغراض. أحدُها ما قُصد من وضعهِ على ألسن بالبهائم غير الناطقة ليتسارع الى قرائته واقتنائه أهل الهزل من الشبَّان فيستميل به قلوبَهُم لأن هذا هو الغرض بالنوادر من حيل الحيوانات. والثاني إظهار خيالات الحيوانات بصنوف الألوان والأصباغ ليكون أُنساً لقلوب الملوك ويكون حرصهم أشد للنزهة في تلك الصور والثالث أن يكون على هذه الصفة فيتخذهُ الملوك والسُّوقَةُ فيكثر بذلك انتسَاخُهُ ولا يبطل فيخلُق على مرور الأيام ولينتفع بذلك المصوِّر والناسخ أبداً. والغرض الرابع وهو الأقصى وذلك يخص الفيلسوف خاصةً.

114 H. J. Blackman, *the Fable as Literature*, London and Dover: The Athlone Press 1985, 16.

115 See Jallad, "Translator's Forward," 25.

# Short Stories in Classical Arabic Literature: The Case of *Khālid* and *Umm Salama*

*Jaakko Hämeen-Anttila (University of Helsinki)*

In his lifetime, the courtier, orator and tribal nobleman Khālid ibn Ṣafwān (d. 135/752)[1] was rather famous. Stories circulated about his witty answers and extemporized jokes, his masterful use of language in both panegyrizing and satirizing people was admired, or feared, and his sometimes outspoken sermons to the high and mighty reminded the Caliphs and their court of the basic religious truth that there is more to life – and death – than meets the mortal eye. In a lighter vein, he was also known, and laughed at, for his misogyny and his avarice, *bukhl.* Yet he left us no written works.

Until the mid-eighth century, little prose literature had been written in Arabic. The epistolary genre was taking its first steps and translations from Persian had started to be made. However, one cannot as yet speak of any developed prose literature during this time. Later in the eighth century, philologists started systematically collecting verses, rare words and ancient expressions, writing down stories and sayings derived from the mouths of the uncouth but at the same time unspoiled Bedouins, the genuine speakers of Arabic. Historians started working with script, collecting oral lore from those who still remembered, or had heard of, earlier events which had been crucial in moulding the emergent Arab-Islamic empire, and writing these *akhbār* down. Historical monographs were compiled on the birth of Islam, the early internal wars in the empire and various other subjects.

It was probably historical interest that led Abū l-Ḥasan ʿAlī ibn Muḥammad al-Madāʾinī (d. between 215–235/830–850)[2] to collect a great deal of material that was in circulation at his time and to compile several monographs on various events and characters.[3] One of the persons who caught his attention was Khālid

---

1 For the date of his death, see Yāqūt, *Irshād al-arīb ilā maʿrifat al-adīb* (ed. D.S. Margoliouth. I-VII. E.J.W. Gibb Memorial Publications VI. 2nd ed., London: Luzac & Co. 1923-1931), IV, 160–165. I have discussed Khālid in two articles in the early 1990s: Jaakko Hämeen-Anttila, "Unity and Variation in a Medieval Anecdote", in: *The Middle East: Unity and Diversity. Papers from the Second Nordic Conference on Middle Eastern Studies, Copenhagen 22–25 October 1992*, Heikki Palva and Knut S. Vikør, eds., Nordic Proceedings in Asian Studies, no. 5, 1993, 153-164, and "Khālid ibn Ṣafwān - The Man and the Legend", *Studia Orientalia* 73 (1994), 69-166. In the latter I also gave a translation, here revised, of the story discussed in this paper and in the former an analysis of its various versions.

2 Fuat Sezgin, *Geschichte des arabischen Schrifttums*. I. Leiden: Brill 1967, 314–315.

3 For a list of his works, mostly later lost, see, especially, Ibn al-Nadīm, *Fihrist* (I–II, Gustav Flügel, ed., Leipzig: F.C.W. Vogel 1871), 100–104 (translation in: Bayard Dodge, *The Fihrist of al-Nadīm. A Tenth-Century Survey of Muslim Culture*, I-II, Records of Civilization: Sources and Studies LXXXIII, New York: Columbia University Press 1970, 220–227). The mono-

ibn Ṣafwān. In the early ninth century Khālid was still famous, and there were plenty of stories about him still in circulation for al-Madāʾinī to collect.[4] Like so many other works by him and by his contemporaries, this book was lost but not before it had been extensively excerpted by al-Balādhurī (d. 279/892) for his *Ansāb al-ashrāf* (vol. 7/1, 55–89).

Al-Balādhurī's work contains more than 110 stories about Khālid, mainly derived from al-Madāʾinī's lost monograph – in many stories, the *isnād* leads explicitly back to al-Madāʾinī, in many others we have to presume that the stories come from the same source.[5]

Among the stories told by al-Madāʾinī there are some that are of considerable length, the longest being those in *Ansāb* 7/1, 65–67 and 77–79.[6] The first belongs to the genre of *maqāmāt al-ʿulamāʾ*, the latter to tribal *mufākhara* or *maḥāsin wa-masāwī*. Both consist mainly of Khālid's long and eloquent speeches. These stories are more focused on the use of language than on developing narrative structures. It is probable that neither of these anecdotes is an accurate report of what Khālid had actually said, as the speeches are very ornate and complicated and should have been written down immediately after the performance to have been transmitted in an authentic form. We do not know who recreated the versions that found a place in al-Madāʾinī's book and thence in *Ansāb*. But the speeches would probably have been taken as the actual words of Khālid by al-Madāʾinī, as well as by his informants and audience. In this sense, al-Madāʾinī's material is historical.[7]

Most of the stories, however, are rather brief. Two such brief stories deserve our attention in the light of what later became of them. The first (*Ansāb* 7/1, 59) reads:

> al-Madāʾinī from ʿAdī ibn al-Faḍl who told that Khālid said: "Do not marry one wife so that when she menstruates, you will menstruate with her[8] and when she is in childbed,

---

graph on Khālid is mentioned on p. 104 (Dodge, *Fihrist*, 226). Another, later lost, monograph on Khālid was compiled by ʿAbdalʿazīz ibn Yaḥyā al-Julūdī (d. after 330/941), see Ibn al-Nadīm, *Fihrist*, 115 (Dodge, *Fihrist*, 252). The latter monograph seems to be quoted in Abū Hilāl al-ʿAskarī, *Dīwān al-maʿānī*, (I–II, Bayrūt: Dār al-jīl s.a., repr. of ed. al-Qāhira 1352 A.H.), I, 291–292.

4 We have no information on the extent of al-Madāʾinī's monograph but the work was probably a booklet which, perhaps, did not much exceed the article on Khālid in al-Balādhurī's *Ansāb al-ashrāf* (7/1, Ramzī Baʿlabakkī, ed., Bibliotheca Islamica 28i, Beirut: in Kommission bei United Distributing co. 1997), 55–89.

5 This is true especially in cases where we have after one item explicitly derived from al-Madāʾinī others that simply begin with *wa-qāla Khālid*, or the like. In some cases the parallel tradition proves this derivation correct.

6 Both are given in *Ansāb* without an *isnād*, but the closest preceding *isnād* in both cases leads to al-Madāʾinī and the subsequent stories are, thus, probably derived from him.

7 Al-Jāḥiẓ, *Kitāb al-Bayān wa-l-tabyīn* (I–IV, ʿAbdassalām Muḥammad Hārūn, ed., repr. Bayrūt: Dār al-jīl, s.a.) I, 317–318, was confident that both Khālid's and Shabīb ibn Shayba's speeches had been transmitted up to his time in an authentic form, but I cannot share his belief.

8 I.e., during her periods, you will have no legally and ritually pure bedfellow so that you, too, may be said to share her state.

you will be there, too. When she is away visiting someone, you are (when it comes to having sex) as if you were away, and when she travels, it is as if you were travelling, too. When she is sick, it is as if you were sick, too. Do not marry two wives: you would be between two evils (*sharratayn*); nor three: you would be as (a cauldron) on three stones (*athāfī*). Do not marry four wives: they will wear you out (*yujfirnaka*) and make you old and penniless."

Ibn Ribāṭ al-Fuqaymī said to him: "You have forbidden everything that God has allowed!"[9] Khālid answered: "Better than that is having two loaves of bread, two old rags and two jugs, and worshipping God."[10]

The story presents Khālid as speaking against marriage but here he is not so much a misogynist as in some other stories. In this anecdote his adverse attitude towards women is explained in his final words by his piety and asceticism, which are recurrent themes in many Khālid stories. Mostly, however, his frugal life style is related to his meanness, not to a nobler characteristic, and we may perhaps assume that here, too, there is at least a hint at avarice.[11]

The story is told with little context. His interlocutor, (Durust) ibn Ribāṭ al-Fuqaymī, is a little-known contemporary of Khālid. He seems to have had, during his own time, some slight reputation as a poet[12] and he is mentioned in a few anecdotes in connection with the same persons whom we know to have been acquainted with Khālid.[13] Thus, there is nothing inherently unhistorical in the anecdote: moving around in the same society, the two would probably have known each other. Had they not met each other, one cannot easily see what motive there would have been for connecting Khālid with a person scarcely known by later generations. Thus, we may, *a priori*, accept the story as basically historical, even if it may have undergone changes during the period of its oral circulation. The saying of Khālid is also brief enough not to tax the memory of the narrators. If Khālid did not say exactly what the anecdote claims him to have said, he may well have said something like it. And his interlocutor may well have been Ibn Ribāṭ.

---

9 Cf. Q 66, 1, quoted and discussed below.

10 For the last maxim of Khālid, cf. *Ansāb* 7/1, 58, and Hämeen-Anttila, *Khālid*, no. 80. The story about Khālid is very similar to a saying, attributed to an anonymous Bedouin in al-Rāghib al-Iṣfahānī, *Muḥāḍarāt al-udabāʾ* (I–IV, Bayrūt: Dār maktabat al-ḥayāh 1961), III, 202 (and cf. also the previous anecdote in III, 201).

11 Note especially the last item in Khālid's speech against marrying: the wives will make him penniless.

12 Al-Fīrūzābādī, *al-Qāmūs al-muḥīṭ* (I–IV, al-Ṭāhir Aḥmad al-Zāwī, ed., 3rd ed., al-Dār al-ʿarabiyya li-l-kitāb, 1980), s.v. DRST, defines him as a poet. He is probably not to be identified with Durust al-Muʿallim, who lived in Baghdad and is mentioned in al-Ṣafadī, *Kitāb al-Wāfī bi-l-wafayāt* (XIV, Sven Dedering, ed., Bibliotheca Islamica 6n, Wiesbaden: in Kommission bei Franz Steiner 1982), 9–10.

13 Al-Jāḥiẓ, *Kitāb al-Bayān wa-l-tabyīn* (I–IV, ʿAbdassalām Muḥammad Hārūn, ed., Bayrūt: Dār al-jīl s.a., repr.), II, 166 (> al-Ābī, *Nathr al-durr*. I-VII, ʿAlī Muḥammad al-Bajāwī et al., eds., al-Qāhira: al-Hayʾa al-Miṣriyya al-ʿāmma li-l-kitāb 1981-1991, here II, 192), on the authority of al-Aṣmaʿī, mentions him having visited Bilāl ibn abī Burda when the latter was imprisoned. In *Bayān* II, 284, there is an invective verse on Ibn Ribāṭ by al-Farazdaq.

As such, the saying fits well with the pithy nature of most of Khālid's sayings. We may easily conceive this piece having been received as such by al-Madāʾinī from his informant, ʿAdī ibn al-Faḍl.[14] Naturally, though, we cannot prove that it were not a fragment of a longer story which otherwise would have been lost. Yet there is no obvious reason ready at hand as to why the historian al-Madāʾinī would have left out its context, especially if it originally involved a Caliph or some other well-known person.

The second noteworthy passage is located on p. 61:[15]

> al-Madāʾinī from Ibrāhīm ibn al-Mubārak who told: Abū l-ʿAbbās, the Commander of the Believers, said to Khālid ibn Ṣafwān: "People have said so much about women! What kind of woman pleases you most?" Khālid answered: "O Commander of the Believers, I love most a woman who is neither little and frail nor big and old. As to her beauty, I am satisfied if she is stately from afar, pretty from near, her upper part like a palm branch without leaves and her lower part like a sand-hill. She shall have been nurtured in wealth but then poverty shall have befallen her, so that wealth has edified her and poverty made her humble. She should be unrestrained towards her husband, chaste towards her neighbour. When we are alone, we will be people of this world and when separated from each other, people of the world to come."

This passage is unrelated to the first one. Even al-Madāʾinī's informant in this story is different from that in the first one so that we cannot easily derive the two from one larger, fragmented story. Here Khālid, on the Caliph's order, describes his dream woman in a way that is similar in tenor to his speech in the story *Khālid and Umm Salama*, to which we shall soon turn, although in details the two descriptions of women have little in common.

Read together, the two anecdotes combine to make a story of *maḥāsin wa-masāwī*, or *pro et contra*, for and against marriage. Yet in al-Madāʾinī's monograph they are given separately, the only common denominator being the identity of the protagonist. The passage against marriage is contextualized as a mini-sermon to a friend of Khālid, Ibn Ribāṭ, the voluptuous description of a lady is set in the court of the Caliph al-Saffāḥ. No mention is made of the Caliph's wife, Umm Salama.

Both stories are written in elegant language but neither of them would deserve much attention as such. Completely unrelated to them, there is in the *Ṣaḥīḥ* of al-Bukhārī a *ḥadīth* (no. 4913)[16] involving an Umm Salama, one of the wives of the prophet. This *ḥadīth*, cognate to another (no. 5191) called the *Ḥadīth of*

---

14 ʿAdī ibn al-Faḍl Abū Ḥātim al-Baṣrī, d. 171/787, see al-Ṣafadī, *Kitāb al-Wāfī bi-l-wafayāt* (XIX, Riḍwān al-Sayyid, ed., Bibliotheca Islamica 6s, Beirut: in Kommission bei Franz Steiner 1993), 534.

15 There are three further similar stories in al-Balādhurī's *Ansāb* 7/1, 62–63. For other versions of this particular story, see Hämeen-Anttila, *Khālid*, nos. 129–130.

16 *Ṣaḥīḥ al-Bukhārī*, Muḥammad Nizār Tamīm and Haytham Nizār Tamīm, eds., Bayrūt: Dār al-arqam s.a., from *Kitāb Tafsīr al-Qurʾān, bāb Sūrat al-Taḥrīm 1-2.*

*Choice* by Sylvia Akar in her recent dissertation,[17] belongs to a cycle relating to, and explaining, Q 66, 1–5, the passage beginning with: "Prophet, why do you prohibit that which God has made lawful to you, in seeking to please your wives? God is forgiving and merciful."[18]

In this particular *ḥadīth*, ʿUmar ibn al-Khaṭṭāb is displayed as worried when he hears that some of the wives of the prophet are not quiet and obedient but cause their husband trouble. He comes to learn this when his own wife meddles, as he thinks, in his business and she defends her behaviour by referring to the homelife of the prophet: times have changed with Islam and women have their say in family matters. When ʿUmar goes to see his daughter, the prophet's wife, Ḥafṣa, he learns that the wives of the prophet do really sometimes oppose their husband. After leaving Ḥafṣa, he next visits Umm Salama, who turns out to be a lady with firm opinions. Having heard what ʿUmar is up to, she exclaims: "You are a wonder (*ʿajaban laka*), Ibn al-Khaṭṭāb, you put your nose (*dakhalta fī*) in everything! And now you want to come between the Apostle of God and his wives!" Umm Salama makes it clear that she does not welcome any busybodies wishing to influence her husband and his relations with his wives.

Dumbfounded, ʿUmar leaves her. The rest of the *ḥadīth* need not detain us any longer, except for the end. After having been absent for a while, ʿUmar comes to see the prophet and finds him lying on a reed mat with no cushions to soften them, so that the imprint of the reeds is clearly visible on his side. Seeing this, ʿUmar starts crying. When the prophet asks the reason for his behaviour, he answers: "O Apostle of God, the Persian and Byzantine kings (*Kisrā wa-Qayṣar*) have all their luxuries (*fīmā humā fīhi*). You are the Apostle of God, (yet you live in such poor conditions)!" The prophet said: "Does it not satisfy you that they have this world, we have the next world?" Thus, the *ḥadīth* also contrasts the ascetic behaviour of the prophet with the luxuries of earthly rulers.

With this, the *ḥadīth* comes to an end. The *ḥadīth* is explicitly related to the position of women and their behaviour towards their husbands, and it is given to explain the background of a Qurʾanic verse which asks why the prophet prohibits that which God has made lawful to him.

An unknown author seems to have detected the similarities between the situation of al-Saffāḥ, the mighty Caliph, reputedly monogamously married to Umm Salama, and the prophet Muḥammad, also married to an Umm Salama, whose relations with his wives were the reason for revealing a Qurʾanic verse. Likewise, this author realized that there is something similar between the behaviour of the

---

17 Sylvia Akar, *But if You Desire God and His Messenger. The Concept of Choice in Ṣaḥīḥ al-Bukhārī*, Studia Orientalia 102, 2006, 76. In this paper, I will use the title *Ḥadīth of Choice* in speaking about *ḥadīth* no. 4913.

18 The translation is based on N.J. Dawood's *The Koran*, Penguin Books 1956.

courtier Khālid ibn Ṣafwān describing women to the Caliph and that of ʿUmar ibn al-Khaṭṭāb in his role as an outsider coming between the prophet and his wives.

We have no way of knowing who this author was. What we do know is that no later than the middle of the tenth century a longer story emerged, here called *Khālid and Umm Salama*. This story involves Khālid, the Caliph al-Saffāḥ and Umm Salama, the wife of the Caliph, and this story was enthusiastically received by other literati. The earliest extant sources for this story are al-Masʿūdī's (d. 345/956) *Murūj al-dhahab*, and al-Bayhaqī's (early fourth/tenth century) *al-Maḥāsin wa-l-masāwī*. The two versions deviate from each other so widely that they have to be taken as independent versions, making it less probable that either of their authors would have been the first author of *Khālid and Umm Salama*. Had one of them been its first author, the other should have received the story from a written and well-known contemporary source and would perhaps have been less ready to modify it at will.[19] There is also a third version, found in Ibn Badrūn's *Sharḥ qaṣīdat Ibn ʿAbdūn*, which can be derived from neither al-Masʿūdī nor al-Bayhaqī. Other attestations in various sources are derivable either from al-Bayhaqī or, more often, al-Masʿūdī.[20]

*Khālid and Umm Salama* contains elements from the *Ḥadīth of Choice* and the two Khālid anecdotes translated above. It hardly has any historical background, as it turns up rather late and elements of it are found in other contexts in al-Madāʾinī's monograph on Khālid. In addition, one would be hard put to explain why the story should have been cut into pieces and one piece set in a context involving an obscure Ibn Ribāṭ. The reverse development is, of course, most understandable. Thus, *Khālid and Umm Salama* has to be considered a fictitious narrative, though based on historical sources and ascribed to historical characters. Thus, it merits analysis as an independent piece of fictitious literature, not as a historical report. That it, and similar long anecdotes, have received but little attention seems at least partly due to the anonymity of their authors: we do not know the name of the author who first created this story from various elements and we cannot even be certain whether al-Masʿūdī and al-Bayhaqī are responsible for the versions attested in their books or whether they merely put down a version they found in an earlier source. It seems that, in general, scholars working with Medieval Arabic literary studies prefer well-defined authors, who can be securely dated and placed within their context, to vague and shadowy, anonymous authors about whom we know next to nothing.

---

19 Let it be added that it is immaterial whether the first author of *Khālid and Umm Salama* was al-Masʿūdī, al-Bayhaqī or some anonymous author. The present article concentrates on how the anecdote was created and how it is structured, not on who its author was.

20 For all attestations, see below, footnote 32. The relations between the various versions have been studied in Hämeen-Anttila, *Unity*.

Yet a closer look at many such long anecdotes will show that in Classical Arabic literature prose narratives do exist that have been constructed with care and that exhibit a creative, though anonymous genius. Let us study the case of *Khālid and Umm Salama* more closely.

## *Translation*

One day during Abū l-ʿAbbās al-Saffāḥ's Caliphate, Khālid ibn Ṣafwān was alone with him and said: "O Commander of the Believers, I have thought about you and the extent of your power. Yet a single woman holds sway over you[21] and you are confined by her. If she is sick, you have to be sick with her, and if she is away,[22] you are yourself away. You have prohibited yourself the pleasures of trying other girls, getting to know them and enjoying whatever you want of them. Know, O Commander of the Believers, that among them there are the young and delicate with lofty stature, the tender and white, the dark emancipated, the brown slave, the Berber with her heavy buttocks, the half-breed Medinese who charms you with her conversation and of whom you can enjoy in privacy, too. And what about freeborn girls, O Commander of the Believers! To look at what they have and to speak with them! O Commander of the Believers, if you would but see the tall white, the brown, the red-lipped, the blond, the one with heavy buttocks! And the half-breed Basrans and Kufans who have a sweet tongue, a slender body and a slim waist, golden curls, painted eyes and cup-shaped breasts! Their fine clothes, jewels and shapes! Now, there is something for you to see!" In this way Khālid excelled in description and went on and on with his sweet words and his well-known eloquence.

When Khālid had finished the Caliph said: "Woe to you, Khālid! By God, I have never heard anything as beautiful as what you just said. Repeat your speech;[23] it has affected me indeed!" Khālid repeated his speech even more beautifully than the first time. Then he departed. Abū l-ʿAbbās was still pondering upon what he had heard when his wife, Umm Salama, entered. When she saw him deep in thought and looking worried, she said: "You look strange, O Commander of the Believers: has something bad happened or have you heard a worrying report?" "Nothing of that sort", he answered, and she asked: "Well, what is

---

21 According to a well-known story, Abū l-ʿAbbās had promised his wife neither to marry another wife nor to take concubines, see al-Masʿūdī, *Murūj al-dhahab wa-maʿādin al-jawhar* (I-VII, Charles Pellat, ed., Publications de l'Université Libanaise. Section des études historiques XI. Beyrouth 1966-1979), §2326.

22 Var. "menstruates." The word *ḥāḍat* was considered improper when addressing a king; see al-Thaʿālibī, *Yatīmat al-dahr* (I-IV, Dār al-kutub al-ʿilmiyya 1399/1979), I, 167.

23 The repeating of special witticism to the caliph is a topos found sometimes in similar contexts, cf., e.g., Ibn ʿAbdrabbih, *al-ʿIqd al-farīd* (I-VII, Aḥmad Amīn et al., eds., 3rd ed., Al-Qāhira: Dār al-kitāb al-ʿarabī 1384/1965), III, 211, l. 2.

it then?" Abū l-ᶜAbbās tried to change the subject, but she kept asking him until he had to tell her what Khālid had said. "And what did you say to that son-of-a-bitch!", she cried, but he said: "By God, the man is giving me counsel and you scold him?!" Umm Salama left furious and sent to Khālid some[24] of her Bukharan slaves with their clubs[25] with orders not to leave a single one of his limbs unbroken or sound.

Khālid himself said: So I left the Caliph and headed homewards. I was glad about the effect my speech had had on him. I did not doubt in the least that his gift would soon reach me. It did not take long until those Bukharans came to me while I was sitting in my doorway. When I saw them draw near, I was positive about the present and the gift. They stopped in front of me and asked about me. "I'm Khālid", I said, but then one of them dashed towards me with the club he was carrying. When I saw him coming I jumped up, entered my house and locked the doors behind. I then remained hidden for some time without going out. It crossed my mind that the men might have come from Umm Salama.

Meanwhile, Abū l-ᶜAbbās kept asking for me urgently. All of a sudden some people rushed in and said to me: "Answer to the Commander of the Believers!" I was sure I was going to die! Still, I mounted and rode, being all jelly and no bones! While on my way to the palace several messengers came to me. When I entered and found him alone, I calmed down a little. I greeted him and he beckoned me to sit down. I looked around and saw behind me a door with curtains drawn across it and I noticed some movement behind it.

So Abū l-ᶜAbbās said to me: "Khālid, I have not seen you for three days." "I was sick, O Commander of the Believers", I replied, and he continued: "Woe to you, Khālid, last time you described women and slavegirls to me, and I have never heard a speech more beautiful. Now repeat your words to me!" "It is a pleasure, O Commander of the Believers", I replied, "I told you that the Arabs of the olden days derived the word *ḍarra*, 'second wife', from *ḍarr*, 'harm'.[26] None of them took more than one wife without getting into trouble." "What!", he cried, "that wasn't what you said!" "Oh yes it was, O Commander of the Believers", I insisted, "Moreover, I told you that three wives are like the three stones on which the cauldron boils, and you, too!"[27] Abū l-ᶜAbbās exclaimed: "May I be

---

24 Al-Bayhaqī's version has here the truly gargantuan number of one hundred.

25 *Kāfirkūbāt*. The word is often used in connection with al-Saffāḥ, cf., e.g., al-Maqdisī, *Kitāb al-badʾ wa-l-taʾrīkh* (I–VI, Cl. Huart, ed., Publications de l'École des langues orientales vivantes IVᵉ Série, vol. 16–18, 21–23, Paris 1899–1919, repr. Bayrūt: Dār ṣādir s.a., Arabic text only), VI, 72.

26 The problems inherent in taking a second wife were often described in literature, and the *jinās* between *ḍarrat-* and *ḌRR* did not escape the notice of other authors, e.g., al-Qālī, *Kitāb al-Amālī* (I-II, s.l. & s.a.), II, 35-36; Ibn ᶜAbdrabbih, *ᶜIqd* III, 172, l. 2-3; al-Tawḥīdī, *Kitāb al-Imtāᶜ wa-l-muʾānasa* (I-III, Aḥmad Amīn and Aḥmad al-Zayn, eds., Bayrūt: al-Maktaba al-ᶜaṣriyya 1373/1953), I, 15.

27 The phrase "*taghlī ᶜalayhinna*" is ambivalent in Arabic ('it boils' – 'you boil').

absolved from my relationship with the Messenger of God if I ever heard you say anything like that!"

I went forth: "Yes, and I told you that four wives are the sum of all evil combined for their husband: they turn his hair grey and make him senile and sick." Abū l-ʿAbbās cried: "Woe to you! By God, I have never heard this from either you or anybody else before this moment." I said: "Yes you have, by God!" "Do you call me a liar?", he asked, and I replied: "And you, do you want to kill me (*turīdu an taqtulanī*), O Commander of the Believers?" "Go on", he said, and I continued: "Then I told you that virgin slavegirls are no more than men without a pair of testicles."[28]

I heard laughter from behind the curtain and went on: "Yes, and I told you also that the tribe Makhzūm is the flower of Quraysh and that you have with you one of these flowers.[29] Still, your eye covets freeborn women and slavegirls thereto!" Then a voice came from behind the curtain: "You have said the truth, dear uncle, and been true. So you told the Commander of the Believers, but he altered your words and changed them and put words in your mouth!" Abū l-ʿAbbās said: "What's the matter with you, may God kill you and put you to shame!"[30]

I left him and went out, sure that I was saved. It was but a moment until the messengers of Umm̩ Salama came to me bringing ten thousand dirhams, a robe of honour, a horse and a slave for me.[31] (al-Masʿūdī, *Murūj* §§2327–2330)[32]

---

28 Cf. al-Balādhurī, *Ansāb* 7/1, 88: Khālid said: "Slavegirls are a bad substitute for freeborn women: they are dirtier and have less reason." Someone said to him: "But you, yourself, only marry slavegirls!" Khālid replied: "Have you not heard it said: Accept what the priest says, not what he does."

29 The metaphor *rayḥān* (fragrant basil) for women is very common, cf., e.g., al-Thaʿālibī, *Thimār al-qulūb* (Muḥammad Abū l-Faḍl Ibrāhīm, ed., Dhakhāʾir al-ʿarab 57, Al-Qāhira: Dār al-maʿārif s.a.), 270; al-Jurjānī, *al-Muntakhab min kināyāt al-udabāʾ wa-ishārāt al-bulaghāʾ* (Muḥammad Shamsalḥaqq Shamsī, ed., Ḥaydarābād 1403/1983), 17; Ibn ʿAbdrabbih, *ʿIqd* III, 79, l. 14–15, and III, 158, l. 8 (<ʿAlī ibn abī Ṭālib). Banū Makhzūm are called the *rayḥān* of the Quraysh, e.g., in al-Thaʿālibī, *Thimār*, 298, and Ibn abī l-Hadīd, *Sharḥ Nahj al-balāgha* (I-V, Ḥasan Tamīm, ed., Bayrūt: Dār maktabat al-ḥayāh 1979), V, 395 (+ commentary until p. 411). The Prophet's wife Umm Salama also belonged to Makhzūm (see, e.g., Ibn abī l-Hadīd, *Sharḥ Nahj al-balāgha* V, 409).

30 These are formulaic exclamations of admiration, see, e.g., al-Suyūṭī, *al-Muzhir fī ʿulūm al-lugha wa-anwāʿihā* (I–II, Muḥammad Aḥmad Jād al-Mawlā Beg, Muḥammad Abū l-Faḍl Ibrāhīm, and ʿAlī Muḥammad al-Bijāwī, eds., Bayrūt: al-Maktaba al-ʿaṣriyya 1406/1986), I, 331.

31 These were the usual gifts sent by the magnates, cf., e.g., al-Zajjājī, *Majālis al-ʿulamāʾ* (ʿAbdassalām Muḥammad Hārūn, ed., al-Turāth al-ʿarabī 9, al-Kuwayt: Wizārat al-irshād wa-l-inbāʾ fī l-Kuwayt 1962), 54–55 (a story which contains other similarities with the present stories).

32 Cf. al-Bayhaqī, *al-Maḥāsin wa-l-masāwī* (Friedrich Schwally, ed., Giessen: Ricker'sche Verlagshandlung 1902), 420–422; ps.-al-Jāḥiẓ, *Kitāb al-maḥāsin wa-l-aḍdād* (al-shaykh Muḥammad Sawīd, ed., Bayrūt: Dār iḥyāʾ al-ʿulūm 1412/1991), 221–222; Ibn Hilāl al-Ṣābiʾ, *al-Hafawāt al-nādira* (Ṣāliḥ al-Ashtar, ed., Dimashq: Maṭbūʿāt majmaʿ al-lugha al-ʿarabiyya bi-Dimashq 1387/1967), 101–105; Ibn Badrūn, *Sharḥ qaṣīdat Ibn ʿAbdūn* (R.P.A. Dozy, ed., Leyde: S. et J. Luchtmans 1846), 216–218; Ibn al-Jawzī, *Kitāb al-Adhkiyāʾ*

## *Analysis*

*Khālid and Umm Salama* is a long and elaborate story in comparison to the brief anecdotes in al-Balādhurī's *Ansāb* which derive from al-Madāʾinī's lost work. Al-Madāʾinī was something of a historian or journalist: his stories seem to aim at reporting what the historical Khālid had said or done in various situations, even though he may well have embellished or elaborated his sources. Obviously, al-Madāʾinī not only wanted to educate but also to entertain, these two being the cornerstones of *adab*, but he did this within the limits of historical reports. Anecdotes, witty sayings and longer speeches form the material of al-Madāʾinī, and though at least the authenticity of the exact wording of the speeches may be doubted, one may easily accept that al-Madāʾinī worked more or less *bona fide*, recording what material was circulating about Khālid by his time.

The anonymous author of *Khālid and Umm Salama* worked in a different way. Whereas al-Madāʾinī was a historian, our author created freely a piece of fictitious literature. He must have been aware that what he tells is not the plain truth, and that he is dealing rather liberally with his sources. In using the *Ḥadīth of Choice* as his intertext and in creating a story around the figures of Khālid and Umm Salama, the wife of al-Saffāḥ, he consciously stepped outside of the historical into the fictitious. Historical material provided him with usable elements but from these he freely created a new story which probably contains little historical fact. His relation to his historical, or would-be historical, sources was

(Bayrūt: al-Maktab al-tijārī li-l-ṭibāʿa wa-l-tawzīʿ wa-l-nashr s.a.), 116–117; al-Itlīdī, *Iʿlām al-nās* (Bayrūt: Dār ṣādir 1410/1990), 46–48; al-Shirwānī, *Nafḥat al-Yaman* (Kabīraddīn Aḥmad, ed., Calcutta 1278), 64–66; Ibrāhīm al-Aḥdab, *Dhayl Thamarāt al-awrāq* (in the margins of: al-Ibshīhī, *al-Mustaṭraf fī kull fann mustaẓraf*, I-II, Bayrūt: Dār al-fikr s.a.), II, 292–296. The story is translated in Max Weisweiler, *Arabesken der Liebe. Früharabische Geschichten von Liebe und Frauen* (Leiden: Brill 1954), no. 67. The story is referred to also in *Dīwān Abī Tammām bi-sharḥ al-Khaṭīb al-Tibrīzī* (I–IV, Muḥammad ʿAbduh ʿAzzām, ed., Dhakhāʾir al-ʿarab 5, al-Qāhira 1965–1972), I, 403 (*wa-ḥadīthuhu mashhūr maʿa Umm Salama imraʾat Abī l-ʿAbbās*), and Abū l-ʿAlāʾ al-Maʿarrī, *Risālat al-Ṣāhil wa-l-shāḥij* (ʿĀʾisha ʿAbdarraḥmān [Bint al-Shāṭiʾ], ed., Dhakhāʾir al-ʿarab 51, al-Qāhira: Dār al-maʿārif 1404/1984), 360. See also Ulrich Marzolph, *Arabia Ridens. Die humoristische Kurzprosa der frühen adab-Literatur im internationalen Traditionsgeflecht* (I-II, Frankfurter Wissenschaftliche Beiträge. Kulturwissenschaftliche Reihe 21/1-2, 1992), II, 104–105, no. 420 (< al-Damīrī, *Ḥayāt al-ḥayawān al-kubrā*, 5th ed., al-Qāhira: Maṭbaʿat Muṣṭafā al-Bābī al-Ḥalabī 1398/1978, 170–172, s.v. *birdhawn*). The same story is later told about Hārūn al-Rashīd, Lady Zubayda and Abū Nuwās in several popular *Nawādir Abī Nuwās* collections, e.g., *Nawādir Abī Nuwās* (Silsilat "al-ḍāḥikūn", Bayrūt: Maktabat al-maʿārif s.a.), 33–40; *Nawādir Abī Nuwās* (Bayrūt s.a.), 3–6; *Dīwān Abī Nuwās, ḥayātuhu, tārīkhuhu, nawādiruhu, shiʿruhu* (Bayrūt: Dār al-kutub al-ʿilmiyya, s.a.), 21–27; W.H. Ingrams, *Abu Nuwas in Life and Legend* (Port Louis, Mauritius 1933), 36–38. A popular story with some similar features may be found, e.g., in Inea Bushnaq, *Arab Folktales*, Penguin Folklore Library (Penguin Books 1987), 274 = Ingrams, *Abu Nuwas*, 42–43. For another story of contest between the Caliph and Umm Salama, see, e.g., al-Thaʿālibī, *Thimār*, 201–202 (with ʿUmāra ibn Ḥamza).

probably the same as Shakespeare's: we are not to take Shakespeare's history plays as accurate versions of history as understood at his time but as free elaborations only vaguely based on the historical sources the author was using.

The author of *Khālid and Umm Salama* substituted the more famous protagonist, the Caliph Abū l-ʿAbbās al-Saffāḥ, for the scarcely-known Ibn Ribāṭ of *Ansāb* 7/1, 59. Incidentally, in some late versions Hārūn al-Rashīd, Lady Zubayda and Abū Nuwās have been substituted for the original protagonists: it is a general tendency in *adab* and especially popular stories for famous characters to draw around themselves material that fits their character but originally derives from elsewhere. The same happened in poetry, which is why Abū Nuwās, Abū l-ʿAtāhiya and ʿUmar-i Khayyām are credited with verses that are by less famous authors.

The author combined anecdotes that originally had nothing to do with each other. He perhaps noticed the opportunity provided by the name of the Caliph's wife being the same as that of the prophet's, Umm Salama. He used this coincidence to play with a religious intertext, and selected Umm Salama, the wife of al-Saffāḥ, as another protagonist in the story. The *ḥadīth* may even have inspired him to create the story in the first place.

When we turn to inspect the literary structures of, and devices used in, the story, we immediately come across a wealth of features, beginning with subtle allusions and double-entendres and ranging to intertexts. We see that *Khālid and Umm Salama* is not a simple anecdote but an elaborate piece of literature with an intricate net of allusions and careful and subtle characterization.

To start with, the author has selected a speech by Khālid (*Ansāb* 7/1, 59) which in its original context is a refutation of marriage in general. In *Khālid and Umm Salama* he turns the tables around: what originally was the beginning of a speech against marriage is now introduced as an admonition against taking only one wife. This is achieved by postponing the rest of *Ansāb* 7/1, 59, to Khālid's second speech, where the further arguments of Khālid, and *Ansāb* 7/1, 88, are used to create a case against marrying more than one wife.

The two parts of *Ansāb* 7/1, 59, have thus been separated from each other. They have been given two different foci, neither of which was found in the original. Instead of asceticism and celibacy, we find first polygamy and then monogamy exulted. The end of this latter part is close in tenor to the *maqāmāt al-ʿulamāʾ*, admonitions to the high and mighty, which are attested in the Khālid corpus. Thus, standing against a Caliph and opposing his lowly instincts was not unheard-of, when it comes to Khālid, though in the *maqāmāt al-ʿulamāʾ* it is, obviously, never the protagonist himself who kindles the flame of temptation to begin with. If we were to read *Khālid and Umm Salama* in the framework of *maqāmāt al-ʿulamāʾ*, it would sound like a parody, the same person first leading the Caliph into temptation and then criticizing him for falling into such temptation.

The protagonists of *Khālid and Umm Salama* have been given specific characterizations which make them alive and distinct, unlike the stereotypical characters found in many anecdotes. The Caliph is described as a person wide open to influence. In the beginning, he seems to be quite satisfied with his life with just one wife, but once Khālid has had his say, the idea of polygamy begins to haunt the Caliph's mind. When she later enters, Umm Salama finds her husband "deep in thought and looking worried".[33] It seems that the ascetic feature of monogamy – when all the lovely young women would be available – is not so much al-Saffāḥ's conscious choice, as the avoidance of luxury by the prophet is certainly to be understood to be in the *ḥadīth*, but something he has merely accepted without further ado: the active role must have fallen to his energetic wife, Umm Salama.[34] Once reminded of the luxury of polygamy, al-Saffāḥ, contrary to the example set by his ancestor, is tempted by it. Far from being content with leaving the luxury to others and claiming the world to come as his, he wants his share of the luxury once his courtier has pointed it out for him. Ironically enough, the Caliph himself refers, though only rhetorically, to the ties between himself and the prophet being severed ("May I be absolved…"). In fact, it is his own morally ambivalent behaviour that absolves him, morally at least, from his relationship with the prophet. Unknowingly, he pronounces his own verdict.

Yet even lust cannot entice the Caliph out of his passivity. He does not do anything during the story, except for wishing to hear the first speech again and again and uttering weak exclamations of wonder or indignation during the second speech. These exclamations, moreover, only incite Khālid to an escalating series of statements against polygamy and, in the end, to the exultation of Umm Salama along with respective blame on the Caliph. After the first speech, the Caliph may be burning for these Basran and Kufan beauties, not to mention young concubines, yet he does not act. He does not reward his courtier, as the latter seems to have expected. This is not spelled out in the story but is clearly inferred: it is the private army of Umm Salama that comes to see Khālid, not gift-bearers from the Caliph, and these, it should be emphasized, never appear on the scene, not even after the servants of Umm Salama have paid their nefarious visit to Khālid's house. Later, the Caliph simply remains agape when Khālid impertinently lies to his face. The Caliph knows that the story went differently, but Khālid may fearlessly turn everything upside down: the Caliph does not punish him for his lies and impudence, as he should have done. He cannot push him-

33 Incidentally, this resembles the beginning of the *Ḥadīth of Choice* where the wife of ʿUmar ibn al-Khaṭṭāb comes in and finds her husband pondering on some matter of importance. When she volunteers her opinion, the story is set in motion.

34 Note that this is not a historical fact but the implicit context of the fictitious *Khālid and Umm Salama*. According to al-Masʿūdī, *Murūj* §2326, al-Saffāḥ, after his recovery from temporary impotence during their wedding night swore not to marry other wives or to take concubines. Reading this in the light of *Khālid and Umm Salama*, one might suggest that the idea was not his own but put into his head by Umm Salama.

self into any action, either rewarding or punishing the courtier.[35] And, naturally, he could not, on his own initiative, send for the belles Khālid had described.[36] His greatest feat is to send for Khālid to repeat his sweet description of girls. When at first he does not find his courtier, he can again do nothing more than send his servants to search for him, although, in fact, it was not Khālid the Caliph ultimately wanted but the beautiful girls. But to reach out for them was too much for him, especially without further incitement from Khālid.

The Caliph does not have one of the brightest minds, either. During his second speech, Khālid tries to hint at his real situation, at the same time insinuating that the behaviour of the Caliph himself is reprehensible, but the Caliph notices neither, since they are not spelled out by Khālid. In Arabic, Khālid's crucial phrase is ingeniously ambivalent. What he says is "*wa-turīdu an taqtulanī*", where *taqtulanī* may as well be 2nd person masculine ("Do you want to kill me?") as 3rd person feminine ("Do you want her to kill me?"). Khālid is making one last effort to wake up the Caliph. When this goes unnoticed, he rather openly moves over to side with Umm Salama.

In this phrase, there is also a clear allusion to Q 28, 19, where Moses is addressed by a man who fears for his life: *Yā Mūsā a-turīdu an taqtulanī kamā qatalta nafsan bi-l-amsi? In turīdu illā an takūna jabbāran fī l-arḍi wa-mā turīdu an takūna mina l-muṣliḥīn* (Moses, would you kill me as you killed that wretch yesterday? You are surely seeking to be a tyrant in this land, not an upright man). The subtle allusion seems to evade the Caliph, who is not infuriated by Khālid actually insinuating that he is aspiring to become a tyrant, as he did not realize that Khālid is desperately trying to refer to the secret presence behind the curtain. And when Umm Salama is, in the end, satisfied, and she and Khālid join forces, the Caliph can hardly do more than whine. The reader starts feeling that the Caliph in his impotency does not deserve the beautiful wives and concubines Khālid had been describing. In fact, in *Murūj* §2326, al-Masʿūdī does refer to al-Saffāḥ's reputed temporary impotence on his wedding night. Al-Saffāḥ's physical impotence is mirrored in his impotence in taking any independent action.

The real al-Saffāḥ may have been quite a different person. More importantly, in later literature he is generally described as brisk and active. The usual image arises from pseudo-al-Jāḥiẓ's *Kitāb al-Tāj*,[37] 40: a Caliph who rewards his entertainers and companions without the slightest delay. This was the received image

---

35 The phrase "may God kill you and put you to shame" may have yet another implication if taken literally (cf. above, footnote 30): instead of acting himself, al-Saffāḥ can only wish someone else to take the action which he is unable to in his passivity.

36 In the version of al-Bayhaqī, we have a very vivid picture of the Caliph "tapping the inkwell in front of him with his pen", obviously totally absorbed in the thoughts Khālid has implanted. Was he thinking of writing to his agents to procure the girls his verbose courtier had described to him? If he was, he never proceeded from thoughts to action but was waiting for Khālid to come and prompt him once more.

37 *Kitāb al-Tāj* (Fawzī ʿAṭawī, ed., Bayrūt: al-Sharika al-lubnāniyya li-l-kitāb 1970).

of al-Saffāḥ, and the change in his characterization was made purposefully by the author of *Khālid and Umm Salama* and is, thus, highly significant: he is not using some traditional way of describing al-Saffāḥ as an inert daydreamer and weakling but is startling the reader by presenting a surprising characterization. He is creating a character far removed from the historical person who bore the same name.

Umm Salama, the Caliph's wife, on the other hand, is an active protagonist. Even before the story begins she has made her husband feel her influence and forego the pleasures of polygamy. Once she realizes that there is something suspicious going on, she very determinedly first squeezes the story out of her husband and then quickly acts upon it, sending his servants with their *kāfirkūbāt* to beat the poor Khālid and to give him a lesson. Later, when Khālid is confronted with both the Caliph – who is quite unaware of the presence of his wife – and Umm Salama, who dominates the situation from behind the curtains, Khālid knows who really is the boss in the house – or palace – and acts accordingly, giving no more than lame excuses to the Caliph. When the Caliph asks whether he calls him a liar, Khālid does not choose to answer properly but replies by asking his own question: "And do you want to kill me?" The reply is, on the surface, insolent ("well, if you don't like it, go ahead and kill me") and below the surface either again insolent (if the Caliph picks up the allusion to Moses) or a desperate call for help – which the Caliph, needless to say, does not notice. Nor does he realize that his wife is overhearing their discussion.

Here we are far from the atmosphere of the *Ḥadīth of Choice*. The *ḥadīth* grew out of an ultimatum from God (Q 66, 1–5) towards refractory wives and the well-known end of the story was the surrender of the wives to the will of God and His prophet. When our story ends, the Caliph remains inert. Either he has not been following what happens and remains uncertain as to what is actually going on, or he is too weak to do anything when the conspiracy between Umm Salama and Khālid is laid bare before his, and the reader's, eyes.

Khālid is right in siding with Umm Salama. Hardly has he returned home after his second speech, when Umm Salama's servants arrive, this time with gifts. Umm Salama knows how to use both the stick and the carrot. The Caliph should have done this very thing after the first speech but instead began daydreaming. After his second speech, there is nothing for Khālid to be afraid of: no punitive expedition will be sent by the passive Caliph. Umm Salama is the active one in the palace, thus reversing the traditional roles of men and women. There were active ladies in the Abbasid palace but basically it was a man's world. Thus, again the author has reversed the expected situation and characterized a historical person in a novel way.

Khālid, the courtier, is described as promoting his own interests. First he thinks that the Caliph is the right person to have on his side, but when he realizes the power relations between him and Umm Salama, he loses no time in switching sides. He knows which way the wind blows. The historical Khālid – or the Khālid of al-Madāʾinī, to be more exact – had been suspicious of women, finding divorce one of his greatest joys.[38] The protagonist of this story is, in the beginning, quite different, finding his pleasure in describing charming women.

On the other hand, Khālid's character is perhaps the truest to history of these three. The historical Khālid was witty and quick to comprehend and to react; he had a way with words and loved describing things, be they women or something else. Perhaps the main innovation concerning the historical person derives from the *ḥadīth*: in this story, Khālid is shown meddling in business not his own and getting bettered by a woman.

Although there is always a danger of over-interpretation, I would nevertheless like to draw attention to the parallelism in *Khālid and Umm Salama* and Q 66, 1, between the role of Khālid and that of God. Khālid begins by taking God's role in admonishing the Caliph to do as the prophet was admonished to in the Qurʾanic verse. Seen in this light, the story becomes a tale of hubris. Forgetting that he cannot act towards the Caliph as God had acted towards His prophet, Khālid goes to the Caliph to prompt him so that he should search for female pleasures instead of prohibiting that which God had made lawful to him. This hubris nearly leads to a downfall, which Khālid avoids only by withdrawing to the seclusion of his house. It is only when Khālid resumes his more servile position – not vis-à-vis the Caliph but his wife – that he gets out of harm's way and is even rewarded.[39] Instead of emulating God, he meekly listens to the words from behind the curtain and obeys this *lisān al-ghayb*. Khālid is not a god but the servant of an unseen, yet dominant character. That this was ever in the mind of the author of *Khālid and Umm Salama* or his Medieval audience is far from obvious, but it does add some piquancy to the story as we read it.[40]

The characterization of the protagonists is carefully drawn and essential for understanding the story. The description of the protagonists is not, and does not aim at being, historical. The author of *Khālid and Umm Salama* is drawing a picture that does not claim to be historical and is not following the received image. He is freely using his imagination to devise a good story.

In addition to characterization, the author is using structural devices to make his story as impressive as possible. One such feature relates to the change in point of view in the middle of the story. The first part is narrated in the third person, as told by an omniscient narrator. The second part is of heightened ten-

---

38 Cf. *Ansāb* 7/1, 86 (Hämeen-Anttila, *Khālid*, no. 125).

39 After the first part, Khālid was nearly beaten with *kāfirkūbāt*, "unbeliever-smashers' (from Persian *kūftan*, *kūb* - 'to smite'). Now, he is no more *kāfir*, 'ungrateful' (towards Umm Salama) but a *muslim*, resigning himself to the will of Umm Salama.

40 In general, one should be careful about reading modern ideas into Medieval texts. There is more in these texts than meets the eye but that does not mean that we may let our interpretative mind roam freely. The reader should, thus, take this paragraph as an example of how we *might* interpret such longer and more complicated stories in Medieval literature but not how they necessarily *should* be interpreted.

sion and is, respectively, told in the first person, from Khālid's point of view. His surprise when the Bukharans arrive, his horror when he is summoned to the palace and, finally, his realization of the situation are all told in his own words. This makes the tension even more palpable than it would perhaps have been had the story been told, as in the first part, by an omniscient and detached narrator who can neither be surprised nor emotionally involved.[41]

The change of viewpoint is also useful in showing the gradual growth of Khālid's understanding. It first crosses his mind that the servants might have been sent by Umm Salama but he remains uncertain of this. When he sees movement behind the curtain, the suspicion grows that Umm Salama is not only behind the curtain but behind the whole affair. The laughter from behind the curtain finally settles the question, and Khālid proceeds to the climax of his second speech, a eulogy of Umm Salama and a direct accusation of the Caliph for being lascivious.[42] To achieve this gradual movement most effectively, the author appropriately chose first person narration.

The story is also symmetrically structured. It is basically divided into two, and the division is marked by the change of narrator in the middle. We can further divide both parts into four movements, which mirror each other:[43]

| | | |
|---|---|---|
| 1. | Khālid comes to meet the Caliph | Khālid comes to meet the Caliph |
| 2. | Khālid speaks to please the Caliph | Khālid speaks to please Umm Salama |
| 3. | Khālid returns to his house | Khālid returns to his house |
| 4a. | (Nothing comes from the Caliph) | A gift comes from Umm Salama |
| 4b. | A punishment comes from Umm Salama | (No punishment from the Caliph) |

The expectations of Khālid change diametrically in the two parts of the story. The first part shows him confident in his expectations of being rewarded by the Caliph, the nexus between the parts presents his disillusionment and in the sec-

41 One might also note that in the *ḥadīth* ʿUmar tells his story in the first person singular in the same way as Khālid tells the second part of his, and the first person narration may have been inspired by the *ḥadīth*. There are also some further similarities between the *ḥadīth* and *Khālid and Umm Salama*: After ʿUmar has been sent away by Umm Salama, he tells that he stayed away (*ghibtu*) from the prophet (cf. Khālid staying away from the palace after Umm Salama's action). Later, ʿUmar is propelled into action by a knock at the door (*fa-idhā ṣāḥibī l-anṣārī yaduqq al-bāb*), in the same way that Khālid is activated by people rushing in. As such, these parallels are not conclusive but added to the other similarities they strengthen the case of seeing here a conscious use of an intertextual relation between the two texts.

42 Incidentally, the accusation is not false: the Caliph does lust for these women, though only after Khālid has himself put the idea into his head.

43 The implied events which are not explicitly stated are given in brackets. We could also see this structure as cyclical (expectation of reward – speech – return home – close escape from being beaten – return to palace – speech – reward) but I am doubtful as to whether this would contribute anything new to the analysis or whether the author built his story with a cyclical structure in mind.

ond part, he has changed his attitude. It would be too much to say that his character develops in a modern sense but there is a certain growth in his understanding. What he learns in the story is that it is Umm Salama who is to be flattered, not the weak Caliph: their real power relation becomes clear to him as the events unravel. Khālid basically remains the same throughout the narrative: this is not a story of his growth to become a new man. Yet in relation to the Caliph and Umm Salama, Khālid has changed, now knowing who it is he must beware of and please. Had there been a second episode to this anecdote, we would have met a new Khālid.

Thus far we have analysed al-Masʿūdī's version. In its main lines, al-Bayhaqī's version does not much differ from al-Masʿūdī's and one may, roughly, take the above analysis to fit both and, thus, in broad lines, the original *Khālid and Umm Salama*. Al-Bayhaqī reinterpreted the focus of the story by appropriating it into his work dedicated to *maḥāsin wa-masāwī* stories.[44] In al-Masʿūdī, the story was narrated for its comic effect. In al-Bayhaqī, the same reason, obviously, is important, but the story has been classified on the basis of the juxtaposition of Khālid's two speeches, listing, first, the good points of polygamous life and then the bad points of the same. Al-Bayhaqī's version is, though, artistically clearly inferior to that of al-Masʿūdī.

The original author of *Khālid and Umm Salama* was a creative writer. He took several Khālid anecdotes, connected these with a *ḥadīth* and seasoned his story with allusions to the Qurʾan and other sources. He worked with his sources much in the same way as early Renaissance European authors, such as Boccaccio or the other authors of *novelle.*

Al-Bayhaqī, however, still has a predilection for historical writing. He retains the names of the protagonists and creates a story which has some historical verisimilitude: the events described in the story could have taken place, and the characters do bear a certain resemblance to the historical persons behind them. The historical, i.e., al-Madāʾinī's, Khālid had a reputation for stories connected with women and the historical al-Saffāḥ reputedly did confine himself to monogamy.[45]

Thus, the author has not quite freed himself of history and would, perhaps, not have felt that he was working within a genre completely detached from history. Despite many embellishments and considerable freedom concerning his sources he is, after all, producing a *khabar*, a piece of historical information, and

---

44 The story could also be classified under *al-faraj baʿd al-shidda*. Al-Madāʾinī is credited (Sezgin, *Geschichte* I, 314, no. 6) with a short text on the theme but there is nothing to suggest that the present story would have been included in this work.

45 One might note here a certain parallelism with the prophet Muḥammad, who was monogamous during the life of Khadīja. The story, told by al-Masʿūdī in *Murūj* §2326, of how al-Saffāḥ came to marry Umm Salama resembles the story of the prophet Muḥammad and Khadīja and may well have been modelled on it.

his story was later used as such. Al-Masʿūdī is a historian, though a charmingly loquacious one, and his *Murūj al-dhahab* is not a collection of *novelle* but a historical work. Had al-Masʿūdī thought that the story is clearly unhistorical, he would probably not have included it in his *Murūj al-dhahab*, at least not without a word of warning. The author of Khālid and Umm Salama was a creative writer in spite of himself.

This trend of rather free composition of stories is typical of the period around 800–1000. Arabic prose literature of the period created few stories from nowhere – as a modern author is generally supposed to do – but it freely used stories and elements derived from written or oral sources and modified these. Al-Tanūkhī is a name which we know but many other authors have remained anonymous. *Khālid and Umm Salama* is one example of anonymous but highly developed literature and the anecdote collections and other *adab* works contain many other such long narratives which come close to early Renaissance *novelle* in their artful use of structure and literary devices. The story of the *Weaver of Words*[46] is another example of some fame, but these stories have usually received little attention despite their merits as rare pieces of prose *belles lettres* from Medieval times.

Most authors seem to have worked with characters and plots which had some connection with historical persons and events, such as in *Khālid and Umm Salama*. Al-Tanūkhī, for example, besides using written sources, collected oral stories from persons he knew, thus remaining within the limits of the historical or pseudohistorical. The final step in this direction was taken by al-Hamadhānī in his *maqāmas*.

Badīʿazzamān al-Hamadhānī sifted traditional *adab* sources, as well as, perhaps, folklore, to find suitable plots for his *maqāmas*. He took the decisive step outside of history by replacing the original characters of the stories by characters he himself had created and who, thus, had no real historical basis.[47] Moreover, when he reattributed anecdotes, he left this undisguised: what he wrote was literature, not history by any standard, and he did not try to convince his readers that they were reading historical *akhbār*. He also combined anecdotes which originally were completely unrelated to each other and built from these multiepisodic *maqāmas* where two or more stories are narrated within one *maqāma*, the protagonists continuing their adventures from one episode to another. The author of *Khālid and Umm Salama* took a step towards this by fusing together elements taken from different sources, but he did not go beyond a single, though bipartite, episode.

***

46 For which, see Jaakko Hämeen-Anttila, *MAQAMA. A History of a Genre*, Diskurse der Arabistik 5, Harrassowitz: Wiesbaden 2002, 80–82, and Jaakko Hämeen-Anttila, "Al-Hamadhānī and the Early History of the Maqāma", in: *Philosophy and Arts in the Islamic World*, Urbain Vermeulen and Daniel de Smet, eds., Orientalia Lovaniensia Analecta 87, 1998, 83-96.

47 On the lack of his protagonists' historicity, see Hämeen-Anttila, *Maqama*, 41–43.

As is commonly known, Medieval Arabic literature did not favor long, fictitious prose genres. In prose, it concentrated on the short and witty anecdote – basically, a *nukta* with, or without, its background story, *sālifa* – which it preferred to be historical or, at least, in a historical guise. Such stories were either based on historical events or purported to be, the only major exception being stories that were not told about individuals but about types ("a Bedouin", "a pretty slavegirl") and which were accordingly ahistorical.

*Khālid and Umm Salama*, the *Weaver of Words* and the works of al-Tanūkhī and al-Hamadhānī distanced themselves from this model of literature which had handicapped Arabic prose literature and had directed the attention of authors towards history and away from fiction. Their works were admired during their time, were eagerly read but, for some reason, not further developed. Later authors shifted their focus more on the exquisite use of language and less on the narrative itself. *Maqāma* authors did continue writing unhistorical stories but beginning with al-Ḥarīrī their main interest usually lay in rhymed prose with all its tropes and delicacies. Occasional attempts were made, especially in Islamic Spain, to reorient the genre towards fiction, but these were exceptions to the rule. Some *risāla* writers, especially those writing hunting *risālas* (*risāla ṭardiyya*),[48] created plots which do not seem to derive from any pre-existing model but are truly artistic creations *ex nihilo*. Yet, in the final analysis, such overtures remained marginal and mainstream literature steered away from longer prose narratives.

Yet there were attempts at producing long narratives in Medieval Arab society. These, however, were reduced to a secondary role by being limited to genres that were not considered serious or suitable to a well-read, civilized audience. Popular *sīras* with their "faulty" language – from a Classical point of view – never attained high status but remained confined to being popular entertainment, not worthy of the attention of the literati. Animal tales, such as *Kalīla wa-Dimna*, and other popular stories, such as those incorporated into the *Arabian Nights*, did, for a while, receive some attention but they, too, fell out of vogue at about the same time as anecdotal literature stopped creating longer and more complex prose narratives.

In geographical literature, the same period produced many tall tales of *ʿajāʾib*[49] but these, too, were marginalized as non-serious literature. Thus, Classical Arabic literature never produced longer prose genres, despite the fact that all the elements were there and certain authors between 800 and 1000 did start the development with promising results. It seems impossible exactly to pinpoint the reasons for this: it is always easier to explain why something happened than why

[48] Cf. Hämeen-Anttila, *Maqama*, 213–215.

[49] Syrinx von Hees, *Enzyklopädie als Spiegel des Weltbildes. Qazwīnīs Wunder der Schöpfung – eine Naturkunde des 13. Jahrhunderts*, Diskurse der Arabistik 4, Wiesbaden: Harrassowitz 2002, and Syrinx von Hees,"The Astonishing: A Critique and Re-Reading of ʿAǧāʾib Literature", *Middle Eastern Literatures* 8/2 (2005), 101–120.

something did not. One might search for reasons for this non-occurrence from the high regard enjoyed by exquisite language which it is difficult, though not impossible, to maintain over a long period.

One might also turn to an extra-literary reason. In a manuscript culture, long narratives demand much effort not only from the writer but also from the copyist. As is well known, Arab copyists preferred anthologies, abridgements, and rewritings. Naturally, Arabic and Persian literature can boast of huge works consisting of scores of volumes. But all these works were highly prestigious. Dictionaries, select anthologies, religious works, biographical dictionaries and world histories were copied and recopied despite their length because they were considered handbooks or otherwise specially valuable works. It would have been far more difficult to get one's novel of entertainment copied. A long novel may make good reading but few would be prepared to copy it by hand or to pay for the copyist. The technical problems of reproduction may partly explain why long narrative forms were not prone to develop in Classical Arabic literature. In Europe, too, the novel began to flourish only after the invention of printing.

Whether it was a matter of taste or economy, or both, Medieval Arabic literature did not develop genres such as the short story or the novel. It could have done so, as this essay has aimed to show: all the necessary elements were present and the skill of Medieval Arab authors is not to be doubted. A similar reluctance towards longer genres may be noticed in poetry. Arab poets were able to write highly complicated poetry and in Persian epics they even had a model of epic poetry before their eyes, yet they did not find it necessary to create Arabic epics.

But it is perhaps a misplaced question to ask why such genres were not developed. It might be more just to question the universality of Western genres. Even though longer prose narratives are met with in world literature – Japanese and Chinese novels for example – they are far from self-evident in developed literature. Western literature did not develop any genres equivalent to the Japanese *haiku* or *tanka* and we accept this non-development without problems: Why should Western literature have developed such exotic genres? Why, then, should one expect to see a universal drive towards short stories or novels in non-Western literatures?

# Literary Criticism as Literature

*Geert Jan van Gelder (University of Oxford)*

There is no compelling reason why literary criticism should itself be literary, part of *belles-lettres*. A description or a scientific study of an object, say food, or a phenomenon, such as religion, does not resemble either food or religion. However, if a description is a form of representation, the links become closer, especially if the medium is similar or identical. Thus, a visual representation of a tree by a painter (it might be called a "study" of a tree) does resemble a real tree; a composer's imitation of bird-song, though it will not fool any bird, will show some acoustic correspondences with the real thing. If the medium is language and style, such as in literature, we could also expect some resemblance, even though the analogy is not perfect. The history of literary criticism and theory abounds with examples and counter-examples. Horace's *Ars poetica* is itself a good poem, but nobody will find anything particularly poetic in Aristotle's *Poetics*, apart from the verses quoted in it. English literary criticism and poetics in prose boast many influential works that firmly belong to literature itself, often written by those who were poets (the names of Sidney, Dryden, Shelley, and Empson spring to mind); there is no need to list examples of the less readable forms of LitCrit.[1] It may be an advantage for literary criticism to be itself literary, because then, ideally, it teaches by example as well as by instruction and it practises what it preaches. The advantages are sometimes outweighed by disadvantages, however, because literary texts often lack the clarity and precision that are found in plain, scholarly prose.

The case is not different throughout the history of Arabic literature. "Literary criticism", *al-naqd al-adabī*, is a modern term, used here for the rather heterogeneous collection of works on poetics, rhetoric and stylistics *(ʿilm al-balāghah)* and practical criticism of poetry *(naqd al-shiʿr)*. These are often found together in various admixtures, combining the descriptive and the prescriptive, and often accompanied by an anthological element (which may contribute to the "literary" character of a work as a whole) or by a linguistic and philological component, insofar as this can be distinguished from literary criticism. To define "literary" in the context of medieval Arabic is another difficulty, and one that is so central to the present volume that I shall not venture to offer my own version, other than adopting the editors' term, "artistic". Roughly, "literary prose", or "artistic prose", is what the early critics themselves would have called *kalām* (or *nathr*) *balīgh*; any prose employing rhyme *(sajʿ)* should be considered literary prose, or at least

---

1 Satire and parody are effective means of elevating unreadability to highly entertaining literature, as demonstrated by Frederick Crews, *Postmodern Pooh*, London: Profile Books 2002, a scathing sequel to his equally entertaining but milder *The Pooh Perplex: A Freshman's Casebook*, New York: E.P. Dutton 1965.

prose with literary aspirations. *Sajʿ* is by no means a necessary component but merely one of the numerous stylistic and rhetorical devices that contribute to the literary character of a text, such as metaphor, simile, irony, allusion, forms of repetition and parallelism and other figures, tropes and schemes, and fiction. The term *adab*, often close to "literature" (but always with connotations of ethics and edification), is too vague to be very useful for our purpose. When Ibn Khaldūn (d. 808/1406) discusses *ʿilm al-adab*, he says that

> We have heard from our teachers in their lectures that the fundamental cornerstones of this discipline are four compilations: *Adab al-kātib* by Ibn Qutaybah [d. 276/998], *al-Kāmil* by al-Mubarrad [d. *c.* 285/898], *al-Bayān wa-l-tabyīn* by al-Jāḥiẓ [d. 255/868-9], and *al-Nawādir* [usually entitled *al-Amālī*] by Abū ʿAlī al-Qālī al-Baghdādī [d. 356/967]. All works other than these four are dependent on them and derived from them.[2]

It is sometimes concluded from this passage that the works mentioned are themselves examples of *adab*, but it should be noted that Ibn Khaldūn calls them the cornerstones, not of *adab* itself but of "knowledge" *(ʿilm)* or the study of *adab*: they are sources of literary prose and verse rather than literary works. With the exception of al-Jāḥiẓ, the personal style of the authors is not particularly artistic, if this style can be discerned at all, submerged as it is by copious quotation. In fact, in *al-Bayān wa-l-tabyīn* itself, although it is concerned with literary style and communication in general, al-Jāḥiẓ's stylistic qualities are less conspicuous than in some of his other works. Nevertheless, in view of al-Jāḥiẓ's many perceptive and often seminal remarks about literary style, poetics and rhetoric, not only in *al-Bayān wa-l-tabyīn* but also in *al-Ḥayawān* and other works, he must be considered as an early master of Arabic "literary literary criticism", to coin a rather inelegant expression.

Even al-Jāḥiẓ's *al-Bayān wa-l-tabyīn*, which deals with "clear exposition" or "clarity" *(bayān)* and "eloquence" *(balāghah)*, should not be automatically consigned to the category of *belles-lettres*, as James Montgomery has argued convincingly in a recent article: al-Jāḥiẓ's theory of rhetoric and eloquence is part and parcel of his Muʿtazilite ideas on religion.[3] The purpose of eloquence and ora-

---

2 Ibn Khaldūn, *al-Muqaddimah*, ed. ʿAlī ʿAbd al-Wāḥid Wāfī, Cairo: Lajnat al-Bayān al-ʿArabī 1962, vol. 4, 1267-1268; cf. Franz Rosenthal's translation, *Ibn Khaldûn, The Muqaddimah: An Introduction to History*, Princeton: Princeton University Press 1967, vol. 3, 340-341. See also the very similar saying, attributed to Abū Isḥāq (Ibrāhīm b. Qāsim) al-Aʿlam al-Baṭalyawsī (d. 642/1244-5 or 646) in Ibn Saʿīd al-Andalusī, *al-Muqtaṭaf min azāhir al-ṭuraf*, ed. Sayyid Ḥanafī Ḥasanayn, Cairo: al-Hayʾah al-ʿĀmmah li-l-Kitāb 1984, 217: *"In kāna gharaḍuka iqrāʾ al-adab wa-l-ishtihār bi-kutubihi fa-ʿalayka bi-arkān al-adab al-arbaʿah*: al-Bayān *li-l-Jāḥiẓ wa*-l-Kāmil *li-l-Mubarrad wa*-l-Amālī *li-l-Qālī wa*-l-Zahrah *li-l-Ḥuṣrī."* The last-mentioned work is *Zahr al-ādāb* by al-Ḥuṣrī al-Qayrawānī (d. 413/1022); this literary anthology is obviously more appropriate than Ibn Qutaybah's *Adab al-kātib*, which is more concerned with linguistics and lexicography (Ibn Khaldūn should rather have mentioned Ibn Qutaybah's *ʿUyūn al-akhbār*).

3 James E. Montgomery, "Al-Jāḥiẓ's *Kitāb al-Bayān wa al-Tabyīn*", in: *Writing and Representation in Medieval Islam: Muslim Horizons*, Julia Bray, ed., London & New York: Routledge 2006, 91-152.

tory is never merely aesthetic and always includes elements of edification, instruction, paraenesis, homily, and other non-literary matters. Nevertheless, it is possible to speak of "literariness", as a quality of texts in which the form (style, diction, structure) has obviously been given special attention, as a means to convey the meaning. Thus poetry, with its strict, formal characteristics, its density of tropes and figures of speech, is far more obviously "literary" than most prose genres. Al-Jāḥiẓ's prose, when he discusses matters of style and eloquence (or anything else), is often itself eloquent and stylistically arresting.

The earliest artistic forms of literary criticism, however, antedate al-Jāḥiẓ. Poets themselves include in their own poetry interesting snippets of criticism and reflection on their art; but since the present volume deals with prose, criticism in the form of poetry will have to be ignored.[4] As for prose, the pithy, eloquent, impressionistic judgments recorded from the mouths of the first consumers of pre-Islamic and early Islamic poetry, the Bedouin, are often of an undoubted literary character.[5] Such sayings employ arresting metaphors, as when the Umayyad poet ʿUmar ibn Lajaʾ al-Taymī boasts (in prose) to another poet: "I am a better poet than you, because I put a verse next to its brother, and you put a verse next to its cousin";[6] or in the famous if slightly obscure statement in rhymed prose by al-Akhṭal on the merits of the other two of the Umayyad triad of great poets: "Jarīr scoops from a sea, al-Farazdaq hews from a rock" *(Jarīr yaghrifu min baḥr, wa-l-Farazdaq yanḥitu min ṣakhr)*.[7] Many such sayings are, like these, concerned with ranking poets and making comparative judgments. Other sayings are more general. When Isḥāq ibn Ibrāhīm al-Mawṣilī (d. 235/850) asked an anonymous Bedouin, "Who is the best poet?" he replied in *sajʿ* (imitated in my translation): "He who composes fast without delays. When he is fast he will amaze. He makes people listen to what he says. When speaking in praise, he will raise. When he inveighs, he will debase *(alladhī idhā qāla asraʿ, wa-idhā asraʿa abdaʿ, wa-idhā takallama asmaʿ, wa-idhā madaḥa rafaʿ, wa-idhā hajā waḍaʿ)*".[8] The main inspirations for

---

4 For a much later "literary" form of poetics written in verse, see e.g. my "The Antithesis of *urjūza* and *badīʿiyya*: Two Forms of Arabic Versified Stylistics", in: *Calliope's Classroom: Studies in Didactic Poetry from Antiquity to the Renaissance*, M.A. Harder, A.A. MacDonald and G.J. Reinink, eds., Leuven: Peeters 2006, 153-172.

5 See on this material Nabia Abbott, *Studies in Arabic Literary Papyri, III: Language and Literature*, Chicago: University of Chicago Press 1972, 108-148 (chapter "A Bedouin's Opinion of Jarīr's Poetry as Expressed to the Caliph Hishām", section "Modes of Early Literary Criticism", 122-148).

6 Quoted in many sources and also ascribed to others, such al-Rāʿī; see Abbott, *Studies*, 131, G.J. van Gelder, *Beyond the Line: Classical Arabic Literary Critics on the Coherence and Unity of the Poem*, Leiden: Brill 1982, 26-27.

7 See e.g. Ibn Sallām al-Jumaḥī, *Ṭabaqāt fuḥūl al-shuʿarāʾ*, ed. Maḥmūd Muḥammad Shākir, Cair: Dār al-Maʿārif 1952, 387, 408, al-Jāḥiẓ, *al-Bayān wa-l-tabyīn*, ed. ʿAbd al-Salām Muḥammad Hārūn, Cairo: al-Khānjī 1968, vol. 2, 117, 273; cf. Abbott, *Studies*, 134-136 (wrongly having *yanʿatu* for *yanḥitu*).

8 Ibn Rashīq, *al-ʿUmdah fī maḥāsin al-shiʿr wa-ādābih*, ed. Muḥammad Muḥyī l-Dīn ʿAbd al-Ḥamīd, repr. Beirut: Dār al-Jīl 1972, vol. 1, 123.

poetry are summed up in the answer given by the poet Arṭāh ibn Suhayyah to the caliph ʿAbd al-Malik who had asked for a poem: "By God, I feel no emotion, I am not angry, I am not drinking, I desire nothing. Poetry comes only with one of these things." Again, rhyming prose is used: *Wa-llāhi mā aṭrab, wa-lā aghḍab, wa-lā ashrab, wa-lā arghab.*[9] Such aphorisms remain a staple part of Arabic writings on literature. In many works of literary criticism they alternate with more discursive passages.

Between the short adage, which is often part of an anecdote, and the treatise one finds more sustained passages in prose on specific matters related to criticism or eloquence. There are several examples of such longer passages that deal with eloquence and oratory; it is not surprising that texts on eloquence should themselves be eloquent. When al-Jāḥiẓ quotes answers to the question "what is eloquence?" *(mā l-balāghah)*, he gives both kinds. Short and eloquent, though somewhat cryptic, are for instance the answers given by "a Persian": eloquence is "knowing disjunction from junction" *(maʿrifat al-faṣl wa-l-waṣl)*, "a Greek": "making sound divisions and selecting speech" *(taṣḥīḥ al-aqsām wa-khtiyār al-kalām)*, and "a Byzantine": "apt conciseness in extemporizing and abundance on a day when length is needed" *(ḥusn al-iqtiḍāb ʿinda l-badāhah, wa-l-ghazārah yawm al-iṭālah)*;[10] one notes the use of *sajʿ* and parallelism. Much longer, however, are passages on eloquence and oratory by Ibn al-Muqaffaʿ, by Sahl ibn Hārūn, by an unknown Indian, and by Bishr ibn al-Muʿtamir, all of them quoted by al-Jāḥiẓ; to each of these I shall turn in due course. When Ibn al-Muqaffaʿ (d. *c.* 137/155) is asked the identical question, his answer, as quoted by al-Jāḥiẓ, is one hundred words long.[11] Its literary character is less obvious than in the bon-mots quoted above; it is found in the subtle balance between phrases and the clarity of thought and is not in need of *sajʿ*:

> Eloquence is a word that brings together meanings applying to many different aspects. Some of it lies in silence and some in listening; some in allusion *(ishārah)* and some in argumentation; some of it is replying, and some is initiating; some of it is poetry, some

---

9 Ibn Rashīq, *ʿUmdah*, vol. 1, 120, which has the fullest version; compare the versions in e.g. Ibn Qutaybah, *al-Shiʿr wa-l-shuʿarāʾ*, ed. Aḥmad Muḥammad Shākir, Cairo: Dār al-Maʿārif 1966-1967, vol. 1, 80, Ibn Ṭabāṭabā, *ʿIyār al-shiʿr*, ed. ʿAbd al-ʿAzīz ibn Nāṣir al-Māniʿ, Riyadh: Dār al-ʿUlūm 1985, 206, al-Marzubānī, *al-Muwashshaḥ*, ed.ʿAlī Muḥammad al-Bijāwī, Cairo: Dār Nahḍat Miṣr 1965, 377-378, Ibn ʿAbd Rabbih, *al-ʿIqd al-farīd*, ed. Aḥmad Amīn, Aḥmad al-Zayn, Ibrāhīm al-Abyārī, repr. Beirut: Dār al-Kitāb al-ʿArabī 1983, vol. 5, 326, Abū l-Faraj al-Iṣfahānī, *al-Aghānī*, Cairo: Dār al-Kutub / al-Hayʾah al-Miṣriyyah al-ʿĀmmah 1927-1974, vol. 13, 31. In some versions one finds *lā arhab* "I am not afraid" or even non-rhyming elements: *lā aḥzan* "I am not sad".

10 Al-Jāḥiẓ, *Bayān*, vol. 1, 88; the sayings are often quoted in later works.

11 Al-Jāḥiẓ, *Bayān*, vol. 1, 115-116; also quoted in later sources such as Abū Hilāl al-ʿAskarī, *Kitāb al-Ṣināʿatayn*, ed. ʿAlī Muḥammad al-Bijāwī and Muḥammad Abū l-Faḍl Ibrāhīm, Cairo: ʿĪsā al-Bābī al-Ḥalabī 1971, 20. The original speech may have included other sayings by Ibn al-Muqaffaʿ, quoted after what is obviously an explanatory interruption either by al-Jāḥiẓ or his source, Isḥāq ibn Ḥassān al-Qūhī.

of it is *sajʿ* and speeches, and some is epistles. Collectively, these various kinds should reveal *(waḥy)* or allude to *(ishārah)* the meaning.[12] Concision *(ījāz)*: that is eloquence; but in formal orations,[13] or (speeches) for the reconciliation of discord, use prolixity without garrulity, length without causing boredom. Let there be in the beginning of your words an indication of your business, just as the best verse in poetry is a verse of which, as soon as you have heard the beginning, you know its rhyme-word.

The syntactic and semantic balancing in this passage is not of the rigid and predictable kind – one would have expected, for instance, "silence" to be balanced by "speech" rather than "listening", but "speech" may have been too obvious for inclusion. The series of opposite or complementary pairs (allusion vs. explicit argumentation, revelation vs. allusion, concision vs. prolixity) is interrupted by the triad poetry – oratory – epistles (where it should be noted that rhymed prose is still associated with oratory only and not yet with epistles, which in a later age it would come to dominate). The last sentence is self-descriptive in that the word "rhyme-word" may be anticipated by the listener.

Half a century after Ibn al-Muqaffaʿ's death, an Indian physician called Bahlah was asked about Indian eloquence. Instead of giving his own views, he produced a page or sheet *(ṣaḥīfah)*[14] written in Indian (presumably Sanskrit), which was duly translated into Arabic.[15] Here follows a translation of the passage as quoted by al-Jāḥiẓ:[16]

---

12 Instead of "or allude to the meaning", the version of *al-Ṣināʿatayn* has "but alluding to the meaning is more eloquent".

13 *al-khuṭab bayn al-simāṭayn*, lit. "speeches between the two rows", referring e.g. to a court situation where the ruler is flanked by two rows of attendants.

14 Although *ṣaḥīfah* could mean "scroll" (cf. Q 74:52 and 81:10) it is here probably a loose leaf or folio. The Indians did not use scrolls but codices (as my colleague Prof. Christopher Minkowski informs me).

15 Bahlah is said to be one of the Indian doctors "imported" in the days of the Barmakid vizier Yaḥyā ibn Khālid, who retired from office in 181/797. One of Bahlah's Indian colleagues mentioned by al-Jāḥiẓ's informant (*Bayān*, vol. 1, 92) is Mankah, who was also active as a translator from "Indian" into Persian and Arabic according to Ibn Abī Uṣaybiʿah, *ʿUyūn al-anbāʾ fī ṭabaqāt al-aṭibbāʾ*, ed. Nizār Riḍā, Beirut: Dār Maktabat al-Ḥayāt n.d., 475 and (Ibn) al-Nadīm, *al-Fihrist*, ed. Gustav Flügel, Leipzig 1871-1872 repr. Beirut: Khayyāṭ n.d., 245. It is doubtful whether he is responsible for the polished Arabic prose of the present translation.

16 al-Jāḥiẓ, *Bayān*, vol. 1, 92-93, in a story told by the rather obscure Muʿtazilite called Muʿammar ibn al-Ashʿath in (Ibn) al-Nadīm, *Fihrist*, 100 (Yāqūt, *Muʿjam al-udabāʾ*, repr. Beirut: Dār Iḥyāʾ al-Turāth al-ʿArabī n.d. vol. 14, 127, reads Maʿmar). Parts of the text are found in numerous other sources, all going back to al-Jāḥiẓ (Ibn al-Mudabbir, *al-Risālah al-ʿadhrāʾ*, Ibn Qutayba, *ʿUyūn al-akhbār*, al-Bāqillānī, *Iʿjāz al-Qurʾān*, al-Ḥuṣrī, *Zahr al-ādāb*, al-Ābī, *Nathr al-durr*, Abū Ṭāhir al-Baghdādī, *Qānūn al-balāghah*, Ibn Abī l-Iṣbaʿ, *Taḥrīr al-taḥbīr*). The text is discussed at some length by Abū Hilāl al-ʿAskarī in his *al-Ṣināʿatayn*, 25-43. The passage has been translated into Russian by Kratchkovsky, who thinks that the text is unlikely to be a straightforward translation from an Indian text: Игнатий Юлианович Крачковский (I. Y. Kratchkovskij), "Фрагмент индийской реторики в арабской передаче", *Избранные Сочинения*, Том II, Москва – Ленинград: Издателство Академии Наук 1956, 309-316; and into French by Charles Pellat, "Djâhiz et la «littérature comparée »", *Cahiers algériens de la littérature comparée*, 1 (1966), 94-108 (see 104).

The beginning of eloquence is that all the tools[17] of eloquence come together. This happens when the orator is composed, his body motionless, his glances few [does not look around too much], his diction well-chosen. He should not address the master of a slave-girl[18] with the words of the slave-girl, nor kings with the words of the common people. It should be in his powers to deal with every class. He will neither refine the meanings (thoughts, ideas) too much nor polish the expressions overmuch, nor[19] purify them thoroughly nor revise them excessively, but only do [all] this when he meets a wise man or a learned philosopher, someone who has made it his habit to delete any superfluous speech and to omit words that share more than one meaning; someone who has studied the art of speech[20] as an art and as a means to come across,[21] not in order to raise objections and to be pedantic[22] (?), or to make a curious point and to be witty.
He(?) said:[23] To do justice to a meaning the word (chosen for it) should correspond to it and this(?) situation be in accordance with it. The word used for it should give neither too much[24] <nor too little>, it should neither fall short, nor be a homonym, nor be made to imply (other meanings).[25] One should, in addition to this, remember the point made at the beginning of one's speech. One should pay as much attention to what one has come from as to what one will arrive at. One's words should be pleasing and one should make oneself accustomed to the stress (lit. "terror") of these speech situations. The whole matter revolves around making oneself understood by each group of people to the extent of their ability and imposing on them according their stations. His tools should be easily available to him and his instrument should be free to act together with him (?).[26] He should be just in doubting[27] himself, and be frugal in thinking well of

---

17 "tools": the Arabic *(ālah)* is singular.

18 The editor vocalises the word as *amah*; most others either leave it unvowelled or read it as *ummah* "people", as do Kratchkovsky ("народа …народу"), and Pellat ("la nation"). But there can be little doubt that the former reading is correct, since *sayyid al-amah* is a common expression, e.g. in Islamic legal texts.

19 The negative *lā*, here and at the next verb, is not found in all parallel texts.

20 *ṣināʿat al-manṭiq* apparently does not mean "(the art of) logic" here.

21 *ʿalā jihat … al-mubālaghah*. The usual meaning of *mubālaghah* ("exaggeration, hyperbole") does not seem to fit here; I have connected it with *balāghah* "eloquence", from *balagha*, "to reach, come across".

22 *al-iʿtirāḍ wa-l-taṣaffuḥ*: The literal meaning of *taṣaffuḥ* is "turning over the pages" *(taqlīb al-ṣafaḥāt)*; derived from this is the meaning "to scrutinise, examine critically, pay attention", on which my conjectured translation is based. But Pellat may be correct with his "par hazard et superficiellement" (connecting the words with *ʿaraḍ* and *ṣafḥah*, "surface", respectively), which in a sense is the opposite of my interpretation. Note that *taṣaffuḥ* is used later in the passage as "paying attention".

23 The speaker is presumably the anonymous author of the passage, as was apparently believed also by al-ʿAskarī and some others who quote this passage. Some others who quote from Bahlah's text, however, end here or slightly before, as if they believe that another speaker takes over.

24 The words *wa-lā mafḍūlan*, not found in all MSS and therefore put between brackets by the editor (and here between <>), is also absent from most other versions.

25 *lā mushtarakan wa-lā muḍammanan*; Pellat: "ni ambigu, ni incomplet". The word *muḍamman* and the verbal noun *taḍmīn* have several meanings, including "enjambment", which is how al-ʿAskarī and following him Pellat, it seems, interpret it, although normally this applies to poetry rather than prose.

26 Pellat: "que son outil se plie à ses exigences".

27 cf. Pellat ("Il ne doit douter de lui-même"), probably better than "accuse, suspect himself".

himself. For if he accuses himself unduly he does himself an injustice and consigns to himself the humiliation of those that are wronged; and if he thinks well of himself unduly he gives himself (false) assurance and consigns to himself the ignominy of those who feel assured. All this implies a certain amount of work *(shughl)*; every work implies a certain measure of weakness, and all weakness implies a certain degree of ignorance.

Kratchkovsky doubts whether the ideas in this passage do in fact have an Indian source, and both its style and its ideas make a thoroughly Arabic impression, even though some of the ideas may also be found in Indian rhetoric.[28] One could almost suspect that al-Jāḥiẓ wrote or revised it himself. Despite some clumsy repetitions[29] its style is undoubtedly "literary", marked as it is by a restrained use of rhyme *(laḥẓ / lafẓ, ḥakīmā / ʿalīmā, ṭibqā / wafqā, ālātuh / adātuh)*, by an extensive use of syntactic and semantic parallelism often with assonance (e.g. *lā yudaqqiqu l-maʿāniya kull al-tadqīq / wa-lā yunaqqiḥu l-alfāẓ kull al-tanqīḥ* ...), and by its conclusion with a *catena* or *gradatio*, a chain of aphorisms. It seems to ramble a bit, jumping from the orator (O) to his speech (S), from there to the audience (A), and so forth; but even here it may be possible to detect some order, for the passage seems to have a symmetrical structure (OSASASO). One could argue that it sins against some of its own precepts, for it is not free of repetition and redundancy. Yet, the Arabic text has obviously been carefully refined and polished, as if the reader were to be flattered by thinking himself to be the "wise man or a learned philosopher" mentioned in the text.

Bishr ibn al-Muʿtamir, an early Muʿtazilite theologian who died in 210/825, also had literary gifts. Some interesting poems are quoted by al-Jāḥiẓ in his *al-Ḥayawān*, and a passage about oratory is found in *al-Bayān wa-l-tabyīn* and other sources.[30] Again, it is a *ṣaḥīfah*, a written page, carefully composed *("min taḥbīrihī wa-tanmīqihī")*, with advice addressed to would-be orators, somewhat rudely given to some young men in the presence of their teacher, Ibrāhīm ibn Jabalah

---

28 I thank my Oxford colleagues Dr Firuza Abdullaeva for her help with Kratchkovsky's Russian and Prof. Christopher Minkowski for his comments on the possible Indian background.

29 e.g. *awwal al-balāghah ijtimāʿ ālat al-balāghah*; instead of *lā yukallim sayyid al-amah bi-kalām al-amah* he could have said *lā yukallim al-sayyid bi-kalām al-amah.*

30 Al-Jāḥiẓ, *Bayān*, vol. 1, 135-139 (or 140? It is not wholly clear where Bishr's text ends). Also quoted in al-Zubayr ibn Bakkār, *al-Akhbār al-muwaffaqiyyāt*, ed. Sāmī Makkī al-ʿĀnī, Baghdad: al-Jumhūriyyah al-ʿIrāqiyyah, Riʾāsat Dīwān al-Awqāf 1972, 163-165, Ibn ʿAbd Rabbih, *ʿIqd*, vol. 4, 55-56, al-ʿAskarī, *Ṣināʿatayn*, 140, Ibn Rashīq, *ʿUmdah*, vol. 1, 212-214. See I. Y. Kratchkovskij, "Мутазилитский трактат VIII в. о литературном творчестве", in his *Избранные Сочинения*, vol. 2, 221-229 (Arabic text and Russian translation); Wolfhart Heinrichs, *Arabische Dichtung und griechische Poetik*, Beirut – Wiesbaden: Franz Steiner 1969, 47-48 ʿAdnān ʿUbayd al-ʿAlī (ed.), "Bishr ibn al-Muʿtamir: shiʿruhu wa-ṣaḥīfatuhu l-balāghiyyah", *Majallat Maʿhad al-Makhṭūṭāt al-ʿArabiyyah* 31 (1987), 503-541. For a partial translation, see Suzanne P. Stetkevych, *Abū Tammām and the Poetics of the ʿAbbāsid Age*, Leiden: Brill 1991, 16-17 (attributing the text to al-Jāḥiẓ rather than Bishr); a useful summary is given by Josef van Ess, *Theologie und Gesellschaft*, vol. 3, Berlin: de Gruyter 1992, 112-115.

al-Sakūnī ("Do not pay attention to him!").[31] The passage, here given in a shortened form, shows some parallels with the page produced by Bahlah the Indian:

> Take for yourself a moment when your mind is full of energy, free of preoccupations, and ready to respond to you; for a little of what is made at such time[32] is more precious, nobler, better to the ear, sweeter to the heart, freer of bad mistakes, and more productive of choice and brilliant things, than many a noble expression and novel idea. Know that this will yield more to you than what a long day of toil, drawn-out exertion, and strained, repeated effort will give you. Whatever you may fail to achieve, you will not fail to make your intended meaning accepted and to be light and easy on the tongue, just as it sprang from its well and came up from its mine. Be careful not to take a rugged path, for the rugged path will deliver you into the hands of tangledness, and tangledness is what will consume your ideas and mar your expressions. Whoever desires a noble idea, let him seek for it a noble expression, for a lofty idea deserves a lofty expression; both deserve to be protected from what may spoil them and debase them…
> Be on (one of) three levels (…) If the first level happens to be out of your reach, if it will not come to you and be available at a first attempt, as soon as you make an effort, when you find that the expressions will not fall in their proper places or settle in their right positions allotted to them, or when a rhyme word will not take its proper place, when it cannot be joined to its like, when it is uncomfortable in its place and loath to stay in its position, then you should not force the expressions to usurp their places and to settle where they are not at home. For if you do not engage in composing metrical verse and if you do not take it upon yourself to produce choice speech in prose, nobody will blame you for not doing so. If, however, you engage in either of them while you are not proficient or naturally talented, no expert who can see the pros and contras of a case, then even those who are more deserving of criticism than you will criticise you, and those inferior to you will deem themselves superior.

The above passages, that of the "Indian" and Bishr's advice, are mainly concerned with oratory, although Bishr also mentions poetry. When the poet Abū Tammām gives advice on composing poetry to his younger colleague, al-Buḥturī, he dwells on similar themes:[33]

---

31 As van Ess remarks, there is some doubt about the story, for this Ibrāhīm ibn Jabalah seems to have been active in the mid-eighth century (see al-Jahshiyārī, *al-Wuzarāʾ wa-l-kuttāb*, Cairo: Muṣṭafā al-Bābī al-Ḥalabī 1980, 82, 106-107) and he was therefore much older than Bishr. But Bishr, who died at an advanced age, could have been a young man.

32 *fa-inna qalīl tilka l-sāʿah*; al-ʿAskarī has *fa-inna qalbaka tilka l-sāʿah*; the editors of *al-ʿIqd* record a variant that has *nafsaka* instead of *qalbaka*.

33 The authenticity of Abū Tammām's "recommendation" *(waṣiyyah)* is not above suspicion, since it is first found in a relatively late work, al-Ḥuṣrī, *Zahr al-ādab*, repr. Beirut: Dār al-Jīl 1972, 152-153; also in Ibn Rashīq, *ʿUmdah*, vol. 2, 114-115 and several later sources. See Jamal Eddine Bencheikh, *Poétique arabe: essai sur les voies d'une creation*, Paris: Anthropos 1975, 88-90, Geert Jan van Gelder, "Inspiration and 'Writer's Block' in Classical Arabic Poetry", in: *Poetica medievale tra oriente e occidente*, Paolo Bagni & Maurizio Pistoso, eds., Rome: Carocci 2003, 61-71 (see p. 66 and note 52 for more references). The version in Ibn Abī l-Iṣbaʿ, *Taḥrīr al-taḥbīr*, ed. Ḥifnī Muḥammad Sharaf, Cairo: Lajnat Iḥyāʾ al-Turāth al-Islāmī AH 1383, 410-411 or al-Nawājī, *Muqaddimah fī ṣināʿat al-naẓm wa-l-nathr*, Beirut: Maktabat al-Ḥayāt n.d., 40-42, is markedly more flowery.

> Choose moments when you have few worries and are free of anxieties. Know that usually, if one wishes to compose or memorize something, one aims at doing so at dawn; for then the soul has taken its share of rest and sleep. If you want love poetry, then make the diction elegant and the ideas subtle. Provide much in the way of displaying ardent love, complaining of the pains of grief, the agitation of yearnings, and the torment of separation. If you embark on praising a munificent patron, then make public his virtues, demonstrate his lineages, and elucidate his known characteristics and the nobility of his status. Arrange[34] your thoughts and be on your guard against those that are unknown. Beware of disfiguring your verse with ugly words. Be like a tailor who cuts the cloth to the measures of the body. If you are confronted with boredom, then rest yourself: only make poetry when your mind is empty.[35] Make your lust[36] for making verse the means towards good composition, for lust is a good helper. In general, compare your poetry with earlier poetry, of those who went before. Seek what the experts deem good and avoid what they reject: then you will follow the right path, if God wills.

It may strike us as surprising that Abū Tammām, the innovative poet, appears so conservative here, in his warning against "unknown" or unfamiliar poetic ideas and his recommendation to hold fast to the canon and critical consensus. His advice is cast in simple but eloquent language, without the far-fetched imagery for which he was notorious.[37] There is a modest use of parallelism and rhyme *(qalīl al-humūm / ṣifr min al-ghumūm, ijʿal al-lafẓ rashīqā / wa-l-maʿnā raqīqā, ṣabābah / ka'ābah, ashwāq / firāq, manāqibah / manāsibah)*. The direct incentive that leads to good poetry is a strong desire ("lust") to make it: it almost sounds as *l'art pour l'art*, even though such a concept hardly existed in medieval Arabic poetry or poetics.

While the use of *sajʿ* is often a clear indication of the literary character of a piece of prose, it is by no means a necessary element. A passage on *balāghah* and the use of *sajʿ* by Abū Ḥayyān al-Tawḥīdī stresses this eloquently, for it is itself eloquent while almost devoid of *sajʿ* :[38]

> I shall mention to you the varieties of eloquence, in a summary by means of which you may find out about the details. Know that the first of its kinds is the speech that is granted by natural talent *(ṭabʿ)*, even though this natural speech is never free of art *(ṣināʿah)*. The second kind is the speech that is obtained by means of art, even though

---

34 *naḍḍid*; Ibn Rashīq has *taqāḍa*, Ibn Abī l-Iṣbaʿ has *taqāṣṣ* the meanings of which are not clear in this context. The clause is lacking in al-Nawājī.

35 Obviously meaning "not preoccupied".

36 He uses *shahwah*, usually associated with either sex or food.

37 One should keep in mind that our only, and perhaps not wholly reliable, source for the text is al-Buḥturī, whose own style is often contrasted with that of his teacher.

38 Abū Ḥayyān al-Tawḥīdī, *al-Baṣā'ir wa-l-dhakhā'ir*, ed. Wadād al-Qāḍī, Beirut: Dār Ṣādir 1988, vol. 2, 68-69. Parts of this passage are also found in al-Tawḥīdī's *Mathālib al-wazīrayn*, Damascus: Dār al-Fikr [1961, date of preface], 94-95, where they are attributed to a Christian *kātib* called Abū ʿUbayd, who is praised for his eloquence (ibid. 93) and who is identical, I suspect, with Ibn [thus] ʿUbayd al-Kātib, an associate of al-Tawḥīdī whom he mentions several times in his *al-Imtāʿ wa-l-mu'ānasah* and other works. See e.g. Joel L. Kraemer, *Humanism in the Renaissance of Islam: The Cultural Revival During the Buyid Age*, Leiden: Brill 1992, 198, 201.

> this artful speech is never free of naturalness. The third kind is the free-flowing continuous speech *(al-musalsal)*[39] that spontaneously comes in the course of the two former two methods. Examples of these varieties will be found in these *Anecdotes and Insights*;[40] if you look for them you will find them. But whatever your own gifts are in this matter, do not be overly fond of *sajʿ*, for it is difficult to achieve if one aims at doing it in its proper place. Neither should you avoid it altogether, for then you will be deprived of half the beauty. The course to follow in this is to aim at a proportion such as that of the embroidered hem *(ṭirāz)* to the robe as a whole, the ornamented border to the silk gown, the beauty-spot to the face, the eye in a human being, the pupil to the eye, or the gesture to movement. For you know that when a face has many moles, to the point of being dominated by them, the extent of the black parts will take away the perfection of beauty. *Sajʿ* runs smoothly in some places but not in others, and free-flowing (unrhymed) speech *(istirsāl)* is a better indication of natural talent (…) Try to be like a goldsmith who takes a gold flake, casts it, then moulds it, then engraves it, then drives it, then embellishes it, and then offers it for sale (…)

During al-Tawḥīdī's lifetime we find the first instances of more sustained compositions of artistic literary criticism: neither the short aphorisms of the earliest times nor the somewhat more extended passages of one or a few pages. Al-Tawḥīdī himself contributed to this trend, for instance in his collection of "essays" entitled *al-Imtāʿ wa-l-muʾānasah*, presented as the faithful record of conversations and discussions in the presence of his patron, the vizier Ibn Saʿdān (d. 374/983) but no doubt carefully edited by the author. One of these sessions ("the seventh night") is a report of al-Tawḥīdī's dispute with Ibn ʿUbayd (the Christian *kātib* mentioned before) on the merits of the two main types of *kātib*, the chancery scribe, standing for *balāghah* and literary art, and the accountant, standing for the utilitarian, "no-nonsense" use of language;[41] another is devoted to the difference between prose and poetry.[42] Both compositions are not meant

---

39 I am not certain of the precise meaning of *musalsal* (literally, "concatenated") here. In *Mathālib al-wazīrayn* it is said that this style is found in al-Jāḥiẓ's works.

40 *Al-Nawādir wa-l-baṣāʾir*; he seems to refer to the present work.

41 Al-Tawḥīdī, *Imtāʿ*, vol. 1, 96-104; for a translation and brief discussion, see Geert Jan van Gelder, "Man of Letters *v.* Man of Figures: The Seventh Night from al-Tawḥīdī's *al-Imtāʿ wa-l-muʾānasa*", in: *Signa Scripta Vocis: Studies about Scripts, Scriptures, Scribes and Languages in the Near East, presented to J. H. Hospers...*, H. L. J. Vanstiphout *et al.*, eds., Groningen: Egbert Forsten 1986, 53-63. The theme was taken up later by al-Ḥarīrī in his 22nd *maqāmah* (*al-Furātiyyah*). It is somewhat paradoxical that Ibn ʿUbayd is presented as attacking artistic prose while al-Tawḥīdī praises him for his eloquence elsewhere (see note 38).

42 Al-Tawḥīdī, *Imtāʿ*, vol. 2, 130-147; see Klaus Hachmeier, "Rating *adab*: Al-Tawḥīdī on the Merits of Poetry and Prose. The 25th Night of *Kitāb al-Imtāʿ wa-l-muʾānasa*, Translation and Commentary", *Al-Qanṭara* 25 (2004), 357-385. The conclusion of the text, some 100 words with statements by Ibn al-Marāghī, Ibn ʿUbayd, and the vizier, is not included in this translation, perhaps because it deals with a topic (aphorisms, *kalimāt qiṣār*) that is resumed in the following, 26th night. However, this truncation somewhat spoils the unity of the text, and Ibn al-Marāghī's remark, corroborated by Ibn ʿUbayd, on the felicitous combination of prose and poetry in one text is surely a fitting conclusion to the debate. See also Ziyad Ramadan az-Zuʿbī, *Das Verhältnis von Poesie und Prosa in der arabischen Literaturtheorie des Mittelalters*, Berlin: Klaus Schwarz 1987, 191-196.

as systematic, scholarly treatises: reading them is, as Klaus Hachmeier said of the latter essay, "an enlightening and entertaining experience"; each is "a work of *adab* about *adab*".[43] They are obviously intended, not merely as collections of aphorisms and appropriate quotations (although they contain much of this), but as unified compositions, each embedded in the framework imposed by the format of *al-Imtāʿ wa-l-muʾānasah* as a whole: a conversation with the erudite vizier, who solicits, prompts, and himself provides opinions.

Al-Tawḥīdī's report of the debate between the "man of letters" *(kātib al-inshāʾ)* and the "man of figures" *(kātib al-ḥisāb)* is prompted by the vizier's question, "I heard you shouting today in the Palace with Ibn ʿUbayd: what was it all about?" In the body of the text al-Tawḥīdī refutes, sentence by sentence, Ibn ʿUbayd's claims for his own profession given at the beginning. At the end, after a particularly eloquent passage by al-Tawḥīdī, in which he finishes, uncharacteristically, with a few maxims in *sajʿ*, the vizier speaks again, expressing his satisfaction with al-Tawḥīdī's refutation and commenting on the latter's career. After a few exchanges, they note that it is midnight and the text ends with one of the closing formulas used in the collection: *wa-nṣaraft* ("and I left").

The same formula ends the debate on poetry *vs.* prose. The topic is suggested by the vizier. Al-Tawḥīdī, at the outset, remarks that "speech about speech is difficult", since "it revolves around itself and is entangled with itself *(innahū yadūr ʿalā nafsihī wa-yaltabis baʿḍuhū bi-baʿḍihī)*".[44] The point made here is crucial to our topic. Just as thinking about thinking or being conscious of being conscious could lead to a kind of vertigo, and just as speaking about speech, or literary criticism of literary criticism, requires the deployment of a different level of discourse (conventionally indicated by the prefix "meta-"), so an artistic, literary expression of ideas on artistic expression runs the risk of being entangled in its own clothes (as eloquently suggested by al-Tawḥīdī's use of the verb *iltabasa*, which combines the concepts of clothing and confusion). But not every passage in the text, in which many different persons are quoted, is equally flowery and artistic, and even if they are "literary" in their use of elegant balancing, parallelism and other devices, this does not necessarily impair their clarity of meaning. Particularly interesting is a long and somewhat puzzling quotation from al-Tawḥīdī's revered master, Abū Sulaymān al-Manṭiqī al-Sijistānī (d. *c.* 375/985), in which he distinguishes between seven different kinds of *balāghah*, eloquence (or rhetoric, as Hachmeier translates): those of poetry, oratory, prose (apparently written prose, as distinct from the spoken prose of oratory), proverb (or parable, *exemplum, al-mathal*), intellect (*al-ʿaql*, perhaps standing for scientific and scholarly discourse), extemporizing *(al-badīhah)*, and exegesis (or interpretation, *al-taʾwīl*).[45]

---

43 Hachmeier, "Rating *adab*", 359.
44 Al-Tawḥīdī, *Imtāʿ*, vol. 2, 131; cf. Hachmeier, "Rating *adab*", 360.
45 Al-Tawḥīdī, *Imtāʿ*, vol. 2, 140-143; cf. Hachmeier, "Rating *adab*", 377-379.

The categories seem to overlap, for one could imagine that "extemporizing" and "aphorism" could be combined, for instance, with "oratory". And – to take the one most relevant to the present volume – what is "eloquence of prose" (*balāghat al-nathr*)? According to Abū Sulaymān it implies that

> its expression *(lafẓ)* should be readily understood *(mutanāwal)*, its meaning *(maʿnā)* well-known, its text refined, the composition *(taʾlīf)* should be simple, the intent *(murād)* should be sound, it should be shining brightly and of gentle appearance, its blades should be polished, analogies (parables, or examples? Arab. *amṯāl*) should be easy to grasp, the "necks" *(al-hawādī)* should be connected, and the "hind quarters" *(al-aʿjāz)* set apart [?].[46]

The translator's final parenthesized question mark is justified, for the passage begins with phrases that are straightforward and easily understood but then plunges into a series of disparate metaphors that are by no means wholly clear. One can see what is meant by *rawnaq* (lustre, splendour), but what about the *ḥawāshī* ("borders, seams") that should be *raqīqah* ("thin, fine, delicate"),[47] and what precisely are the burnished "blades" or "swords" (*ṣafāʾiḥ*, probably an allusion to written pages, *ṣaḥāʾif*) or the "necks" and "hindquarters" of the text? Why should the necks be connected *(muttaṣilah)* but the hindquarters set apart or separated *(mufaṣṣalah)*? It is this unfocused imagery and obscurity that can make artistic literary criticism alternately a source of admiration (when one grasps the general drift) and irritation (when one grapples with the details of interpretation). Similarly, Abū Sulaymān's distinction between various kinds of styles, each requiring different standards of excellence, is valid and useful, but the apparent lack of logical rigour can only rub in the fact that literary criticism is not a science.

Literary criticism in the 4th/10th century takes on other extended forms that, in one way or another, belong to artistic prose. The earliest monographs, dating back to the end of the preceding century, do not fall into this category. Although Ibn al-Muʿtazz was himself an important poet and also produced some highly literary prose,[48] his seminal treatise on literary devices and rhetorical or poetic embellishments *(Kitāb al-Badīʿ)*, written in 274/887, is written in a factual, unadorned style, as is his practical criticism in other works.[49] Another proficient poet, Ibn Ṭabāṭabā (d. 322/934), wrote his *ʿIyār al-shiʿr* ("The Standard of Poetry)

---

46 Al-Tawḥīdī, *Imtāʿ*, vol. 2, 141, as translated by Hachmeier, "Rating *adab*", 377-378.

47 *raqīq al-ḥawāshī* is in fact a very common expression for anything that is delicate and refined.

48 See for instance the short passages on *bayān* and *balāghah*, in *Rasāʾil Ibn al-Muʿtazz fī l-naqd wa-l-adab wal-ijtimāʿ*, ed. Muḥammad ʿAbd al-Munʿim Khafājī, Cairo: Muṣṭafā al-Bābī al-Ḥalabī 1946, 62-64.

49 e.g. in his *Ṭabaqāt al-shuʿarāʾ al-muḥdathīn*, ed. ʿAbd al-Sattār Aḥmad Farrāj, Cairo: Dār al-Maʿārif 1968, and his *Risālah ʿalā maḥāsin shiʿr Abī Tammām wa-masāwīh* (On the Good and Bad Points of Abū Tammām's Poetry), quoted in al-Marzubānī, *al-Muwashshaḥ*, ed. ʿAlī Muḥammad al-Bijāwī, Cairo: Dār Nahḍat Miṣr 1965, 470-490, also in *Rasāʾil Ibn al-Muʿtazz*, 19-31.

in the form of a series of essays on poetry and poetics, such as the poetic process, descriptions and similes, good and bad poetry depending on either the ideas or the expression, far-fetched motifs, transitions between themes. Although some passages may be called literary, the style of the book as a whole is not. Even less so is the first true poetics in Arabic literary history, *Naqd al-shiʿr* (Criticism of Poetry) by Qudāmah ibn Jaʿfar (d. perhaps 337/948). In subsequent centuries Qudāmah is sometimes called a paragon of eloquence,[50] yet his own style is that of the scholar rather than the *adīb*. The titles of the books by Ibn Ṭabāṭabā and Qudāmah are "literary" in that they employ metaphor: both are derived from testing coins, but the analogy between monetary and literary currency was already conventional[51] and not particularly literary. In the following I shall briefly discuss some longer texts that qualify, by my standards. The discussion will not be exhaustive but is intended merely to highlight a hitherto somewhat neglected aspect of texts that have been studied by many scholars in some detail but rarely with an eye to their literary characteristics.

Abū Bakr al-Ṣūlī (d. *c.* 335/947), all-round courtier, unrivalled chess-player, court historian, editor of the poetry of several of the most important "modern" poets, also wrote several valuable works of literary criticism. Some of these have an anthological or biographical character, such as his monographs on Abū Tammām and al-Buḥturī. His own style may be appreciated in a remarkable and lengthy epistle addressed to a certain Abū l-Layth Muzāḥim ibn Fātik, about whom nothing is known. It is prefixed to his book on Abū Tammām[52] and deals with the controversial status of that poet and compares him, favourably, with that of younger contemporaries such as al-Buḥturī and Ibn al-Rūmī. The significance of this epistle or essay has been stressed by several recent scholars, for instance by Stetkevych[53] and Ouyang;[54] it is an important document in the controversy about Abū Tammām that inspired many works of literary criticism. But not only its contents are interesting: its style, as may be expected from an epistle that is addressed to a specific person and deals with the personal preferences of the writer, contrasts with that of the author's monographs. It is more rhetorical, more personal, and altogether more "literary". To give a short example: when al-Ṣūlī wanted to say that his patron, apparently, had an unstated demand, he could have written simply something like "I saw that you wanted something else

---

50 e.g. by al-Ḥarīri in his introduction to his *Maqāmāt* (ed. A.I. Sylvestre de Sacy, Paris: Imprimerie Royale 1847-1853, 11): "... even if one possessed the eloquence of Qudāmah".

51 See Ibn Sallām al-Jumaḥī, *Ṭabaqāt*, 6-7, 8.

52 Abū Bakr Muḥammad ibn Yaḥyā al-Ṣūlī, *Akhbār Abū Tammām*, ed. Khalīl Maḥmūd ʿAsākir et al., Cairo: Lajnat al-Taʾlīf 1937; for the the *risālah* to Muzāḥim ibn Fātik see 1-56.

53 Suzanne Pinckney Stetkevych, *Abū Tammām and the Poetics of the ʿAbbāsid Age*, Leiden: Brill 1991, 38-48.

54 Wen-chin Ouyang, *Literary Criticism in Medieval Arabic-Islamic Culture: The Making of a Tradition*, Edinburgh: Edinburgh University Press 1997, 138-140.

from me, but did not say so, perhaps to spare me further trouble". Such a statement would be personal but plain. Instead, he expresses himself as follows, in a manner distinctly literary by the standards of his own time:

> Then the eye of thought showed me there was something left in your mind which your tongue did not reveal to me, either because you were unwilling to trouble me or fearing that you would add to my labour, what with all that was allotted to me: the injustice of Time *(jawr al-zamān)*, the harshness of the ruler *(jafāʾ al-sulṭān)*, and the altered attitude of friends *(taghayyur al-ikhwān)*.[55]

When he embarks on actual literary criticism he remains personal, giving his own views in a straightforward manner rather than by quoting other people's opinions and hiding behind them. He rarely uses *sajʿ*, high-flown metaphors or far-fetched similes but his style is rhetorical and artful, with exclamations, innuendos, rhetorical questions and syntactic suspensions, as in a passage also quoted by Stetkevych:[56]

> If these people knew what others have condemned in skilled poets, ancient and modern alike, there would be so much that whatever they blame Abū Tammām for would dwindle, if only they believed in being fair and looked at it fairly. Someone who blames Abū Tammām – a leading poet who began a new school followed by every good poet after him, but without reaching his level, so that people speak of "the Ṭāʾite school", someone to which every skilled poet after him is traced back, following his footsteps – he has a rank so lowly that Blame itself should be safeguarded from mentioning it: lowland would rise above it![57] Before Abū Tammām poets would come up with something original in one or two verses in a whole poem; this was reckoned to be a token of their most sublime excellence. Then Abū Tammām put his mind to it and drove his talent to be original in the greater part of his poetry. And so he did, by my life, and well did he do it! Even if he had fallen short in a small portion – but he did not – this would have drowned in the seas of his excellence. Who is so perfect in a thing that he is not allowed to make a mistake? Only someone without sense would imagine that.

This eminently readable epistle (partisanship is often more attractive than sober impartiality) concludes with a conventional apology for having been long-winded: "I have written such a long epistle – God give you strength – because I took such delight in addressing you and being passionate to provide what you desired".[58] The excuse sounds genuine.

Polemical criticism informs some of the more literary works of criticism of the generations following al-Ṣūlī. The obsessively literate statesman of the Būyids, al-Ṣāḥib ibn ʿAbbād (d. 385/995), composed a treatise on that other great and controversial poet, al-Mutanabbī (d. 354/965). *Al-Kashf ʿan masāwī al-Mutanabbī* (Ex-

---

55 Al-Ṣūlī, *Akhbār Abī Tammām*, 5.
56 ibid., 37, cf. Stetkevych's translation, *Abū Tammām*, 44-45 (with some differences on minor points).
57 Stetkevych's "lower than the lowest bog" sounds even better but may be somewhat less precise for *yartafiʿu ʿanhā l-wahd*.
58 Al-Ṣūlī, *Akhbār Abī Tammām*, 56.

posing al-Mutanabbī's Faults) is also a *risālah*, addressed to an unnamed person.[59] In the introduction he depicts himself as an unbiased critic, normally loath to find fault but reluctantly doing so on this occasion, having been provoked by an uncritical admirer of the poet. As Pellat says, Ibn ᶜAbbād was most noted, and sometimes criticised, for his fondness of *sajᶜ*, but he did not employ it indiscriminately.[60] In the present treatise he hardly uses it. The literary character lies in the style not only of the introduction but also where he criticises individual verses. Whereas many critics would express their condemnation in plain terms such as "this is extremely ugly" and might deploy their philological skills to explain the failing in some detail, al-Ṣāḥib regularly has a mocking quip or an original scathing remark and mostly omits scholarly pedantry. A verse by al-Mutanabbī is said to be "ugly like love lyrics by old men".[61] Of the poet's hemistich "... and No! to you when you ask, No, O No, No!"[62] he says, "I had heard of the *faʾfāʾ* [a stammerer who says *fa-fa-fa-* 'and-and-and'] but I had not heard of the *laʾlāʾ* [by analogy, someone who says *lā-lā-lā* 'No no no']".[63] Another verse he declares fit to be inscribed on talismans and charms, apparently because of the ungrammatical *illāka* (for *illā anta*, "except you").[64] When the poet changes Jibrīl (Gabriel) into Jibrīn for the sake of the rhyme, Ibn ᶜAbbād wonders if the archangel would be pleased with this distortion of his name. Of the striking opening verse "Was it single, or sextuple in a single, / our sweet night...?" *(Uḥādun am sudāsun fī uḥādī / luyaylatunā ...)*[65] Ibn ᶜAbbād says, with some justification, that it perplexes the mind and transcends ordinary arithmetic; it resembles the speech of the Jikil (Chigil, a central Asian Turkic people) or the jabber of the Zuṭṭ (Gypsies).[66] And so, relentlessly, he goes on, entertaining the reader.

A contemporary critic, author of a valuable work on stylistics and poetics[67] and himself an accomplished poet and prose-writer, Abū ᶜAlī al-Ḥātimī (d. 388/998)

59 Published as an appendix to Abū Saᶜd Muḥammad ibn Aḥmad al-ᶜAmīdī, *al-Ibānah ᶜan sariqāt al-Mutanabbī*, ed. Ibrāhīm al-Dasūqī al-Bisāṭī, Cairo: Dār al-Maᶜārif 1969, 239-270.

60 C. Pellat, "Al-Ṣāḥib Ibn ᶜAbbād", in: *ᶜAbbasid Belles-Lettres*, Julia Ashtiany *et al.*, eds., Cambridge: Cambridge University Press 1990, 110.

61 Ibn ᶜAbbād, *Kashf*, 258.

62 *Wa-lā laka fī suʾālika lā alā lā*; al-Mutanabbī, *Dīwān*, ed. F. Dieterici, Berlin: Mittler 1861, 221.

63 Ibn ᶜAbbād, *Kashf*, 260.

64 Ibid., 260-261.

65 Al-Mutanabbī, *Dīwān*, 137.

66 Ibn ᶜAbbād, *Kashf*, 262. Instead of al-Jikil (on which see e.g. Yāqūt's geographical dictionary *Muᶜjam al-buldān*, *s.v.*) some later quotations (al-Badīᶜī, *al-Ṣubḥ al-munabbī ᶜan ḥaythiyyat al-Mutanabbī*, ed. Muṣṭafā al-Saqqā *et al.*, Cairo: Dār al-Maᶜārif 1963, 305 and al-Thaᶜālibī, *Yatīmat al-dahr*, ed. Muḥammad Muḥyī l-Dīn ᶜAbd al-Ḥamīd, Cairo: Maktabat al-Ḥusayn al-Tijāriyyah 1947, vol. 1, 147) have *al-ḥukl* "voiceless insects, e.g. ants" (which is less likely on several obvious grounds).

67 Abū ᶜAlī Muḥammad ibn al-Ḥasan al-Ḥātimī, *Ḥilyat al-muḥāḍarah fī ṣināᶜat al-shiᶜr*, ed. Jaᶜfar al-Kattānī, Baghdad: Dār al-Rashīd 1979.

also attacked al-Mutanabbī in a polemical treatise.[68] Its title has been translated as "illustrative treatise on the mention of the appropriations of Abū al-Ṭayyib al-Mutanabbī and that which is worthless of his poetry";[69] but it is nastier than that, for *mūḍiḥah*, in addition to its "normal" sense of "revealing", also means "laying bare the bone", said of inflicting grievous wounds, as the author himself reminds us: he intends it to be a "hatchet job".[70] Al-Ḥātimī wrote this lengthy "epistle" (which runs to nearly 200 pages in a modern edition) in the form of a report of his dispute, or rather a series of disputes with the poet that took place, attended by a gathering of students, in the poet's house in Baghdad around the year 352/963. Bonebakker calls it "perhaps one of the most accomplished pieces of caricature from mediaeval Arabic literature".[71] Opinions on al-Ḥātimī's own stylistic gifts are divided. Whereas al-Thaᶜālibī praises him as an excellent stylist in prose and poetry,[72] al-Tawḥīdī is far less positive and criticizes him for his lack of smoothness and his "rough" diction, more appropriate to a Bedouin than a city-dweller; al-Ḥātimī "is intoxicated with speech, but when he is sober again he has a hangover".[73] The tone of *al-Mūḍiḥah* is set in the introduction, with a satirical portrait of the haughty and disdainful poet, clad in seven robes, each of a different colour, in the heat of summer.[74] Without any deference to the poet's fame or seniority, the young al-Ḥātimī launches an attack, choosing a verse that in his view (and by most modern standards, too) seems tasteless:[75] "Tell me about your verse, 'Fear God! Cover that beauty with a veil, / for if you showed yourself, young women in their chambers would menstruate!'[76] – is this how one speaks about lovers?" The poet defends himself by referring to an interpretation of a

68 Abū ᶜAlī al-Ḥātimī, *al-Risālah al-mūḍiḥah fī dhikr sariqāt Abī l-Ṭayyib al-Mutanabbī wa-sāqiṭ shiᶜrih* , ed. Muḥammad Yūsuf Najm, Beirut: Dār Ṣādir / Dār Bayrūt 1965. For shorter versions, see the text given as an appendix in al-ᶜAmīdī, *Ibānah*, 271-290 (entitled *al-Risālah al-Ḥātimiyyah wa-hiya l-munāẓarah bayn al-Ḥātimī wa-l-Mutanabbī bi-madīnat Baghdād*) and that quoted in Yāqūt, *Muᶜjam al-udabāʾ*, ed. Aḥmad Farīd Rifāᶜī, Cairo: Dār al-Maʾmūn 1936-1938, vol. 18, 159-179 and in al-Badīᶜī, *Ṣubḥ*, 130-142.

69 Ouyang, *Literary Criticism*, 149. On al-Ḥātimī and his polemics with al-Mutanabbī see S.A. Bonebakker, *Ḥātimī and his Encounter with Mutanabbī: A Biographical Sketch*, Amsterdam: North-Holland Publishing Company 1984; also, Amidu Sanni, "The Historic Encounter Between al-Mutanabbī and al-Ḥātimī: Its Contribution to the Discourse on *ghuluww* (Hyperbole) in Arabic Literary Theory", *Journal of Arabic Literature* 35 (2004), 159-174.

70 Al-Ḥātimī, *Mūḍiḥah*, 4-5.

71 Bonebakker, *Ḥātimī*, 6.

72 al-Thaᶜālibī, *Yatīmah*, vol. 3, 103.

73 *Imtāᶜ*, vol. 1, 135.

74 al-Ḥātimī, *Mūḍiḥah*, 9-10.

75 ibid., 13-14.

76 al-Mutanabbī, *Dīwān*, 126, in an ode praising a patron, where the text has *dhābat* "would melt (of desire)"; the variant *ḥāḍat* "would menstruate (prompted by sexual desire)" is mentioned by the commentator, al-Wāḥidī. Al-Qāḍī al-Jurjānī says that the poet changed *ḥāḍat* to *dhābat* ("would melt") after having being criticized (*al-Wasāṭah bayn al-Mutanabbī wa-khuṣūmih*, ed. Muḥammad Abū l-Faḍl Ibrāhīm and ᶜAlī Muḥammad al-Bijāwī, Cairo: ᶜĪsā l-Bābī al-Ḥalabī n.d., 90).

Qur'anic expression from the story of handsome Yūsuf/Joseph when he is shown to the women of the town: "When they saw him, *akbarnahū*";[77] most commentators think that the last word means "... they thought much of him" but another interpretation is "... they menstruated".[78] Al-Ḥātimī rejects this and when al-Mutanabbī asks him "to forgive" this expression for the sake of the quality of the following verses, al-Ḥātimī goes on to point out how many motifs of these verses were taken from earlier poets. Seemingly impartial and unbiased, he stresses that al-Mutanabbī has one or several undeniably good verses in every poem, but regularly couples them with verses that are silly *(sakhīfah)* in meaning and expression, verses that "raid on the (good) meanings and expressions like hairless wolves on roaming sheep ...; it is one of the worst failings when one expression is a bad companion to its sister".[79] Here al-Ḥātimī seems to suggest that mixing good and bad verses is somehow worse than composing uniformly bad poems; it does not help the poet that his good lines are compared to sheep, or even "sheep of inferior quality" (the word used is *naqad*). Thus al-Ḥātimī employs various rhetorical means to belittle his famous adversary. It is obvious that the text cannot be a faithful rendering of what was said in the debate; as Bonebakker notes, the sarcasm is too strong at times to be believable in a "polite" debate in al-Mutanabbī's own surroundings[80] and it is unlikely that the proud poet would have suffered repeated public humiliation in the manner described.[81] In short, the debate is a fine specimen of rhetorical fiction which, in spite of its obvious partiality and the equally obvious pettiness of some of the carping, is remarkably effective: as Bonebakker admits, "one almost ends up feeling that Mutanabbī was, after all, a mediocre poet who was not only lacking in originality, but also had insufficient competence in grammar, lexicography, and rhetoric, and sometimes gave evidence of incredibly bad taste."[82]

Badīᶜ al-Zamān al-Hamadhānī (d. 398/1008), younger contemporary of al-Ḥātimī and originator of the fictional prose genre *par excellence* in Arabic, the

---

77 Q 12: 31.

78 This interpretation is already found (and rejected) in Abū ᶜUbayda's *Majāz al-Qurʾān*, ed. Fuʾād Sazkīn (Fuat Sezgin), Cairo: Maktabat al-Khānjī 1970, vol. 1, 309. Al-Zamakhsharī and al-Bayḍāwī mention it in their Qur'an commentaries without rejecting it; they quote al-Mutanabbī's verse. Although it is intriguing from a literary point of view to connect the blood shed by the ladies' cutting their fingers with menstrual blood, al-Ḥātimī is surely right in his rejection; the context and the syntax make the other explanation more plausible (how to explain, for instance, the object suffix *-hū* in *akbarnahū*? The explanation given in *Lisān al-ᶜarab* is very contrived: it is said to be a pausal *-h*, not an object suffix).

79 al-Ḥātimī, *Mūḍiḥah*, 22.

80 Bonebakker, *Ḥātimī*, 46, on the critic's reaction to a striking line, a metrical *tour de force*, by the poet: "He is a showery cloud, son of a showery cloud, son of a showery cloud, son of a showery cloud": "I suppose Abū l-Ṭayyib (al-Mutanabbī) conversed with the stars all night long until the morning greeted him, when he composed this verse!" (*Mūḍiḥah*, 35; rain was supposed to be caused by constellations).

81 Bonebakker, *Ḥātimī*, 52.

82 ibid., 44.

*maqāmah*, used the form for literary criticism on a few occasions, in which he was followed by subsequent *maqāmah* writers. Unlike most of the texts discussed so far in this essay, the literary character of the *maqāmah* has been discussed extensively; the contribution of the genre to literary criticism has received less attention, which is not altogether surprising since it is relatively slight, with a few exceptions. It is not known who ordered al-Hamadhānī's collection as we know it today, but perhaps it is not wholly a coincidence that the *maqāmah* that opens it is entiteld *al-Qarīḍiyyah* ("Of Poesie", in Prendergast's rendering). It consists of a series of aphoristic characterizations of poets such as were discussed above, in *sajᶜ* as the genre demands, put into the mouth of the trickster-hero, Abū l-Fatḥ al-Iskandarī. The narrative interest is slight (Abū l-Fatḥ is rewarded for his eloquence), as is the critical content: all is conventional. In *al-Jāḥiẓiyyah* the famous prose writer, after being praised by a gathering of banqueters, is criticised by the same Abū l-Fatḥ for not being a competent poet and because his prose is relatively unadorned with metaphor and other embellishments. It is sometimes taken for granted that Abū l-Fatḥ's views are identical with those of al-Hamadhānī, but there is no reason to believe that the latter necessarily agrees with the otherwise ill-mannered Abū l-Fatḥ: he may have wanted to show that it is possible to advance contrasting views.[83] *Al-Shiᶜriyyah* ("Of Poetry") and *al-ᶜIrāqiyyah* ("Of Iraq") are not strictly concerned with criticism; both contain a series of riddle-like questions about well-known and not-so-well-known lines of poetry, e.g. "What is the verse that cannot be touched?", the answer being a verse attributed to Abū Nuwās: "A breath of fragrance in a shirt of water; a stature of light in a skin of air".[84] In his study of the *maqāmah* genre, Jaakko Hämeen-Anttila classifies these texts as "philological and aesthetic maqamas".[85] Their main aim seems to be, not to contribute seriously to critical debates or literary theory, but to display wit and *esprit*, and to provide the reader or listener with striking lines of poetry that could profitably be memorised and used at suitable occasions. The same may be said of some of al-Ḥarīrī's *Maqāmāt*, such as *al-Ḥulwāniyyah*, on poetic similes and metaphors, among them the often-quoted verse by al-Waʾwāʾ on a weeping girl: "She let pearls [tears] rain from narcissuses [eyes], watering the roses [cheeks] and biting the jujube fruits [henna-dyed fingers] with hail-stones [teeth]".[86]

---

83 See Mohamed-Salah Omri, "'There is a Jāḥiẓ for Every Age': Narrative Construction and Intertextuality in al-Hamadhānī's *Maqāmāt*, *Arabic and Middle Eastern Literatures* 1 (1998), 31-46.

84 Badīᶜ al-Zamān al-Hamadhānī, *Maqāmāt*, with comm. By Muḥammad ᶜAbduh, Beirut: Dār al-Mashriq 1973, 144, 149; *The Maqámát of Badíᶜ al-Zamán al-Hamadhání*, translated by W.J. Prendergast, repr. London: Curzon 1973, 114, 117 (with a rather different translation). I have not found the verse in Abū Nuwās' *Dīwān*; it is ascribed to al-Khubzaruzzī in al-Thaᶜālibī, *Thimār al-qulūb*, ed. Muḥammad Abū l-Faḍl Ibrāhīm, Cairo: Dār al-Maᶜārif 1985, 600.

85 Jaakko Hämeen-Anttila, *Maqama: A History of a Genre*, Wiesbaden: Harrassowitz 2002, 58.

86 Al-Ḥarīrī, *Maqāmāt*, 29.

A more sustained piece of literary criticism in *maqāmah* form, with a fictional narrator who provides brief characteristics of numerous poets, was composed by Ibn Sharaf al-Qayrawānī (d. 460/1068),[87] who lived in the fifth Islamic century and therefore falls outside the scope of the present volume. It is the same with several other interesting writers of that century, such as Abū l-ʿAlāʾ al-Maʿarrī (449/1058), who packs much of literary criticism into his various eccentric masterpieces such as *Risālat al-ghufrān* (The Epistle of Forgiving) and *Risālat al-ṣāhil wa-l-shāḥij* (The Epistle of Neigher and Brayer), and ʿAbd al-Qāhir al-Jurjānī (d. 471/1078), who is often dubbed the greatest and most perceptive of medieval Arabic literary theorists and critics, and whose own style in *Asrār al-balāghah* (The Secrets of Eloquence) is remarkably eloquent. Whereas al-Maʿarrī has been studied extensively for his literary rather than his literary-critical qualities, it is the reverse for ʿAbd al-Qāhir, whose literary gifts would deserve further attention.

Although the Andalusian poet and prose writer Ibn Shuhayd (426/1035) also wrote just outside the allotted time span – he wrote his *Risālat al-tawābiʿ wa-l-zawābiʿ* probably *c.* 417/1026 – I may be allowed to include him in this survey. His *Epistle (or Treatise) of Familiar Spirits and Demons* is an imaginative essay in fiction and literary criticism.[88] As Monroe has put it in the introduction to his translation, it is "a voyage to the medieval Arab Parnassus, in the course of which the author will make value judgments and indicate his own literary preferences and ideas".[89] Monroe goes on to analyse the critical ideas in the epistle (discovering Neoplatonic ideas about poetic creativity and aesthetics) as well as Ibn Shuhayd's own poetry; less is said about the author's prose style.

The principal literary quality of *al-Tawābiʿ wa-l-zawābiʿ* is to be found in the inventive conceit that forms the scaffolding of the composition as a whole: the dialogues of the author's persona with the inspiring "demons" *(jinn)* of pre-Islamic and Islamic poets and prose writers of the past, while he is being guided by another "demon" on a black horse. In the case of the poets these dialogues consist mainly of an exchange of poetic recitations: first poetry by the older poet, followed by that of Ibn Shuhayd, who is obviously meant to be the supe-

---

87 Published several times, as *Rasāʾil al-intiqād*, ed. Ḥasan Ḥusnī ʿAbd al-Wahhāb, Beirut: Dār al-kitāb al-jadīd 1983 (orig. published 1911, also incorporated in *Rasāʾil al-bulaghāʾ*, ed. Muḥammad Kurd ʿAlī, Cairo: Lajnat al-taʾlif 1954, 300-343); as *Aʿlām al-kalām*, ed. ʿAbd al-ʿAzīz Amīn al-Khānjī, Cairo: Maṭbaʿat al-Nahḍah 1926; and (with French translation) as *Masāʾil al-intiqād / Questions de critique littéraire*, ed. & tr. Charles Pellat, Alger: Editions Carbonel 1953. The *maqāmah* remained a vehicle of literary criticism, witness e.g. the *maqāmah*s on poets and on poetry vs. prose by al-Saraqusṭī Ibn al-Ashtarkūwī (d. 538/1143), *al-Maqāmāt al-luzūmiyyah*, ed. Badr Aḥmad Ḍayf, Alexandria: al-Hayʾah al-Miṣriyyah al-ʿĀmmah 1982, 353-383 and 547-565, transl. by James T. Monroe, Leiden: Brill 2002, 307-330, 403-417.

88 Ibn Shuhayd, *Risālat al-tawābiʿ wa-l-zawābiʿ*, ed. Buṭrus al-Bustānī, Beirut: Maktabat Ṣādir 1951, translated by James T. Monroe, *Risālat at-tawābiʿ wa z-zawābiʿ / The Treatise of Familiar Spirits and Demons*, Berkeley: University of California Press 1971.

89 Monroe, *Risālat at-tawābiʿ*, 19.

rior one. Thus the composition as a whole is an example of the old poetic mode of *fakhr*, vaunting or boasting, in a novel form. Most of the ideas on criticism and poetics are implied rather than stated. On a smaller scale the text is enlivened by numerous, and often humorous, digressions on incidents or descriptions of persons and locations that have little or nothing to do with literary criticism or aesthetic theory. When he does turn to criticism he often uses lively metaphors and similes. As Hämeen-Anttila observes,[90] in its theme and style the work comes close to what he terms the "aesthetic maqama", yet without belonging to the genre; for one thing, rhymed prose is used only occasionally – except when he wishes to show off in a set piece such as the amusing "epistle on sweets" or the descriptions of a flea and a fox, embedded in the text.[91]

In spite of the scarcity of *sajᶜ* in the main flow of the text, the familiar spirit of al-Jāḥiẓ rebukes Ibn Shuhayd for his fondness of it: "You are truly a gifted orator, a skilled weaver of words – were it not that you are seduced by *sajᶜ*; your speech is poetry, not prose!" This prompts Ibn Shuhayd to inveigh against the literary standards of his own time. Then the familiar spirit of ᶜAbd al-Ḥamīd ibn Yaḥyā (d. 132/750), one of the founders of Arabic prose style, interferes, accusing Ibn Shuhayd of affecting the unaffected, unrhymed style of al-Jāḥiẓ, upon which Ibn Shuhayd directs his invective to him, accusing him of Bedouin coarseness and alluding to the contrast between Umayyad primitiveness and Abbasid sophistication:

> Your bow is made of hard *nabᶜ* wood, the sap of your arrow is poison: what are you hunting, a wild ass or a human being? What do you seek, a loud noise or eloquent clarity *(bayān)*? By your father, eloquence is a difficult thing and you are dressed in a cloak of it that exposes the arses of your ideas, just as a goat's tail exposes its arse. It is warmer now, not cold, and fine speech is that of Iraq, not Syria. I can see the blood of jerboas upon your hands and I can spot the tail-fat of lizards on your mandibles![92]

As we saw before, it is often in invective and debunking criticism that our literary critics tend to be most entertaining and eloquent, and often their negative criticism is more trenchant and illuminating than the flowery praise, fulsome yet empty, that fills much of the literary anthologies of later times. Nevertheless, although the Arabic words most commonly used for eloquence stress the conveying of information *(balāghah)* and clarity *(bayān)*, it is obvious that highly literary and rhetorical criticism is normally less precise and clear than plain, unadorned scholarly prose. The scurrilous image just quoted may serve as an example: what does Ibn Shuhayd mean precisely by saying that the ideas or topics of the prose of ᶜAbd al-Ḥamīd Ibn Yaḥyā (who certainly was not a Bedouin and probably not even an Arab) are exposed like a goat's arse and that its author has donned a

---

90 Hämeen-Anttila, *Maqama*, 219-229.

91 Ibn Shuhayd, *Risālat al-tawābiᶜ*, 162-166, 170-72, tr. Monroe, 74-76, 78-79.

92 Ibn Shuhayd, *Risālat al-tawābiᶜ*, 158-161, cf. tr. Monroe, 71-73.

Bedouin cloak? How can this be reconciled with the opinion of Ṭāhā Ḥusayn that "there has perhaps never been any writer to equal ʿAbd al-Ḥamīd in purity and euphony of language, clarity of concept and aptness of style",[93] or that of J.D. Latham, who speaks of the formal perfection achieved in his epistolary prose and who observes that he uses relatively few rare or *recherché* words?[94] Ibn Shuhayd unfairly bases his obloquy on the prose that he himself put into the mouth of ʿAbd al-Ḥamīd's familiar spirit Abū Hubayra, and in which he lets him produce a grammatical mistake, as Monroe has noted.[95] It is the prerogative of the writer of fiction, not of the serious critic, to deploy such devious rhetorical stratagems.

It is here that, finally, I must turn to the passage on oratory by Sahl ibn Hārūn (d. 215/830), mentioned before as being quoted by al-Jāḥiẓ. Responding to the opinion voiced by an unnamed Indian who stresses that a handsome appearance is a great asset to the orator, Sahl ibn Hārūn (himself good-looking, as al-Jāḥiẓ notes) rejects this. In an eloquent passage he points out that if two people speak or argue, one being handsome and imposing and the other puny and ugly, while their eloquence and the soundness of their ideas are equal, then people will generally come out in favour of the latter: the amazement caused by the unexpected, the paradox of the beautiful coming from the ugly, turns into admiration and tips the balance.[96] I am not entirely convinced that Sahl was right or wholly serious (he had a penchant for defending paradoxical or unpopular views), but it is an interesting thought and one that could be applied to our topic: ultimately, literary criticism couched in beautiful, literary language may not always be more convincing for that reason, even though one may be carried away at times by the lure of the language and the rhetoric of the orator. "Literary literary criticism" (to use for the last time this ungainly phrase) is a dubious genre, but it has enriched Arabic *belles-lettres* and even literary criticism.

---

93 Ṭāhā Ḥusayn, quoted (without giving source) by J.D. Latham, "The Beginnings of Arabic Prose Literature: The Epistolary Genre", in: *Arabic Literature to the End of the Umayyad Period*, A.F.L. Beeston et al., eds., Cambridge: Cambridge University Press 1983, 154-179 (see 165). In his *Min ḥadīth al-shiʿr wa-l-nathr*, Cairo: Dār al-Maʿārif 1975, 40-46, Ṭāhā Ḥusayn argues that ʿAbd al-Ḥamīd was strongly influenced by Greek thought and stylistics.

94 Latham, "Beginnings", 164, 176.

95 Ibn Shuhayd, *Risālat al-tawābiʿ*, 160, tr. Monroe, 73; Abū Hubayra says "*lā li-l-aʿrābiyyah lā tūmiḍ*" where he should have said "*mā li-l-aʿrābiyyah …*"

96 Al-Jāḥiẓ, *Bayān*, vol. 1, 89-90.

# Love in the Time of Pilgrimage or A Lost *Maqāma* of Ibn Durayd?[1]

*Philip F. Kennedy (New York University)*

In his eloquent and well-received anthology of translations and commentaries on *Medieval Hebrew poems on the Good Life* (also known as *Wine, Women and Death*[2]), Ray Scheindlin writes, amid a discussion of the "stylization that prevails" in love poetry, that "[we] if should not blame the poets for our frustration at not finding in their poetry the hard biographical data one seeks; their purpose was to write poetry, not autobiography" (p. 78). It is as well to remember this caution when we read the plentiful narratives of the life of Abū Nuwās whose poetry is often coupled with aetiological anecdotes in the *Akhbār*, which act as if to foist enlightening, and more often simply entertaining, concrete facts upon vague (though sometimes quite theatrical) poetic sentiment. Just as *asbāb al-nuzūl* accrued traditionally around individual clusters of verses of the Qur'ān, so a similar explanatory literature (though one far less prestigious and rigorous in its transmission mechanisms) was accreted to the literary persona of Abū Nuwās. In the paper that ensues we will narrate in a full translation, and then discuss, one particularly striking anecdote that closes the first section devoted to the *Naqā'iḍ* of Ḥamza al-Iṣfahānī's recension of *Dīwān Abī Nuwās*. It is uncharacteristically long, cuts an unusual image of the poet, and displays several intertexual, prosimetrical and stylistically ornate literary features that combine to give off the flavor of enhanced fiction far more than "hard fact". The subject, however, is not that exceptional in summary form: the pilgrimage as a setting and occasion for love and poetry.

* * *

Though Abū Nuwās (d. *ca* 814 C.E.) is not known for matters of religion, except in their breach, he must have visited Mecca on pilgrimage at least once in his life, perhaps from Basra initially, following the tracks of his beloved Janān (sometime before 786 C.E.), and possibly also thereafter from Baghdad, accompanying the Abbasid prince al-ʿAbbās ibn Jaʿfar.[3] The evidence lies in several celebrated anecdotes about this (or these) occasions, and a handful of poems which treat

---

1 This article is dedicated to Professor Raymond Scheindlin on the occasion of his 65th birthday.

2 *Wine, Women and Death: Medieval Hebrew Poems on the Good Life* (Philadelphia: The Jewish Publication Society, 1986).

3 See *Dīwān Abī Nuwās*, ed. Ewald Wagner (vol. 1, Wiesbaden and Cairo, 1958), pp. 148-50.

the *Ḥajj* as an excuse for erotic and literary play.[4] These poems are indeed interesting as variations upon a theme[5] that had its marked precedent in the poetry of ʿUmar ibn Abī Rabīʿa (born *ca* 644 C.E.), a century earlier.

The *Dīwān* of ʿUmar, who was a prominent Meccan of the tribe of Makhzum (and for whom finding a woman to leer upon lyrically during the pilgrimage season was apparently as easy as shooting fish in a barrel), is suffused with detailed language and imagery that is unmistakably, and often quite arrestingly, Islamic.[6] Indeed, he offers an important contemporary gauge of the extent to which Arabic had utterly absorbed the language of the Qurʾān and Islamic practice by the mid-seventh century. The *Ḥajj* provides a good example of this, offering in one instance linguistic and factual details for a solemn oath:

*By the One for whom the pilgrims enter the sacred state*
*and then by the place of offerings and by the sacrificial beasts;*
*By the House lying in its ancient valley*
*and its covering of the finest Yemeni cloth;*
*By the shaven-headed one[s] shouting* labbay-ka *and doing the* ṭawāf
*between al-Ṣafā and the* maqām *and the pillar;*
*And by Zamzam and the pebbles when they are thrown*
*and the two* jamras *which are in the valley [at Minā]*[7]

More typical of ʿUmar's persona as an avatar of philandering poets are treatments of the *Ḥajj* that are impious, certainly, but quite sensuous:

*When he comes in the afternoon, embrace*
*the stone as he does his* ṭawāf.
*Make yourself show through your clothes for him,*
*to stir his yearning when he sees you.*[8]

And the following brief cameo, taking place now outside Mecca, is a comedy of errors, spoiling the solemnity of religious ritual yet wryly accomplished in showing up a man flustered by infatuation:

*A sun covered by Yemeni cloth showed herself to me with*
*the pilgrimage at* al-Muḥaṣṣab *at* Mīnā*;*

---

4 There is always the possibility that some of this evidence is either apocryphal or falsely attributed; but the interest for us lies not so much in what the evidence shows as the very enhanced literary nature of the evidence itself.

5 It is tempting to label this theme facetiously *mutʿat al-ḥajj*; the religious and socio-historical significance of which will be discussed at the end of this essay.

6 See Alan Jones, "Central but Skewed: the Qurʾān, Islam and ʿUmar ibn Abī Rabīʿa" (forthcoming). – "ʿUmar is particularly interesting because he has no one to please but himself and his friends. If he and they take Islam for granted, it can only be because it was natural to do so"; "it is quite staggering that of the 440 poems and fragments in his *Dīwān*, roughly 190 have at least one phrase that stands out as Islamic, and a good many of them have much more than that."

7 *Dīwān*, Beirut: Dār Ṣādir 19, p. 423, lines 1-4. (trans Jones)

8 Ibid. p. 187, lines 13-14. (trans Jones)

*On the day that she threw the pebbles a wrist appeared*
*and a hand adorned with fingers dyed with henna.*
*When we met on the pass, she greeted me,*
*and my accursed mule refused to obey my directions;*
*And by God, I do not know, though I am good at counting,*
*whether I threw seven pebbles or eight!*[9]

(The more one exercises oneself about the profound numerological significance of the number seven, the more deftly silly and mischievous this becomes, as if handing the Devil a pebble to cast back in the pilgrim's face.)

* * *

Abū Nuwās composed several short poems in a similar vein. The occasion for the most celebrated of these is given thus, on the authority of Jammāz and Sulayman Sakhṭa:[10]

> We made the pilgrimage the same year as Abū Nuwās, and we all gathered together to perform the circumambulation of the Kaᶜba. He stepped out in front of me and I saw him following a woman round, though I didn't yet know who she was. I then progressed to the Black Stone and beheld the woman kissing listen the stone and there he was kissing it alongside her in such a way that their cheeks touched. I said to myself, 'He is the most perverse of people!' Then I realized this was Janān. When they had departed, I met up with him and told him, 'You wretch! Does not even this holy site bring you to your senses!' He answered that I was a fool to think that he would have crossed so many deserts and desolate tracts for any other reason! And how[11]

Abū Nuwās then recited his poem about his encounter with Janān:[12]

*Two lovers' cheeks wrapped together*
*while they kissed the Black Stone;*
*Their passion felt reprieve, without sin being committed,*
*as if they were on a tryst*
*And if it were not for the people heaving at them*
*they would have stayed entranced forever.*

***

*We tarried there, each of us hiding his face*
*from his neighbor with his hand*
*Doing in the mosque what others*
*were not doing in the mosque!*

---

9 Ibid. p. 399, lines 1-4. (trans Jones)

10 *Dīwān* IV:42-4; the full reference to the five volume critical edition is: *Dīwān Abī Nuwās*, vols 1-3 and 5 ed. Ewald Wagner; vol. 4 ed. Gregor Schoeler, (Wiesbaden and Cairo, 1958; Wiesbaden and Beirut, 1972-2005); the anecdote is told identically but on the authority of Jạmmāz only, omitting Sulaymān Ṣakhṭa, in Ibn Manẓūr's *Akhbār Abī Nuwās* (Cairo 1924), vol. 1, pp. 195-6.

11 *Dīwān* IV:58, poem 72 offers further evidence that Abū Nuwās made the pilgrimage to follow Janān.

12 Al-Ṣūlī considered this poem wrongly attributed to Abū Nuwās-; however, we should remark that al-Ṣūlī's judgments on the subject of authenticity appear often overly cautious and conservative.

Conceivably this is the same occasion that drove the poet to compose the less captivating erotic *lamiyya* of *Dīwān* IV,[13] 302-3 which contains the line *lam yunsi-nī l-saʿyu wa-l-ṭawāfu wa-lā / l-dāʿūna lammā btahaltu wa-btahalū // qaḍība bāni* ....[14] (Neither the running [at Safa and Marwa] nor the ritual circumambulation, nor even those invoking God and supplicating, could make me forget this branch of a Ben tree ...)

The tone of all these verses is, in any case, happier than those he is said to have composed by Hātim al-Sijistānī when he espied (perhaps a few weeks earlier) her tribe, the Thaqafiyyun of Basra, processing out of the Mirbad on their way to Mecca[15] – verses in which he thus aped the manner of the pre-Islamic poets, often forlorn witnesses of seasonal decampings, describing himself in the upshot as a soulless body, having neither movement nor rest.[16]

* * *

13 Also relayed in Abu Hiffān's *Akhbār Abī Nuwās*, pp. 98-9; according to this anecdote, told on the authority of Yūsuf ibn Dāya, Abū Nuwās while on the *Ḥajj* in 190 h spotted Muḥammad ibn Ismāʿīl performing the *ṭawāf* and composed the poem beginning *lam-yunsi-nī l-saʾyu* ... about him.

14 Simple logic (mention of one "Ḥasan" rather than Janān) would suggest that the short *nūniyya* on page 363 of *Dīwān* IV was written on a quite different occasion, not necessarily when Abū Nuwās was on the *Ḥajj* – rather upon the pilgrimage of "Ḥasan" whose folk the poet addresses with the words "*yā ayyu-hā l-nafaru l-ḥujjāju* ..."

15 Ibid., 114-5.

16 There are also instances when the *Ḥajj* is said to have been simply one of the occasions when he recited some of his verses. See e.g. *Dīwān* IV, 121-2. In this instance the use of the root *ḥurma* in the first line may have crafted a spurious link between the ensuing verses (about trying to keep love under wraps yet being a talking point of gossip) and the *Ḥajj*, with its obvious association with *iḥrām*. *Iḥrām* is specifically mentioned, in fact, in another poem (*Dīwān* V, 50): *wa-ghazālin yasbī l-nufūsa idhā huttika // minhu maʿāziru l-iḥrāmi*. Other references to the *Ḥajj* include *Dīwān* V 162 ("Dearer to me than prodding my mount on to the curtain-draped Holy House ... is to go on pilgrimage to the tavern-monastery of Māsarjusānā"); *Dīwān* V 206 (amid a long and unusually truculent poem, containing advice, e.g., to throw a recalcitrant lover "off a mountain summit" we find the prohibition, quite in spirit with the poem, "Do not go near the Holy House; leave it be till the time of *Iḥlāl* comes round"); and *Dīwān* V 212 (*wa-bayta in ḥajjū fa-ḥujja mubādiran // ḥānūta khammārin wa-ʿuj shahrā*).

Anecdote 69 (the final anecdote) in Abū Hiffān's *Akhbār Abī Nuwās*, ed. ʿAbd al-Sattār Aḥmad Faraj (Cairo: Maktabat Miṣr n.d.) should also be noted, pp. 119-20: "Abū Hiffān relays: Abū Muslim Ibrāhīm ibn ʿAbdullāh said: Abū l-Mughīth Mūsā ibn Ibrāhīm al-Rāfiqī related to me: I went on the *Ḥajj* one year; when we arrived in Mecca we were told that Sufyām ibn ʿUyayna was there and giving audiences. My brother Abū l-Ḥārith Aḥmad ibn Ibrāhīm had come on the pilgrimage with me. I would go and frequent the sessions of Sufyān ibn ʿUyayna in order to listen to what he had to say; while I was at his *majlis* one day, and he had just finished dictating, a young boy came up to me saying: 'Young man, I was listening with you but had nothing to write; would you lend me your note book so that I can make a copy of what you heard and noted down?' I handed him my note book and he sat a little way off then returned it to me. So I placed it in my sleeve and set off to see my brother Abū l-Ḥārith. He said to me, 'What did you hear today from Sufyān?' So I handed him my note book, which he began to read; he smiled then said to me, 'Did this note book ever leave your hand and find its way into someone else's?' I told him, 'Yes, a young boy from Iraq sat next to me; he told me he had listened with me and

Most readers and students of classical Arabic literature are aware of the above material, either in part or in their entirety,[17] and have an impression of the robust literary persona they portray and, in some measure, exemplify – the persona of a poet who postured strongly, often mischievously, with religion as his foil, either to channel the expression of intense emotions or to show that he had none (none, that is, for the sensibilities of the pious). But less well known is the long anecdote that forms the core of this short article: a "likely" story about Abū Nuwās that has the *Ḥajj* as its frame. It smacks of utter fiction, as we will discuss in a brief commentary after a full translation. The episodes given above are likely to be fictive and spurious, but the poetry associated with them is at least probably genuinely by Abū Nuwās. The anecdote below emits the flavor of pure and enhanced concoction all round, both in form and content. It is given, somewhat curiously as already indicated, at the tail end of the section on *naqāʾiḍ* in the redaction of Ḥamza al-Iṣfahānī.

## *Translation*[18]

"Abū Bakr Muḥammad ibn Durayd related to me: ← Makhlad ibn al-Qāsim told me: ← Ismāʿīl ibn Naybakht related to me: ← Abū Nuwās told me:[19] I went on the pilgrimage with al-Faḍl ibn Rabīʿa. When we had reached the territory of the Banū Fazāra,[20] during the first days of spring, we stopped to pitch camp in an area of luscious vegetation adjacent to their desert holdings. The land ... was covered in a splendid mantle of flowers that competed with the cushioned and orderly idylls of Paradise [described in Sūra 88 of the Qurʾān].[21] The scene was a

---

asked me to lend it to him, so I did.' He replied, 'God curse all wickedness! That was Abū Nuwās. He never lets up his licentious ways, anywhere.' Then he returned the book to me, in which [Abū Nuwās] had written:

O namesake of the one summoned by the flanks of Mount Sinai (i.e. Mūsā)
– Of the one who spent time with the tribe of Midian;
O you whose byname has been coined after the rain (i.e Abū l-Mughīth)
... Come to us and go easy!

17 Ewald Wagner discusses the issue of Abū Nuwās and the *Ḥajj* briefly in his study *Abū Nuwās. Eine Studie zur Arabischen Literatur der frühen ʿAbbāsidenzeit*, Wiesbaden 1965, pp. 43-5.

18 *Dīwān* I 98-105. The subsection of this "bāb" is entitled "*fī riwāyāt li-abī nuwāsin alḥaqtu-hā bi-ākhiri hādhā l-bābi wa-fīhi qaṣīdatāni la-hu*".

19 This *isnād* will be discussed below.

20 The geography implicit in this anecdote is quite plausible. The *Banū Fazāra* were denizens of *Wādī al-Rumma* (not to be confused with Wādī Rūm in modern day Jordan), an area situated on the pilgrimage route from Iraq, north east of Medina midway between the Hijaz and Jabal Shammar, due south of Ḥāʾil and the "great Nafūd" beyond that. Wādī al-Rumma is indeed a verdant valley – a fact visible to the eye from publicly accessible satellite photos (see Google Earth at 25° 39'32.36 North 42° 36'15.76 East, elevation 2395 feet).

21 See Qurʾān 88, verses 1-7 describing Hell and verses 8-16 describing a heavenly idyll. The Arabic here *[al-arḍu] ltaḥafat fī anwāʿi zakhrafi-hā l-bāhiri bi-mā yaqṣuru ʿan-hu l-namāriqu l-maṣfūfatu wa-lā yudānī bahjata-hā l-zarābiyyu l-mabthūthatu* evokes Qurʾān 88: 15-16: *[fī jan-*

pleasure to gaze upon and left [our] hearts in rapture to its fragrance; with its low canopy of clouds auguring rain and vegetation, it was redolent of a scene described by the great pre-Islamic poet, ʿAbid ibn al-Abras ...[22]

*[It was] a laden cloud that skirted close above the ground,*
*So near one could almost push it away with one's palm*

The sky now shed tears in a drizzle, then released a shower, and then a heavy downpour all of which flooding left the hill tops scoured like ravines; the cloud then dispersed and left crevices brimful as pools and the lowlands a luscious vibrant carpet of gardens and vegetation from which wafted a fragrant scent – the flowers now in bloom beamed at us luxuriantly such that had you wanted to liken the scene to another in a simile the object compared would force you to return the compliment to the object compared. .. I was enraptured by the beauty of the sight and breathed in the perfume that wafted pleasantly like a heady musk. Then I said to my companion:

"Damn it, man! Let's make for those tents. We may find someone to tell us a choice and authentic story worth telling when we return to Baghdad."[23] When we had reached the outlying habitations we found ourselves in front of a tent at whose entrance sat a servant girl wearing a Bedouin veil (*burquʿ*). She was gazing with such eyes as cause the malady of passion to stir: they were languid and brimful of magic. She stretched out a dyed hand that was as delicate as the tongue of a bird. Then a gust of breeze blew and lifted the veil from her face to reveal a woman[24] as beautifully white as an ostrich egg.[25] I said to my friend:

---

*natin ʿāliyatin] ... wa-namāriqa masfūfatin / wa-zarābiyyu mabthūthatun.* Sūra 88 is evoked in the Maqāma Iblīsiyya of Badīʿ al-Zamān al-Hamadhānī in a similar way; this is relevant in a pointed way since other features of this long anecdote about Abū Nuwās recall features of the Maqāma genre, in general, and the Maqāma Iblīsiyya, in particular (see below).

22 Al-Aṣmaʿī attributes these verses and the poem they are excerpted from to ʿAws ibn Ḥajar. The lines of ʿAbīd (let us say) quoted here evoke, because of the context in which they are set, the last line of the original *qaṣīda*: *fa-aṣbaḥa l-rawḍu wa-l-qīʿānu mumriʾatan // min bayni murtafiqin fī-hi wa-minṭāḥī* . This is a form of deliberate literary allusion. See *Dīwān ʿAbīd ibn al-Abraṣ* (Beirut: Dār al-Kitāb al-ʿArabī), 1994), pp. 44-8.

23 There may seem to be something forced and self-reflexive about this statement. It is an old narrative device, though, and one still used, that the story of the search for a story becomes the story that was being sought. *Barton Fink* (1991), the film by the justly celebrated "Coen Brothers," is a delightful recent example on the silver screen.

24 When we encounter the wind in cahoots with the author to reveal the face of a woman we are encountering a medieval romance topos; an enchanting example of this is found in Nizami's *Haft Paykar.* See Nizami, *Haft Paykar. A Medieval Persian Romance*, trans. and introduced by Julie Scott Meisami, Oxford: OUP, 1995, p. xviii: "In the third tale (section 34: the Green Dome/Moon/Monday) Bishr falls in love with a passing woman *whose veil is lifted by the wind.* He goes on pilgrimage to Jerusalem to purify himself of temptation; on his return journey he is accompanied by a godless know-it-all named Malikha, who meets a suitably gruesome end when he drowns in a well which he mistakes for a jar of water buried in the desert. When Bishr returns Malikha's belonging's to his wife, *he finds that she is the same woman by whom he was tempted*; impressed by his honesty, she persuades him to marry her."

"She has an entrancing look for which there is no incantatory cure. Get her to speak!"

"How am I to do that?" he replied.

"By asking for water," I suggested.

He thus approached her and asked for drink.

"Why of course! You are both most welcome!"

Then she rose and walked off, twisting gently in her gait like the branch of a Ben tree or a stem of bamboo ... I was in complete thrall to what I saw. She brought us water. I took it, drank some, then poured the rest upon my hands; and then said:

"My friend, too, is thirsty."

So she took the water vessel and went into the tent. I said to my companion, alluding to the way her face had been exposed to us:

*If ever God blesses an item of clothing,*
*May he yet never bless the* burquᶜ
*It shows you the eyes of a cute girl, unsuspecting,*
*Then reveals a sight more deadly [in its effect]*

She returned having taken off her *burquᶜ*, donning instead a black scarf, reciting verses in her turn:

*Greet two travelers[26] whom I once saw tarry long,*
*not knowing what they wanted*
*Asking for water though not thirsty so as to look with pleasure*
*upon the girl who served them*
*They vilified the wearing of the* burquᶜ *just as a merchant*
*pours scorn on goods he seeks to buy!*

Her speech was like a necklace of pearls whose string has grown weak and breaks to let them spill. The words came from her with a sweet and soft timbre. Their sound was like a dew that would cause even mute rocks to yield water; at this I remembered the words of the Umayyad poet, Dhū al-Rumma(d. 735):[27]

---

25 The archetype of this image of beauty is in the Muᶜallaqa of Imruʾ al-Qays, as part of the descriptive passage that forms the final part of his lengthy *nasīb*.

26 It is only rarely we witness the formulaic dual form of address lyrical poetry having actual relevance to the scene the poetry evokes. This is a minor point, but already the woman who recites the verse is shown to be deft in manipulating her art to suit the situation.

27 Abū Nuwās often quoted other poets in his own verse, among them notably al-Aᶜshā, Jarīr, Abū Miḥjan al-Thaqafī – and Dhū al-Rumma, whose full name was Ghaylān ibn ᶜUqba. For a full discussion of this subject see: Andras Hamori, "Convention in the Poetry of Abū Nuwās", *Studia Islamica*, 30 (1969), 25-6; and Alan Jones, "Final *Taḍmīm* in the Poems of Abū Nuwās", *Arabicus Felix* (Oxford, 1991), 61-73. We might note here also an anecdote in Ibn Manẓūr's *Akhbār Abī Nuwās* featuring Abū Nuwās (and Dhū al-Rumma)- in a context quite different from a pilgrimage journey; see *Akhbār* p. 202: it tells how Abū Nuwās once spent the night in prayer was spooked by a voice from a grave. Returning form the tavern through a graveyard he had spontaneously uttered a verse by Dhū al-Rumma, "At Ṭayzanābādh are vines I have never passed by without being astonished at those who

*When we met tears poured from our eyes*
*Which we staunched with our fingers*
*And we were treated to a speech that seeped unctuously from her mouth*
*Like the honey harvest of bees mixed with the water from rain clouds*[28]

She had a brilliant face which darkened the light of our thoughts; which made our hearts cower with fear; and which even sound minds would have failed to grasp. It would perturb all who glance upon its splendor … I could not help but prostrate myself before her without reciting any formulae glorifying God ( – as one usually does in prayer).[29]

"Raise your head," she said, "You'll receive no recompense for such prostration, and be on your way carrying off the burden of your sin! Never again disparage the *burquᶜ*. For how often – in other ways – is that which puts rout to sleep and diminishes your strengths exposed without attainment of the object of pleasure and desire. In such instances death is simply fated and hope preordained for disappointment."

I was tongue-tied and unable to reply to her, and completely perplexed as to what was most appropriate to say or do.[30] My friend glanced at me and, when he saw how agitated I was, he said, as if to console me from what was wilting me:

"What is this impertinence from a face that shines so brightly with beauty? It seems impossible to know what lies beneath it. Have you not heard the line of Dhu al-Rumma:

*Mayy's face has a touch of prettiness,*
*But under her clothes lies shame,*
*If only you could see it …?*"[31]

The woman retorted:

"What are you aiming at, you bastard?! No, rather I resemble his other verses:

---

drink water"; the ghostly voice riposted "In Jahannam there is water which no man can drink and keep hold of his guts!"

28 These verses are in *Dīwān Dhī al-Rumma* ed. al-Maktab al-Islāmī li-l-Ṭibāᶜa wa-l-Nashr (Beirut 1964), 447-8, lines 14-15; it may conceivably be that the *burquᶜ* has brought Dhū al-Rumma initially to mind, since he mentions *barāqiᶜ* elsewhere in poetry of similar sentiment (ibid. p. 336) *ka-annā ramat-nā bi-l-ᶜuyūni llatī badat // jaʾādhiru hawḍā min juyūbi l-barāqiᶜi.*

29 This is something of a topos in Abū Nuwās. See *Dīwān* III, pp. 178-9, poem 148; this is an 11-line narrative *khamriyya* recounting a long bout of indulgence, ending *wa-ḥāna minnā ṣalātu-nā l-ḍuḥan // qumnā nuṣallī bi-ghayri takbīrī.*

30 Being bested in expression is a topos, as is being impotent to describe a person's beauty.

31 According to one anecdote in the *Kitāb al-Aghānī* of Abū al-Faraj al-Iṣfahānī this verse was ascribed falsely to Dhū al-Rumma, a fact which incensed him due to its (relatively) lewd content (Beirut: Dār al-Thaqāfa 17:327). In another fuller anecdote, which appears to be more intertextually pertinent to this tall tale of Abū Nuwās, it was part of a brief exchange in a contretemps between Dhū al-Rumma and Mayya: upon hearing this verse she bared her body (*kashafat thawba-hā ᶜan jasadi-hā*) and asked: "Do you then see any shame? You bastard!" (ibid. 17:329). It is the baring of a body that resonates meaningfully within this anecdote.

*She is gorgeous and spoiled, with intensely black eyes,*
*Her waistband draped upon quivering hips*
*Below a slender middle ...*"[32]

She then lifted her clothes up to her neck, beyond her shoulders, to reveal a torso that resembled a silver branch whose sap was a liquid gold, trembling upon a fleshy dune-like hip. Her chest was like a polished silver tray with two pomegranates upon it, like two (round) ivory caskets, that would fill the hand of him who touches them. She had a slender waist tapering upon a plump backside, and a navel so exquisitely round it is quite beyond me to describe it ...

She then said: "Do you see any flaws?"[33]

"By God, no!" I replied, "I see only what will accelerate my anxiety and sickness."

At this point an old woman emerged from the tent, saying:[34]

"You man! Be off on your business. Anyone smitten by her will stay unavenged. There is no ransom or release for those whom she captivates!" And the girl added:

"Leave him be, for he fits the description of Ghaylān (Dhū al-Rumma) when he wrote:

*... Though you might slake [the thirst of my longing] for only an hour*
*Just a fraction of that [time] would benefit me*"[35]

The old lady turned away, reciting:

*You can have nothing to do with her,*
*Except that your eyes fornicate with hers.*[36]
*...But will this benefit you, I wonder?*[37]

---

32 These verses are not in the *Dīwān* of Dhū al-Rumma, though clearly this anecdote which is highly sensitive to his poetry and literary persona considered that they were part of his tradition, and this excerpt is to be taken as a well-judged quotation.

33 See note 28.

34 For a fascinating discussion of the variable tradition of an Old Woman, Go-Between or *Alcahueta*, featuring in the relationship and exchanges between men and women, see Cynthia Robinson *Medieval Andalusian Courtly Culture in the Mediterranean* (New York: Routledge 2007).

35 *Dīwān* 634, line 14.

36 This is something of a motif; in a one erotic poem by Abū Nuwās about a *dīwān* boy "people made love to him with their eyes, and if he passed by them when they slept they [made love to him] in their dreams;" cf. also *Dīwān* IV, p. 300, poem 233 (recurring identically on p. 309, poem 253) *marra bi-nā wa-l-ʿuyūnu taʾkhudhu-hu // tajraḥu min-hu mawāḍiʿa l-qubalī*; and ibid. p. 272, poem 187, *wa-idhā aqbala kādat aʿuyunun // naḥwa-hu tajraḥu fīhi bi-l-ḥadaqī*; and ibid. p. 260, poem 171, *wa-rakhīmi l-dalāli kāda mina l-riqq // - -ati yudmī adīma-hu waqʿuṭarfī*; ibid. p. 206, poem 87, line11; ibid. p. 196, poem 70, *ṭarfu-ka zānin qultu damʿī idhan // yajlidu-hu akthara min ḥaddī.*

37 In Arabic: *fa-mā la-ka min-hā ghayra anna-ka nākiḥun // bi-ʿaynay-ka fa-hal dhāka nāfiʿū*; this is not in Dhū al-Rumma's *Dīwān* yet it may be a rude and deliberate evocation of his more chaste: *fa-mā l-qurbu yashfī min hawā ummi sālimin // wa-mā l-buʿdu ʿanhā min dawāʾin bi-nāfiʿī* (*Dīwān* 447 line 11).

While we were thus embroiled we heard the drum beat to announce the caravan's imminent departure and so we hastened to depart afflicted by a fatal anguish and an inner sorrow. I thus recited:

*All traces of sleep are effaced from my eyes,*
*Worn away by duration of tears over you…*[38]

When we had completed our pilgrimage and were returning home, we passed by that spot. The vegetation had intensified and was enhanced in its beauty, attaining a perfect splendor. So I said to my companion:

"Let us go and see that lady friend of ours."

When we were close by the tents, walking through a garden where drops of dew flirted with the flowers, their eyes wide-open upon emerald stems, a Zephyr breeze blew and the branches of the trees shook twisting like ebullient drunkards. There we climbed up a hillock and down the other side into a ravine where, all of a sudden, we saw her among five women none of whom she was fit to serve [so exquisite were they]. They were picking flowers amid the plants, and flouncing about on the grass that covered the land like a turban. When we saw them we stood still, and I greeted them. She alone among them greeted me back, then she told them my story. So they said to her:

"Shame on you! Have you not provided him with something to heal his pains?"

She replied:

"Rather I have provided him with an attendant despair and an anxious mind."

The girl who had the most graceful cheeks, elegant build and most charming disposition now said:

"You've behaved badly from start to finish, requiting the man evilly, failing to return his affection. I can see that he is fond of you and longs to meet with you. There is nothing to stop you from coming to his aid since the place is deserted, no one around to spread gossip about you."

She answered:

"I will do no such thing unless you join in with me, for better or worse."

The other woman replied:

"That would be an iniquitous division.[39] It is you who have waxed proud and humbled the man, refusing him any return, yet you order me to do that which you in fact have an appetite for and I am more inclined to sneer at. This is injustice in both word and deed."

---

38 *Dīwān Abī Nuwās* IV 93-4. Oddly (or ironically) Abū Nuwās is said, according to Ḥamza al-Iṣfahānī, to have composed these verses about Janān having followed her on the *Ḥajj*, as we know (see above). Thus the citation here is either wry and humorous or clumsy concoction, or conceivably it contrives to be the former because of the latter.

39 The Arabic here is extremely significant: *tilka idhan qismatun ḍīzā*. To the letter, this is verse 22 of Qur'ān, Sūrat al-Najm (53). For more on the intertextual and hermeneutic significance of this verse in the precise context of this anecdote, see the commentary below.

The women then approached me and asked: "What have you come for?"

I replied: "I have come to slake a thirst and put out the fire of a longing that has set my liver alight, melted my body, eviscerated my guts, and joined my days to my nights."

They asked me if I had composed any poetry about this. I replied that I had and recited:

*I went on pilgrimage in the hope of reward,*
*To unburden the guilt of grave sins*
*Yet return an empty handed wretch,*
*With feelings that pay no dividend in heaven*
*The young woman afflicts me with her eyes;*
*Her face is brilliant as the sun, though languid of gaze*
*Were she to appear before the decayed bones of a dead man,*
*He would return among the living, in full body*
*If she were the light of the moon,*
*No other star could appear in the sky*
*She is like an ostrich egg bred*[40] *by the Banū Fazāra*
*For the people of the highlands, the Banū ʿĀmir and Sulaym*
*If she gives I shall attain all my hopes,*
*If she refuses I shall visit the graves*[41]

They responded to this by drawing lots for me and the lot fell to the most charming among them ... They told me to make for a recess where I waited impatiently for one of them. Then, lo, in walked a black man as dark as a night cloud, with a large stick in his hand.

"What do you want?" I asked.

"To fornicate with you!" He said.

Terrified, I called for my companion, who only just managed to save me from him. We ran from the cave and saw the women darting towards their tents like pearls spilling from a broken string, laughing and dangling between themselves the ropes upon which my heart had been strung. I left that place dejected."

---

40 The Arabic here (*mina l-bīḍ tunmī-hā fazāratu lil-ʿulā)* takes us back to the description of the Fazārī woman as *bayḍatu naʿāmin taḥta ummi riʾālin* at the outset of the first encounter (p. 100 line7). A reductionist view, but also a tenable one, would see this detail of the poem as giving rise to the full complex version of the anecdote as we have it here, with Abū Nuwās as its main player. This is the least satisfying view of intertextuality in the anecdote, but it should not be ignored.

41 This poem is only relayed in this anecdotal setting. Since the anecdote is an intertextual concoction, and a complex variation of a motif, the fact might argue for the poem's lack of authenticity: it survives only within a fiction. That argument is not conclusive, however.

## *Commentary*

This is something of a "shaggy-dog-story" – a long-drawn-out narrative of a largely jocular tone that holds us in suspense, intensifying its descriptive idyll and multiplying the sources of temptation, only to deliver bathos and an anti-climactic joke at the poet's expense just when he seems posed to enjoy some requital. The poet was certainly capable of laughing at himself.[42] Here, however, even though he is said to have narrated the story himself, he is not, in all likelihood, the principal propagator of the literary prank. Abū Nuwās escapes a scene in the end which he probably never attended. The anecdote stands out, indeed, as something of an anomaly in a number of ways: stylistically, in its use of enhanced rhyming prose to set the idyllic scene at the outset;[43] thematically, in what it says about the poet's sexuality; and, more essentially, in the way it reflects at least some *perceptions* about that sexuality already in Abbasid times. That is to say, the quite exceptional nature of the anecdote in fact tells us more about the variables of posthumous perception than about actual biographical events.

These are the elements of the story that are markworthy:

(i) The "intertextual" element: the interlacing of poetic quotations within the sequence of events, and, in particular, the repeated evocations of the legendary love affair between the Umayyad poet, Dhū al-Rumma, and his beloved Mayy. The event, given the category of poetry in which it is relayed in the *Dīwān* by al-Iṣfahānī (the "satirical flytings"), is principally viewed as a poetic exchange. But it is only mildly invective by the normal standards of *naqāʾiḍ* literature, and thus our attention is drawn to the more purely intertextual aspect of the exchange, privileging the erotic register. Real love is evoked with mention of Dhū al-Rumma, striking an amorous note which the narrative ultimately fails to live up to. Yet in fact even to say "ultimately" is misleading, for things go tonally awry long before the end of the story. When the woman, unabashed, bares her body before her two interlocutors, well before the denouement of events, it happens with little warning and we are struck by the abruptly permissive element – by the exposure. What are we being exposed to exactly? It seems unlikely at first blush that a figure like Mayy, or any other *ʿudhri* beloved, would behave so brazenly. The least we might expect at this point is that the men's physical desire, which lies transparently below the surface of infatuation, will be consummated. Yet it is not in *this* way – in consummation – that the anecdote flouts *ʿudhri* convention.

And the fact is, Mayy *did* bare herself once, according to one account, in response to the very same verse that piques the young girl in this story (as re-

---

42 See Philip F. Kennedy *Abū Nuwās: A Genius of Poetry* (Oxford: Oneworld 2005), 48-9.

43 The anecdote is reminiscent of the opening of the Maqāma Iblīsiyya by Badīʾ al-Zamān al-Hamadhānī, in this respect. For more comment on the textual significance of this see below.

marked already in note 28). Here in full are the two mutually-exclusive variants of the occasions on which this verse was recited in the *Aghānī* (they may of course both be anecdotal concoctions – certainly at least one of them must be):

Version I. … Kathīra was a servant girl adopted by the Āl Qays ibn ʿĀṣim (the family of Mayy); she was Umm Sahm ibn Burda the thief killed by Sinān ibn Mukhayyas al-Qushayrī in the days of Muḥammad ibn Sulaymān. Now Kathīra composed the verses:

*Mayy's face has a touch of prettiness,*
*But under her clothes lies shame,*
*If only it were visible!*
*Do you not see that water can have a nasty taste,*
*Even though it may look limpid to the eye?*

She then attributed them falsely to Dhū al-Rumma; he was furious about this, and vowed, upon his faith, that he had not composed them: "How could I compose such verses when I have spent my whole existence and expended my youth making love to her in verse and praising her. And now I'm supposed to have said this!?" He then learnt that Kathīra had composed them and attributed them to him.[44]

Version II. Mayy had spent a long time without seeing Dhū al-Rumma, although during this period she heard his poetry and swore to slaughter a sacrificial camel for him upon seeing him [again]. When she then saw that he was a swarthy and ugly man, while she was one of the most beautiful of creatures, she exclaimed, "O woe – how terrible! What a waste of a sacrificial camel!" So Dhū al-Rumma recited:

*Mayy's face has a touch of prettiness,*
*But under her clothes lies shame,*
*If only it were visible!*

She then lifted her robes from her body and said: "Do you see any blemishes, you bastard!?" He continued:

*Do you not see that water can have a nasty taste,*
*Even though it may look limpid to the eye?*

She then said, "Well, you've seen what lies under these robes and know that there are no blemishes; it remains simply for me to tell you: 'Just try and taste what lies behind it! By God, you never will!'" He then recited:

*What a waste of my persistent poetry, when the upshot*
*With Mayy left my heart far from obtaining what it sought.*

Then matters were patched up between them and his love for her resumed as before.[45]

Whichever version might be alluded to (the latter being the more credibly evoked), what is clear is that this long anecdote about Abū Nuwās has deliberate and pointed intertextual associations and resonances. It is in a sense an extended literary *clin d'oeil* and reenactment; and it may also, in this respect, be a riddle

44 Abū al-Faraj al-Iṣfahānī, *Kitāb al-Aghānī* (Cairo reprint 1993) vol. 18 pp. 25-6.
45 Ibid. p. 28. This version in the *Aghānī* quotes Ibn Qutayba's *Kitāb al-Shiʿr wa-l-Shuʿarāʾ*.

developed upon the following verse of Dhū al-Rumma, which is, we might well aver, conspicuous by its absence:

*The Ḥajj is only complete when your mounts*
*Have halted before Kharqāʾ, her veil lifted and bare of face*[46]

This needs some explanation. There is a curious interlude in Dhū al-Rumma's amorous poetry during which he wrote for Kharqāʾ, a mature woman of the Banū ʿĀmir. Several explanations exist for this interlude (see *Aghāni* 18:36 ff.). One version has it that she was a *Kaḥḥāla* who cured an ailment in his eyes; when he asked her how she wanted to be recompensed she requested ten verses of erotic poetry so that men might still consider her desirable. Most anecdotes about her paint the picture of a woman with unusual charm and wit, including the following story which shows her skilled in genealogy and, more to the point, explains the verse quoted above in a way highly relevant to our study:

> [Abū al-Faraj al-Iṣfahānī records] I have copied out from Muḥammad ibn Ṣāliḥ ibn al-Naṭṭāḥ's book the following anecdote: "Muḥammad ibn al-Ḥajjāj al-Asadī al-Tamīmī – and I know no one of Tamīm more knowledgeable than he – said to me: I had been on the pilgrimage and was leaving Marrān, when, lo!, there appeared before me a young man with dusty hair shepherding his sheep; I approached him and asked him to recite some poetry, but he replied, 'Go away, I am busy!' But I insisted, so he replied, 'I will tell you who can give you what you want. See that house in front of you – there your need will be requited. That is the house of Dhū al-Rumma's Kharqāʾ.' So I went towards it and said hello from a distance. The woman replied, 'Come closer.' So I approached, and she asked, 'You are a town dweller, but who are you exactly?' I said, 'From the tribe of Tamīm, thinking that she had no knowledge of peoples and their genealogies.' She then asked, 'From which clan of Tamīm?' So I told her, and she kept on asking me for precise details until I had traced my genealogy to my father, at which she said, 'al-Ḥajjāj ibn ʿUmayr ibn Yazīd?' 'Yes,' I replied. She then said, 'God have mercy on Abū al-Muthannā, we had hoped that he would inherit from ʿUmayr ibn Yazīd.' 'Yes,' I said, 'but death overtook him as a young man.' 'God give you life!' she went on, 'Where do you come from now?' 'From the *Ḥajj*,' I said, at which she retorted, 'Why then did you not come to me then, when I am one of the rituals of the *Ḥajj*? Your pilgrimage is deficient, so set it aright, or would you deny one of its precepts?' 'How so?' I asked; she said, 'Have you not heard the words of Ghaylān ibn ʿUqba [Dhū al-Rumma]:
>
> *The Ḥajj is only complete when your mounts*
> *Have halted before Kharqāʾ, her veil lifted and bare of face …*'"[47]

(This is simply the most involved and artful of a number of anecdotes cast from similar elements: an encounter with Kharqāʾ upon a return from the *Ḥajj* and her insistence on the occasion that she is one of the *manāsik*. According to Ibn Qutayba, al-Mufaḍḍal al-Ḍabbī related a similar episode about himself.)

---

46 *Tammāmu l-ḥajji an taqifa l-maṭāyā // ʿalā kharqāʾa wāḍiʿata l-lithāmi.*

47 *Aghānī*, 18:39-40.

It would seem rash to deny that this verse of Dhū al-Rumma about Kharqāʾ is intentionally evoked by the anecdote.[48] More conjectural is the intertextual use made by the anecdote of the Qurʾān. When the women, towards the tail end of the story, rebuke the young lady by whom Abū Nuwās has been enticed with the words *tilka idhan qismatun ḍīzā* ("that would be an iniquitous division!") we have already noted the word for word quotation of Qurʾān Sūrat al-Najm (53), verse 22. On one level this simply makes for a linguistically rich, indeed prestigious, way of saying, "That would be unfair!" Perhaps, indeed, nothing more is to be made of the phrase. However, we should also note that in the Qurʾān the phrase is set into the following passage about the three pagan idols of Mecca:

> *Q. 53:18-22. Have you considered al-Lāt and al-ʿUzza; and Manāt, the other one – the third of them? Are you to have the male and He the daughters? That would be an iniquitous division!*

The contextual point seems to be quite clear: we are taken in the story with these words straight back to Mecca, from which the pilgrims have just returned, and strange menacing female figures are evoked. The pagan Meccans had thought they were gods; if they existed at all, they were other than gods – demons of some kind. Just what kind of devilish women, we seem justified to ask ourselves, do Abū Nuwās and his companion really have dealings with in this story? On this level of association the story is akin to those tales of ominous encounters with Jinn during journeys in far flung parts, mostly on abandoned desert tracts.[49] And the exchange that ensues in such encounters often turns upon the subject of poetry, a fact which the *Maqāma Iblīsiyya* of al-Hamadhānī celebrates in a relatively rich game of literary allusion. Doubts about the women thus subliminally stirred are justified at the close.

(ii) Stylistically, with its strikingly polished passages of rhyming prose, the anecdote is hardly of a piece with the bulk of roughly hewn anecdotes that survive about Abū Nuwās (themselves of doubtful authenticity in the majority of cases, precisely because they tend to be more jocular than naturalistic). The finest aesthetic element of the narrative – one that scarcely comes across in translation – is the passage that evokes the Qurʾānic description of Heaven in Sūra 88. The anecdote reads much more convincingly as an example of stylistically sophisticated 10th century *adab* prose (of the kind that Ibn Durayd and Badīʿ al-Zamān al-Hamadhānī were either composing or recording as bookends to that century). At times, and arguably in its entirety (depending on what view one takes of the shape

---

48 One is even tempted to suggest, more rashly, that the fact that the name Wādī al-Rumma, home of Banū Fazāra, is so acoustically close to "Dhū al-Rumma" is intentionally toyed with; – which fact might combine with the contextually striking effect of the word *rimma* (meaning 'cadaver') in the long poem of Abū Nuwās.

49 For a bibliography on this subject see Philip F. Kennedy, "Some Demon Muse: structure and allusion in al-Hamadhānī's *Maqāma Iblīsiyya*, in *Arabic and Middle Eastern Literatures*, vol. 2, No. 1, 1999.

of the whole yarn), it reads like an early Maqāma. It is the enhanced texture of the rhyming prose at the outset which gives this impression, albeit rhyming prose, or *sajᶜ*, is not a sustained effect. In short, because of this stylistic aspect, the attribution to Ismāᶜīl ibn Abī Sahl of the Al Nawbakhyt, with whom Abū Nuwās had close dealings of patronage towards the end of his life, can hardly be taken seriously. He, and other members of his family, would have provided a convenient source for forgers and false attributors of apocryphal materials.

Yet while we might fault Ḥamza al-Iṣfahānī for his sense of authentic anecdotage, in this case, he can hardly be faulted for his taste. The anecdote is a superb narrative curio.

(iii) How does the anecdote reflect Abū Nuwās' sexuality? Is the biggest clue to its lack of authenticity the fact that it depicts Abū Nuwās as heterosexually attracted to, first one exquisitely beautiful woman, then a whole group of them? If this is deemed anomalous, then how is the fact distinct from those many other poems and anecdotes that establish Abū Nuwās' heterosexual love for Janān in Baṣra, and ᶜInan, *et al* among the elite circle of *qiyān* (singing girls) in Baghdad? And what are we then to make of the apparently homophobic feint with which the episode ends? Or is the final lewd point rather a racist one? Is the ending, indeed, a deliberate dig at what became standard fare in tawdry depictions (and confessions) of Abū Nuwās's sexual antics? These are all fair questions, and they are all equally unresolvable. The anecdote is ambiguous in all respects. There are various perceptions about Abū Nuwās conveyed in this story, we simply cannot be sure exactly which one holds sway, other than that at some point in his life (or afterlife) it would not have seemed at all queer for him to be attracted to a group of strange young women. We should note simply that the quite deliberate sting in the tail[50] of this anecdote works by virtue of the nature of the heterosexual subject matter that has gone before.

(iv) Love in the time of pilgrimage was something of a motif for Abū Nuwās, as we know. Here at least it was not at the Kaᶜba itself that the poet indulged his desire. There is some tension between religion and love, but really not that much, as the spheres of religion and love are kept physically apart. And when "*al-fahisha*" is mentioned at the end the intention is to force it grotesquely upon the poet.

The literary quality of the story centers, in fact (it seems to me), on two related images, which reflect the way events unfold: the first is that in which the woman is described when she speaks as spilling pearls that are loosened from her, their metaphorical string. These are ordered pearls breaking from their necklace as she speaks. It is hard to detect a threat or caution in the evocative beauty of the image. Yet in the closing image of the story the women are seen racing home, laughing at

---

50 A homosexual threat only by virtue of the fact that Abū Nuwās would presumably have the passive rather than active role.

the poet's expense, like pearls scattering from a broken string. The pleasing promise of the first image is routed and dispersed – almost literally – by the second, and with them, finally, the misplaced hopes of Abū Nuwās. It is this finely enhanced internal consistency of imagery, together with the delicate and veiled allusions to Dhū al-Rumma, which suggests that the whole story is an accomplished literary contrivance. The story holds us, for the larger part, to the false hope of poetry ("ordered pearls") and delivers us to a prosaic and burlesque ending, where the promise of amorous and erotic verse falls apart. And the *Ḥajj* is a faded memory.

* * *

Three issues remain to be discussed. 1. The significance of Ibn Durayd in the chain of transmission; 2. The formal and stylistic aspects of the narrative that are redolent of the Maqāma; and 3. The possible relevance to the fantasist's general theme of love and pilgrimage of the formal subject in Islamic law and ritual of *mutᶜat al-ḥajj*.

The first two subjects are linked. For one of the more puzzling, and unresolved, issues of Arabic literary history is Ibn Duryad's (d. 924) role, according to al-Ḥuṣrī (d. 1022), as a precursor to Badīᶜ al-Zamān al-Hamadhānī (d. 1008) in developing the Maqāma as a genre. The whole subject, which is in the end something of a *cul-de-sac* in literary history, has recently been reviewed helpfully and in detail by Jaakko Hämeen-Anttila in *Maqama. A History of a Genre.*[51] What follows is deeply indebted to Hämeen-Anttila's judicious review, with which this author is largely in accord, simply wishing to add the significance of this conspicuous anecdote into the mix.

These are the main points: In a now famous passage of his *Zahr al-Ādāb* the North African *littérateur* al-Ḥuṣrī, avowedly a great admirer of al-Hamadhānī's newly minted Maqāmāt, quoting them severally during the course of his rich discursive anthology, made the following statement about the origins of the new genre:[52]

> [al-Hamadhānī] saw that Abū Bakr ibn Durayd al-Azdī had composed forty novel stories (*aghraba bi-arbaᶜīna ḥadīthan*) and had mentioned that he had extracted them from the fountains of his own heart and had selected them from the mines of his own thought. He had disclosed them to both eyes and insights and conducted them (as a bride) for both thoughts and minds in Persian garments (*maᶜāriḍ ᶜajamiyya*) and curious (*ḥūshiyya*) expressions. However, the minds (of the readers) shied away from most of what he had produced (*aẓhara*) and they did not open their ears to it because he had used words and their meanings in different ways and in everchanging patterns. [al-Hamadhānī] countered (*ᶜāraḍa-hā*) them with four hundred maqamas on mendicancy (*fī l-kudya*) ...[53]

[51] Wiesbaden: Harrassowitz Verlag 2002, pp. 66-73.

[52] Abū Isḥāq Ibrāhīm Ibn ᶜAlī al-Ḥuṣrī al-Qayrawānī, *Zahra al-Ādāb wa-Thamar al-Albāb*, ed. ᶜAlī Muḥammad al-Bajāwī (Cairo 1970), 2 vols; vol. 1, p. 261.

[53] Trans. Hämeen-Anttila p. 67 (with minor emendations).

The passage is intriguing; though, in the end baffling – because al-Ḥuṣrī is not at all clear about identifying the *arbaʿīn ḥadīth*. This locution does not seem to allow one to understand this as reference to a single work, such as "The Forty Stories"; he is referring rather, seemingly, to forty stories – or simply a fair few stories. He then qualifies them. They owed much to his own invention ("extracted from the fountains of his own heart"), which is significant in so far as we know the Maqāma to have been fictional, and were full of "curious expression". This makes sense from what we know concretely about Ibn Durayd, the greatest repository in his day of Arabic philological lore.

All writers who have commented on the *Maqāmāt* during the last century have been apprised of this passage.[54] Most have dismissed it as a confusing dead end, unable to explain what precisely in Ibn Durayd's writing may have fed al-Hamadhānī's inspiration. Only Zakī Mubārak in his 1931 *La Prose arabe au quatrième siècle de l'hégire* clung enthusiastically to the significance of this passage; naively, he seems to have taken *ʿarabīna ḥadīth* as the title of a specific work – a transparent mistake; and he trawled a number of works to find examples of these misplaced – but surviving – anecdotes of Ibn Durayd, persuaded particularly by the evidence of anecdotes relayed in the *Āmālī* of al-Qālī, a student of the former, as examples of the kind of literature al-Ḥuṣrī may have been alluding to. Few recent authors have been convinced; as Hämeen-Anttila puts it: "Mubarak chose forty stories quoted in *Amālī* on the authority of Ibn Durayd which had a distant resemblance to the maqamas of al-Hamadhānī. ...Al-Qālī's work does contain several lengthy stories transmitted on the authority of Ibn Durayd, but in none of these is Ibn Durayd considered an author on his own; Ibn Durayd was an important transmitter of philological material which included longer prose anecdotes, but so were many others, too, al-Aṣmaʿī (d. 213/828) being the foremost philologist under whose name prose narrative circulated."[55]

On the basis of the evidence that Mubarak provides, Hämeen-Anttila suggests in conclusion that "the theory of Mubarak has been proven wrong, the discussion has died out, and Ibn Durayd has been buried deep in the field of maqama studies."[56] (Though a caveat to such a view is helpfully noted in the words of Malti-Douglas: "In all fairness, we must conclude that there is a considerable

---

54 These authors have been conveniently listed, in a (by no means dismissive) discussion of the relevance of this passage to the study of theories of fiction in medieval Arabic literature, by Rina Drory in *Models and Contacts. Arabic Literature and its Impact on Medieval Jewish Culture* (Leiden: Brill 2000), p. 14, note 7. (They include Prendergast in 1915, Margoliouth in 1927, Balchère et Masnou in 1957, Beeston in 1971, Kilito in 1976, Bosworth in 1976, Pellat in 1986, Malti-Douglas in 1985 and Richards in 1991.)

55 Op. cit. p. 67-8.

56 Ibid. p. 68.

possibility that the *Maqāmāt* of al-Hamadhānī were instigated by a series of stories by Ibn Durayd, apparently no longer extant."[57])

Indeed, Hämeen-Anttila is himself ambivalent, adding a question as a rider to his own conclusion, "Yet, has he really received the fate due to him?" It seems that no matter how much one tries to bury Ibn Durayd, with regard to his role as a forefather of the *Maqāma* genre, a hand or foot pokes alluringly out of his literary grave. In lieu of the anecdotes in al-Qālī examined earlier by Mubarak, for which Ibn Durayd was simply a transmitter rather than a source, the Finnish scholar offers for scrutiny a book which was actually composed by Ibn Durayd, "certainly circulating under his name" – the *Kitāb Waṣf al-Maṭar wa-l-Saḥāb* (anecdotes about rain, clouds and rain augury among the Bedouin tribes).

This is a gem of medieval Arabic literature – well worth perusal in its own right. And suffice it to say here that Hämeen-Anttila's presentation is quite persuasive in highlighting shared formal features with certain *Maqāmāt* of al-Hamadhānī. Anecdote 9 of *Waṣf al-Maṭar* recalls significant elements al-Hamadhānī's *Dīnāriyya*; for our purposes, we might note that in Ibn Durayd's anecdote 16 "we have, after a short *isnād*, a story about a Bedouin stopping by a group of pilgrims." The pilgrimage is a backdrop, as one would expect, of all sorts of encounters, fictional or otherwise, that are given a literary rendering. In addition to 9 and 16 (in the light of Hämeen-Anttila's argument), we can further suggest the relevance of anecdote 12 in which scouts from three clans of the southern tribal group of Saᶜd al-ᶜAshīra are dispatched to espy grassland after rain.[58] They each return and give account of their sightings in simple eloquence, characterized by attractive (i.e. not overburdened) rhyming prose, at times reminiscent of what we know of the utterances of the pagan *kāhins*; language, as well as being descriptive, is thus competitive, agonistic and seeks to persuade, – it is this tone that is germane to some of the antics of the *Maqāma* in its standard form.

In summarizing his argument about the relevance of *Waṣf al-Maṭar*, anecdote 9, Hämeen-Anttila singles out eight formal features that are redolent of the maqāma: 1. Ample use of rhymed prose; 2. *Isnād*; 3. Some kind of story [i.e. they are not exclusively of philological interest]; 4. Philological interest; 5. A ragged but eloquent hero; 6. First person narration; 7. A travel theme; 8. All encounters are standing ones as opposed to seated learned sessions.

All of these features are loosely present in Abū Nuwās's unlikely "pilgrim's progress", whose proto-*maqāma* traits we should now focus on, having alluded to them only intermittently thus far.

---

57 Fedwa Malti-Douglas, "Maqāmāt and adab: "al-Maqāma al-Maḍīriyya" of al-Hamadhānī", in *Journal of the American Oriental Society*, 105:247-258 (citation from pp. 248-9).

58 Abū Bakr Muḥammad ibn al-Ḥasan ibn Durayd al-Azdī, *Kitāb Waṣf al-Maṭar wa-l-Saḥāb*, ed. ᶜIzz al-Dīn al-Tanūkhī (Damascus 1963), pp. 46-52.

The *isnād* is a spurious one – in so far as it cannot authenticate the narrative, which is clearly fictional as told. But the "*rijāl*" of the *isnād* are real enough, we know. The only one not mentioned in passing in the foregoing essay is Makhlad ibn al-Qāsim al-ʿAtakī, Ibn Durayd's informer for the anecdote. He is (apparently) unheard of in medieval Islamic literature with this particular *nisba*; with the *nisba* al-Balkhī, however, we find mention of him in Ibn Ḥajar al-ʿAsqallānī's *Lisān al-Mīzān* (as well as his *Mīzān al-Iʿtidāl*) as a highly unreliable source; apropos the sole tradition he had a role in reporting, Ibn Ḥajar comments that he was considered "*ḍaʿīf*" by al-Dārquṭnī. The *isnād* of our anecdote is, in short, problematic. Perhaps Ibn Durayd did make this all up – "mine it from his heart," as al-Ḥuṣrī might have said.

(Ibn Durayd himself was not always a very reliable source either, we can observe in passing.) Yāqūt al-Ḥimawī records the following about him in the *Irshād al-Arīb ilā Maʿrifat al-Adīb: Muʿjam al-Udabāʾ*:

> Abū Manṣūr al-Azharī has said in the Introduction of *Kitāb al-Tahdhīb*: "Among the people of our time who compose books, and concoct the Arabic language, inventing words, inserting in them that are not the genuine speech of the Arabs is Muḥammad ibn Durayd the author of the *Kitāb al-Jamhara*, *Kitāb Ishtiqāq al-Asmāʾ* and the *Kitāb al-Malāḥin*. I have attended his house in Baghdad more than once and seen him transmitting information from Abū Ḥātim [al-Sijistānī], al-Rayāshī and ʿAbd al-Raḥmān al-Aṣmaʿī's nephew. I asked Ibrāhīm ibn Muḥammad ibn ʿArafa about him and he said he paid no attention to him, finding him an untrustworthy transmitter. I myself have found him drunk despite his age unable to control his tongue from intoxication; I have perused his book which he entitled *al-Jamhara* and not found any acumen there or fine scholarly instinct; indeed I have come across many locutions I find unacceptable – I do not know what his sources were and have made a note for myself (and others) to investigate them." (This sounds familiar.)

There is rhymed prose in our anecdote; it is not sustained throughout but quite remarkable in the introductory section that sets the scene, that part which carries by association the prestige of the Qurʾānic scene it alludes to and whose language it borrows (see note 18). As Julia Bray has discussed in a detailed study the partial, inconsistent use of rhymed prose may be a feature and indicator of incipient, or proto, *Maqāma* materials that were (or might have been) stylistically enhanced with time.[59]

It is striking (though it may be due to happenstance) that the scene setting of our anecdote is both stylistically *and* thematically that part which reminds one of the *Maqāma Iblīsiyya* of al-Hamadhānī, itself a studied and literary working up of pre-existing proto materials and generic anecdotal norms of desert encounters with inspiring demons (the jinn that were the familiars of poets according to pre-

---

59 See "Julia Ashtiany [Bray], "*Isnād*s and Models of heroes: Abū Zubayd al-Ṭāʾī, Tanūkhī's Sundered Lovers and Abū 'l-ʿAnbas al-Ṣaymarī", in *Arabic and Middle Eastern Literatures* 1, pp. 7-30.

and early Islamic belief). The subject matter rings a bell when we think of Abū Nuwās's fantastic encounter; and the familiar resonance is intensified when we consider that each story has a "sting in the tail" that involves instructions for the protagonist to make for a dark cave to find what he is looking for (camels in one case and sex in the other). These are inconclusive, perhaps tendentious, details; the point is simply that it is consideration of the *Maqāma Iblīsiyya* in particular that allows one to taste the flavor of the *Maqāma* genre in the anecdote Ibn Durayd relayed to Ḥamza al-Iṣfahānī.

In the light of all these remarks about the scene setting, an essential further point should now be made: Abū Nuwās' description of the luscious natural scene he comes upon, where he is entranced by rich vegetation then distracted by the pluvial downpour from a thickly layered low-hanging cloud, etched in the kind of detail only the Arabic language can muster so eloquently, would have appealed to Ibn Durayd; indeed, the passage spanning from page 99 line 10 to page 100 line 2,[60] itself enriched by an apt quotation from the pre-Islamic luminary ʿAbīd ibn al-Abraṣ, could be aptly transplanted to his *Kitāb Waṣf al-Maṭar* (which Dr. Hämeen-Anttila has so pertinently guided us to, exulting as it does in the often mesmerizing linguistic celebration of rain and the vegetation it brings).

The arguments of this essay have been rehearsed on three occasions: at the School of Abbasid Studies (St. Andrews University, June 2006); at the Yale Arabic Colloquium (October 2006); and at Chicago University's Center for Middle Eastern Studies (April 2007). On each occasion the proposition that Abū Nuwās's anecdote can be deemed a proto-Maqāma in some of its aspects has received varied responses. It is not an unassailable position to adopt. Yet on the whole, it would seem, stylistically there is something helpful to be salvaged from the proposition in our understanding of the development of Arabic prose before the end of the 9$^{th}$ century C.E. On one of these occasions that Dr Julia Bray suggested intuitively (and helpfully, I think) that one might reconsider the debate about Ibn Durayd in the light of the anecdote.

Zakī Mubārak's zeal in positing Ibn Durayd as exemplar for al-Hamadhānī has meant that some details of his views have passed below the radar screen in recent overviews of his work. They contain the following astute hunch:

*"Quelles sont ses oeuvres en prose?"* That is, what are the works in prose that Ibn Durayd had a role in transmitting which could be considered proto *maqāma* material? *« J'ai beaucoup cherché pour les retrouver; ... Celui qui raconte le pèlerinage d'Abou-Nowas est un récit très vivant parfaitement digne d'avoir inspire le genre maḳâmât ; et c'est d'une manière sûre, un des quarante d'Ibn-Doraïd. »* Mubārak gives a further brief account of this anecdote, without adequately, and therefore persuasively, setting out those features that would allow one to think of a work *"digne d'avoir inspiré le genre*

60 *Dīwān Abī Nuwās*, ed. Ewald Wagner, vol. 1.

*du makâmât*". It is a shame only in so far as Mubārak short changed himself, as it were. Upon careful scrutiny, his instinct seems entirely justified. We do not in the end know what al-Ḥuṣrī meant exactly by *arbaʿīn ḥadīth* of Ibn Durayd. Mubārak was perhaps too fanatical in wanting to give exact form to lines only loosely drawn by the comments of the *adīb* from Kairouan. But to look for elements of literature simply redolent of the *Maqāma* in works that Ibn Duryad had a part in relaying, seems now entirely justified on the basis of al-Ḥuṣrī's comment (and indeed in general, beyond the work of Ibn Durayd, since al-Hamadhānī was certainly influenced and inspired in many different ways by much of the literature that pre-dated him – the *Maqāmāt* did not arise *ex nihilo*[61]). In a sense, regarding specific elements, we have come full circle since Zakī Mubārak's 1931 publication.

## *Epilogue*

One might assume that the coupling of the themes of love and pilgrimage is a fantasy that has left traces in anecdotal literature and poetry only. There may be more to it, though? Consideration of the issue of *mutʿat al-ḥajj* offers tantalizing possibilities. The concept of *mutʿat al-ḥajj* has its origins in Qurʾān, Sūrat al-Baqara, verse 196:

> *Wa-atimmū l-ḥajja wa-l-ʿumra li-llāhi fa-in uḥṣirtum fa-mā staysara mina l-hady … fa-ishā amintum fa-man tamattaʿa bi-l-ʿumrati ilā l-ḥajji fa-mā staysara mina l-hady …*
>
> (Complete the *ḥajj* and the *ʿumra* for God, and if you are prevented [i.e. by enemies, illness, etc.] then [offer] whatever sacrifices that can be obtained with ease … And when you are secure, then whoever derives enjoyment from the ease … And when you are secure, then whoever derives enjoyment from the *ʿumra* until the *ḥajj* shall [offer] whatever sacrifice that can be obtained with ease.)

The simplest definition of what is intended here by *tamattuʿ* (which came to be referred to most commonly as *mutʿat al-ḥajj*) is that: "it is one of three methods of performing the *ḥajj*: the pilgrim deconsecrates himself between the *ʿumra* and the *ḥajj*, the former being performed upon arrival at Mecca during the *ḥajj* months (i.e. Shawwāl, Dhū 'l-Qaʾda and Dhū 'l-Ḥijja) and the latter commencing on the eighth of Dhū 'l-Ḥijja."[62] During the period of deconsacration the pilgrim may indulge in activities forbidden in a state of *iḥrām*.

---

61 For a recent review of some aspect of these influences and the way they were distilled into al-Hamadhānī's Maqāmāt see Philip F. Kennedy, "The *Maqāmāt* as a Nexus of Interests: Reflections on Abdelfattah Kilito's *les Séances* and Other Writing" in Julia Bray (ed.) *Writing and Representation in Medieval Islam* (London:Routledge 2006).

62 Arthur Gribetz, *Strange Bedfellows:* Mutʿat al-nisāʾ *and* Mutʿat al-ḥajj. *A Study Based on Sunnī and Shīʿī Sources of* Tafsīr, Ḥadīth *and Fiqh* (Berlin: Schwarz Verlag 1994), p. 1.

Some scholars have averred that confusion between *mutʿat al-nisāʾ* and *mutʿat al-ḥajj* have colored our understanding of the latter; thus J. Burton:

> It may be a forgivable assertion to state that the Muslims simply did not understand the meaning of the Qurʾān's undefined term *tamattuʿ*. Certainly, the confusions in the *tafsīr*, *ḥadīth* and *fiqh* discussions of this term do nothing to shake that assertion ... What is demonstrated in the foregoing [study] is the gradual convergence and ultimate intersection of originally independent exegeses of two unrelated and unconnected statements in the Holy Qurʾān [i.e. 2:196 (referring to *mutʿat al-ḥajj*) and 4:24 (believed to refer to *mutʿat al-nisāʾ*), owing to the quite fortuitous circumstance that each of the two verses featured a function of the Arabic root *m t ʿ*.[63]

Arthur Gribetz's monograph is in large measure an attempt to refute Burton's view: "Although the confusion may have been fostered by the linguistic coincidence of two distinct practices being called *mutʿa*, the connection between them was based on more solid ground. This connection will [...] be in investigated, thereby refuting Burton's claim that the two *mutʿa's* are unrelated other than in name."[64] In one or two significant *ḥadīth*s there was, it appears, confusion between the two *mutʿa*s. Gribetz deals with these confusions lucidly on pages 35-40 of his study. What follows that section of his study is more important to us here, to wit, "The Connection between the Two Mutʿas" (pp. 40 ff.). The sociology of this connection is partly conjectural but certainly worth noting:

> A concrete question, which if answered, could determine the connection between the two *mutʿa*s, is the identity of the women (*nisāʾ*) who crop up in so many of the *ḥajj* traditions. Are these the men's wives who are engaged in sexual intercourse during *mutʿat al-ḥajj*, or are they other women who contract temporary marriages for the occasion? .... In light of the social liberties traditionally associated with Mecca and the pilgrimage, the idea of *mutʿat al-nisāʾ*'s connection with the *ḥajj* is by no means far-fetched ... The less-than-ascetic character of the *ḥajj* during the first century of Islam is portrayed, for example, by al-Fākihī (d. after 272/885). He describes the *ṭawāf* as a parade ground for eligible young women and slave-girls who would circumambulate in beautiful clothing and jewelry, with uncovered faces, while prospective husbands and masters would observe. This fashion of selling slave-girls was apparently encouraged by ʿUmar ...[65]

With the following remark we come full circle yet again: "Prostitution is known to have existed in Mecca during the *ḥajj* season. Stories are related about Kharqa from Banū ʿĀmir who reserved herself for pilgrims and prided herself on being "one of the rites (*anā mansik min manāsik al-ḥajj*)."[66] From what we know already about the lady in question this seems too unambiguous in its glossing; Dhū al-Rumma, at least, was more poetic about this.

---

63 John Burton, "*Mutʿ*, *tamatttuʿ* and *istimtāʿ* – a confusion of *tafsīr* s," *Union Européenne des Arabisants et Islamisants*, Tenth Congress, Edinburgh, 1980. *Proceedings*, ed. Robert Hillenbrand (Edinburgh, 1982), pp. 9-10. Quoted in Gribetz op. cit. p. 2.

64 Gribetz, op. cit. p. 2.

65 Op. cit. p. 40-1.

66 Op. cit. p. 41.

# *Tawqīʿ* (Apostille): Royal Brevity in the Pre-modern Islamic Appeals Court

*Beatrice Gruendler (Yale University)*

## *I. Introduction*

In his anthology of modern poets, which he was not to complete, al-Ṣūlī bent the rules and interrupted the section on poets beginning in *alif* (and their talented kin) with a writer of prose, namely, the chief secretary of al-Maʾmūn, Aḥmad b. Yūsuf (d. 213/828) and his family. This deviation allegedly satisfied the request of an unidentified noble and it also reflected the taste of al-Ṣūlī, who devoted to it well over a hundred pages. Not only did he include the accounts and poetry of the Āl Ṣubayḥ but also their prose, among it a number of apostilles written or received by them, which thus attained the same literary status as poetry.[1] Al-Ṣūlī (d.c. 335/946) was not unique in gathering apostilles of rulers and scribes. His contemporaries al-Jahshiyārī (d. 331/942-3)[2] and Ibn ʿAbdrabbih (d. 328/940), and later al-Thaʿālibī (d. 429/1038), likewise devoted sections of their books to *tawqīʿāt*, and Ibn ʿAbdrabbih, who ordered his anthology as a necklace, placed them next to the sermons that formed the center. The lexicographer and poetic critic Abū Aḥmad al-ʿAskarī (d. 382/993)[3] and his more famous student Abū Hilāl (d.c. 400/1010)[4] placed prose on a par with poetry, and

1 al-Ṣūlī (1401/1982), *al-Awrāq: Akhbār al-shuʿarāʾ al-muḥdathīn*, ed. Heyworth Dunne, London: Luzac 1934, repr. Beirut: Dār al-Maṣīr (hereafter *Awrāq*), 143. See the apostilles received by Yūsuf b. al-Qāsim to pleas made to his three successive employers, al-Manṣūr's uncle ʿAbdallāh b. ʿAlī, al-Mahdī's vizier Yaʿqūb b. Dāwūd, and Yaḥyā b. Khālid for whom he substituted in recording apostilles (ibid., 147-8, 153-4, 156-6) and apostilles composed by him (ibid., 158, 159-60, an example for a characteristically impassive description of feelings, 161, 162). For apostilles by his son, gathered in a separate chapter, see ibid., 229-31, esp. on not wanting to repeat himself, 229; on writing having the impact of speech, 230; and on mistrust of elaborate arguments as usually misrepresenting facts, 230. An excuse for giving a petitioner (*mustamīḥ*) a present beneath his rank (ibid., 231) resembles one such apostille by his father (ibid., 161). Al-Ṣūlī mentions an earlier and longer collection of Aḥmad's apostilles in his *Book of Viziers* (ibid., 231), which has not survived.

2 See Muḥammad b. ʿAbdūs al-Jahshiyārī (1357/1938), *al-Wuzarāʾ*, ed. Muṣṭafā al-Saqqā, Ibrāhīm al-Abyārī and ʿAbd al-Ḥafīẓ Shalabī, Cairo: Muṣṭafā al-Bābī al-Ḥalabī, 205 for the collected apostilles of Yaḥyā b. Khālid.

3 See Abū Aḥmad al-ʿAskarī (1402/1982), *al-Maṣūn fī l-adab*, ed. ʿAbdassalām Hārūn, Kuwait 1960, repr. Cairo, 113-15 for a chapter of pithy sayings by Yaḥyā b. Khālid. For an apostille by Abū ʿUbaydallāh Muʿāwiya b. ʿUbayd, vizier of al-Mahdī, see ibid., 107.

4 See Abū Hilāl al-ʿAskarī (1971) *K. al-Ṣināʿatayn al-kitāba wa-l-shiʿr*, ed. ʿAlī Muḥammad al-Bijāwī and Muḥammad Abū l-Faḍl Ibrāhīm, Cairo 1952, repr. 1971.

in this expansion of the concept of literary art, the apostille exemplified the ideal of brevity in eloquence (*ījāz*). "(One definition of eloquence is) the gathering of many meanings into few words."[5] In this essay, I will focus on the minimalistic genre that received such distinction by the poetic critic al-Ṣūlī.

The following lays no claim to offering an exhaustive study of the apostille (*tawqīʿ*) but rather a brief characterization of its salient literary qualities as a basis for further inquiry. I limit myself to the two early meanings of *tawqīʿ* as (the recording of) a verdict in a tort redress or audit and a written edict, leaving aside the other early meanings of a signature or motto concluding a letter (also *ʿalāma*)[6] and the postclassical meanings of an appointment letter and the looped, continuous script employed therein.[7]

### *I.1 History*

To believe the Arabic sources, tort redress begins with the Sasanians, where it took three different forms. Periodically the early Sasanian kings held audiences in an open space to allow victims of injustice to approach them and submit their cases without being hindered by the rules and personnel of the palace. In a two-step procedure, local leaders likewise gathered grievances at the beginning of each month and submitted them to the king for adjudication.[8] A more formal event was that of the annual royal audiences on the occasion of the *Nawrūz* and *Mihrgān* festivals, described in detail in the *Kitāb al-Tāj*.[9] People were given advance notice to prepare their cases (*qiṣṣa, ḥujja*) in written notes (*ruqʿa*), to be col-

---

5 See Abū Aḥmad al-ʿAskarī (1418/1998) *al-Tafḍīl bayna balāghatay al-ʿarab wa-l-ʿajam*, ed. Ḥamd b. Nāṣir al-Dukhayyil, Barīda, Saudi Arabia: Nādī al-Qaṣīm al-Adabī, 121 and 132. The quotations are comments on the preceding apostilles by Jaʿfar b. Yaḥyā and Sasanian kings; ibid., 120, 130-2. See also Abū Hilāl al-ʿAskarī, *al-Ṣināʿatayn*, 43, 162 and 181 and idem (1424/2003), *Dīwān al-maʿānī*, ed. Aḥmad Salīm Ghānim, 2 vols., Cairo, II:831-4.

6 See, e.g., al-Ṣūlī (1341), *Adab al-kuttāb*, ed. Muḥammad Bahja al-Atharī, Cairo: al-Maṭbaʿa al-Salafiyya, 134-5. See also in this meaning, the Abbasid *dīwān al-tawqīʿ* (which certified all royal edicts, not only tort cases) in the following section and n. 19.

7 F. Babinger and C.E. Bosworth (2000), art. "Tawqīʿ," in: *The Encyclopaedia of Islam*, new ed., Leiden: Brill, vol. VI: 933-5 (hereafter EI$^2$).

8 Arthur Christensen (1936), *L'Iran sous les Sassanides*. Annales du Musée Guimet: Bibliothèque d'Études, vol. 48, Paris and Copenhague: Geuthner and Munksgaard, 296 and 298 based on Niẓām al-Mulk (1340HS/1962), *Siyar al-mulūk (Siyāsatnama)*, ed. H. Darke, Tehran: B.T.N.K., 19 and (1960), *The Book of Government or Rules for Kings*, trans. H. Darke, repr. Surrey: Curzon 2002, 14. See also Niẓām al-Mulk's exemplary tales on the auditing of tax collectors and the invention of tort redress by (A)nūshirwān, *Siyāsatnama*, 29-52/*Book of Government*, 22-42.

9 Pseudo-Jāḥiẓ (1332/1914), *al-Tāj fī akhlāq al-mulūk*, ed. Aḥmad Zakī Bāshā, Cairo: al-Maṭbaʿa al-Amīriyya, 159-63/(1954), *Le livre de la couronne*, trans. Charles Pellat, Paris: Société d'Édition Les Belles Lettres, 179-82. This anonymous Arabic work on Sasanian culture relied on (probably translated) Pahlavi sources and was dedicated to al-Mutawakkil's familiar, al-Fatḥ b. Khāqān. Cf. also Christensen, *Iran* 296-7.

lected at the beginning of the meeting. Obstruction to access was punishable by law. The audience opened with a ceremonial submission of the king to the high priest, and the trial of any grievance against the king himself preceded all others. This form of tort redress was abolished by Yazdagird II (r. 439-57). A third procedure appears in the purported autobiography of Kisrā b. Qubād, or Anūshirwān (r. 531-79), who recounts how he delegated trusted envoys and judges to gather cases of fiscal abuses by local governors at the beginning of his rule.[10] After a twenty-eight-year interval he had the situation reviewed (first through delegation to the high priest, then, after the conclusion of his campaigns, taking charge himself[11]); he dispatched new trustees who were to examine cases of grievances together with local judges (but without the governors' knowledge) and to send back the claimants with their sealed case files to the capital. The judging of the cases was then conducted in full audience and without requiring proof against high-placed defendants, as the king always assumed (with two very unequal litigants) the guilt to lie with the powerful party. Cases were tried immediately, except for complex ones that required local judges and witnesses. In that event the king dispatched a threefold delegation of a chancellery scribe, legal expert and trusted envoy together with the claimant to his hometown to adjudicate the case there.[12] Anūshirwān thus used the priesthood, the judiciary and his personal envoys as parallel powers to control the fiscal administration.

Arab geographers report a similar practice from China. The anonymous *Akhbār al-Ṣīn wa-l-Hind* from 235/851 tells of a tort redress system in all Chinese cities. A uniquely Chinese feature is to ring a bell on the king's head attached to a wire stretched along the road outside of the royal palace, which any victim of injustice could pull to alert the king to his case.[13] Al-Idrīsī (d.c. 555/1162) presents a more elaborate version, according to which only the supreme king Baghbūgh in the city of Khānfū adjudicated torts weekly in full audience with all his viziers.[14] Al-Idrīsī's added detail of a set of stairs reserved for victims of injustice to ascend directly to the king echoes the Sasanian guarantee of uninhibited access, while the Friday date, the submission of the claims in written form, and the direct, immediate royal verdict reflect Islamic customs.[15] The Chinese prac-

10 Miskawayh (1379HS/2001), *Tajārib al-umam*, ed. Abū l-Qāsim Emāmī, 3 vols., Tehran: Soroush I:190-1 reproduced in al-Nuwayrī (1369/1949), *Nihāyat al-ʿarab fī funūn al-adab*, vol. 15, Cairo: Dār al-Kutub, 197. For the autobiography, see Miskawayh, *Tajārib al-umam* I: 188-204, reproduced almost verbatim in al-Nuwayrī, *Nihāya* XV: 195-207.

11 Miskawayh, *Tajārib* I:194-5 and al-Nuwayrī, *Nihāya* XV: 200-1.

12 Miskawayh, *Tajārib* I:195-7 and al-Nuwayrī, *Nihāya* XV: 201-2.

13 Anon. (1948), *Akhbār al-Ṣīn wa-l-Hind*, ed., trans. and comm. Jean Sauvaget, Paris: Société d'Édition Les Belles Lettres, 18-19.

14 The name derives from Parthian *bghpwhr* "son of God," which arrived via Soghdian into Arabic (with the Persian variant Faghfūr) and was understood to render the Chinese royal title *T'ien tzu* "Son of Heaven"; see Editors (1991), art. "Faghfūr," in EI$^2$ II: 738.

15 al-Idrīsī (n.d.), *Nuzhat al-mushtāq fī ikhtirāq al-āfāq*, 2 vols., ed. R. Rubinacci, U. Rizzitano et al., Napoli: Istituto Universitario Orientale 1970, repr. Port Said, I: 97-8.

tice of tort redress, documented from the 3rd century CE through the Tang period (618-907 CE) and institutionalized in the Sung period (960-1276 CE), rather employs a drum and a box outside the city gates where petitions were deposed and then investigated by officially designated censors. The bell seems to be a folkloric elaboration of what was originally a suspended lung-shaped stone in countries surrounding China, such as Japan and Siam, which adopted the practice. In the Arabic sources the bell's inventor is Anūshirwān and it is also designated with a Persian term *(darā)* in the *Akhbār al-Ṣīn wa-l-Hind.*[16] The collected *tawqīʿāt* contain Chinese and Sasanian samples, but these do not deviate from the Arabic ones in substance and style and must have been (at the very least) reformulated.[17]

Before the advent of Islam, the Quraysh had redressed abuses that occurred in Mecca under their authority. The prophet later condoned the pagan practice and made it legal in Islam. But redress of torts (*maẓālim*) was not officially regulated before the Umayyads, when abuses by governors and leaders justified the creation of a specific office that combined administrative and judicial authority. ʿAbdalmalik treated abuses still behind closed doors, ʿUmar II presided personally over a *maẓālim* court. The Abbasids al-Mahdī, al-Hādī, al-Rashīd, al-Maʾmūn and al-Muhtadī continued the practice.[18] With al-Rashīd, tort redress was for the first time delegated to a vizier, Yaḥyā b. Khālid. Thereafter it alternated between constituting a separate *dīwān* or being assumed by the vizier, who often delegated it to a substitute (for example by Yaḥyā to Yūsuf b. al-Qāsim) or requested the help of legal experts.[19] During the Abbasid Muʿtazilite intermezzo

---

16 Edward Kracke (1976), "Early Visions of Justice for the Humble in East and West," *JAOS* 96, 492-8; Henri Maspéro (1927), *La chine antique*, Paris: de Boccard, vol. IV: 87 and 149-50, and Chunyan Huang (2004), "Songdai dengwengu zhidu [On the System of Appealing to the Emperor in the Song Dynasty]," *Zhongzhou xuekan (Academic Journal of Zhongzhou)* 6: 112-16; I am indebted to Hyunhee Park for the references on the Chinese tort system.

17 For Sasanian apostilles, see, e.g., Abū Aḥmad al-ʿAskarī, *Tafḍīl*, 130-2, Ibn ʿAbdrabbih (1359-72/1940-53), *al-ʿIqd al-farīd*, 7 vols., ed. Aḥmad Amīn, Aḥmad al-Zayn and Ibrāhīm al-Abyārī, IV: 222-3 (hereafter *ʿIqd*) and al-Thaʿālibī (1414/1994), *Khāṣṣ al-khāṣṣ*, ed. Maʾmūn al-Janān, Beirut: Dār al-Kutub al-ʿIlmiyya, 124-5 (hereafter *Khāṣṣ*). For one specimen attributed to a Chinese king called Yaʿbūr (corruption of Faghfūr), see *Khāṣṣ*, 123. Cf. also the recent collection by Muḥammad al-Durūbī and Ṣalāḥ Jarrār (1421/2001, Jamharat tawāqīʿal-ʿarab, 3 vols., al-Ain, U.A.E.), compiled from ca. 200 premodern literary, biographical and historical sources.

18 al-Māwardī (1409/1989), *al-Aḥkām al-sulṭāniyya wa-l-wilāyāt al-dīniyya*, ed. Khālid Rashīd al-Jumaylī, Baghdad, 129-31/(1915), *Les statuts gouvernementaux ou Règles de droit public et administratif*, trans. E. Fagnan, Algiers: Adolphe Jourdan, 160-4 and Abū Yaʿlā b. al-Farrāʾ (1386/1966), *al-Aḥkām al-sulṭāniyya*, ed. Muḥammad Ḥāmid al-Fiqī, Cairo: Muṣṭafā al-Bābī al-Ḥalabī, 59-60. For a historical overview, see Jørgen S. Nielsen (1991), art. "Maẓālim," EI$^2$ X: 392-3.

19 In the *dīwān al-tawqīʿ* requests on any subject together with the caliphal decisions were drawn up as formal documents for the *dīwān al-dār* to be dispatched for execution to the respective office in charge (taxation, estate, treasury, stipends, etc.); Qudāma b. Jaʿfar (1981), *al-Kharāj wa-ṣināʿat al-kitāba*, ed. Muḥammad Ḥusayn al-Zubaydī, Baghdad: Minis-

and the Buyid rule, the courts fell under religious authority. After a Tulunid lapse the Fatimids restored the practice. The Ayyubids formalized the procedure including standard wording to be used for the petitions, which were dealt with administratively more often than in public session. Later the process became increasingly bureaucratized; Zangids and Mamluks housed it in a specific building, the *dār al-ᶜadl*, where its ceremonial function came to take precedence over the granting of justice to individuals.

*I.2. Procedure*

The earliest detailed description of *maẓālim* in Islam belongs to the brief restoration of the caliphate under al-Qādir (r. 381-422/991-1031) and al-Qāʾim (r. 422-67/1031-75), when manuals of rulership (*aḥkām sulṭāniyya*) produced for the latter emphasized the caliphal role in ensuring universal justice.[20] The short pronouncements of caliphs or viziers that were collected as quotable literature form only a fraction of the irretrievable proceedings, described in detail by al-Māwardī (d. 450/1058) and Ibn al-Farrā' (d. 458/1066). The head of the court, unless the caliph or vizier performed this function themselves, was a judge chosen for his probity, sense of justice, and kindness towards people.[21] In comparison with a civil judge, the *maẓālim* judge enjoyed greater latitude in accepting evidence, summoning witnesses and expediting procedures. The activity of the *maẓālim* court relied on the presence of clerks (summoning the powerful defendant), judges (aware of the litigants' rights), jurisconsults, scribes and witnesses. In the presence of all these and the parties involved, cases were heard and tried immediately; it was a public performance of the exercise of justice at the highest level of appeal. Not all cases required the individual leveling of a complaint (*ẓulāma*). Review of governors (*wulāh*), tax agents (*ᶜummāl*), accountants (*kuttāb*), and public pious endowments (*wuqūf*), was automatic. Individual complaints in turn were necessary to restitute or expedite missing government stipends (*dīwān al-ᶜaṭāʾ*). The same applied to property confiscated by the authorities or taken by force (*ghuṣūb*), the former requiring only the consultation of the registry of deeds, the latter additional evidence. Individual complaints were further needed to review

try of Culture, 53-4 and Dominique Sourdel (1959-60), *Le vizirat ᶜabbāside de 749 à 936 (132 à 324 de l'Hégire)*, Damascus, I: 228-9, 272, 280-1, 297, 307. On the *maẓālim* office, see al-Jahshiyārī, *Wuzarāʾ*, 177, al-Ṣūlī, *Awrāq* 158-60, Walther Björkman (1928), *Beiträge zur Geschichte der Staatskanzlei im islamischen Ägypten*, Hamburg: De Gruyter, 6-7, and Sourdel, *Vizirat* II: 640-4.

20 See Eric Hanne (2004), "Abbasid Politics and The Classical Theory of the Caliphate," in: B. Gruendler and L. Marlow, eds., *Writers and Rulers: Perspectives from Abbasid to Safavid Times*, Wiesbaden: Reichert, 49-71, esp. 56 and 67. For a later period see the detailed study by Jørgen S. Nielsen (1985), *Secular Justice in an Islamic State: Maẓālim under the Baḥrī Mamlūks, 662/1294-789/1387*, Istanbul: Nederlands Historisch-Archeologisch Instituut.

21 Qudāma b. Jaᶜfar, *Kharāj*, 63.

private pious endowments. Finally the *maẓālim* court acted as an authority executing verdicts or enforcing laws vis-à-vis powerful individuals who had resisted lower judges or market overseers, and the courts also mediated between litigants and supervised public religious festivals.[22] A case either received its final verdict in the *maẓālim* court or was referred (*iḥāla*) to another party with more or less specific instructions, such as to grant and carry out the petitioner's claim or to investigate the truth of his allegation – and a number of the literary apostilles indeed take this form.[23] Both verdict and referral are designated as *tawqīᶜ*. Beyond the procedural specifics, the rules of the Abbasid era share the principles of speed and direct access to the highest authority with the tort redress of later periods.

The preserved apostille collections list the decisions, accompanied by a terse introduction of the initiator, the accused and the accompanying circumstances. The *tawqīᶜāt* thus create the impression that the hearing, examination, verdict and enforcement, were all accomplished in one sitting. The entire procedure appears as a one-stop event with the ruler dispensing and recording his decision *ad hoc*. This must be understood as a literary abbreviation, in a similar way *adab* accounts of literary gatherings (*majālis*) select a few high points from an entire evening. The reality of *maẓālim* justice certainly included prior attempts to obtain justice from regular courts. At times the apostilles may have simply reopened a case and that led to further (protracted or abortive) procedures at a lower court. Some *tawqīᶜāt* explicitly indicate the dependence of the ruling on certain conditions or evidence or contain instructions for further action or examination.[24]

The procedures did not exclude the possibility that justice was immediately granted, especially when an apostille was accompanied by the action of the caliph or the sitting judge. But it is vital not to confuse the actual redress of torts with its literary products and depiction. What we have before us are those rulings and responses that have been selected for their literary merit and potentially reformulated (as can be seen in extant variants). This does not mean however, that the language of a plea came as an afterthought, for it was the prime tool to gain the attention of the judge. Al-Ṣāḥib b. ᶜAbbād once rewarded a good formulation with the granting of its petition, whereas the bad language of another had the opposite effect.[25] Irritated by a language error al-Manṣūr annotated a letter from his governor of Ḥims with "Replace you scribe or be replaced" (*ᶜIqd* IV: 212 #12).[26]

---

22 al-Māwardī, *Aḥkām*, 132-6/*Statuts*, 164-72 and Ibn al-Farrāʾ, *Aḥkām*, 60-3.

23 al-Māwardī, *Aḥkām*, 149-52/*Statuts,* 193-8. See also next note.

24 E.g., *ᶜIqd* IV: 221 al-Ḥasan b. Sahl #2 (to a complainant) and *ᶜIqd* IV: 222 Ṭāhir #6 (to an informer) and other examples in section II.4. make the truth of the allegations a condition.

25 See *Khāṣṣ*, 139 Ṣāḥib #22 and ibid., 137 Ṣāḥib #1, respectively. In the second example he declined the services of a preacher who misplaced a *hamza*.

26 In the following, apostilles will be referenced by a short work title, the quoted speaker, and the serial number (author's addition) in the collection.

Alongside with the apostilles proper, the collections also contain edicts, i.e. orders dispatched or responses given to queries by governors, tax collectors, generals and foreign monarchs. They have become part of the *tawqīʿāt* chapters because of their identical authorship, resemblance in form, and thematic overlap. Edicts concern issues such as delayed land tax shipments, strategic advice on uprisings and battles, building construction, stipends, and other personal matters of officials. But they differ in tone, ranging from impatient to threatening or abusive, always suspicious of the recipient's slothfulness, corruption or insubordination.[27] The edicts will be included in the discussion in as far as they concern matters raised in petitions.

### *I.3. Media*

The *tawqīʿ* is a written form of literature, even if the personal appearance before the court was a vital condition. As opposed to poetry, the whole process of tort redress defined itself from the beginning by the writing material, papyrus or later paper, on which claims were submitted and afterwards preserved as legal evidence. By the late 2nd/8th century, paper became more widely available and cheaper than the papyrus produced under government monopoly. Nonetheless in times of crisis, paper (*kawāghid*, sg. *kāghad, kāghid*) was hard to come by even for the government; police prefect Muḥammad b. ʿAbdallāh b. Ṭāhir (d. 253/867), under siege in Baghdad with al-Mustaʿīn, cautioned his scribes, "Make fine the pen and short the speech! There is no requesting of sheets (*qarāṭīs*, sg. *qirṭās*). Peace!" (*Khāṣṣ*, 134). The *tawqīʿ*'s sparseness was dictated by the encounter, in the tiny space of a scrap note, between the highest and lowest ends of society. This economy of the medium is mirrored by that of the language: an elliptic phrase, perfectly fitted to the practical limits of its writing support.

Petitions (*qiṣṣa, ruqʿa, risāla*) were drawn up ahead of time (later in Ayyubid and Mamluk times a distinct formulary had to be followed) and submitted (*rufiʿa*) in writing by the petitioner either previous to, or on the audience day (usually a Friday). Qudāma b. Jaʿfar (d. 337/948) describes the collection of petitions ahead of time into a folder with annotated summaries of each case prepared by the head of the redress court. The personal appearance of the complainant (*mutaẓallim*) needed to be accompanied with a written document through which the claim could be processed. In the actual session, the caliph could choose to read the whole original or an attached summary. He annotated the case (or its précis) with his ruling, or *tawqīʿ*, either directly underneath the

27 For instance, *ʿIqd* IV: 212 al-Manṣūr #13 (a figurative warning), *ʿIqd* IV: 213 al-Hādī #2 (an insult), and *ʿIqd* IV: 213 al-Rashīd #4 (a figurative threat). But note also al-Maʾmūn's humorous edict dispensing stipends to his companions on ʿĀshūrāʾ (*ʿIqd* IV: 216 #15).

text or on the back of the note (*waqqaʿa fī asfalihā/ẓahrihā*).[28] The order of cases was normally that of the petitioners' appearance, except under al-Mustahdī, who scrambled the order by having people deposit complaints in a box ahead of time to forestall any manipulation. The verdict was often a two-step procedure: the caliph (or his depute) gave the gist of the decision (*maʿnā*) in a short phrase (*jumla*) which was then reformulated as a longer explanation (*sharḥ*) in easily comprehensible language (*yaqrubu min al-ʿāmmati fahmuhā*) for the uneducated petitioners.[29] This is detailed in one instance, when general ʿAlī b. ʿĪsā b. Māhān, having been appointed governor of Khurasan in 180/795-6, troubled al-Rashīd with further demands. The caliph gave his secretary Yūsuf b. al-Qāsim b. Ṣubayḥ (Aḥmad's father) the essence of his answer, "Let him know the extent of what I did for him, for I think he is not aware of it," and Yūsuf composed the actual apostille:

> We gave you enough with [the land] we made you govern. Khurasan is ample for you as long as life is ample for you.
>
> *qad kafaynāka bimā wallaynāka wa-Khurāsānu tasaʿuka mā wasiʿaka ʿumr*
>
> (al-Ṣūlī, *Awrāq*, 161).

Al-Maʾmūn also stipulated brevity when requesting from his secretary ʿAmr b. Masʿada (d. 217/832; depute of Aḥmad b. Abī Khālid in the *tawqīʿāt* office) not to exceed one line in his instruction to a governor to restore a wronged man's right. The writing must have been small to fit within this space. ʿAmr composed:

> My letter to you is the letter of one who trusts to whom he is writing, is concerned for the one about whom he is writing, and between trust and concern, the one in charge will not err.
>
> *kitābī ilayka kitābu wāthiqin bi-man kutiba ilayhi, maʿniyyun bi-man kutiba lahu, wa-lan yaḍīʿa bayna l-thiqati wa-l-ʿināyati ḥāmiluhu*
>
> (Abū Aḥmad al-ʿAskarī, *Tafḍīl*, 120).

The Barmakid vizier Yahyā b. Khālid in turn delegated an answer to household members who had demanded higher allowances to Anas b. Abī Shaykh (executed with Jaʿfar 187/803), and the wording Anas chose, "A little [pay] that lasts is better than a lot that stops" found Yaḥyā's high praise (*Khāṣṣ*, 135 Yaḥyā #7).

After the conclusion of the *maẓālim* hearings, the case summaries (or the full petition texts) and the names of the complainants (*rāfiʿūn*) were entered into the court records, lists of case folders established, and any supporting materials used by the judge and his assistants copied. The apostilles, if noted down onto summaries, were transcribed into the original complaint notes, and returned to the claimants as evidence of the hearing and decision. Repeated visits by one peti-

---

28 Qudāma, *Kharāj*, 63-4. Once the formulation *kataba fī faṣl* is used (al-Ṣūlī, *Awrāq*, 162)

29 al-Jahshiyārī, *Wuzarāʾ*, 210.

tioner were kept in one file.[30] In some cases, copies of the apostilles were forwarded to a third party, typically the official accused by petitioners of wrongdoing. Regarding one complainant, al-Manṣūr is described to have "recorded in his petition to [the attention of] the governor (*waqqaʿa fī qiṣṣatihi ilā l-ʿāmili),* 'Help me in his case lest I help him in yours'" (*Khāṣṣ,* 130 al-Manṣūr #1).[31] Similarly, Yaḥyā b. Khālid wrote "into the note of a complainant, so that the apostille would be shown to the one he accused":

> Be just to him over whom you rule, lest he who rules over you will be just to him (*anṣif man walīta amrahu wa-illā anṣafahu man yalī amraka*; *Khāṣṣ,* 135 #4).

The large amount of cases and small size of the documents dictated the concision of the rulings. But the aesthetic of *ījāz* came to the encounter of the material on which the apostille was registered, and it grew to be an end in itself (see section II.2.). In practice, the claim of the *maẓālim* institution to accord justice to every candidate on an individual basis was a logistical impossibility. This is evident for instance in Jaʿfar b. Yaḥyā creating a blank ruling for a complicated case he could not himself bring to term on a busy day.[32] Without having completely understood the problem, he wrote underneath, "This is to be treated as its like according to the rules and intent of the law and the goal and method of equity, God willing."[33]

## *II. Apostilles as Literature*

Viewed as literature, *tawqīʿāt* bequeath us portrayals of rulers by themselves and thus complement the numerous literary genres (panegyrics, advice literature and historiography) that convey royal iconology as fashioned by the sovereigns' inferiors.[34] In this sense the apostilles add a small but unique perspective from above. In the following I have relied on the *tawqīʿāt* preserved in *adab* sources of the early Abbasid period from al-Ṣūlī to al-Thaʿālibī,[35] and focused in their discussion on those themes that most frequently recur. The pronouncements ascribed to historical figures are thus not taken at face value but rather as literary reflections of rulers' acts of speech and as examples of the literary genre of *tawqīʿ*.

---

30 Qudāma, *Kharāj,* 63-4, Björkman, *Staatskanzlei,* 7 n. 3, and Ḥamdī ʿAbd al-Munʿim (1408/1988), *Dīwān al-maẓālim, nashʾatuhu wa-taṭawwuruhu wa-khtiṣāṣuhu muqāranan bi-l-nuẓum al-quḍāʾiyya al-ḥadītha,* Beirut: Dār al-Jīl, 141-2.

31 See further examples in section II.4.

32 al-Jahshiyārī, *Wuzarāʾ,* 211.

33 Ibid., 210.

34 For case studies on these and other genres, see Gruendler and Marlow, *Writers and Rulers* (see n. 20).

35 For full citation of the sources used, see nn. 1-6, 8 and 17.

### *II.1. Composition*

Despite their diminutive size, the apostilles encompass a whole universe of literature, and they also derive effect from what remains unsaid. *Tawqīʿāt* can certainly fall back on a formulary but in capable hands they vary considerably in two respects: the directness of the decision on an issue brought forward and the literary ornament employed. Regarding the former aspect, the decision comes in three degrees of directness: first, it may specify the issue and personally address the recipient; second it may specify the issue but use an impersonal address, mentioning the recipient in the third person if at all; third, it may remain implicit, replacing both issue and recipient by a general statement or quotation whose relevance to the case at hand must be inferred. This leaves to the recipient the interpretation and, if he is an official, also the execution. The statement may draw on Islamic tenets, principles of government, or ethics of rulership. The first and third option, i.e., a direct pronouncement and its underlying rationale, are often combined, such as in ʿUmar II's rebuff of an overeager adviser "If you remembered death it would occupy you more than giving advice" (*ʿIqd* IV: 209 ʿUmar II #13). Some rulings remain ambiguous, either intentionally so or through loss of context, while in others the apparent ambiguity is clarified by an accompanying action.

Stylistically the apostille tends to be simple, matter of fact and bare of decorum; however certain situations require longer texts. Literary ornament may be a quotation from the Qurʾān, poetry or a proverb. Thus ʿUmar II approves of a Kufan governor's following a decision of ʿUmar I with the citation of Q. 6: 90: "Those whom God guides, their guidance follow!" (*ʿIqd* IV: 209 ʿUmar II #6). The Qurʾānic apostrophe in the second person is easily reapplied to the addressed official. Poetry is rare but adds a specific dimension where it appears, and its complex relationship with apostilles is discussed in section III. A preferred figure of style is antithetical parallelism, both syntactic and semantic. The splitting of the world into black and white, right and wrong, suited the apodictic tone of the apostille, offering the recipient the choice between obedience and disobedience without any room for disagreement. The binarism also sufficed the occasional need to leave a verdict conditional, should further inquiry be necessary to try the case. Other tropes, such as analogues and metaphors are infrequent, though later Abbasid and Buyid rulers developed a predilection for paronomasia and rhyme.

### *II.2. Linguistic Economy*

The predominant feature of style, however, is to drive to an extreme the *tawqīʿ*'s characteristic brevity. As initially mentioned the apostille finds entrance into the canon of literature, side-by-side with proverbs and quotable single verses under the ideal of concision (*ījāz*). Abū Aḥmad al-ʿAskarī (and based on him, al-Ṣūlī, in his chapter on *tawqīʿ* and *ījāz*) reports that Jaʿfar b. Yaḥyā advised brevity to his scribes by positing the model of *tawqīʿ* (here in the meaning of motto, signature). Abū Aḥmad explains, "[Jaʿfar] thereby exhorted them to extreme ellipsis and concision (*ḥadhf, ikhtiṣār*)." Jaʿfar chose for the form of this injunction the apostille itself, recording it at the bottom of his scribes' letters and obeying the very brevity he commanded (Aḥmad al-ʿAskarī, *Tafḍīl*, 120 and al-Ṣūlī, *Adab*, 134).

In his chapter on correspondence, Abū Hilāl al-ʿAskarī comments that apostille-like brevity gives letters a greater affirmative power in conveying orders and prohibitions.[36] In the chapter on concision and prolixity, he compares the Qurʿānic verse on the legal principle of the *lex talionis*, "In retribution is life for you" (*lakum fī l-qiṣāṣi ḥayāt*; Q. 2: 179), favorably against the pre-Islamic Bedouin formulation, "Death best prohibits death" (*al-qatlu anfā li-l-qatl*) on several accounts: the scripture explains both the underlying principle of retribution and the goal of protecting life, it evokes desire and fear more powerfully, and above all its fewer graphemes and avoidance of repetition give the language a greater impact.[37] Unsurprisingly, the verse is used in countless apostilles rejecting pleas of pardon for convicted criminals (see the following section).

The economy and eloquence of *tawqīʿ* suited the ideology of power. A ruler (or high official) had no need to show deference by elaborating on his decisions. His elliptic manner expressed his superior power by subjecting the addressee to exerting his or her mind (some address women, often wives of convicts) to understand the message properly. Thus the ruler affiliated himself with the elliptic divine word, while he granted his audience, i.e., his subjects, a minimum of social etiquette. At the same time, the economy of words represented a literary challenge (*ījāz* and *taḍmīn*) worthy of an educated ruler: he had to compress a maximum of meaning within a minimum of language to produce the trumping speech act.

In apostilles brevity finds its extreme. Al-Maʾmūn's one-line request from ʿAmr b. Masʿada (see section I.3.) was not truly a feat. Among those apostilles transmitted in the *adab* collections, many do not exceed three words, such as Jaʿfar b. Yaḥyā's rejection of a prisoner's plea for early release:

There is Scripture for every term.
*li-kulli ajalin kitāb* (*ʿIqd* IV: 219 Jaʿfar #1)

The usage of two words is rarer, such as ʿUmar's response, likewise to the plea of an imprisoned criminal:

Repent to be released!
*tub tuṭlaq* (*ʿIqd* IV: 209 ʿUmar II #11)

---

36 al-ʿAskarī, *al-Ṣināʿatayn*, 162.
37 Ibid., 181-6.

Al-Mahdī responded to a petitioner in dire straits:

Help has arrived.
*atāka l-ghawth* (*ʿIqd* IV: 213 al-Mahdī #7)

The notoriously terse Iraqi governor Ziyād b. Abīhi denied pardon to a thief with the verdict:

Cutting is your recompense.
*al-qaṭʿu jazāʾuka* (*ʿIqd* IV: 217 Ziyād #9)

Elsewhere he minimized the number of letters in a two-word apostille addressed to a victim of injustice, affirming his support:

I am with you.
*ana maʿaka* (*ʿIqd* IV: 215 Ziyād #5)

One mere word was enough for a reassuring answer to another victim of injustice:

You have been helped.
*kufīta* (*ʿIqd* IV: 217 Ziyād #15)

The pinnacle of brevity was reached by the Buyid vizier and littérateur al-Ṣāḥib b. ʿAbbād (d. 385/995) in a gloss to a plea for financial support, "If our lord considered granting what I requested he would do so" (*in raʾā sayyidunā an yunʿima bimā saʾaltuhu faʿala*; *Khāṣṣ*, 137 al-Ṣāḥib #4). The puzzled petitioner could not find any answer on his returned letter. But with the help of a second pair of eyes, he decoded the awarding of his request: the vizier simply inserted an *alif* before the final verb form and changed it from the third person of the conditional mood to the first person of the future tense, "I will do so" (*afʿalu*). Of course one might top this by a denial through silence, but this lacked literary finesse and clarity, for it might be misconstrued as negligence. Ṭāhir b. al-Ḥusayn (d. 207/822) thus needed to explain to a returning petitioner that "Lack of an answer is an answer" (*tarku l-jawābi jawāb*; *Khāṣṣ*, 133 Ṭāḥir #2). Repetition was a thing abhorred in apostilles, and if discussed, it usually conveyed a threat. The secretary Aḥmad b. Yūsuf admonished a corrupt tax collector with, "Do not compel me to repeat it to you, there is after this offer to you but the power of defense to you" (*lā tuḥwijnī ilā muʿāwadatika fa-laysa baʿda l-tadqimati ilayka illā saṭwatu l-inkāri ʿalayka*; al-Ṣūlī, *Awrāq*, 229).

*Tawqīʿāt* were addressed to a wide range of recipients, from the bottom of the social hierarchy, such as overtaxed farmers and convicts, to the top, such as courtiers and high officials. Caliphal edicts dispatched to governors and local officials or informers followed the style of apostilles. Governors, close in hierarchy to the caliphs, were likewise expected to use the same concision and leave aside the elaboration that marked literary offerings from inferiors, such as court poets. The Buyid vizier ʿAlī b. ʿĪsā thus showed impatience with a governor who painstakingly enumerated his stored-up treasures: "Spare me your agile mouth and gullet and your pretended eloquence with someone who is your equal. Speech is brief, pithy and not bothersome" (*Khāṣṣ*, 138 #1). But in special cases, caliphs who addressed high officials, or viziers who wrote to their professional colleagues, chose length to convey respect for the recipient. The Abbasid ʿAbdallāh b. ʿAlī responded with a ten-line apostille to a poem by his scribe Yūsuf b. al-Qāsim inquiring about his withheld stipend. In it ʿAbdallāh reused the word "kindness" (*birr*) from the scribe's poem:

> The delay of my kindness was neither for stinginess or miserliness nor for lack of care or forgetfulness, but it was the oversight of him who affirms, who knows, your right (*ḥaqq*), and who is distracted from you by the share his heart reserves you, relying on your knowing this and on your extending your excuse to him ... (al-Ṣūlī, *Awrāq*, 147-8)

In similar detail al-Maʾmūn, soon after his own proclamation as caliph in 196/812, officially awarded viziership and a fief to al-Faḍl in an edict:

> You have, O Faḍl b. Sahl, eliminated my concern with your support for me in obeying God and establishing my might, so I saw it fit to eliminate your concern. You have preceded people present and absent, so I wanted to precede [you] in writing with my own hand what I saw fit in my soul... (Jahshiyārī, *Wuzarāʾ*, 306; cf. Sourdel, *Vizirat* I: 201).

Both apostille and edict are addressed by Abbasid leaders to their immediate inferiors, redefining their relationship as one of mutual indebtedness, which al-Maʾmūn draws out particularly well in his parallel prose. The distinction is owed in both cases to the officials' actions and not their status, it is earned and not the result of privilege.

### *II.3. Universal Justice*

The linchpin of tort redress was a sovereign's *universal* justice: it sought out complainants across the realm, it crossed social hierarchies, it was public, and it offered a recourse above any other legislative and executive power. The enforcement of universal justice stood against the concept of mercy. Both are the cardinal virtues of rulership that also receive the bulk of attention in panegyrics, but with the balance there tilting more towards mercy (and generosity).

The concern to grant justice to every individual (see section I.1.) figures prominently in the above-mentioned autobiography of Kisrā Anūshirwān, who used executive, judicial and religious powers to control the regional fiscal administrations:

> My concern to establish [the redress of wrongs] was so immense that, if it were not for the foes and borders I was keeping track of, I would assume myself in person the issue of land tax and subjects, village by village, familiarizing myself with it and speaking with every single man in my kingdom (Miskawayh, *Tajārib* I: 194-5, al-Nuwayrī, *Nihāya* XV: 200).

The rationale for justice is not only divine obedience but the palpable prosperity of the kingdom. In one of the apostilles attributed to Anūshirwān in the Arabic sources, which captures the gist of his autobiography, he explains to a tax collector: "(Land tax is the mainstay of the realm, and) nothing increases land tax like justice, and nothing decreases it like injustice" (*ʿIqd* IV: 222 #5). Jaʿfar b. Yaḥyā would later reuse this saying (*Khāṣṣ*, 134 #1, expanded with the sentence in parentheses). A longer elaboration is contained in two speeches of Anūshirwān to his officials in the etiological tale of the appeal bell's invention, cited by Niẓām al-Mulk. The Sasanian king squarely states, "The peasants are the givers and the soldiers are the takers; so the door ought to be open wider for the giver than for the taker."[38] As with other elements of government, the ethics of Sasanian tort redress can be recognized in many caliphal and vizieral pronouncements of the Abbasid period, which speak to the ideological purpose of the institution more directly than do the procedural details of the government manuals.

In the autobiography, Anūshirwān deplores the impossibility of ensuring justice everywhere himself and emphasizes the careful selection, and eventually the failure, of his trustees.[39] In three separate initiatives the monarch either sends trustees or corresponds with local judges throughout his realm and has delegations with difficult legal cases dispatched to him. Here the voice of the disenfranchised is protected in many ways: secrecy from the local administration, the double sealing of the recorded hearings that are forwarded to the king by the investigating local judge, and the inclusion of members of the rural underclass among the delegation of local representatives.[40]

Justice is served in the *maẓālim* for instance by upholding the convictions of heavy criminals, such as murderers and robbers. Pleas for pardon by condemned criminals are a frequent topic and an opportunity for a ruler to broadcast his protection of the law. More often than not (in two thirds of the sample[41]) pleas are denied. Rulers are not mollified by pleading wives of prisoners, responding for example: "The law imprisoned him" (*al-ḥaqqu ḥabasahu;ʿIqd* IV: 209 ʿUmar II #15), "His verdict belongs to God" (*ʿIqd* IV: 217 Ziyād b. Abīhi #10). They make justice, not mercy, the decisive factor, "Right (*ḥaqq*) imprisons him and justice (*inṣāf*) releases him" (*ʿIqd* IV: 220 al-Ḥasan #3). Justice is not a part of mutual actions but unconditional; al-Ṣāḥib writes to a criminal asking for justice: "Your kind receives justice without practicing it" (Khāṣṣ, 138 #5). Justice is exercised harshly and unflinchingly by Ziyād, who responds to a thief: "Cutting is your reward"; to a man

38 Niẓām al-Mulk, *Siyāsatnāma*, 42-3 and 49-50/*Book of Government*, 33-4 and 39-40. See also nn. 8 and 16. The elements of the governors' incorrigibility, their responsibility for correct taxation, and justice as producing prosperity recur in ʿAbdallāh b. Ṭāhir's speech to his subgovernors (*Khāṣṣ*, 133-4, quoted in II.4.).

39 Miskawayh, *Tajārib* I:195, al-Nuwayrī, *Nihāya* XV: 200.

40 Miskawayh, *Tajārib* I:190-7, al-Nuwayrī, *Nihāya* XV: 197-202.

41 Cf. n. 35.

who caused injury: "The recompense is injury"; to a grave-robber: "He will be buried alive in his grave"; and to burglars who pierced (*naqabū*) a wall: "Their backs will be pierced by misfortune (*tunqabu*)" (*ʿIqd* IV: 217 Ziyād #9, 18, 12 and 11).

More often rulers cite the Qurʾān, the primary source of divine law, to motivate their denial of pardon, as does ʿUmar II with a murderer: "The Book of God is between me and you" (*ʿIqd* IV: 209 #12) and al-Maʾmūn's vizier al-Faḍl b. Sahl, "God's Book is more worthy to be followed" (*ʿIqd* IV: 220 #12). Jaʿfar, and in the variant his father, declines a plea for early release from prison by "There is a Scripture for every term" (Q. 13: 38; *ʿIqd* IV:219 Jaʿfar #1 = Khāṣṣ, 135 Yaḥyā #2), and Hishām b. ʿAbdalmalik explains to a condemned convict: "The Scripture has revealed your lashing" (*ʿIqd* IV: 209 #5). Some rulings even state the exact verse on which the verdict rests. For murder, this is the *lex talionis*, which serves to reject a murderer's plea for pardon: "In retribution there is life for you, O you who reflect" (Q. 2: 179;*ʿIqd* IV: 213 Mahdī #10 = *Khāṣṣ*, 135 Yaḥyā b. Khālid # 1). Al-Faḍl also cites a divinely stipulated punishment to uphold the condemnation of a band of highway robbers: "This is the recompense of those who fight against God and His Messenger, and hasten about the earth to do corruption there" (Q. 4: 33[42];*ʿIqd* IV: 220 al-Faḍl #11).

In the case of Rashīd's toppling of the Barmakids, he had to wrest from his vizier the moral right to do so. Feeling death approach, Yaḥyā b. Khālid had written: "The enemy preceded to the place of decision, but you are at the root. God is the just arbiter, and you will be judged first and you will know." Al-Rashīd countered this with claiming God's law for his own side, "The arbiter you approve of for the other world is the one who roused the enemy against you in this world. His verdict cannot be rejected nor his judgment averted" (*ʿIqd* IV: 215 al-Rashīd #18).

In apostilles of pardon, the collections never specify the crimes, which must have been lesser than the above-treated theft and murder. Pardon was a ruler's unilateral choice, but it might reward the individual's remorse, and show the ruler's grace in accepting it: "Repent to be released!" (*ʿIqd* IV: 209 ʿUmar II #11), "Hostility [var. crime] confined him and repentance sets him free" [var.: "Justice confines him"] (al-Jahshiyārī, *Wuzarāʾ*, 205 Jaʿfar b. Yaḥyā #5 =*ʿIqd* IV: 219 Jaḥfar b. Yaḥyā #2 and 9); "He who repents for a sin is like him who did not sin" (*ʿIqd* IV: 217 Ziyād b. Abīhi #19); "He who seeks refuge with God is saved" *(man lajaʾa ilā llāhi najā; ʿIqd* IV: 214 al-Rashīd #7); and "One cannot harm those who do good" (*ʿIqd* IV: 218 al-Ḥajjāj #4). A rare exception is al-Faḍl b. Sahl's conditional pardon to a man who broke into the treasury, if indeed he had a rightful claim, presumably a withheld stipend or confiscated property: "Punishment is warded off him if he has a [rightful] share in it" (*ʿIqd* IV: 220 #6).[43]

42 Implied is the verse's continuation "...they shall be slaughtered, or crucified, or their hands and feet shall alternately be struck off, or they should be banished."

43 No reason for the release is given in *ʿIqd* IV: 222 Ṭāhir #7.

In a political case of pardon by al-Maʾmūn for his uncle, the failed counter-caliph Ibrāhīm b. al-Mahdī, repentance is associated with Ibrāhīm's submission to his nephew's reestablished power. Ibrāhīm wrote, "If you pardon it is by your grace, and if you take [my life] it is by your right." Thus acknowledged as sovereign, al-Maʾmūn (who already had the killing of a brother to account for) could pardon his uncle without losing face, "Power eliminates anger, repentance is part of pardon, and between the two lies the grace of God" [var. "repentance is pardon"] (*ʿIqd* IV: 216 al-Maʾmūn #13 = *Khāṣṣ*, 130 al-Maʾmūn #4).

Another frequent subject of individual pleas is for missing or withheld sustenance, which gives the sovereign the occasion to demonstrate his magnanimity, make good his promises, and show gratitude to those loyal to him.

### *II.4. The Leveling of Social Hierarchy*

It lies in the nature of tort law to expect mishandling of justice from the authorities. The ruler's supreme authority gives him (or his delegate) the responsibility to detect instances of this. But to sit as judge over his own appointees, who normally enjoy great privilege, a ruler must disassociate himself from them. Al-Maʾmūn thus cautions his general Ḥumayd al-Ṭūsī (d. 210/825), after someone complained of his injustice, "O Abū Ghānim, do not let your station with your *imām* deceive you, for you and the lowest of his servants are equals before the law" [var. "Abū Ghānim[44] ... you and one of my subjects are equal to me before the law"] (*ʿIqd* IV: 215 al-Maʾmūn #7 = *Khāṣṣ*, 131-2 al-Maʾmūn #2; cf. the close parallel *ʿIqd* IV: 209 Yazīd b. ʿAbdalmalik #1 addressed to the governor of Khurasan).

This denial of privilege before the law applies to an even higher degree to the ruler's family. To show the ruler as unbiased in the exercise of justice, kinship is declared irrelevant. To his brother Abū ʿĪsā, when someone complained of his injustice, al-Maʾmūn wrote, "When the horns are blown, on that day there is no kinship between them, and they will not ask each other questions" (Q. 23: 101;*ʿIqd* IV: 215; #6 cf. also *ʿIqd* IV: 212 al-Mahdī #1). The same caliph excused himself from a case against his son brought forth by a widow (in a versified plea). Al-Maʾmūn remained present, but surrendered the decision to the chief *qāḍī* (or in a variant, the vizier).[45] The strongest leveling of hierarchy occurs in the Sasanian ceremonials, when the king accepts complaints against his own person first, submits himself to the high priest's supreme verdict, and encourages him to show no mercy.[46] According to an apostille attributed to Anūshirwān, when reading an accusation of himself he responded with, "Injustice does not behoove the king, it is justice that one seeks from him; nor does stinginess [behoove him], it is

44 Emendation of Abū Ḥāmid.
45 al-Māwardī, *Aḥkām*, 138-9/*Statuts*, 175-6.
46 Pseudo-Jāḥiẓ, *Tāj*, 159-63/*Livre de la couronne*, 179-82.

generosity that one expects from him." Then he summoned the petitioner to appear together with himself before the [high] priest *(mūbadh)* for trial (*ᶜIqd* IV: 223 #6).

But the ruler does not stop at leveling the social hierarchy before the law; he literally inverts it by stepping into the position of his lowest subjects and shouldering their plight. He takes the stand of the socially weakest against the strongest. Anūshirwān concludes the narrative of his *maẓālim* initiatives with, "He who oppressed them [sc. the subjects] oppressed me, and he who wronged them wronged me."[47]

Jaᶜfar b. Yaḥyā echoes this sentiment to two different complainants about officials, responding to them, "I did you injustice, not he" and "I am [unjust] like him indeed until he will grant you justice" (*ᶜIqd* IV: 219 #8, 15). The Abbasid vizier takes upon himself the guilt of the perpetrator and the responsibility for righting the plaintiff's wrong. Hishām rhetorically reverts the roles, placing the complainants in the judge's position, while he takes their place as plaintiff, "Let us put you in charge of the case (*la-nufawwiḍannakum*), for I am the adversary on your behalf" (*ᶜIqd* IV: 210 #8). The meting out of justice to those who are usually barred access to it against the high and mighty epitomizes the mission of the *maẓālim* courts.

Petitions about mistreatment by authorities come both in individual and collective form. In most cases the ruler accedes to them with a general assurance that he will restore justice, responding: "Justice is your *imām*" (*ᶜIqd* IV: 209 ᶜUmar II #10), "You have been helped" (*ᶜIqd* IV: 217 Ziyād b. Abīhi #15), or with a Qurʾānic quote, "Those who do wrong shall surely know by what overturning they will be overturned" (Q. 26: 227; *ᶜIqd* IV: 209 Yazīd b. ᶜAbdalmalik #2). At the same time rulers use the self-reflective apostilles, spelling out the principles upon which they are formulated, to broadcast their own role. Al-Mahdī praises complainants requesting that he recall their oppressive governor for seeking help at the right place: "He did right who challenged the Banū Qāra [renowned archers] in archery" (*ᶜIqd* IV: 212 al-Mahdī #9).

The official accused of injustice, usually a tax collector or governor, may only vaguely be referred to or treated in the third person in the response to the complainants: "Even if [my own son] ᶜĪsā were your governor, I would guide him to the right like a camel is goaded by a nose ring" (*ᶜIqd* IV: 212 al-Mahdī #1) and "My covenant shall not reach the evildoers" (*ᶜIqd* IV: 212 al-Manṣūr #5).[48] The context of the Qurʾānic quote Q. 2: 124 in which God bans the unjust among Abraham's offspring from rulership underscores the edict's message that governance must be just. By which further procedures justice would reach the com-

---

47 Miskawayh, *Tajārib* I: 197/al-Nuwayrī, *Nihāya* XV: 202).

48 Cf. the variant dispatched directly to the governor complained about: "I would not ever take those who lead others astray to be My supporters" (Q. 18: 51; *ᶜIqd* IV: 211 al-Saffāḥ #6)

plainants is left open in such summary verdicts, except for those that contain immediate action, such as al-Rashīd's decision dispatched to a man he knew to be a victim of gubernatorial ill-treatment: "We have put you in his place, avoid his behavior" (*ʿIqd* IV: 214 al-Rashīd #11).

On other occasions the decision was directly imparted to the perpetrator. In such cases a copy of the physical document including the recorded apostille must have been forwarded as in the next example. In some forwarded verdicts, the ruler specifies the plaintiff to the addressee and makes his satisfaction a condition for the accused: "Be just to the one you are in charge of, lest he who is in charge of you will be just to him" (*Khāṣṣ*, 135 Yaḥyā b. Khālid #4) or more briefly, "Help me in his case lest I help him in yours" (*Khāṣṣ*, 130 al-Manṣūr #1; see section I.3.). Al-Maʾmūn identifies to his general al-Ḥusayn b. ʿAmr al-Rustamī a case of unjust debt: "It is not virtue that I load you with gold and silver, while your debtor is deprived and your neighbor hungry" [var. "while you neighbor is deprived and your debtor howling"] (*ʿIqd* IV: 215 al-Maʾmūn #3 = *Khāṣṣ*, 131 al-Maʿmūn #1). A longer description of a case illustrates the desire of his chief secretary, Aḥmad b. Yūsuf, to give his writing to an absent governor the force of a face-to-face interview: "I am full of care and seriously concerned about so-and-so, and I wanted that the letter in what regards him, which I give your eyes to peruse, be as if it were entrusted to your ears through my speech" (al-Ṣūlī, *Awrāq*, 230). Unusual was the forwarding of the opposite verdict, such as ʿUmar's rejection of a group of Egyptian subjects' grievance against Marwān b. al-Ḥakam.[49] ʿUmar sent it to him with the gloss: "If they disobey say 'I am innocent of their actions'" (Q. 26: 216; *Khāṣṣ*, 126 ʿUmar I #2).

In non-specific apostilles on petitioners' notes forwarded to governors and other officials, justice is the foremost demand, as expressed here by al-Maʾmūn to his secretary ʿAmr b. Masʿada, "ʿAmr, cultivate with justice the favor you enjoy – injustice ruins it," and to Muḥammad b. al-Faḍl al-Ṭūsī,[50] "We have born your foul tongue and intractable nature, but your injustice towards the subjects we will not countenance" (*ʿIqd* IV: 215 al-Maʾmūn #4 and 11). Jaʿfar b. Yaḥyā, or in the variant al-Manṣūr, combines for another governor antithesis, parallelism and paronomasia into a rhetorical diamond with not a word to spare, "Many complain about you, few are grateful to you, be just or be deposed" (*qad kathura shākūka wa-qalla shākirūka fa-immā ʿadalta wa-immā ʿtazalta*; *ʿIqd* IV: 219 #4 = *Khāṣṣ*, 130 al-Manṣūr #2 without the clause *qalla shākirūka*). Only al-Ṣāḥib could be terser, using for a governor instead the formal unity of imagery, "Curb your bridle from wrongful deeds, lest we draw against you the sword" (*Khāṣṣ*, 138 al-Ṣāḥib

49 The caliph in question was more likely Marwān's cousin ʿUthmān, whom he served as secretary and during whose reign he participated in the North African campaigns; C.E. Bosworth (1991), "Marwān II," EI² VI: 621-3.

50 Perhaps identical with the governor of Mawṣil under al-Mahdī; al-Ṭabarī (1960-9), *Taʾrīkh*, ed. Muḥammad Abū l-Faḍl Ibrāhīm, 10 vols., Cairo: Dār al-Maʿārif, VIII: 151.

#16). For some governors it was too late, as in two of al-Ṣāḥib's dismissals, "Your dismissal is the better of your two states, and your banishment the more effective of your two bonds" (*Khāṣṣ,* 138 al-Ṣāḥib #13 and the close parallel #10).

Not always could an immediate decision be handed down, such as when further oral or written evidence was required. Al-Maʾmūn's vizier al-Ḥasan b. Sahl (r. 202-18/812-18) thus responds to one complainant: "The petition will be looked into. The true right (*ḥaqq*) is unassailable, otherwise, the recovery of the sick is the cure of the disease" [var. *ᶜIqd* "The matter of the healthy is the cure of the disease"] (*ᶜIqd* IV: 220 al-Ḥasan b. Sahl #1), and to a group of complainants about a governor "[The right befits us and justice is our goal.] If it is correct what you allege against him we will depose him [var. remove him] and punish him" (*ᶜIqd* IV: 220 al-Ḥasan b. Sahl #2 = *ᶜIqd* IV: 209 Hishām b. ᶜAbdalmalik #2 without the sentence added in brackets). The following apostille by Hishām b. ᶜAbdalmalik shows the risk a false accusation posed and allows the plaintiff a way out: "Help arrives if you have spoken true and punishment falls if you lied – advance now or retreat" (*ᶜIqd* IV: 209 #1 = *Khāṣṣ,* 128 without the last phrase).[51]

Few cases were rejected, either by stating that justice had been served or by referring the plaintiff to the higher authority of God. Instances of the first are "Justice has not been transgressed with you" (*ᶜIqd* IV: 214 al-Rashīd #8) and "The law is ample for you" (*al-ḥaqqu yasaᶜuka; ᶜIqd* IV: 217 Ziyād b. Abīhi #13); and of the second, "God suffices as a helper to the victim of injustice" or "Be content, for God is with him who suffers injustice," both being adaptations of Qurʾānic phrases (*ᶜIqd* IV: 220 al-Faḍl b. Sahl #5 and 9).

Not all types of grievance were accepted with equal openness. Citizens of Kufa, because of their historical proneness to rebellion, were not given the benefit of a doubt when complaining about a governor: "Such as you are you have been given a ruler" (*ᶜIqd* IV: 212 al-Manṣūr #4; cf. also *ᶜIqd* IV: 209: ᶜUmar II #8). ᶜAlids were problematic in a different way, they occupied a paradoxical position being both politically precarious and socially noble, and thus they did not fit the mould of the lowly petitioner or further the ideology of the *maẓālim* court. They were mostly rejected with the comment that those in power must be magnanimous and tolerate abuse. As for family disputes, which were by no means rare, judges might offer exhortation or reprimand but for the most part choose not to get involved (*ᶜIqd* IV: 209 Yazīd b. ᶜAbdalmalik #3, *ᶜIqd* IV: 217 Ziyād b. Abīhi #16).

As certain grievances repeated themselves, the semi-independent governor of Khurasan, ᶜAbdallāh b. Ṭāhir (d. 230/844), composed a summary *tawqīᶜ* to subgovernors who had failed him, stressing in it, "Reflect for yourselves and treat

[51] The beginning is reused by al-Mahdī as a two-word response for an indigent petitioner (*ᶜIqd* IV: 213 #7). Likewise *qīla buᶜdan...* (Q. 11: 44) is used elsewhere for an unjust governor and vanquished rebels. The formulaic nature and brevity of the apostilles, understood within the context, made Qurʾānic citations a useful option for time-pressed judges.

well those who till the earth because God has made their hands a sustenance for us, their tongues a reverent greeting, and mistreatment of them a sin, 'and what is with God is better and more enduring. Will you not understand?'" (Q. 28: 60; *Khāṣṣ*, 133-4). Al-Maʾmūn's last secretary Muḥammad b. Yazdād, reflecting on the *maẓālim* court, stresses the importance of incessant government oversight, "The gates of kings are mines for needs and homesteads for requests, and in order to see them find success and fulfillment, there is only patience and diligence and morning visit and evening visit" (*Khāṣṣ*, 136 #1). The few examples make clear that the single case of grievance was more than one right to restore; it was a means to show the ruler's all-embracing justice to the weakest and against those closer to him in kinship and hierarchy who would be wont to corrupt it.

### *Acts of God*

Other common issues for rulers to step in and broadcast their ethics were nature catastrophes, such as spoilt harvests and flooding, or loss, of estates, whether caused by nature or human intervention. In the apostilles, Sasanian rulers pleased themselves in the role of making up out of their own treasuries for devastating acts of God. In a crisis that engulfed the kingdom, Ardashīr (r. 224-39) decreed to petitioning farmers, "It is justice that the king shall not be happy when his subjects are in sorrow" and ordered that the content of his treasuries be distributed in the regions (*ʿIqd* IV: 222). In a parallel, also ascribed to Narsī b. Bahrām (r. 293-302; he was actually the son of Shāpūr I), he addressed the people of his capital Iṣṭakhr (near Persepolis) with "When no rain falls the clouds of the king pour generously" [var. "When the sky is stingy with drops the hand of the king pours generously. We have ordered you to receive what sets your broken bones and frees you from poverty"] (Abū Aḥmad al-ʿAskarī, *Tafḍīl*, 130 = *Khāṣṣ*, 124 Narsī #1). Kisrā Anūshirwān reacted similarly, "My kindness and my grace go out to the subjects, for I and they are equals in the benefit from this" (Abū Aḥmad al-ʿAskarī, *Tafḍīl*, 131).

Some Muslim rulers imitated this and likewise sacrificed momentary tax income for their subjects' future survival, taking upon themselves the losses from droughts and locust plagues. Al-Mahdī acceded with a tax reduction to a collective petition of drought-stricken peasants, "In a year of drought and in the year thereafter, they will be apportioned sustenance" (*ʿIqd* IV: 212 al-Mahdī #4). Al-Maʾmūn welcomed with grandeur the victims of a locust plague that had destroyed the harvest of the Sawād, "We are more suited to host locusts than the people of the Sawād. Half of their land tax shall be rescinded" (*Khāṣṣ*, 132 #8). When governors conveyed such difficulties on behalf of their populations, the response was similar. Al-Ḥajjāj advised the governor of Khurasan, Qutayba b. Muslim (d. 96/715), on the loss of a harvest to locusts, "When the land tax is due consider what is in the best interest of your subjects, because the treasury is more resilient in this [sc. the drought] than a widow, an orphan, or a breadwinner for a household," describing the petitioners with the (adapted) Qur'ānic phrase for the socially weak[52] (*ᶜIqd* IV: 217-18 al-Ḥajjāj #1). Al-Mahdī reacted with practical advice to the governor of Khurasan who complained of price inflation, "Hold them to justice in measuring volume and weight" (*ᶜIqd* IV: 212 al-Mahdī #11). This sympathy for governors was exceptional; many more edicts to governors demanded instead a speedy delivery of the revenue, "Beware of distractions until you have fully delivered your land tax!" (*ᶜIqd* IV: 212 al-Ḥajjāj #6); "Maḥfūẓ [tax collector of Egypt], deliver the land tax whole – such as you are! (*wa-anta anta*)" (*ᶜIqd* IV: 212 al-Rashīd #13); "Hurry to us the sum of revenues that have gathered on your side, do not delay it..." (Abū Aḥmad al-ᶜAskarī, *Maṣūn,* 107, Abū ᶜUbaydallāh Muᶜāwiya b. ᶜUbayd, vizier of al-Mahdī). Ṭāhir b. al-Ḥusayn barely hid his impatience for overdue land tax in verses addressed to prince al-ᶜAbbās b. Mūsā al-Hādī, governor in Kufa, "One in charge does not spend the night sleeping but he spends the night in the saddle" (*ᶜIdq* IV: 222 #5).

On other occasions, Muslim rulers did not feel compelled to correct acts of God, but rather deferred to His higher jurisdiction. Ziyād b. Abīhi thus rejected a petition of people whose estates had been flooded with, "We do not appear in matters that belong to God alone," and of peasants whose fields had suffered a locust swarm with, "There is no verdict in what God has chosen" (*Iqd* IV: 217 #20 and 21). Some caliphs even seized the occasion to interpret the damage as divine punishment that had to be atoned for. To a subgovernor deploring scarce rain in his province, Hishām b. ᶜAbdalmalik commanded, "Order them to ask God for forgiveness" (*ᶜIqd* IV: 209 #9), and al-Manṣūr exhorted the governor of Egypt who had alerted him to a low Nile, "Clean your army camp of mischief, so the Nile will hand you its rope [to guide it]" (*ᶜIqd* IV: 212 #11).

Human destruction of estates, however was not tolerated by caliphs, in contrast to Anūshirwān, who had accepted that "Slight specific damage is born in conjunction with greater general good" when digging a canal in Madā'in (Ktesiphon) *(Khāṣṣ,* 124 #1). Al-Saffāḥ condemned the flooding of people's estates in the area of Kufa with an implied reprimand of the governor, "It is said the unjust people shall be remote" (*ᶜIqd* IV: 21). The Qurᶜānic quote (11: 44) he aptly used refers to the sinners swept away by the deluge. To citizens of al-Anbār whose homes had been confiscated without compensation for a public construction project al-Saffāḥ himself had ordered, he let it be known that this was unacceptable: "Such building is not grounded upon piety" (*ᶜIqd* IV: 211 al-Saffāḥ #1 and 7). The exact course of remedial action, however, remains unclear. In all these apostilles and edicts, the public justifications given are not to be taken at face value, as the decisions certainly obeyed motivations that escape us. However the pronouncements served to advertise a ruler's just self-image.

---

52 *Dhū l-qurbā/al-aqrabūna wa-l-yatāmā wa-l-masākīn;* Q. 2: 177, 2: 215, 8: 41, and 59: 7.

The leniency shown subjects in distress is contrasted by the strictness in curbing governors' lavish construction projects. After the victory of general Saʿd b. Abī Waqqāṣ (d.c. 50-8/670-8) over the Sasanians in Qādisiyya, ʿUmar allows only the bare minimum at Saʿd's request to construct a garrison in Kufa (whose first governor he became), "Build what shelters you from the midday heat and the damage of rain" [var. "what hides from the sun and shelters from the rain"] (*ʿIqd* IV: 205-6 #1 = *Khāṣṣ*, 126). Muʿāwiya ridicules the aspirations of Rabīʿa b. ʿIsl al-Yarbūʿī, tax collector in Khurasan, for financial support with procuring 12,000 palm trunks (*jidhʿ*) for his Basrian residence: "Is your palace in Basra or is Basra in your palace?" (*ʿIqd* IV: 207 #4).[53] ʿUmar II used faith to restrict his governors' ostentatious architecture. Upon a request for a city restoration, he admonished, "Build her with justice and purify her streets from injustice" (*ʿIqd* IV: 208 #1), and on another city's need for a garrison he declared, "Fortify her and your soul with the fear of God" [var. "Fortify her with justice. Peace!"] (*ʿIqd* IV: 208 #2 = *ʿKhāṣṣ*, 128 #1). The Medinan governor's request for a building site is declined with "Beware of death" (*ʿIqd* IV: 209 #9). Likewise al-Ḥajjāj cut a planned garrison of Qutayba b. Muslim (whom he had helped with the locust plague) with, "See to it that your army [var. the people of your army camp] recite the Qurʾān; this is a better defense than your garrisons" (*ʿIqd* IV: 218 #5).[54]

As with overreaching authorities above, harm suffered by the peasant class is corrected within the powers of the ruler, who takes responsibility for his lowest subjects. Those closer in hierarchy are, when pleading their own causes, met with admonition, mistrust and rejection. Their strict treatment is the obverse of the sovereign's care for the weak and the necessary complement to it in the iconology of universal justice.

### *Intermediaries*

The same attitude is articulated with a third category of persons, namely those who would come in-between rulers and their subjects as unsolicited advisers (*mutanaṣṣiḥ*), informers (*mukhbir*) or calumniators (*sāʿī*). The principle of *maẓālim* rejects precisely such meddling; it is the presiding ruler, supreme judge or vizier who listens and adjudicates. Accordingly, volunteered information is presumed to serve the interest of the interfering party and rejected in the harshest terms.

The Sasanian Anūshirwān is credited with most instances of rejecting calumny. He bluntly rejected a note listing supposedly ill-intentioned courtiers among his retinue, by stating his principle: "I rule outward bodies not intentions, I judge with justice not desire, and I examine actions not secret thoughts

---

[53] Al-Ṭabarī reports this event however as part of a conversation; *Taʾrīkh* V: 333.

[54] Perhaps the citadel he eventually built in Bukhara 94/712-13 after conquering the city; $EI^2$ V: 541.

[var. secrets]" (*ʿIqd* IV: 220 #1 = *Khāṣṣ*, 125 #7). He indirectly blamed a noble who denounced a commoner for improperly lavishly hosting (which the noble had himself enjoyed): "We praise you for your advice and blame your friend (sc. the commoner) for his bad choice of brethren," (Abū Aḥmad al-ʿAskarī, *Tafḍīl*, 132). Anūshirwān reprimands an overeager informer who reported that some drunken courtiers had blamed the king: "If they spoke with different tongues, you have assembled their vices upon your tongue, so the injury through you is deeper and your tongue more false" (*ʿIqd* IV: 220 #3). Another man who had forwarded false accusations the king threatened with, "Use your tongue to protect your head" (*ʿIqd* IV: 220 #9). His dislike for calumny was so intense that he dismissed a long-serving high official because of it (*Khāṣṣ*, 125 #5).

Muslim rulers and governors expressed similar attitudes. The Umayyad governor Ziyād b. Abīhi rejected offered information with a line of poetry:

> [*qālat wa-lam taqṣid li-qīli l-khanā*]
> *mahlan faqad ablaghta asmāʿī*
>
> [She said, not intending [playful] licentiousness,]
> 'Slowly! You have reached my ears'
>
> (*ʿIqd* IV: 217 #14, with added first hemistich)

The full verse by Abū Qays b. al-Aslat al-Anṣārī (d.c. 1/622) from the beginning of his *Mufaḍḍaliyya* no. 76 is a lady's unflirtatious rejection of a hoary suitor, in the same way Ziyād roundly rejected the indiscretion. ʿUmar indirectly reprimanded a meddling counselor with, "If you remembered death it would occupy you more than giving advice" (*ʿIqd* IV: 209 #13), while Jaʿfar openly blamed such a person: "Sincerity is sometimes ugly" (*ʿIqd* IV: 219 #3).[55]

If rulers acted on information obtained through indiscretion, they did so wisely. To a treasurer who accused a tax collector of theft and wanted to expose him, Ibn al-Muʿtazz advised instead, "Make him whom you appoint too rich to steal, for he whom you do not suffice will not suffice you" (*Khāṣṣ*, 134 #1). Al-Faḍl b. Sahl reacted more drastically; he blamed the district head of Hamadhān for listening to a scribe who had verified in the records that his master (a postmaster) had assigned himself a large portion of the fief income, "Accepting calumny is worse than calumny, because calumny is an indication, but acceptance its permission..." (Jahshiyārī, *Wuzarāʾ*, 308 #2). Here again the concern for truth reigns supreme. The sovereign shows himself skeptical of allegations and demonstrates his justice by not giving credence to privileged underlings but discerning their self-serving intentions. Ṭāhir counters a would-be informer with the Qurʾānic citation, "Now we will see whether thou hast spoken truly, or whether thou art amongst those that lie" (*sa-nanẓuru a-ṣadaqta am kunta mina l-kādhibīn*; Q. 27: 27) with which king Solomon questioned the hoopoe bird's account of the queen of

[55] Cf. also *Khāṣṣ*, 130 al-Manṣūr #3, reprimanding a judge for calumny.

Sheba (*ʿIqd* IV: 222 #6 = *Khāṣṣ*, 133 #1). ʿAbdalmalik threatens another individual to desist should he not be truthful: "If you are sincere we praise you, if you lie we punish you, and if you wish we will drop the matter" (*Khāṣṣ*, 128 #3).

There were of course exceptions, such as the unveiling of an Alid plot, for which al-Rashīd richly rewarded the Zubayrid governor of Medina, Bakkār [b. ʿAbdallāh b. Muṣʿab] (d. 176/792), "May God give Faḍl [b. Yaḥyā] the best reward for choosing you. The caliph rewards your good intention with 100,000" (*ʿIqd* IV: 212 #12). The caliph is careful to stress in his response the informer's "good intention."[56] As a rule however intermediaries are rejected, and this is done publicly to demonstrate the sovereign's impartiality.

### *II.5. Performance*

The task of the apostille was not complete with its passing of the verdict, but rather lay in its proclamation of doing so. It was exemplary justice for public consumption. The legal verdict is the perfect representative of John Austin's performative, or John Searle's declarative speech act, which describes the very state that it brings about. Each *tawqīʿ* played a role beyond the specific case as a proclamation of a ruler's ethics, and the otherwise terse texts make pronouncements on equality before the law and suchlike that are superfluous to the legal matter at hand, but which are the true point of holding a *maẓālim* court. The Saljuq vizier Niẓām al-Mulk (d. 485/1092) stresses that the selective performance of exemplary justice had a multiplicatory effect, deterring officials from abuses, because they were aware of the corrective higher court.[57] For this reason the sovereign's physical involvement, his direct accessibility (for instance by a frequent and regularly held outdoor venue), and the absence of intermediaries were a *sina qua non* to make the performance credible and effective. These aspects are emphasized over and over in accounts of Sasanian and Muslim rulers, such as the insistence of the Samanid Ismāʿīl b. Aḥmad (r. 279-95/892-907) on snow days to wait alone on horseback in the square of his capital Bukhara for fear of missing a single complainant.

## *III. Apostille vs. Ode*

Petitions and *tawqīʿāt* employ elaborate parallel and rhyming prose and prosified poetic motifs, such as al-Rashīd's warning to the tax collector of Fars to think of him "as a night of sudden raids," recalling al-Nābigha al-Dhubyānī's classical topos for the ruler's ubiquity (*ʿIqd* IV: 214 #4).[58] But poetry too appears at differ-

---

56 But see al-Ṭabarī (*Taʾrīkh* VIII: 244-7) on Bakkār's ambivalent role in the plot. Cf. also Anūshirwān (Abū Aḥmad al-ʿAskarī, *Tafḍīl* 131) and ʿAbdallāh b. Ṭāhir (*Khāṣṣ*, 133 #1).

57 Niẓām al-Mulk, *Siyar al-mulūk*, 19/*Book of Government*, 14.

58 For a warning of actual nocturnal attacks, see *ʿIqd* IV: 209 Marwān #3.

ent junctures in the redress of torts. Petitioners avail themselves of this subtle, powerful medium to gain the ear of the sitting judge.[59] One such case is the widow who had been defrauded by a son of al-Maʾmūn and who alluded to the high-placed suspect with "To you appeals, O Pillar of the Kingdom, a widow whom a lion has attacked against whom she is powerless." Al-Maʾmūn grants her a hearing that day with an improvised poetic response (*ijāza)*, only to find out that the defendant is his own son.[60]

Authors of apostilles and edicts use poetry first as a way of communicating with members of their household and their professional class, especially among *kuttāb* of any rank, such as the poetry in the responses of Yaḥyā b. Khālid (Jahshiyārī, *Wuzarāʾ*, 205 #1, 2 and 4) and his son Jaᶜfar (*ᶜIqd* IV: 219 #7), though this is not a rule. Second, poetry carried a special emphasis either in conveying appreciation[61] or rebuke for an addressee who had shown himself unworthy of his status. Al-Rashīd shamed in verse his Baṣrian governor Sulaymān b. Abī Jaᶜfar al-Manṣūr who had failed to quell an uprising:[62]

> I am ashamed of an old man born of al-Manṣūr, who flees from those born of Kinda and Ṭayyiʾ. Why did you not meet them face forward, show them the broadside [of your sword], and act like your cousin Marwān when he went forth with his blank sword, citing as his example the verse of al-Jaḥḥāf b. Ḥakīm [al-Sulami]:[63]
>
> *mutaqallidīna ṣafāʾiḥan hindiyyatan*
> *yatrukna man ḍarabū kaʾan lam yūladi*
>
> Girding themselves with Indian broadsides
> that left him whom they struck as if he had not been born.
>
> [Why were you not like him who] fought till he was killed? How excellent is the mother who bore him and the father who made him rise!
>
> (*ᶜIqd* IV: 214 #16).

The verse, composed by one battle leader and cited by another who died in battle combined with his ancestral praise, makes the Sulaymān's pusillanimity appear dishonorable in contrast. In a like fashion the vizier Abū ᶜUbaydallāh

---

59 See for example the successful petitions of al-Wāqidī and Abū Ḥafṣ al-Warrāq (*Khāṣṣ*, 132 al-Maʾmūn #5 and *Khāṣṣ*, 139 al-Ṣāḥib b. ᶜAbbād, respectively), the latter using the motif that even the rats have abandoned his house. A poet's dream told in verse also finds fulfillment by al-Ḥasan b. Sahl (*ᶜIqd* IV: 220-1 #5).

60 al-Māwardī, *al-Aḥkām*, 138-9/*Statuts*, 175-6 (cf. n. 18).

61 E.g., ᶜAbdallāh b. Ṭāhir's verses to a general's request in the form of a dream (*Khāṣṣ*, 136 #4).

62 Probably in the Syrian upheavals during the first decade of al-Rashīd's reign. Sulaymān had also deplored the bloodshed and abstained from battle in an Alid revolt in Mecca, when leading the *ḥajj* caravan in 169/785; al-Ṭabarī, *Taʾrīkh* VIII: 196-9, 204, and 346.

63 Chief of the Banū Sulaym and leader in their battle (*yawm* Bishr) in 73/626-3 in eastern Syria against the Taghlib and the poet al-Akhṭal; EI$^2$ I: 1241 and al-Iṣfahānī (1374/1955), *al-Aghānī*, 24 vols., Beirut: Dār al-Thaqāfa, XII: 194-206. With "cousin" the caliph possibly referred to Marwān II who fell in Būṣīr in 312/750 in a skirmish with the rising Hāshimiyya.

Muʿāwiya b. ʿUbayd warns one of al-Mahdī's tax collectors not to adopt his neighbor's delay tactics with a verse of ʿAdī b. Zayd (d.c. 600 CE) on the effect of bad company on one's character (Abū Aḥmad al-ʿAskarī, *Maṣūn,* 107). Governor Ziyād b. Abīhi sarcastically dismisses calumny with a *nasīb* verse addressing a hoary would-be lover (section II.4.).

But the apostille is most damning when criticizing the ode. The panegyric genre, by nature lengthy and verbose is literally cut down to size. Anūshirwān, in an apostille to a note containing an encomium (designated with the Arabic generic term *madḥ*), responds cautiously with a blessing for the praised one (*mamdūḥ*) who deserves it and for the claimant who fulfills its demands, implying that he does not accept it as his portrayal (*ʿIqd* IV: 222 #2). Elsewhere he who responds to a long-winded ode displaying all the different styles (*madḥun aṭnaba bihi wa-ashaba wa-dhahaba kulla madhhab*) with blame for choosing items of praise that rather ought to be blamed (Abū Aḥmad al-ʿAskarī, *Tafḍīl,* 131). Al-Mahdī goes a step further and registers his disapproval of poetic exaggeration not only in a *tawqīʿ* but with an underpayment of the reward that inversely mirrors the excess of the praise (*ʿIqd* IV: 213 al-Mahdī #5). In terms of genre, the *tawqīʿ* is an unfair adversary for the *qaṣīda*, as its aesthetic of brevity exactly contrasts the *qaṣīda* whose length is one of its merits. The legal and administrative functions of the *tawqīʿ* produce a straightforward and lapidary style, which differs from the *qaṣīda*'s indirect way of achieving (often equally practical) goals.

Moreover the relation to truth in the prose of apostilles is a direct and factual one. In the world of government and court where it belongs, the word has power only when it coincides with acts. Aḥmad b. Yūsuf thus chastises the delay tactics of a tax collector by accusing him:

> ...You do not accompany your speech with acts, nor do you follow up your promise with execution (*mā tuṣḥibu qawlaka fiʿlan wa-lā tutbiʿu waʿdaka injāzan*). For you have withheld an installment of money whose delivery is due until its like has become incumbent. Dispatch then three installments, so that what you advance becomes the fulfillment of what you delayed (al-Ṣūlī, *Awrāq*, 230-1).

The truth of an ode, in contrast, is an aesthetic correspondence between sitter and portrayal, and a negotiation between author and recipient.[64] Finally, as an act of speech, the *tawqīʿ* comes invested with its writer's supreme authority (which lies outside its sparse language and empowers it), while the *qaṣīda* must build its own authority precisely through the poetic word.

Beyond the ode, the *tawqīʿ* expresses a general unease with ornate rhetoric. For Aḥmad b. Yūsuf the mere excellence of the argument with which a man defended ownership of an estate (which he had taken in the owner's absence) made

---

64 Regarding one sophisticated concept of panegyric truth, see Beatrice Gruendler (2003), *Medieval Arabic Praise Poetry: Ibn al-Rūmī and the Patron's Redemption*, London and New York: RoutledgeCurzon, 247-62.

him suspicious. The lack of substantiation then voided his well-wrought claim completely. The secretary adumbrates his principle of decision:

> The novelty of a right does not fade even if it has long endured lies. If you articulately voice your need and clearly remove the complication – though [var. to my mind and in my experience] this is often the means of one who wrongfully appropriates and the argument of one who tries to win – right is amply granted to you and led to you without an effort. But if you rely on the clarity [*bayān*] of words [alone] and stop at argumentation, then his (sc. the adversary's) argument by proof is higher and his claim worthier, God willing (al-Ṣūlī, *Awrāq*, 230).

The *tawqīᶜ* is the rhetoric of those who need no fancy ornament to empower themselves, and the genre's clipped prose implicitly criticizes those other genres and styles that rely on length and a different type of fit between word and act, most notably the ode.

## IV. Conclusion

It is always risky to deduce social circumstances from the limited purview of a literary transmission. Apostilles paint a picture of rulers' sense of justice, impartiality and incorruptibility, which is as idealized as their lavish generosity extolled in odes. At the same time, the *maẓālim* court's mere existence proves that more often the opposite of justice went on at the lower echelons of the administration. The logistical limitations of a single court with one or two weekly sessions could not have had a significant remedial effect. Nonetheless by creating even a theoretical possibility of stemming excesses of injustice in select cases, apostilles provided a "pressure valve" for the status quo. At the same time the performance of tort redress substantiated a ruler's claim to uphold universal justice. Even if only a representative minority attained hearings, and a fraction of those actually had their abuses corrected, their stories would surely be told. It is here, in the word and act of the apostille, that literary and political expediency coincide: less was surely more.

## Bibliography

### Sources

anon. (1948), *Akhbār al-Ṣīn wa-l-Hind*, ed., trans. and comm. Jean Sauvaget, Paris: Société d'Édition Les Belles Lettres.

al-ᶜAskarī, Abū Aḥmad (1402/1982), *al-Maṣūn fī l-adab*, ed. ᶜAbdassalām Hārūn, Kuwait 1960, repr. Cairo.

– (1418/1998) *al-Tafḍīl bayna balāghatay al-ᶜarab wa-l-ᶜajam*, ed. Ḥamd b. Nāṣir al-Dukhayyil, Barīda, Saudi Arabia: Nādī al-Qaṣīm al-Adabī.

al-ʿAskarī, Abū Hilāl (1971) *K. al-Ṣināʿatayn al-kitāba wa-l-shiʿr*, ed. ʿAlī Muḥammad al-Bijāwī and Muḥammad Abū l-Faḍl Ibrāhīm, Cairo 1952, repr. 1971.

*Awrāq* = al-Ṣūlī (1401/1982), *al-Awrāq: Akhbār al-shuʿarāʾ al-muḥdathīn*, ed. Heyworth Dunne, London: Luzac 1934, repr. Beirut: Dār al-Maṣīr.

Ibn al-Farrāʾ, Abū Yaʿlā (1386/1966), *al-Aḥkām al-sulṭāniyya*, ed. Muḥammad Ḥāmid al-Fiqī, Cairo: Muṣṭafā al-Bābī al-Ḥalabī.

al-Idrīsī (n.d.), *Nuzhat al-mushtāq fī ikhtirāq al-āfāq*, 2 vols., ed. R. Rubinacci, U. Rizzitano et al., Napoli: Istituto Universitario Orientale 1970, repr. Port Said.

*ʿIqd* = Ibn ʿAbdrabbih (1363/1944), *al-ʿIqd al-farīd*, vol. 4, ed. Aḥmad Amīn, Aḥmad al-Zayn and Ibrāhīm al-Abyārī.

al-Iṣfahānī (1375/1955), *al-Aghānī*, 24 vols., Beirut: Dār al-Thaqāfa.

*Khāṣṣ* = al-Thaʿālibī (1414/1994), *Khāṣṣ al-khāṣṣ*, ed. Maʾmūn al-Janān, Beirut: Dār al-Kutub al-ʿIlmiyya.

al-Māwardī (1409/1989), *al-Aḥkām al-sulṭāniyya wa-l-wilāyāt al-dīniyya*, ed. Khālid Rashīd al-Jumaylī, Baghdad.

al-Māwardī (1915), *Les statuts gouvernementaux ou Règles de droit public et administratif*, trans. E. Fagnan, Algiers: Adolphe Jourdan.

Miskawayh (1379HS/2001), *Tajārib al-umam*, ed. Abū l-Qāsim Emāmī, 3 vols., Tehran: Soroush.

Niẓām al-Mulk (1340HS/1962), *Siyar al-mulūk (Siyāsatnama)*, ed. H. Darke, Tehran: B.T.N.K.

– (1960), *The Book of Government or Rules for Kings*, trans. H. Darke, repr. Surrey: Curzon 2002.

– (1984), *Traité de gouvernement*, trans. Ch. Schefer, Paris: Sindbad.

– [Nizāmulmulk] (1959), *Das Buch der Staatskunst. Siyāsatnāma*, trans. K.E. Schabinger von Schowingen, repr. Zürich: Manesse, 1982.

al-Nuwayrī (1369/1949), *Nihāyat al-arab fī funūn al-adab*, vol. 15, Cairo: Dār al-Kutub.

Pseudo-Jāḥiẓ (1332/1914), *al-Tāj fī akhlāq al-mulūk*, ed. Aḥmad Zakī Bāshā, Cairo: al-Maṭbaʿa al-Amīriyya.

– (1954), *Le livre de la couronne*, trans. Charles Pellat, Paris: Société d'Édition Les Belles Lettres.

Qudāma b. Jaʿfar (1981), *al-Kharāj wa-ṣināʿat al-kitāba*, ed. Muḥammad Ḥusayn al-Zubaydī, Baghdad: Ministry of Culture.

al-Ṣūlī (1341), *Adab al-kuttāb*, ed. Muḥammad Bahja al-Atharī, Cairo: al-Maṭbaʿa al-Salafiyya.

al-Ṭabarī (1960-9), *Taʾrīkh*, ed. Muḥammad Abū l-Faḍl Ibrāhīm, 10 vols., Cairo: Dār al-Maʿārif.

*Wuzarāʾ* = al-Jahshiyārī, Muḥammad b. ʿAbdūs (1357/1938), *al-Wuzarāʾ*, ed. Muṣṭafā al-Saqqā, Ibrāhīm al-Abyārī and ʿAbd al-Ḥafīẓ Shalabī, Cairo: Muṣṭafā al-Bābī al-Ḥalabī.

*Critical Literature*

ᶜAbd al-Munᶜim, Ḥamdī (1408/1988), *Dīwān al-maẓālim, nashʾatuhu wa-taṭawwuruhu wa-khtiṣāṣuhu muqāranan bi-l-nuẓum al-quḍāʾiyya al-ḥadītha*, Beirut: Dār al-Jīl.

Babinger, F. and C.E. Bosworth (2000), art. "Tawḳīᶜ," in: *The Encyclopaedia of Islam*, new ed., Leiden: Brill, vol. VI: 933-5.

Björkman, Walther (1928), *Beiträge zur Geschichte der Staatskanzlei im islamischen Ägypten*, Hamburg: de Gruyter.

Christensen, Arthur (1936), *L'Iran sous les Sassanides*, Annales du Musée Guimet: Bibliothèque d'Études, vol. 48, Paris and Copenhague: Geuthner and Munksgaard.

Editors (1991), art. "Faghfūr," in: *The Encyclopaedia of Islam*, new ed., Leiden: Brill, vol. II: 738.

Gruendler, Beatrice (2003), *Medieval Arabic Praise Poetry: Ibn al-Rūmī and the Patron's Redemption*, London and New York: RoutledgeCurzon.

Huang, Chunyan (2004), "Songdai dengwengu zhidu [On the System of Appealing to the Emperor in the Song Dynasty]," *Zhongzhou xuekan* [*Academic Journal of Zhongzhou*] 6: 112-16.

Kracke, Edward (1976), "Early Visions of Justice for the Humble in East and West," *JAOS* 96, 492-8.

Maspéro, Henri (1927), *La chine antique*, Paris: de Boccard, vol. IV.

Nielsen, Jørgen S. (1985), *Secular Justice in an Islamic State: Maẓālim under the Baḥrī Mamlūks, 662/1294-789/1387*, Istanbul: Nederlands Historisch-Archeologisch Instituut.

– (1991), art. "Maẓālim," in: *The Encyclopaedia of Islam*, new ed., Leiden: Brill vol. X: 392-3.

Roemer, H.R. (1986), art. "Inshāʾ," in: *The Encyclopaedia of Islam*, new ed., Leiden: Brill, vol. 3:1241-4.

Sourdel, Dominique (1959-60), *Le vizirat ᶜabbāside de 749 à 936 (132 à 324 de l'Hégire)*, Damascus.

# The Aesthetics of Pure Formalism: A Letter of Qābūs b. Vushmgīr[1]

*Everett K. Rowson (New York University)*

According to an oft-repeated dictum, the art of fine writing (*kitāba*) in Arabic began with ʿAbd al-Ḥamīd and ended with Ibn al-ʿAmīd.[2] ʿAbd al-Ḥamīd was the celebrated Umayyad secretary of the mid-second/eighth century,[3] and Ibn al-ʿAmīd the famous Būyid *wazīr* of the mid-fourth/tenth;[4] by *kitāba* is meant the art of the secretaries, and specifically the artistic prose displayed in their official and private correspondence. When we look at what survives of this prose, however, such a statement seems hardly justified; and indeed, Ibn al-ʿAmīd appears to represent less the end of an era than the beginning of one. Although we have evidence for the collection and publication of the correspondence of many writers in the two centuries before the *wazīr*, none of these collections seem to have survived in integral form;[5] yet from Ibn al-ʿAmīd's own generation and that of his immediate successors there are no less than eight collections of letters extant in manuscript.[6] Four of these come from Būyid officials – two *wazīr*s, Ibn al-ʿAmīd himself[7] and

---

1 This essay represents a somewhat revised version of a talk delivered at the annual meeting of the Middle East Studies Association of North America in November 1988. I am grateful to Professor Vahid Behmardi and Bilal Orfali for inviting me to include the essay in this volume. I hope I have managed to sweep away most of the cobwebs from the original talk, but cannot pretend to have dealt adequately with all the relevant scholarship that has appeared in the meantime.

2 *Budiʾat al-kitāba bi-ʿAbd al-Ḥamīd wa-khutimat bi-Ibn al-ʿAmīd*, reported ("*wa-kāna yuqāl*") by al-Thaʿālibī, *Yatīmat al-dahr*, ed. Muḥammad Muḥyī l-Dīn ʿAbd al-Ḥamīd (Cairo, 1956), III, 158, and repeated in many later sources.

3 The definitive edition and study of the extant epistles of ʿAbd al-Ḥamīd (d. 132/750) is that of Iḥsān ʿAbbās, *ʿAbd al-Ḥamīd ibn Yaḥyā al-Kātib wa-mā tabaqqā min rasāʾilihi wa-rasāʾil Sālim Abī l-ʿAlāʾ*, Amman, 1988.

4 On Abū l-Faḍl Ibn al-ʿAmīd (d. 360/970) see *EI2*, s.v. Ibn al-ʿAmīd (Cl. Cahen).

5 See the second *fann* of the third *maqāla* in al-Nadīm, *al-Fihrist*, ed. R. Tajaddud (Beirut: Dār al-Masīra, 1988), 129-155; A. Arazi and H. Ben-Shammay calculate (*EI2*, s.v. Risāla) that al-Nadīm lists a total of seventy published collections of epistles by individual authors.

6 For an illuminating analysis of this change in survival patterns, see Klaus U. Hachmeier, *Die Briefe Abū Isḥāq Ibrāhīm al-Ṣābi's (st. 384/994 A.H./A.D.): Untersuchungen zur Briefsammlung eines berühmten arabischen Kanzleischreibers mit Erstedition einiger seiner Briefe* (Hildesheim, 2002), 15-44.

7 See Hans Daiber, *Naturwissenschaft bei den Arabern im 10. Jahrundert n. Chr.: Briefe des Abū l-Faḍl Ibn al-ʿAmīd (gest. 360/970) an ʿAḍudaddaula* (Leiden, 1993), for an edition and German translation of seven letters on topics of natural science. The situation with regard specifically to Ibn al-ʿAmīd's diplomatic letters remains unclear, but it would appear that collections of them survive in a number of manuscripts; see ibid., p. 5, n. 4, and Hachmaier, *Briefe*, p. 17, n. 15.

his successor the Ṣāḥib Ibn ʿAbbād (d. 385/995),[8] and two heads of the chancery, ʿAbd al-ʿAzīz b. Yūsuf (d. 388/998)[9] and Abū Isḥāq al-Ṣābiʾ (d. 384/994)[10] – and it is precisely these four that the Ṣāḥib himself, in another famous (and rather immodest) saying, identified as the "secretaries of the world" or world-class stylists (*kuttāb al-dunyā*).[11] Of the other four collections, three belong to celebrated private littérateurs, Abū Bakr al-Khwārazmī (d. 383/993),[12] Badīʿ al-Zamān al-Hamadhānī (d. 398/1008),[13] and the Qāḍī al-Azdī al-Harawī (d. 440/1048),[14] and the fourth is that of an *amīr*, Qābūs b. Vushmgīr (d. 403/1012-13), the ruler of Jurjān.[15]

Clearly, later generations recognized that the late fourth/tenth century was a turning-point in the development of Arabic artistic prose; and when we look at these letters ourselves, a rapid increase in the elaborateness and rhetorization of style is immediately apparent. Not that it is particularly easy to look at them: two of these eight collections have never been published; only one, that of the Ṣāḥib, has been both completely and critically edited; and despite some valuable recent

8 *Rasāʾil al-Ṣāḥib b. ʿAbbād*, ed. ʿAbd al-Wahhāb ʿAzzām and Shawqī Ḍayf (Cairo, 1947), from a Paris manuscript, representing a substantial but far from complete collection of his correspondence.

9 See J. Christoph Bürgel, *Die Hofkorrespondenz ʿAḍud ad-Daulas und ihr Verhaltnis zu anderen historischen Quellen der frühen Būyiden* (Wiesbaden, 1965), a historical analysis based on a collection of ʿAbd al-ʿAzīz's official letters in a Berlin manuscript, the text of which remains unpublished.

10 Hachmaier, *Briefe*, reviews all previous scholarship, discusses the eighteen known manuscripts of al-Ṣābiʾ's letters, and edits a substantial selection of them.

11 Al-Thaʿālibī, *Yatīma*, II, 246.

12 His *Rasāʾil* are preserved in numerous manuscripts, and have been published repeatedly (notably, Constantinople, 1297, and Beirut, 1970), but never critically; on him, see Aḥmad Amīn Muṣṭafā, *Abū Bakr al-Khwārazmī, ḥayātuhu wa-adabuhu*, Cairo, 1985.

13 Ibrāhīm al-Aḥdab al-Ṭarābulsī, ed., *Kashf al-maʿānī wa-l-bayān ʿan rasāʾil Badīʿ al-Zamān*), Beirut, 1890; full details in D. S. Richards, "The *Rasāʾil* of Badīʿ al-Zamān al-Hamadhānī," in *Arabicus Felix: Luminosus Britannicus: Essays in Honour of A. F. L. Beeston on his Eightieth Birthday*, ed. Alan Jones (Oxford, 1991), 142-162.

14 He has been totally neglected by modern scholarship, despite the apparent survival of a collection of his letters assembled by al-Maydānī (d. 518/1124) under the title *Munyat al-rāḍī bi-rasāʾil al-qāḍī*; see C. Brockelmann, *Geschichte der Arabischen Litteratur* (2nd ed., Leiden, 1943), I, 96, and *Supplement* (Leiden, 1937), I, 154f. On him see al-Thaʿālibī, *Yatīma*, IV, 348-350; idem, *Tatimmat al-Yatīma*, ed. ʿAbbās Iqbāl (Tehran, 1353), II, 46-53; and al-Bākharzī, *Dumyat al-qaṣr*, ed. Sāmī Makkī al-ʿĀnī (Baghdad and Najaf, 1971), II, 89-99.

15 It would perhaps be appropriate to add to this list the slightly earlier but elusive writer Abū l-Ḥusayn al-Ahwāzī (Muḥammad b. al-Ḥusayn), for whom see Brockelmann, *GAL* I, 96, and *GALS* I, 153. His *K. al-Durar wa-l-ghurar* (preserved in a Leiden manuscript but unpublished) is intended as a stylistic manual for secretaries, with all the model letters (or pieces of letters) presented being from his own pen; while many or most of these are artifical (composed only for the book), some are real letters, with the addressees identified. Al-Ahwāzī is also the author of a collection of pithy phrases, in rhymed prose, for the use of aspiring littérateurs with the title *al-Farāʾid wa-l-qalāʾid*, which is misattributed in some manuscripts (and published editions) to quite a variety of other authors, including Qābūs and al-Thaʿālibī, and with a variety of other titles; but the correct author and title would appear to be established by the excerpts from it that al-Thaʿālibī included in his *Siḥr al-balāgha* (Damascus, n.d., p. 200).

work scholarship in this area remains distinctly thin. The reason for such neglect is not hard to find – beneath the elaborate rhetoric lies, on the whole, an extraordinary banality of content. In his historically (rather than literarily) focused study of the correspondence of ʿAbd al-ʿAzīz b. Yūsuf, J.-Ch. Bürgel comments on the letters' vagueness, allusiveness, and lack of concrete detail,[16] an observation even more applicable to the other collections. For diplomatic correspondence, such vagueness was no doubt often intentional, more concrete and sensitive details being entrusted to the messenger as an oral communication which would leave no record; many of the private letters convey such generalized sentiments as - congratulations and condolences, and specificity either is avoided or has been suppressed by later redactors, who often substitute "*Fulān*" for personal names, sometimes including those of the addressees. Interest in content certainly had little or nothing to do with the preservation of these documents.

In fact, the situation is analogous to that of poetry in the same period. A generalized and immediately comprehensible sentiment – the *gharaḍ* or "genre" – is made the basis for a stylistic *tour de force*. The redactor normally informs the reader of the *gharaḍ* at the head of the letter, labelling it *taʿziya*, condolence, or *ʿitāb*, reproach, for example, so that the point may be presupposed, just as a poem in an anthology will be labelled *marthiya*, elegy, or *hijāʾ*, abuse. Even in official letters, such as the Ṣāḥib's announcement of a Būyid victory in Jurjān, concrete detail is kept to a minimum and the content subordinated to the recognized structure of a *kitāb fatḥ*, or victory proclamation. This parallelism between artistic prose and poetry is of course a traditional idea, articulated throughout the history of Arabic literature; the discussion of the relative merits of poetry and prose was a particularly prominent topos in the late fourth/tenth and early fifth/eleventh centuries, as illustrated, for example, by a chapter of al-Tawḥīdī's (d. 414/1023) *al-Imtāʿ wa-l-muʾānasa*,[17] a letter by al-Ṣābiʾ,[18] and Abū Hilāl al-ʿAskarī's (d. after 395/1005) *Kitāb al-Ṣināʿatayn*, or *Book on the Two Arts*, *kitāba* and *shiʿr*, epistolography and poetry.[19] It is also in this period that monographs on prosification of poetry (and, secondarily, versification of prose) began to appear, including al-Āmidī's (d. 370/980) *Nathr al-manẓūm* (not extant), al-Nayramānī's (d. 403/1012) *Manthūr al-manẓūm li-l-Bahāʾī*,[20] and al-Thaʿālibī's (d. 429/1037) *Nathr al-naẓm wa-ḥall al-ʿaqd*.[21]

---

16 Bürgel, *Hofkorrespondenz*, 48.

17 Al-Tawḥīdī, *al-Imtāʿ wa-l-muʾānasa*, ed. Aḥmad Amīn and Aḥmad al-Zayn (Cairo, 1953), II, 130-147.

18 Text and discussion in Albert Arazi, "Une épitre d'Ibrāhīm b. Hilāl al-Ṣābiʾ sur les genres littéraires," in *Studies in Islamic History and Civilization in Honour of Professor David Ayalon*, ed. M. Sharon (Jerusalem-Leiden, 1986), 473-505.

19 See George J. Kanazi, *Studies in the Kitāb al-Ṣināʿatayn of Abū Hilāl al-ʿAskarī*, Leiden, 1989.

20 Facsimile edition, Frankfurt, 1984.

21 Numerous editions, most recently Beirut, 1990. On the genre, see the monograph by Amidu Sanni, *The Arabic Theory of Prosification and Versification*, Beirut-Stuttgart, 1998.

If style is all in the letters of this period, and style meant mainly rhetoric, perhaps it is worth looking at a sample, preferably an extreme one, to see how this rhetoric functioned and where its appeal lay. Of the eight collections mentioned above, the two displaying the most elaborate rhetoric are certainly those of Badīʿ al-Zamān and Qābūs, a view supported by a statement by Ibn Shuhayd (d. 426/1035) in Spain, only a few years after their deaths, singling these two out as representatives of a new (and admirable) style.[22] Badīʿ al-Zamān's letters are well known and have received a certain amount of scholarly attention,[23] but those of Qābūs have been largely neglected; for present purposes, they have the additional advantage of offering probably the best examples from this period of the triumph of style over content. (The one significant recent study devoted to them, by Adrian Gully and John Hinde, is a valuable but rather narrowly focused quantitative analysis of the "rhythm" of short and long syllables in Qābūs's prose; the observations offered below are directed more at broader structural aspects of his style.)[24]

About Qābūs himself and his rather turbulent career only a few basic facts need be presented here.[25] He came to the throne of Jurjān in 366/977, but lost it to the Būyids four years later and spent the following eighteen years in exile in Nishapur, before returning in 388/998 and reigning again for fourteen years. In a rebellion in 403/1012-13 he was again dethroned, imprisoned, died shortly thereafter of exposure, and was buried in the magnificent mausoleum he had built for himself, the Gunbadh-i Qābūs. One of the intellectual luminaries of the age, he was host to both Ibn Sīnā (d. 428/1037) and al-Bīrūnī (d. after 442/1050), who dedicated his *al-Āthār al-bāqiya* to him, and was an intimate of many other literary contemporaries. Al-Thaʿālibī presumably got to know him well during his exile in Nishapur, and after his restoration twice visited his court in Jurjān, dedicating to him at least two of his major works.[26] Badīʿ al-Zamān probably also met him in Nishapur and apparently also later spent time in Jurjān; he composed at least two panegyrics on him, and among his extant letters is one requesting admission to his salon (*majlis*).[27]

---

22 Ibn Bassām, *al-Dhakhīra fī maḥāsin ahl al-jazīra*, ed. Sālim Muṣṭafā al-Badrī (Beirut, 1998), I, 147.

23 See, in particular, Richards, D. S., "The *Rasāʾil* of Badīʿ al-Zamān al-Hamadhānī," (Oxford, 1991), 142-162.

24 Adrian Gully and John Hinde, "Qābūs ibn Wushmagīr: a study of rhythm patterins in Arabic epistolary prose from the 4th century AH (10th century AD)," *Middle Eastern Literatures* 6 (2003), 177-197.

25 See C. E. Bosworth in *EI2* s.v. Ḳābūs b. Wushmagīr b. Ziyār.

26 See *EI2*, s.v. al-Thaʿālibī, Abū Manṣūr, and M. A. al-Jādir, *al-Thaʿālibī nāqidan wa-adīban* (Baghdad, 1976), noting the dedications to Qābūs of his *al-Mubhij* and *al-Tamthīl wa-l-muḥāḍara*. See also the section on Qābūs in the *Yatīmat al-dahr*, IV, 59-61.

27 *Dīwān Badīʿ al-Zamān al-Hamadhānī*, ed. Yusrī ʿAbd al-Ghanī ʿAbdallāh (Beirut, 1987), 58, 111-13; Ibrāhīm Efendī al-Aḥdab al-Ṭarābulusī, *Kashf al-maʿānī wa-l-bayān ʿan rasāʾil Badīʿ al-Zamān* (Beirut, n.d.), 130f.

A selection of Qābūs's letters was collected and published at some unknown time, but probably not too long after his death, by an otherwise unknown ʿAlī b. ʿAbd al-Raḥmān al-Yazdādī, with the title *Kamāl al-balāgha*, and this text is available in an edition made from two manuscripts in private hands and published in 1922.[28] The collection comprises twenty-seven letters to *wazīr*s and other high officials, including ten to the Ṣāḥib, for which, exceptionally, al-Yazdādī provides also the latter's replies – included, he says, in order to show Qābūs's obvious superiority to the famous Būyid stylist. An appendix reproduces five "philosophical" epistles by Qābūs (discussed briefly below). There is also a short - introduction, in which al-Yazdādī heaps lavish praise on the *amīr* and gives a list of new prose "figures," illustrated from Qābūs's letters and presented as a supplement to the figures identified by the critic Qudāma b. Jaʿfar (d. 337/948) in the previous century.

Because al-Yazdādī does not elaborate on what Qudāma has already said, it is impossible to determine with certainty which of the latter's works he means. He may well be referring to the brief introduction to the *Jawāhir al-alfāẓ*, in which Qudāma lists fourteen prose figures; this possibility is supported by the fact that al-Yazdādī's list also comprises fourteen figures and could be an attempt to "match" Qudāma.[29] On the other hand, al-Yazdādī mentions Qudāma's presentation of illustrative *fuṣūl*, a term probably referring to longer examples than those given in the *Jawāhir*, which he would probably have called *fiqar* or *qarāʾin*; perhaps then he has in mind rather the presumably more elaborate discussion in the lost third section of Qudāma's *Kitāb al-Kharāj wa-ṣināʿat al-kitāba*.[30] In any case, the point to be stressed here is that the predominance of what may be called "structural" over "ideational" figures, arguably already the case in Qudāma's list in the *Jawāhir*, is unmistakeable in al-Yazdādī. A few examples should serve to clarify this distinction.

The two fundamental structuring principles of ornate prose are *izdiwāj*, parallelism of phraseology, and *sajʿ*, rhyme; of secondary importance are parallelism of syntax (*bināʾ*) and of rhythm (*wazn* or *ittizān*), the latter normally presupposing the former.[31] Qudāma's first three figures in the *Jawāhir* are defined accord-

---

28 ʿAbd al-Raḥmān b. ʿAlī al-Yazdādī, *Kamāl al-balāgha*, Cairo, 1341. I am grateful to Wolfhart P. Heinrichs for first drawing this text to my attention.

29 Qudāma b. Jaʿfar, *Jawāhir al-alfāẓ*, ed. Muḥammad Muḥyī l-Dīn ʿAbd al-Ḥamīd (Beirut, 1985), 2-8.

30 See *EI2*, s.v. Ḳudāma b. Djaʿfar, and Paul L. Heck, *The Construction of Knowledge in Islamic Civilization: Qudāma b. Jaʿfar and His* Kitāb al-kharāj wa-ṣināʿat al-kitāba, Leiden, 2002.

31 *Sajʿ*, and prose generally, do not loom large in medieval Arabic literary theory and criticism, which are mostly focused on poetry. After Qudāma, the most important contributions are Abū Hilāl al-ʿAskarī, *Kitāb al-Ṣināʿatayn* (presumably unknown to al-Yazdādī), and, much more substantively, Ḍiyāʾ al-Dīn Ibn al-Athīr (d. 637/1239), *al-Mathal al-sāʾir fī adab al-kātib wa-l-shāʿir* (ed. Aḥmad al-Ḥūfī and Badawī Ṭabāna, Cairo, n.d., especially I, 210-62). For secondary literature, see *EI2*, s.v. Sadjʿ; Devin Stewart, "*Sajʿ* in the Qurʾān: Prosody and Structure," *Journal of Arabic Literature* 21 (1990), 101-39; and Maḥmūd al-

ing to the degree of concord of these factors: *tarṣīʿ*, the "best" alternative, requires both internal and final *sajʿ*, as well as strict parallelism of *wazn* (and syntax), as in the example:

> *ḥattā ʿāda taʿrīḍuka taṣrīḥā / wa-ṣāra tamrīḍuka taṣḥīḥā*
>
> until your allusions become plain statements, and your aggravation becomes conciliation...

(Whether Qudāma considered the semantic oppositions which are also part of this example essential to his definition is unclear.) The second alternative lacks internal *sajʿ*, but preserves the other factors; the third retains only parallelism in rhythm at the ends of the periods, without *sajʿ* (but with, implicitly, parallelism of syntax).

Most of al-Yazdādī's "new" figures, which he claims more or less as inventions by Qābūs, involve further and more complex combinations of these elements. Two examples should suffice as illustrations. In al-Yazdādī's *mutazāwij*, *every* word in two paired phrases rhymes:

> *innī muʾammilu ghamām / ghayri jahām // wa-muʿmilu ḥusām / ghayri kahām*
>
> I put my hopes in a cloud not devoid of water, and set to work a sword not blunt.

In the *mutawʾam*, the "twinned," the same consonantal substitution is made in each word of the paired phrases:

> *(al-dahr) qāṣim al-aṣlāb / wa-qāsim al-aslāb*
>
> (Fate is) the breaker of backs, and the divider of spoils.

The point here is not to assess the adequacy or accuracy of al-Yazdādī's analysis of constructions such as these, but to show what sort of thing it was that he appreciated in Qābūs's style, as well as what sort of rhetorical ornament it is that dominates, nay, pervades the latter. I have called these devices "structural" as opposed to "ideational," rather than using "*lafẓī*" and "*maʿnawī*" or other terminology from within the tradition, to emphasize that even semantically-dependent figures are generally employed in a "mechanistic" way: Qābūs does not often come up with original metaphors, or manipulate metaphors to create striking new associations of *meaning*, for example, but rather combines hackneyed metaphors with paronomasia or unusual rhythmical structures to create his effects.[32]

---

Masʿadī, *al-Īqāʿ fī l-sajʿ al-ʿarabī* (Tunis, 1986), whose quantitative analyses are the starting point for Gully and Hinde's study.

32 Not all of Qābūs's metaphors are hackneyed, to be sure; but those that could be dubbed original seem usually to be serving structural rather than ideational ends, as should become clearer from the following analysis. Nevertheless, it is worth noting that Abū Hilāl al-ʿAskarī follows up his quotation of the letter analyzed here with the comment that "In some of the *alfāẓ* of this letter there is artificiality (*takalluf*), but I have cited it because of the exaltedness (*ʿuluww*) of its *maʿānī*" (*Dīwan al-maʿānī*, Beirut, 1989, 104).

Now many people would call this sort of thing vapid, and ask first of all whether al-Yazdādī does justice to Qābūs with analysis of this sort. Whatever one may think of al-Yazdādī's literary-critical sophistication, however, there would seem to be little room for doubt that he is appreciating Qābūs's style the way Qābūs intended it to be appreciated. But then if it is true that Qābūs's letters lack any great originality in *maʿnā* at either the macro or the micro level – in content or in "ideational" figures – does this mean that Qābūs himself is simply a vapid writer?

As a response to this question, I would like to look briefly at a single entire letter and its structure. For my sample I have chosen the letter which seems to entrance al-Yazdādī most, an unusually long one addressed by Qābūs to his maternal uncle the Iṣbahbadh of Ṭabaristān, which is also quoted in full, with some variants, in the *Dīwān al-maʿānī* of Abū Hilāl al-ʿAskarī.[33] It is perhaps not entirely characteristic, being more specific in its intention than a run-of-the-mill letter of condolence or congratulation; al-Yazdādī labels its *gharaḍ* as "reproach and coaxing" (*fī l-ʿatb wa-l-istimāla*), explaining that Qābūs had been unable to fulfill a request by the Iṣbahbadh, with the result that the latter cut off relations with him in anger. Typically, we learn nothing more than this about the situation.[34] (Abū Hilāl quotes the letter in his chapter on self-praise (*iftikhār*) – appropriately enough, as Qābūs's reproaches include a long section describing his own exaltedness, which the Iṣbahbadh has been foolish enough to disregard – and labels the letter itself one of "self-praise and reproach" (*fī l-iftikhār wa-l-ʿitāb*).)

The content of the letter can be summarized, leaving out nothing of significance, as follows:

> Why do you insist on being so unfriendly? This is not right of you. How can you be stand-offish with someone so powerful and lofty as me? This is stupid and wrong of you. You think that you do not need me, but you underestimate me. I am not asking for your friendship because I need you, but because you need me. But if you prefer your present abasement, I will gladly forget you.

---

33 Al-Yazdādī, *Kamāl al-balāgha*, 52-57; Abū Hilāl al-ʿAskarī, *Dīwān al-maʿānī*, 102-4. Al-Yazdādī's text is clearly superior to that of Abū Hilāl, which will not be taken into consideration here. (A more recent edition of the *Dīwān al-maʿānī*, ed. Aḥmad Salīm Ghānim, Beirut, 2003, offers for this particular letter (I, 230-32) a text no better than that of the earlier edition.) For a recent overview of the *Dīwān al-maʿānī*, see Beatrice Gruendler, "Motif vs. Genre: Reflections on the *Dīwān al-Maʿānī* of Abū Hilāl al-ʿAskarī," in *Ghazal As World Literature I: Transformations of a Literary Genre*, ed. Thomas Bauer and Angelika Neuwirth (Beirut, 2005), 57-85.

34 Our historical sources are of little help here. The Iṣbahbadh can be identified as the Bāwandid Shahriyār b. Sharwīn, whom al-ʿUtbī twice mentions as an ally of Qābūs, without noting their familial relationship (*al-Yamīnī*, ed. Iḥsān Dhanūn al-Thāmirī [Beirut, 2004], 230, 239); but Bāwandid history and genealogy are a hopeless muddle (cf. Wilferd Madelung in *The Cambridge History of Iran IV: The Period from the Arabi Invasion to the Saljuqs*, ed. R. N. Frye [Cambridge, 1975], 212-19), and any more specific identification of the situation prompting this letter seems quite unattainable.

How have these simple sentiments been expanded into a letter of significant length, with a total of fifty-four *qarāʾin* (paired rhyming phrases)? (In his edition, al-Yazdādī notes at the beginning of each letter the number of *qarāʾin* which it contains, in order, he says, to prevent abridgement or interpolation by copyists.) Without attempting a full rhetorical analysis of the text (which would be much longer than the letter itself, of course), I would like to draw particular attention to its architecture – the way its *sajʿ* clauses are laid out in a hierarchy that is at the same time complex and transparent, serving most of all to produce a compelling rhythm through the coordinated exploitation of rhyme, assonance, and semantic parallelism (and opposition). Here is the Arabic text, with the *qarāʾin* numbered, and with indentations intended to highlight its syntax, followed by an English translation observing the same convention.

1 الإنسان خُلق ألوفا * وطُبع عطوفا

2 فما للإصبهبذ سيّدي لا يحنى عُودُه * ولايُرجى عَوْدُه

3 ولا يُخال لفيئته مخيلة * ولا يُحال تنكُّرُه بحيلة

4 أمن صخر تدمر قلبه فليس يليّنه العتاب * أم من الحديد جانبه فلا يميّله الإعتاب

5 أم من صفاقة الدهر مِجَنّ نبوّه فقد نبا عنه غرب كلّ حِجاج *
ام من قساوته مزاج إبائه فقد أبى على كلّ علاج

6 ما هذا الاختيار الذي يَعُدّ الوهم فهما

7 وهذا التمييز الذي يحسب الخير شرّا

8 وما هذا الرأي الذي يزيّن له قبح العقوق * ويُمْقِت اليه رعاية الحقوق

9 وما هذا الإعراض الذي صار ضربةَ لازب * والنسيان الذي أنساه كلّ واجب

10 أين الطبع الذي هو للصُدود صَدود * وللتألّف أَلوف وَدود

11 وأين الخُلق الذي هو في وجه الدنيا البشاشة والبِشر * وفي مَبسِمها الثنايا الغُرّ

12 وأين الحياء الذي يُجَلّى به الكرم * وتُحَلّى بمحاسنه الشِيَم

13 كيف يُزْهَد في من ملك عنان الدهر فهو طوع قياده * وتَبَع مراده

14 ينظر أمره ليمتثل * ويرقب نهيه فيعتزل

15 وكيف يُهْجَر من تضاءلت الأرض تحت قدمه * وصارت في الانقياد له كخدمه

16 اذا رأت منه هشاشة أعشبت * وإن أحسّت منه بجفوة أجدبت

17 وكيف يُستغنى عمّن خيله العزمات والأوهام * وأنصاره الليالي والأيّام

18 فمن هرب منه أدركه بمكائدها * ومن طلبه وجده في مراصدها
19 وكيف يُعْرَض عمّن تُعْرِض رفاهة العيش بإعراضه * وتنقبض الأرزاق بانقباضه
20 وأضاء نجم الإقبال اذا أقبل * وأهلّ هلال الجَدَّ اذا تهلّل
21 وكيف يُزْهى على من تحقر في عينه الدنيا * ويرى تحته السماء العليا
22 قد ركب عنق الفلك * واستوى على ذات الحُبُك
23 فتبرّجت له البروج * وتكوكبت لعبادته الكواكب *
واستجارت بعزّته المجرّة * وأثْرت بمآثره أوضاح الثريّا
24 بل كيف يهوَّن من لو شاء عقد الهواء * وجسَّم الهباء
25 وفصّل تراكيب السماء * وألّف بين النار والماء
26 وأكمد ضياء الشمس والقمر * وكفاهما عناء السير والسفر
27 وسدّ مناخر الرياح الزَعازع * وطبّق أجفان البروق اللوامع
28 وقطع ألسنة الرعود بسيف الوعيد * ونظم صوب الغمام نظم الفريد
29 ورفع عن الأرض سطوة الزلازل * وقضى بما يراه على القضاء النازل
30 وعرض الشيطان بمعرض الإنسان * وكحل الحور العين بصور الغيلان
31 وأنبت العُشْب على البحار * وألبس الليل ضوء النهار
32 ولِمَ لا يعلم ان مهاجرة من هذه قُدرته ضلال * ومباينة من هذه صفته خَبال
33 وأن من له هذه المعجزات * يُشترى رضاه بالنفس والحياة
34 ومن أتى بهذه الآيات * يُبتغى هواه بالصوم والصلاة
35 ومن لم يتعلّق منه بحبل كان بهيما لا شية له *
ومن لم يأو منه الى ظلّ ظلّ صريما لا عصمة له
36 ولِمَ لا يستردّ عازب الرأي فيعلم انه ما لم يعاود الصلة مأفون *
ويستعيد غائب الفكر فيفهم انه ما دام على الفُرقة مغبون
37 أظنّه يقدّر الاستغناء عنّي هو الغِنى والغَناء *
ولا يدري ان الالتواء عليّ هو البِلى والبَلاء
38 ويخال انه مكتفٍ بجاهه وعِرْضه * ومتعزّز بسمائه وأرضه

39 ولا يشعر أنّي كلٌّ لبعضه * وطولٌ في عَرْضه

40 وأنّ قوّة الجناح بالقوادم والخوافي * وعمل الرماح بالأسنّة والعوالي

41 ليس إلحاحي على سيّدي مستعيدا وصاله * ومستصلحا خصاله

42 وعَدّي عليه هذه العجائب * ووثوبي لاستمالته من جانب الى جانب

43 لأني ممّن يرغب في راغب عن وصلته * او ينزع الى نازع عن خُلّته

44 أو يؤثّل حالا عند من ينحت أَثْلته * أو يُقْبِل بوجهه على من لا يجعله قِبْلته

45 فإني لو علمت انّ الأرض لا تسَفّ تراب قدمي لجنّبتها جنبي *
وأنّ السماء لا تتوق الى تقبيل هامتي لقلبت عن ذكرها قلبي

46 لكني أكره ان يعرى نحره من قلائد الحمد * ويجتنب جبينه إكليل المجد

47 ويظلّ وجه الوفاء بقبضه على يده مسودّا * وركن الإخاء لِفتّه في عضده منهدّا

48 ولا يعجبني ان يكسو ضوءَ مكارمه كلفَ الخمول * ويأذن لطوالع معاليه بالأفول

49 فإنْ فضّل سيّدي الخمود على الوُقود * والعدم على الوجود

50 ونزل من شاهق الى خفض * ومن حالق الى أرض

51 وهاجر بِهَجْره * وأصرّ على صُرْمه

52 ومال الى الملال * ولم يَصْلَ نار الوصال

53 حللت عنه معقود خنصري * وشغلت عن الشغل به خاطري

54 بل محوت ذكره عن صفحة فؤادي * واعتددت ودّه فيما سال به الوادي
ففي الناس إن رثّت حبالك واصل   وفي الأرض عن دار القِلى متحوَّل

1. Man was created sociable, and given a naturally affectionate disposition.
2. Wherefore, then, can my lord the Iṣbahbadh's wood not be bent, nor his return (to his former affection) be hoped for,
3. Nor a cloud be seen promising the blessed rain of his restored equanimity, nor his disaffection be displaced through any stratagem?
4. Is his heart made of the stones of Palmyra, not to be softened by reproach, or his side made of iron, not to be turned by satisfaction rendered,
5. Or the shield of his aversion made of the brazenness of Fate, so that the sharp edge of every protestation glances off it, or the temperament of his scorn made of Fate's harshness, so that it defies every treatment?
6. What is this act of choice that takes fantasy for understanding,

7. And this power of discernment that considers the good to be evil?
8. And what is this faculty of judgment that makes the ugliness of disrespect look fine to him, and renders hateful to him fulfillment of responsibilities?
9. And what is this avoidance that has become a permanent fixture, and this forgetfulness that has made him forget every duty?
10. Where is the nature that is aloof to aloofness, and congenial and amicable to congeniality?
11. And where is the character that is the bright cheerfulness in the face of the world, and the gleaming teeth of its smile?
12. And where is the modesty by which nobility is made manifest, and with whose virtues qualities are adorned?
13. How can one turn away[35] from someone who holds the reins of Fate so that it follows his lead, and submits to his will,
14. Awaiting his command in order to comply, and watchful for his prohibition so it may abstain?
15. And how can one desert someone beneath whose foot the very earth cringes, and in submission to whom she has become as one of his servants,
16. Blooming when she sees him well disposed, and drying up when she senses his displeasure?
17. And how can one do without someone whose cavalry are his resolutions and aspirations, and whose supporters are the nights and the days,
18. So that he catches the one who flees from him by the devices of (the former), and the one who comes after him finds him among the ambush parties of (the latter)?
19. And how can one turn away from someone with whose turning away all comfort of life turns away, and with whose aloofness men's very sustenance holds itself aloof,
20. But with whose receptiveness the star of prosperity shines forth, and with whose welcoming countenance the crescent moon of good fortune appears?
21. And how can one vaunt oneself over someone in whose eyes the earth is contemptibly lowly, and who sees the exalted heavens spread beneath him,
22. Who has mounted the neck of the celestial sphere, and established himself above the star-streaked sky,[36]

---

[35] I read this verb (*yuzhad*), as well as the following parallel verbs (*yuhjar*, *qarīna* 15; *yustaghnā*, 17; *yuʿraḍ*, 19; *yuzhā*, 21; and *yuhawwan*, 24) in the passive, as does the editor of the *Kamāl al-balāgha*. All could also be read in the active, with the Iṣbahbadh as the implicit subject, but this seems, it terms of general tone, to be too pointed and less likely.

[36] The "star-streaked sky" (*dhāt al-ḥubuk*) is an allusion to Qurʾān 41:7, where the phrase is used in a oath. By associating it here with the verb *istawā* Qābūs would appear to be skating dangerously close to blasphemy, given the repeated statements in the Qurʾān that God "*istawā ilā l-samāʾ*" (2:29 and 41:11) and "*istawā ʿalā l-ʿarsh*" (7:54 and often).

23. So that the zodiacal constellations have adorned themselves for him, the planets have come together[37] to serve him, the Milky Way has taken refuge in his glory, and the brilliant Pleides have rejoiced in his splendid achievements?
24. Indeed, how can one have no regard for someone who if he wished could congeal the air, materialize the sunbeams,[38]
25. Undo the structures of the firmament, reconcile fire and water,
26. Dim the light of sun and moon, spare them the trouble of moving and traveling,
27. Block the nostrils of the turbulent winds, close the eyelids of the flashing lightning,
28. Cut off the tongues of the thunder with the sword of his threat, string the rain streaming from the clouds like a strand of pearls,
29. Rid the earth of the assaults of earthquakes, banish with his sound judgment the descending doom,[39]
30. Make Satan himself appear in the guise of a man, daub the eyes of the houris with the forms of ghouls,
31. Cause the seas to bring forth lush herbage, and garb the night in the light of day?
32. And why does he not realize that forsaking one of such power as this is sheer error, and cutting off relations with one of such attributes is sheer folly,
33. And that the good will of one capable of such miracles would be worth purchasing with one's very life and soul,
34. And the affection of one who brings forth such marvels should be sought with fasting and prayer,
35. And anyone who would not attach himself to him with a firm bond is a beast without blemish,[40] and anyone who would not take refuge in his shade remains cut off without protection?
36. And why does he not summon back his wandering judgment and realize that so long as he does not renew this connection he is being senseless, and seek to restore his absent intellect and understand that so long as he maintains this separation he is fooling himself?

---

[37] *Takawkabat*, unattested in the lexical resources available to me. I take this as a denominative verb from *kawkaba*, "group of people" (*jamāʿa min al-nās*) according to various lexicographers.

[38] More literally, "corporealize the dust particles visible only in a brilliant sunbeam."

[39] The precise point of this phrase eludes me, and I do not understand the basis for al-Yazdādī's ecstatic comment on it (*Kamāl-balāgha*, 27) noting the brilliance of putting it in parallel with the "assaults of earthquakes."

[40] This is an echo of Qurʾān 2:71 ("*lā shiyata fīhā*"), in the story of the Red Heifer, followed later in the verse by the phrase "they slaughtered it" (*fa-dhabaḥūhā*).

37. I believe that he considers doing without me wealth and self-sufficiency, not knowing that his perverse behavior toward me means attrition and affliction (for him),
38. And imagines that his status and dignity suffice for him, glorying in his heaven and earth,
39. And not realizing that I am a whole to his part, and a height compared to his breadth,
40. And that the strength of the wing lies in the forefeathers and those immediately below them, and what makes spears effective are their iron points and the necks of the shafts to which they are attached.
41. My pressing of my lord, seeking restoration of relations with him and rectification of his qualities,
42. And my recounting these wonders to him, and eager attempt to persuade him to incline from one side to another,
43. Is not because I am someone who pursues one who avoids contact with him, or yearns for one who is averse to his friendship,
44. Or plants a firm relation with one who strikes at the root of his dignity, or turns his face toward one who does not make him his *qibla*,
45. For if I knew that the ground did not lap up the dust of my feet I would deny it my side, and that the sky did not long to kiss the top of my head I would turn my heart from any thought of it;
46. But rather I am loath to see his throat denuded of the necklaces of praise, and his forehead lacking the diadem of glory,
47. And the face of faithfulness blackened by his seizing its hand, and the foundation of fraternity demolished by his bruising its arm,
48. And I am not pleased that he should clothe the light of his noble deeds with the blemishes of obscurity, and permit the ascending stars of his merits to set.
49. So if my lord prefers dying embers to a blazing fire, and non-existence to existence,
50. And descends from the heights to the depths, and from a peak to a plain,
51. And removes himself in his aversion, and persists in his aloofness,
52. And inclines to weariness (with our relationship), and does not warm himself at the fire of intimacy,
53. I will unbend my little finger crooked in his honor,[41] and distract my thoughts from being occupied with him,

[41] On this phrase – derived from a system of finger-counting in which crooking the little finger signifies "one," so that the gesture came to mean "he is Number One (in his field)" – see R. Dozy, *Supplément aux dictionnaires arabes* (Leiden, 1881), s.v. *khinṣir*.

54. Indeed I will wipe all recollection of him from the page of my heart, and consider his friendship one of those things swept by the torrent down the wadi.
For if ties with you become frayed, there is someone (else) to connect to among the people *
And a place in the world to move to from the abode of hostility.

This letter is obviously carefully structured. The initial *qarīna*, expressing a general sentiment, sets the stage, so to speak:

> *al-insānu khuliqa alūfā / wa-ṭubiʿa ʿaṭūfā*
>
> Man was created sociable, and given a naturally affectionate disposition.

(Qābūs, by the way, unlike some of his contemporaries, seems to avoid three-phrase *sajʿ*-elements.) This short sentence sets the topic. *Qarīna* **2** then poses the first of the relentless series of questions that take up a full two thirds of the letter:

> *fa-mā li-l-iṣbahbadh sayyidī lā yuḥnā ʿūduh /wa-lā yurjā ʿawduh*
>
> Wherefore, then can my lord the Iṣbahbadh's wood not be bent, nor his return (to his former affection) be hoped for?

This sentence continues in the third *qarīna*, with two more phrases introduced with *wa-lā*, "and not." A second set of questions begins with *qarīna* 4, beginning with *a-min* and *am min*, "is...from...or...from?" repeated in both phrases of two *qarīna*s. The rhythm set up begins to build with the next set of questions, *mā hādhā...wa-mā hādhā*, "what is this...?" each extending through both phrases of *four qarāʾin*, with a changing internal structure. Then we have three questions with *ayna...wa-ayna*, "where?" also each extending through an entire *qarīna*, and then a further heightening with four questions beginning with *kayfa*, "how?" each the length of *two qarīna*s, and a fifth extending over *three qarīna*s, and then a sixth, introduced with *bal kayfa*, "*indeed* how...?" which stretches for no less than eight *qarīna*s. Finally, the first part of the letter ends with a kind of winding down: two questions with *lima*, "why?", the first four *qarīna*s in length and the second only a single *qarīna*.

The rest of the letter, from *qarīna* 37 to the end, is composed of four long and complex sentences; again, the number of parallel phrases tends to increase, as in *qarīna*s 49 through 52, with a relatively abrupt conclusion in 53 and 54, capped with a single line of verse as a conclusion.

Of course, within this overarching structure there is much more going on rhetorically as well. Particularly prominent is the heavy use of semantic parallelism, which contributes to the syntactic lucidity but also has its own rhythm. Thus *qarīna*s 6-9 give us four verbal nouns, of which the first three (*ikhtiyār*, *tamyīz*, *raʾy*) are technical (theological and philosophical) terms, but the fourth (*iʿrāḍ*) is not technical at all and not strictly parallel to the other three; and this pattern is repeated in *qarīna*s 10-12, with *ṭabʿ* and *khulq* as semantic parallels followed by the more specific but not parallel *ḥayāʾ*. *Qarīna*s 13-31 (*kayfa...wa-kayfa...bal kayfa*) are more regular, the verbs in their primary clauses being *all* strictly parallel (with the sense of "turning away," "doing without," or "disdaining": *yuzhad*, *yuhjar*, *yustaghnā*, *yuʿraḍ*, *yuzhā*, *yuhawwan*); and so also *qarīna*s 37-40, where we find the parallel verbs referring to cognition *yuqaddir*, *lā yadrī*, *yakhāl*, and *lā yashʿur*. But then in *qarīna*s 46-47 the initial pattern of parallels-plus-final-non-parallel reappears with the anatomical terms *naḥr*, *jabīn*, and *wajh* followed by the non-anatomical *rukn*. All this is clearly not accidental.

When such semantic parallelism simultaneously involves imagery, it constitutes the figure that later theorists termed *murāʿāt al-naẓīr*, of which there are striking examples in the "*kayfa*" section of the latter. This section exhibits a particular density of other rhetorical devices as well and will serve to show how both figures and phraseology contribute to the dynamic rhythm. In *qarīna*s 17-18, the *murāʿāt al-naẓīr* of the martial vocabulary (*khayl*, *anṣār*, *haraba*, *makāʾid*, *ṭalaba*, *marāṣid*) is conjoined with the figure *al-laff wa-l-nashr* (also a later term), where two sets of terms are put in parallel and the listener or reader is expected to match them up (here, *khayl* and *makāʾid*, and *anṣār* and *marāṣid*, respectively).[42] In 19 we have triple and then double *tajnīs*, paronomasia (*yuʿraḍ*, *tuʿriḍ*, *iʿrāḍ*, and *tanqabiḍ*, *inqibāḍ*), and in 20 double and then triple *tajnīs* (*iqbāl*, *aqbal*, and *ahall*, *hilāl*, *tahallal*). The introduction in 20 of the "star" and the "crescent moon" prepares the way for the cosmlogical imagery of 21 and 22, with the "earth," "heavens," "celestial sphere," and "star-streaked sky," climaxing in 23 with a combination of *tajnīs* and *murāʿāt al-naẓīr*, where, uniquely in this letter, the *sajʿ* itself is abandoned and replaced by the *murāʿāt al-naẓīr* of zodiacal constellations, planets, Milky Way, and Pleiades, while the buildup continues by the expansion of the middle of each succeeding phrase, from *lah*, "for him," to *li-ʿibādatih*, "to serve him," to *li-ʿizzatih*, "in his glory," to the *triple tajnīs* (without *ishtiqāq*) of the last phrase (*athrat*, *maʾāthir*, *thurayyā*). At this point, as the reader – or listener – assumes that the climax has been reached and the tension can go no higher, Qābūs introduces his final *bal kayfa*, "indeed how?", followed by a cascade of sixteen short phrases in rapid succession, containing a series of images from the natural world (coming back down to earth here) exploited for the most extravagant self-praise.

Two related points can be made about this kind of writing. First, it is intensely linear. The content, or "*maʿnā*" in the larger sense, while simple and straightforward, and thus to a large extent predictable, does not conform to a full predetermined structure – unlike, for instance, in the classical *qaṣīda*, where the poet may assume his audience's expectations of *nasīb*, *riḥla*, and *madīḥ* sections, or whatever variations thereof may have become standard in a given period. Rather, expectations are created as the letter-writer proceeds, by means of what he has al-

42 Both *murāʿāt al-naẓīr* and *al-laff wa-l-nashr* are briefly defined and illustrated in al-Sakkākī, *Miftāḥ al-ʿulūm* (ed. Nuʿaym Zarzūr, Beirut, 1984), 424f.

ready said; the listener or reader is led to ask (or guess) "what is coming next?" rather than "how is he going to complete this section, and make his transition to the next?" The "anticipation" of cosmological imagery in the above example is one of several ways in which Qābūs plays with this kind of expectation. Besides the basic technique throughout, line by line, of fulfilling – or thwarting and trumping – the audience's expectations of another parallel phrase and another rhyme word, Qābūs on occasion will link phrases with a single *lafẓ*, as in the second half of *qarīna* 35:

> *wa-man lam yaʾwi minhu ilā ẓillin ẓalla ṣarīman lā ʿiṣmata lah*
>
> And anyone who would not take refuge in his shade remains cut off without protection

where *ẓill/ẓall* carries one over the syntactic break in the phrase (unlike, of course, the otherwise syntactically and rhythmically parallel first half of the *qarīna*). Al-Yazdādī also singles out as one of Qābūs's "new" figures what he calls "*ibdāʿ al-qarāʾin*," where the second half of a *qarīna* startles the audience with an originality outdoing the first half and thwarting its expectation of what will balance the latter, as in the example (from a different letter)

> *fa-l-shaykhu man lā yanṭaliqu fī lawmihi lisānu lāʾim / wa-lā tattajihu ʿalayhi ẓinnatun illā min ẓālim*
>
> And the shaykh is one in blame of whom no blamer's tongue wags, and and against whom no suspicious thoughts are directed except from an unjust person[43]

where the "*illā*" is completely unexpected, and gives the parallelism a new twist, not to mention the complex alliteration of *lawm-lāʾim-ẓinna-ẓālim*. A final example of how Qābūs plays with audience expectations can be seen in *qarīna* 10:

> *ayna l-ṭabʿu lladhī huwa li-l-ṣudūdi ṣadūd / wa-li-l-taʾallufi alūfun wadūd*
>
> Where is the character which is averse to aversion, and congenial and amicable to congeniality?

Here the hearer or reader is caught between expecting a second *tajnīs*-pair and the necessary *sajʿ* (if he can think fast enough), and gets both, with *muqābala* (paired synonymity) and *luzūm mā lā yalzam* (double rhyme) on top of the fully predictable *muṭābaqa* (antithesis) of *ṣudūd* and *taʾalluf.*

Linearity and the kinds of expectations it involves is also central to the more general question of the respective lengths of the pairs of balanced phrases. Abū Hilāl al-ʿAskarī echoes a common opinion when he says

> If it is possible to make the two phrases equal in length, it is nicer; if not, then the second phrase should be longer

but then goes on to say

---

43 Al-Yazdādī, *Kamāl al-balāgha*, 20, 35.

> Still, it often happens in the parallelism of eloquent writers that the second phrase is shorter, and this is even frequent in the speech of the Prophet[44]

and gives some examples. From the examples I have already given, it should be clear that this is a question of rhythm, played out against expectations, and variation in the respective lengths of paired phrases is one way of articulating a discourse at a level greater than that of single lines. Abū Hilāl has some sense here that the possibilities are far more complex than a simple prescription by the critics can encompass.

The second point to be made here is that it is precisely the rhetorical expectations of the hearer or reader that make this kind of writing work, and that any - expectations with regard to *content* must be fulfilled at a fairly elementary level if he is not going to be distracted *from* the rhetoric. To put it more simply: in any culture, prose rhetoric is going to flourish most effectively and naturally in forms of discourse in which the *information* to be conveyed is most predictable. Where do we find rhetoric most concentrated in Arabic prose before the fourth/tenth century? Leaving aside the Qur'ān, one would have to say: sermons and formal documents. On the whole, sermons do not convey startling information to their audiences; nor do documents of investiture and the like. In both cases, the effect lies not in what is said but how it is said. Not surprisingly, the most famous Arabic rhetorical prose outside the chanceries in the late fourth/tenth century was that of the sermons of Ibn Nubāta al-Fāriqī (d. 374/984) (which, according to Ibn al-Athīr two centuries later, were as beloved as Ḥarīrī's *Maqāmāt*[45]). As indicated in the comments above on the vagueness of all the letters of this period, and the consequent difficulty in utilizing them as historical sources, there was actually pressure to *reduce* their informational content. The idea is best expressed, again, by Abū Hilāl, in his *Kitāb al-Ṣināʿatayn*:

> The point does not lie in presenting the *maʿānī*, for the *maʿānī* are known, by Arabs and non-Arabs, villagers and Bedouin. Rather, it lies in the excellence and limpidity of the *lafẓ*, its beauty and splendor, purity and refinement, and degree of smoothness and polish, with proper construction and articulation, and freedom from distortion in structure and composition. All that is demanded of the *maʿnā* is that it be correct, but that is not sufficient for the *lafẓ*, which must also be characterized by the attributes which we have described.[46]

---

44 Abū Hilāl al-ʿAskarī, *Kitāb al-Ṣināʿatayn al-kitāba wa-l-shiʿr*, ed. Mufīd Qamīḥa (Beirut, 1989), 288. See also, for the views of Ibn al-Athīr in his *al-Mathal al-sā'ir*, Stewart, "*Sajʿ*," 113-7, and Gully and Hinde, "Qābūs," 182f.

45 Ḍiyā' al-Dīn Ibn al-Athīr, *al-Mathal al-sā'ir fī adab al-kātib wa-l-shāʿir*, ed. Aḥmad al-Ḥūfī and Badawī Ṭabāna (Cairo, n.d.), I, 215. (Ibn al-Athīr did not, however, share his contemporaries' enthusiasm with regard to either author.) On Ibn Nubāta (a collection of whose sermons is extant and has been published) see *EI2*, s.v.

46 Abū Hilāl al-ʿAskarī, *al-Ṣināʿatayn*, 72. Abū Hilāl is not, however, altogether consistent in his view of *lafẓ* and *maʿnā*; see Goerge J. Kanazi, *Studies in the Kitāb aṣ-Ṣināʿatayn of Abū Hilāl al-ʿAskarī* (Leiden, 1989), 93.

If the art lies in working gracefully and elegantly within constraints – many of them self-imposed – the *maʿnā*, in the larger sense of informational content, is the most basic of these constraints, but at the same time the least interesting. That the letter convey a meaning, and a meaning appropriate to the *gharaḍ*, is the *sine qua non*; but with this basic condition fulfilled, it is the rhetoric that counts.

At this point, an appeal to a musical analogy is virtually irresistible. Jaroslav Stetkevych has written compellingly on the analogy of the *qaṣīda* to the sonata form.[47] For rhetorical prose, the importance of *linearity* stressed here seems less reminiscent of classical Western music than of the baroque. Without attempting here to elaborate further, I would simply suggest that the kind of pleasure one derives from hearing or reading an elegant epistle is quite similar in nature to that derived from listening to Bach, in the rich texture of interlaced patterns and the constant interplay of "where is this going?" and "what a perfect twist!" And such thoughts lead me yet further, to use – or indeed, I would grant, abuse – a famous statement by Walter Pater, where he says,

> Art, then, is thus always striving to be independent of the mere intelligence, to become a matter of pure perception, to get rid of its responsibilities to its subject or material; the ideal examples of poetry and painting being those in which the constituent elements of the composition are so welded together, that the material or subject no longer strikes the intellect only...It is the art of music which most completely realizes this artistic ideal, this perfect identification of matter and form. In its consummate moments, the end is not distinct from the means, the form from the matter, the subject from the expression; they inhere in and completely saturate each other; and to it, therefore, to the condition of its perfect moments, all the arts may be supposed constantly to tend and aspire. Music, then, and not poetry, as is so often supposed, is the true type or measure of perfected art.[48]

I am here *abusing* Pater because, of course, he is speaking of a perfect *fusion* of matter and form, not the subservience of the former to the latter; but what he means by the "matter" of music is not clear from his own words, and I am not sufficiently versed in nineteenth-century aesthetics to attempt a guess, although I am unable to suppress a suspicious shudder when I think of some of his own musical contemporaries. The problem of reducing literature (or painting) to music, of course, is that music must reach outside its proper field to "mean," while literature has no choice but to "mean;" program music finds its own resources insufficient, while purely rhetorical prose fails to take advantage of its own inherent resources. Nevertheless, I think the delights of "musical prose" cannot be gainsaid, and the degree to which medieval Arabs revelled in it can hardly be underestimated.

---

47 Jaroslav Stetkevych, *The Zephyrs of Najd: The Poetics of Nostalgia in the Classical Arabic Nasib* (Chicago, 1993), 16-25.

48 Walter Pater, *The Renaissance* (New York, 1959), 97f.

Yet even they – and even Qābūs – found the radical reduction of content I have described unsatisfactory, and the same generation which produced such exquisite verbal music began to look for ways to expand their horizons. After all, no matter how clever your tropes, there are only so many ways to say "I wish you would make up with me" or "I was sorry to hear that your mother died." How much more clever it would be to use all one's rhetorical resources to *say* something, thus imposing yet another constraint to deal with elegantly! In fact, I think we can point to three simultaneous experiments in this direction, with varying degrees of success. Qābūs tried his hand at what al-Yazdādī calls "philosophical letters," of which he appends five to his collection. These deal with the following subjects: a description of the world and its creation; an argument that all animals, not only man, possess rational souls; a refutation of astrology; a eulogy of the Prophet and the four rightly-guided caliphs (meant, in part, as an anti-Shiᶜite polemic); and a provocative attack on the customary use of the *kunya* as a form of address. Despite their elegance, in none of these letters is Qābūs able to maintain the degree of rhetorical complexity displayed in his more conventional *rasāʾil*.

The real challenge, not seriously confronted by Qābūs, was the use of this sort of prose in *narrative*, where new and unexpected information must be constantly conveyed. Two authors, both intimates of Qābūs, attempted it, in ways which were ultimately far more influential than his "philosophical letters." Al-ᶜUtbī (d. after 413/1022), in his *Kitāb al-Yamīnī*, composed a laudatory history-cum-biography of the sultan Maḥmūd of Ghazna and his rise to power. Drawing from conventions of poetic *madīḥ*, as well as such set pieces as victory proclamations (*kutub fatḥ*) with their already-developed techniques for narrating the outcomes of battles (although, to be sure, in terms distressingly vague to modern historians), al-ᶜUtbī created a form which was to influence such later authors as ᶜImād al-Dīn al-Iṣfahānī, al-Qāḍī al-Fāḍil, and innumerable Persian historians – to the despair of their modern successors.[49]

But most noteworthy, and most successful, of all was, of course, the invention by Badīᶜ al-Zamān al-Hamadhānī of the *Maqāmāt*. Picaresque anecdotal literature offered a form with an amusing, and sufficiently simple, narrative line, with plenty of occasions for static set-pieces. Whatever its historical development, the word *maqāma* serves as a reminder that most of these little narratives are built around a set speech, often a sermon, in which predictable content is not allowed to interfere with the profusion of rhetoric. And the plots themselves essentially play with the reader's expectations in a way strictly comparable to that of the rhetoric; we know that the sermonizer is going to turn out in the end to be the old reprobate Abū l-Fatḥ, and if he doesn't, or if he occasionally ends up as victim rather than victimizer, well, that is just one more – delightful – rhetorical trick.

49 al-ᶜUtbī, *al-Yamīnī*, ed. Iḥsān Zanūn al-Thāmirī, Beirut, 2004. See also *EI2*, s.v. al-ᶜUtbī (C. E. Bosworth), noting that al-ᶜUtbī worked for a time early in his career as a secretary to Qābūs.

# Rhetorical Values in Buyid Persia According to Badīᶜ al-Zamān al-Hamadhānī

*Vahid Behmardi (Lebanese American University)*

By the beginning of the 4th/10th century, and geographically in the eastern regions of the Islamic Empire which was ruled by the Abbasid dynasty, Arabic literature, in its broad sense, was divided into two major categories: the first is what may be called 'sciences of literature' or 'sciences of the Arabic language', on the one hand, and 'pure literature', on the other. The former involves literary criticism, rhetoric, prosody, philology, lexicology, ontology and the like, whereas the latter includes poetry and artistic prose, mainly in the form of epistles or letters. The *maqāma* genre, which was introduced by Badīᶜ al-Zamān al-Hamadhānī, can well fit into the second category.

Sciences of rhetoric – *ᶜulūm al-balāgha* – had a substantial material at hand to deal with. However, the theories that are found in the works on literary aesthetics of that age, and which were composed mostly by Iranian rhetoricians, do not portray the literary values of their own society and age. Apparently, they did not consider the Arabic poetry of their contemporaries and, particularly, those who belonged to non-Arabic speaking societies as adequate enough for their purpose.

ᶜAbd al-Qāhir al-Jurjānī, for example, rarely refers in *Asrār al-Balāgha* to the poetry of his contemporary countrymen. Interestingly, when he quotes a hemistich by Abū Bakr al-Khwārizmī, he does that in order to give an example of bad poetry on which he comments: *kalāmun lā yaḥsulu minhu ᶜalā tāʾil* (A speech of no avail).[1] Thus, the Arabic literary product of Persia was undermined by literary critics in favor of the literature of the Arabs.[2] It is worth mentioning that men of letters in the Iranian society under the Buyids were fully aware of the contemporary trends of literary criticism. Some of them, besides being primarily poets or men of letters, were also critics. Al-Ṣāḥib b. ᶜAbbād, who was a man of letters, a poet, a philologist and a critic of literature is one such illustrious figure.

On the other hand, the literature of Arab poets and writers in Syria and Iraq, which formed the main substance for rhetorical sciences and literary criticism, varied in many respects from the literature that was produced in the eastern provinces of the Abbasid Caliphate, and which was neglected by rhetoricians. Therefore, in order to formulate a relatively accurate picture of the literary es-

---

1 Jurjānī, 'Abd al-Qāhir; *Asrār al-balāgha*, el. H. Ritter, Istanbul, 1958. p.66.

2 For more details on the major aspects of literary criticism in the 4th/10th century, see Abbas, Ihsan; *Tārīkh al-naqd al-adabī ᶜind al-ᶜarab*, Beirut, 4th edition, 1983. pp. 127-357; and Gustave E. von Grunebaum, *Themes in Medieval Arabic Literature*, London, 1981. chap. VIII.

thetical values and ideals that were cherished by Iranian men of letters in the 4th/10th century, it is almost imperative to refer to the literary works of those literatures rather than the works on rhetoric. In other words, the rhetorical values in Buyid Persia are found in "literature" and not in the "sciences of literature". The evaluation of literature that one examines in works of pure literature reveals exclusive rhetorical values that are independent from what is found in the works of traditional rhetoricians.

Badīᶜ al-Zamān al-Hamadhānī is taken here as a representative example of a writer and a poet who reflects, in his fictional work, the *Maqāmāt*, and also in his factual writings, the *Rasāʾil*, the rhetorical values which were upheld by men of letters in Iran during the Buyid age. These works by Hamadhānī reflect a relatively clear viewpoint on what was considered by the literati, then and there, as eloquent, or even as popular and unpopular literature with special emphasis on prose rather than poetry.

## *Literature in General:*

The idea of novelty and classicism in Arabic literature is an age-old controversial question, which has always resulted in schism amidst critics and a general state of disagreement among all those who dealt with literature. In the early Abbasid age, due to the rise of works on anthology and philology, anthologists and philologists established a criterion that specifies novelty and classicism in Arabic poetry. They regarded the poets who lived during the Umayyad age as the last heirs and producers of pure antiquity, whereas their Abbasid successors were the modern ones whose poetry was not regarded as genuine material for theories of eloquence or matters of philology.

Hamadhānī, in his turn, was not left out of the on-going debate on the question of novelty and classicism. He was a student of Aḥmad Ibn Fāris who, despite his reputation as an orthodox linguist, was a reformist and propagandist for renovation in literature. In a letter, which he wrote to Muḥammad b. Saᶜīd al-Kātib,[3] Ibn Fāris brings forth his opinion on the question of novelty, and attacks the conservative doctors who opposed renovation in the established literature of the Arabians, claiming, as they actually did, that what was produced by their predecessors was so perfect that no new elements or aspects could or should be added. Ibn Fāris refutes this dogma and argues that as long as people and circumstances are in a process of change, there will always be enough room for the innovation of new literary material. He even goes further to assert that much of what had been introduced by the 'latter ones' – *al-muta'khkhirūn* – can be, in many respects, more profound than that which has been inherited from the predecessors.

---

3 Thaᶜālibī, Abū anṣūr ᶜAbd al-Malik; *Yatīmat al-dahr*, ed. M. Qumaiha, Beirut, 1983. vol. III. pp. 463-468.

Such a consideration of literature as a progressive aspect of human culture, led to the invention of new literary works in Iran which were novel and unique in their time. Hamadhānī was one of those prose writers who followed the course of his tutor Ibn Fāris. Although Shawqi Daif regards the reform in the Abbasid age as a 'reform of old motifs',[4] it is noteworthy that, in the above mentioned letter, Ibn Fāris attacks Abū Tammām; and Hamadhānī, in his *Maqāmāt*, does the same in regard to Jāḥiẓ. This can be seen as a revolt against what was seen as perfect models of Arabic literature.

In the *Maqāma of Poesie*, ᶜIsā b. Hishām asks Iskandarī, who is presented as a master of poetry, about his opinion on modern and ancient poets. Iskandarī's answer is the following:[5]

> The language of the ancients is nobler and they are more possessive of denotations, whereas the modern's artifice [in composition] is more refined – *altafu ṣunᶜan* – and their weaving [of words] more elegant (*araqqu nasjan*).

This is a moderate judgment that could be acceptable, more or less, to advocates of novelty as well as to patrons of classicism. In fact, Hamadhānī did not rule out the nobility, i.e. innateness, of ancient poets in regard to their language. However, what Iskandarī, the mouthpiece of Hamadhānī, mentions in the *maqāma* about denotations, remains questionable.

Concerning Iskandarī's view on what was then modern literature; he gives an accurate description in two words: *al-ṣanᶜa wal-nasj* – craftsmanship and weaving [of words]; two terms that pertain to the external form of literature. This definition of poetry and poets in the 4th/10th century can be reasonably applied to prose as much as it applies to poetry. Hamadhānī can be introduced in this respect as an exemplar of that literary trend, and one of its outstanding advocates.

Artifice – *ṣanᶜa* – is defined as being the style of diversification in expression and the introduction of several similes and metaphors for one substantive.[6] This definition of *ṣanᶜa* is consistent with the characteristic patterns of composition which were introduced into Arabic by the Arabicized Persians since the days of Ibn al-ᶜAmīd. Many scholars have confirmed the role of the Persian scribes in the evolution of artifice in Arabic prose.[7] Others have gone further to say that

---

4 See Daif, Sh., *al-ᶜAṣr al-ᶜabbāsī al-awwal*, Cairo, 7th ed., n.d.. p.159; *al-ᶜAsr al-ᶜabbāsī al-thānī*, Cairo, 3rd ed., n.d.. p.203.

5 To reflect the exact and accurate statement in the above maqāma, Prendergast's translation (*Maqāmāt Badīᶜ al-Zamān*, trans. W.J. Prendergast, London, 1973. p.29), which reads: "The language of the ancients is nobler and their themes more delightful, whereas the conceits of the moderns are more refined and their style more elegant", has been slightly altered. The original Arabic (in M. Abduh's edition, *Maqāmāt Badīᶜ al-Zamān,* Beirut, 1973. p.8) contains specific terms which need to be translated literally in order to preserve the exact significance of the two major terms: *ṣanᶜa* and *nasj.*

6 Bustani, B., *Muḥīt al-muḥīt*, Beirut, 1977. p.521.

7 cf. Khaffaji, Muhammad, *al-Ādāb al-ᶜarabīyya fī al-ᶜaṣr al-ᶜabbāsī*, Cairo, 1975. PP. 40,48.

Hamadhānī, for example, has given Arabic form to Persian themes in his poetry.[8] R. N. Frye believes that 'the perfection of Arabic poetry by the tenth century AD had become almost artificial ... Arabic literature had become very sophisticated but had lost its natural quality and its spontaneous character'.[9] Whatever the case may be, Persians, throughout their literary history, were keen on the use of synonymous similes, duplication in speech and metaphors which lead, as a rule, to prolixity and exaggeration – an almost missing feature in typical writings of native Arabs. Iskandarī, in the *Maqāma* of Jāḥiẓ, attacked al-Jāḥiẓ because his prose did not possess many metaphors – *qalīl al-istiᶜārāt* – and lacked artifice expressions – *lafẓatun maṣnūᶜatun* -.[10] G. Lazard links the refinement of the Iranian courts – *ḥaḍarāt* – in the Buyid period to the literary styles during that age by saying that:[11]

> Manṭiqī of Ray, for example, one of the protégées of the Sāḥib who appreciated his work, is found to have indulged in subtle figures of speech, in contrast with the simplicity of the early masters. This taste for artifice is perhaps less a characteristic of the poet himself than of the court of Ray, where refinements of style were highly esteemed. It was before the Sāḥib that Badīᶜ al-Zamān al- Hamadhānī, the future author of the *Maqāmāt* in Arabic, famous for their florid style, made his first appearance.

To sum up the question of Hamadhānī 's view on literary novelty; we can conclude from what he says in the *Maqāmāt* and the *Rasāʾil* that he, as a writer, was typical of his age, one which was characterized as the age of outer ornamentation in speech. To put it in Hamadhānī 's own words 'weaving words' became such a delicate task for writers to the extent that writing prose or composing poetry became a 'craft' and thus it was called *ṣanᶜa*;[12] something that can be compared to the delicate weaving of a Persian silk carpet.

Hamadhānī's theory of rhetorical writing reflects the general approach of the Iranian literati in the 4th/10th century to rhetoric. The *Maqāma* of Jāḥiẓ provides us with a relatively clear picture of the concept of eulogy at Hamadhānī's age and in his society. "Verily" Iskandarī claims, "Jāḥiẓ limps in one department of rhetoric and halts in the other".[13] Then he goes on to expand this particular point by saying that the true eloquent man is the one "whose poetry does not detract from his prose and whose prose is not ashamed of his verse".[14] Hamadhānī established the trend of alternating poetry and prose in Arabic literature when he invented

---

8 Kik, V., *Taʾthīr-i farhang-i ᶜarab dar ashᶜār-I manūchihrīy-i dāmghānī*, Beirut, 1971. p.30.

9 Frye, R., *The Golden Age of Persia*, London, 1988. p.124.

10 Abduh, *Maqāmāt*, pp. 75,76.

11 Lazard, G., 'Rise of the New Persian Language' in *The Cambridge History of Iran*, vol.IV, ed. R. Frye, Cambridge University Press, 1975. p.619.

12 Daif differentiated between *taṣnīᶜ* and *taṣannuᶜ*; both mean artificiality, but the latter signifies extravagance in that direction. *Taṣannuᶜ* is regarded by Daif as the upshot of *taṣnīᶜ*. Hamadhānī, in the author's opinion, belonged to both schools. He was the heir of *taṣnīᶜ* and the exponent of *taṣannuᶜ*. (see Daif, Sh., *al-Fann wa-madhāhibuh fī al-nathr al-ᶜarabī*, Cairo, 10th edit., n.d.. p.242.)

13 Prendergast, *Maqāmāt*, p.72.

14 Ibid., p.72.

the *maqāma* genre. This was the first real step towards demolishing the boundaries between poetry and prose. Before the *maqāma* was introduced, several works of prose existed which included poetry, but these were adoptions from other poets. Before Hamadhānī, we do not come across any work in Arabic literature that was composed, equally and contingently, of prose and poetry. In Hamadhānī's age, major literators were poets as well as men of letters. However, none of them composed a work of alternate poetry and prose. This style may be regarded as a peculiar feature of the *maqāma*. Even Hamadhānī, himself, did not apply this theory on his letters and set it aside as a distinctive feature of his *maqāma* genre. The best illustration of this style was the fictional figure of Iskandarī, the major character of the *Maqāmāt*, who mastered both branches of literature. The *Maqāma* of Exhortation is most explicit in this respect,[15] where Iskandarī, acting the role of a preacher, gives a sermon in verse and prose in an interpenetrated form. What may be significant about the structure of the sermon is the relative balance between the number of verses, on the one hand, and the number of the sentences in the interposing prose, on the other.

Besides the pattern of bringing together prose and poetry in an alternative manner, Hamadhānī went further in adjoining together the two frames of composition by introducing a new art form in epistolary literature which Qalqashandi calls: *fann al-imtizāj* – the art of intermingling -,[16] which means the twinning of verse and prose in the same text without any apparent distinction between them, as is the case in the *maqāma*. Several such examples can be found among Hamadhānī 's letters.[17] One example is a letter which he wrote to Khwārizmī, and can be regarded as a good example of *fann al-imtizāj*. It reads as follows (The parts between parentheses signalize the hemistiches):[18]

> My condition [in longing] to approach the Master {is like [the condition of] the intoxicated man who is tilted by wine}, and in my gratification to his encounter [I am] {like a bird which trembles under raindrops}, and for attaining his amity, [I hope to be] {like the wine which mixes with cold fresh water}, and in my delight by seeing him, I am {like the damp bough which shakes in the hot wind of summer}.

In the above passage, each two consecutive hemistiches (which are pointed out by parentheses) have the same rhyme, and the four have the same meter. It is very likely that Hamadhānī was the inventor of this style because none of the examples on *fann al-imtizāj*, which Qalqashandī introduces in *Ṣubḥ al-aʿshā*, predates the time of Hamadhānī.

In addition to the above remarks that were mentioned earlier on the characteristics of a perfect writer, Hamadhānī, through Iskandarī's words, points out to

---

15 Ibid., pp.104-110.
16 Qalqashandī, Aḥmad; *Ṣubḥ al-aʿshā fī ṣināʿat al-inshā*, Cairo, 1913-22. vol.I, p.280.
17 See *Rasāʾil Badīʿ al-Zamān*, Beirut, n.d.. pp.128, 129, 139- 141, 292, 375.
18 Ibid., p.128, 129.

what he thought is eloquent by exhibiting the defects in Jāḥiẓ's prose according to his evaluation. They consist of "far-fetched allusions, a paucity of metaphors and simple expressions. He is tied down to the simple language he uses, and avoids and shrinks difficult words".[19] Iskandarī goes on by asking ʿIsā: "Have you ever heard of a rhetorical expression of his or of any recondite words?"[20]

In the above statement, Hamadhānī is referring to what he regards as seven rhetorical defects: (a) far-fetched allusions – *baʿīd al-ishārāt* – which implies little speech with far implications;[21] a literary phenomenon which the Arabs were reputed to be fond of, whereas the Persians were reputed for their prolixity in composition; (b) paucity of metaphors – *qalīl al-istiʿārāt* -; (c) simple expressions – *qarīb al-ʿibārāt* – which is an indication to the use of popular patterns of speech; (d) tied down to simple language – *ʿuryān al-kalām* – which is the style that does not possess ornamentations; (e) shrinks difficult words – *nafurun min muʿtāṣih* -; (f) lack of rhetorical expression – *lafẓatun maṣnūʿa* -; and (g) lack of recondite words – *kalimatun ghair masmūʿa* -.[22]

The Iranians, however, after introducing their own stylistics into Arabic literature, brought forth their own style of prolixity[23] which aimed at avoiding unfathomable indications as much as possible. Nevertheless, this objective was dissipated in the 4th/10th century when the excessive use of metaphors, difficult words, rhetorical expressions, recondite terms and rhymed speech, as Hamadhānī puts it in the *Maqāma* of Jāḥiẓ, dominated simple expressions and clear language.

The seven points on rhetoric, which Hamadhānī mentions in his criticism of Jāḥiẓ's prose, reflect the main features of the rhetorical and over-decorated Arabic literature that prospered in Iran in Hamadhānī's age. Simplicity was considered a flaw or an artistic frailty among the Iranian literati. It can be suggested that the cause of this phenomenon was the confinement of Arabic literature in Iran within the intelligentsia while the rank and file had no knowledge of Arabic and, thus, the Arabic literature of Iran was not initially addressed to them. As a result, the use of intricate and complicated forms of speech, which befitted the intellectual pride of learned men, became more appreciated. The knowledge of strange and uncommon words and expressions was a precondition for any poet laureate. A story about Al-Sāḥib b. ʿAbbād, which was related by Abu Hayyan al-Tawhidi,[24] shows how the former considered the knowledge of obscure words as a testimony to rhetoric excellence.

---

19 Ibid., p.72.
20 Ibid., p.72.
21 Abduh, *Maqāmāt*, p.75n.
22 According to Abduh's comments, another reading exists for (*kalimatun ghair masmūʿa*) which is (*kalimatun masjūʿa*) -rhymed speech-. See Abduh, *Maqāmāt*, p.76n.
23 It may be argued that Jāḥiẓ, a genuine Arab writer, was prolixious in his style. In fact, Jāḥiẓ was more digressive rather than prolixious.
24 Tawḥīdī, Abū Ḥayyān; *Akhlāq al-wazīrayn*, ed.M. Tunji, Damascus, 1965. pp.482-486.

## *Categories of Literature:*

On three occasions in his letters, Hamadhānī points out the types of literary merits that were cherished by his contemporaries. These were the following:[25]

(1) Memorisation (*ḥifẓ*).
(2) Versification (*naẓm*).
(3) Prose writing (*nathr*).
(4) Improvisation (*badīha*).
(5) Narration (*riwāya*).
(6) Epistolography (*tarassul*).
(7) Prosody (*ʿarūḍ*).

These seven aspects of oral and recorded literature can be summed up in four categories: Memorization and narration (1,5), versification and prosody (2,7), prose writing and epistolography (3,6), and improvisation (4).

Arabs had been acquainted with memorization and narration (*al-ḥifẓ wal-riwāya*) since pre-Islamic times. Poets were sometimes associated with a memorizer and a narrator whose responsibility was to memories and preserve the poems orally. That may be why pre-Islamic poets frequently mention verbs in the dual form such as Amriʾ al-Qais did in the first verse of his *Muʿallaqa*. The two addressees may have been his two companions; the *ḥāfiẓ* and the *rāwiya*. This tradition continued in later ages as a tradition. Memorization and narration became two branches of literary sciences, and talented literatures were upgraded for being skilled in them. For example, Abū Bakr al- Khwārizmī was celebrated as a man of memorization. When Hamadhānī rose to debate with him, the former acknowledged his talent in *ḥifẓ* and sought to challenge him in that area. Ibn Khallikān relates that when Khwārizmī headed to the court of Al-Sāḥib b. ʿAbbād, the chamberlain informed his master about a poet who was asking for admission. Al-Sāḥib ordered his chamberlain to tell the poet that he had taken upon himself not to receive any poet who did not know by heart (*yaḥfaẓ*) twenty thousand verses of Arabic poetry. When Khwārizmī was informed about the condition, he asked the chamberlain to return to his master and investigate whether he means verses of Arabic poetry by men or by women. When al-Sāḥib heard that, he said: "That must be Abū Bakr al- Khwārizmī".[26] Hamadhānī was also known by the sobriquet *al-ḥāfiẓ*, and, thus, stood against another eminent *al-ḥāfiẓ*. Qalqashandī says that, in Hamadhānī's time, he was unique in memorization and was regarded as an example in that respect.[27]

---

25 *Rasāʾil Badīʿ al-Zamān*, pp.42, 65, 66, 80.
26 See Khallikān, Aḥmad b.; *Wafayāt al-aʿyān*, ed. I. Abbas, Beirut, 1968. vol.II, p.355.
27 Qalqashandī, *Ṣubḥ al-aʿshā*, vol.I, p.454.

The second branch of literature which Hamadhānī mentions is related to poetry. However, there is some difference between versification (*naẓm*) and poetry (*shiʿr*). Hamadhānī, in one of his letters, differentiated between *shiʿr* and *naẓm* by relating the first to reading and the second to visualization. In other words, poetry is a concept grasped by the mind, whereas versification is a form seen by the eye.[28] The latter indicates to the form of poetry rather than its content. By admitting that Khwārizmī was superior in versification, Hamadhānī was, probably, asserting Khwārizmī's lack of poetic talent. In fact, he was acknowledging Khwārizmī's merits in forming poetry rather than reciting it. Prosody (*ʿarūḍ*), on the other hand, was founded by al-Khalīl b. Aḥmad al-Farāhīdī as a branch of literary sciences; nevertheless, the major works on prosody were composed in the 4th/10th century and during the following centuries. The Arabicized literators in Iran were more enthusiastic, in this respect, than the Arabs; and composed lengthy works on prosody. The reason for such an enthusiasm by Iranians towards prosody may lie in their being aliens to the language that embodied those meters which they had to adopt. For the Arabs it was an innate aspect of their literary life, while for the Persians, it was acquisitive and, therefore, they had to compose theoretic works on what they had to acquire by learning.

As for prose writing and the art of letters (*al-nathr wal-tarassul*) they can be regarded as the most significant literary aspect of Arabic literature in Iran during the 4th/10th century. Persian literature is renowned for being the literature of poetry, whereas, in respect to the Arabic literature of Iran, the composition of letters became its major art form.

Improvisation (*badīha*) was used as a touchstone for men's literary merits. A talented poet was the one who could compose verses without an advance note. The story of Hamadhānī and al-Sāḥib in this respect is quite an expressive example. In 370 AH al-Sāḥib made a visit to Hamadhan,[29] and at that date Hamadhānī was twelve years old. On that occasion, and in Hamadhan, it happened that al-Sāḥib, according to ʿAwfī,[30] examined his literary talents by asking him to compose some verses. When al-Sāḥib was given the choice of form, he suggested the translation of three Persian verses; in the *sarīʿ* meter and with using the rhyme of *ṭāʾ*. The task was accomplished on the spot.[31] Another account,

28 *Rasāʾil Badīʿ al-Zamān*, p.93.

29 See Ibn al-Athīr, *al-Kāmil fī al-tārīkh*, Beirut, 1967. vol.IX, p.4. C. Pellat mentions a slightly different date. He says, about al-Sāḥib's visit to Hamadhān: "In 369/ 976 he was sent to Hamadhān, to the court of Aḍud al-Dawla, who received him with much honor". (See Pellat, C., 'Al Ṣāḥib Ibn ʿAbbād' in *Abbasid Belles-Lettres*, Cambridge University Press, 1990. p.98.)

30 ʿAwfī, Niẓām al-Dīn; *Lubāb al-albāb*, ed. E.G. Browne, Leiden, 1903. vol.II, p. 17.

31 For the details of Hamadhānī's encounter with al-Ṣāḥib, see M. Shakʿa, *Badʿ al-zamān al-hamadhānī rāʾid al-qiṣṣa al-ʿarabiyya*, Beirut, 1983. pp. 160-164.

which is narrated by Hamadhānī himself,[32] states that one day, while he was in the presence of al-Ṣāḥib, a poet recited a poem on the supremacy of the Persians over the Arabs. Al-Ṣāḥib was infuriated and ordered Hamadhānī to reply, and he, on the spur of the moment, composed an anti-Iranian poem.[33] Al-Ṣāḥib was pleased and the poet commented by saying that had he only heard about him, he would have never believed it![34]

## *Artistic Prose:*

It has already been mentioned that the greater part of Arabic literature in Iran, during the 4th/10th century, was in the various forms of prose. Like poetry, prose was a portrait that reflected the artificiality of its own society. Whereas, V. Danner believes that Iranian writers during the Buyid age had "reached the terminal point in Arabic letters",[35] R. Frye says that, during that age, literature had become so sophisticated in Iran that Arabic "lost its natural quality and its spontaneous character".[36] Frye's opinion and conclusion confirm the difference that existed between the innate Arabic literature of the Arabs, on one hand, and that of the Iranians, on the other. The reason behind this difference between the essence of the Arabic literature of the two nations was that Arabic language and literature for the Iranians was not an inherited cultural factor but rather an innovated and acquired one.

Hamadhānī was regarded as one of the leading men of letters in his age. His literary theory on prose that we come across in his letters reflects some of the main motives that led to the development of prose in the 4th/10th century into a sophisticated job that had to be undertaken by proficient writers rather than ordinary ones. The major opinions of Hamadhānī on prose can be formulated in four propositions:

1- Explicitness of expression.
2- Rhymed prose.
3- Harmony between diction and notion.
4- Impact of letters.

---

32 *Maqāmāt Badīʿ al-Zamān*, Cambridge University Library, MS. Qq.118(8), Ff.128(a,b), 129(a); also as a supplement to the *Maqāmāt* (Istanbul edition, 1298 AH), pp.99, 100.

33 This story sheds light on the nature of the Persian/Arab concept in Iran during the Buyid age. What can be concluded from the incident is that, in that age and in that particular society, 'Arabism' was equal to Islam, whereas, 'Persianism' was the equivalent of Magianism. Hamadhānī was very hostile to the Magians and composed a letter to express and justify his hostility. (See *Rasāʾil Badīʿ al-Zamān*, pp.279-284.) His preference of the Arabs to the Persians, which is mentioned on two occasions in the *Rasāʾil* (pp.279, 310), should be justified in the light of the above theory.

34 Both poems are recorded in the source manuscript.

35 Danner,V. 'Arabic Literature in Iran' in *The Cambridge History of Iran*, ed. R. Frye, Cambridge University Press, 1975. vol.IV, p.593.

36 Frye, R. *The Golden Age of Persia*; p.124.

As for the first point, Hamadhānī regarded vague expressions as hodgepodges (*akhlāṭ*) that "deduction can not perceive and even Hippocrates could not explicate".[37] This type of inexplicit speech was not, probably, uncommon in Hamadhānī 's society since he had ridiculed it in more than one occasion in the *Maqāmāt*. The speech of the cupper[38] in the *Maqāma* of Hilwan can be the best illustration of what Hamadhānī meant by the confusion and inexplicitness of speech. The dialogue between ʿIsā b. Hishām and the cupper who turned to be Iskandarī goes as follows:[39] "Then he [the cupper] came in and said: 'Peace be to thee! From which town art thou?' I replied: 'Qum'. He said: 'May God prosper thee! From a land of plenty of comfort, the city of the Sunnis. I was present there in its cathedral mosque in the month of Ramadan when the lamps had been lit and the *tarāwīḥ* prayers were inaugurated, but, before we knew it, the Nile rose and came and extinguished those lights, but God made me a shoe which I put on when it was green, but there was no embroidery produced on its sleeve. And the boy returned to his mother, after I had performed the evening prayer when the shadow is equal. But how was thy pilgrimage? Didst thou perform all its ceremonies as was incumbent? And thy cried out: 'A marvel! a marvel!' So I looked at the beacon, and how light a thing is was- to the spectators! And I found the *harīsa* in the same state, and I knew that the matter was decreed and pre-ordained by God. And how long this vexation? And to-day, and to-morrow, and Saturday and Sunday, but I will not be tedious, but what is this prating? And I like thee to know that Mubarrad in grammar wields a keen razor, so do not occupy thyself with the speech of the common people..."

It is not surprising to read that, after hearing that delirium, ʿIsā realized that "madness had overtaken" the cupper.

It is quite obvious that the whole speech is made of inconsistent statements and is completely malapropos. The cupper described Qum, a city with exclusively Shiite population, as the city of the Sunnis! The Nile rose in Qum! He prayed the evening prayer when the shadow was equal; that is when it was noon time! The rest of the speech proceeds in an incomprehensible manner which can be attributed to the inconsistency between the statements that construct the whole speech. In a reference to the unity of motif which was considered essential by Hamadhānī in any eloquent prose, he, as a matter of fact, had praised a letter that was sent to him by Abu al-Abbas al-Isfrāʾīnī as "having its beginning pending on its end, and its end united with its beginning".[40]

---

37 *Rasāʾil Badīʿ al-Zamān*, p.384.

38 Prendergast has translated (*ḥajjām*) as barber (*Maqāmāt*, p.133) whereas the exact translation would be cupper.

39 Prendergast, *Maqāmāt*, pp.133,134.

40 *Rasāʾil Badīʿ al-Zamān*, p.273.

This malapropos speech of the cupper can clarify the third point in Hamadhānī 's theories on eloquent prose. Harmony between diction and notion (*al-lafẓ wal-maʿnā*) is a relation similar to that between the soul and body. Notion, although exists potentially without diction, nevertheless, it can be manifested in various forms due to the form of speech that brings it into light. In one occasion, Hamadhānī describes meanings as 'eloquent' (*maʿnā faṣīḥ*)[41] despite the established usage of eloquence (*faṣāḥa*) for expressions (*alfāẓ*) rather than notion (*maʿnā*). This may be an implication to the fact that the content of speech is as important as its form with respect to eloquence. This theory of Hamadhānī contradicts the theory of Jāḥiẓ which says that meanings are common property among people and what distinguishes one individual from another in writing is merely the form or, in other words, the way in which meanings are presented.[42]

The second point is related to rhymed prose *(sajʿ)*. Hamadhānī vilified harsh rhyme,[43] yet, degraded common rhymes such as *ikbār* and *inkār* or *ʿibād* and *bilād* or *jannāt al-naʿīm* and *nār al-jaḥīm*.[44] These were very common and ordinary rhymes that everybody knew. Writers, as it can be deduced from Hamadhānī's words, were supposed to produce original rhymes, which people did not know yet! This may be regarded as a trend of rhythmic refinement and peculiarity, which Hamadhānī did not fail to effectuate in his *maqāma* genre.

Hamadhānī's solicitude with rhythmic refinement reflects the important role that words, and even letters (point 4), possessed in his literary theory. In one of his letters, he mentions the letter *mīm* (M) as always being associated with words of exaltation (*kull-u shaiʾ ʿalā al-mīm fī bāb al-tafkhīm*)[45] such as *ʿaẓīm* (great), *jasīm* (immense) and *karīm* (generous). A survey in Hamadhānī's works affirms his approach to letters as indicative particles rather than being mere phonetic characters. This phenomenon must have been an impact of Ibn Fāris, Hamadhānī's teacher, on his pupil. The former was the first philologist who paid attention to the indicative qualities of letters in a systematic method. His book, *Maqāyīs al-lugha*, though considered a dictionary, is, virtually, the earliest work on Arabic phonetics. It was described by Ṣafadī as "an unprecedendent noble work" (*jalīl lam yuṣannaf mithluh*).[46] Ibn Fāris believed that Arabic letters implied specific denotations. For instance, he argued that the two letters *jīm* (J) and *nūn* (N) when found in a word respectively, indicate invisibility and disappearance such as the words (*junūn*) which indicates the disappearance of the mind, or (*junayna*) which is a garden made invisible by a wall, or (*jinn*) who were believed to be invisible beings, and (*janīn*), the invisible embryo in the womb.

---

41 Ibid., p.273.
42 See Abbas, I. *Tārīkh al-naqd al-adabī ʿind al-ʿarab*, Beirut, 1983. p.99.
43 *Rasāʾil Badīʿ al-Zamān*, p.492.
44 Ibid., p.77.
45 Ibid., p.240.
46 Safadi, Ṣalāḥ al-Dīn, *al-Wāfī bil-wafayāt*, ed. S. Derdering, Weisbaden, 1972. vol.VII, p.279.

Hamadhānī's treatment of words in accordance with their indicative letters was influenced by his teacher's concept. For example, the 5th *Maqāma* is centered on the idea of invisibility or occultation. Therefore, it was not coincidental that he chose *Kūfa* as the sitting for this theme since the two letters *kāf* (K) and *fā'* (F) indicate coverage.

This interest, even in the letters that writers would use, demonstrates the intensive punctiliousness that Iranian men of letters were displaying in the 4th/10th century; a fact that made the geographer Muqaddasī testify that the Arabic used in Khurāsān was the purest and highest standard Arabic he ever heard in his travels throughout the Muslim world.[47]

## *Epistolography* "Tarassul":

Hamadhānī, in his account of his debate with Khwārizmī, refers to four hundred types of letters, but gives only eleven examples![48] Those examples, which Hamadhānī suggested to Khwārizmī in a challenging manner, consist of:

1- A letter that provides its own reply simultaneously.
2- A letter written simultaneously with a poem on the same theme.
3- A letter that can be comprehensible if read backwards.
4- A letter whose lines, if read backwards, form its own reply.
5- A letter without disconnected characters such as *dāl*, *dhāl*, *rā'* and *zāi*.
6- A letter without *alif* and *lam* (the).
7- A letter without undotted characters.
8- A letter whose lines begin with *mīm* (M) and end with *jīm* (J).
9- A letter that changes into a poem if read in a twisted manner.
10- A letter that can be interpreted as being satire or praise simultaneously.
11- A letter that can be memorized without being re-read.

Unsurprisingly, Khwārizmī's reply to Hamadhānī's suggestion to compose such letters at the spur of the moment was that such letters were 'jugglery'. However, Hamadhānī's reply to this accusation was that his opponent did not master except the composition of artless letters which were current among all people. This justification for favoring the extreme artificiality in the art of letter writing echoes Hamadhānī's earlier opinion on rhymed prose where common rhymes were degraded.

---

47 Muqaddasi, Muhammad; *Aḥsan al-taqāsīm fī maʿrifat al-aqālīm*, ed. M. J. De Goeje, Leiden, 1876. p.32.

48 *Rasā'il Badīʿ al-Zamān*, p.74-76.

## *Descriptive Literature:*

Literature, in general, is the description of outer phenomena, abstract realities or human inner sentiments. However, the descriptive literature in Iran during the 4th/10th century had an unprecedented phenomenon which reflected the elaborative course that literature was heading towards.

Arabic descriptive literature, which embodied, since the pre-Islamic age, the bulk of the Arab's literary product, became systematically categorized in the 4th/10th century. Hence, a social or natural phenomenon was described, in poetry or prose, in the most detailed manner. Afterwards, all the descriptions of the proposed phenomenon would form one unity with a title that refers to the described object. For example, several poets would describe an elephant and, afterwards, the totality of the poems would be called '*al-fīliyyāt*'.[49] The same principle would be applied to a house or a hackney, and the Descriptive poems or prose on those two objects would be called '*al-dāriyyāt*' and '*al-bardhawniyyāt*'. Many of Hamadhānī's *maqāmas* can be observed in the light of this phenomenon which was common in Iran during the Buyid age. His 30th *Maqāma* was known as *Maqāmat al-faras* (the *Maqāma* of Horse).[50] It is a descriptive *maqāma* of the horse, exactly as the elephant or the hackney were described. This aspect reflects the illustrative and prolixious trend in Hamadhānī's literature which exemplified the general literary trend of his age and society.

To sum up the rhetorical values that Hamadhānī upheld and promoted, it should be said that, for him, novelty was not a shift towards simplicity, but rather a turn towards elaboration and sophistication. The use of Arabic in literature, after being oriented by the Arabicized Persians in Iraq towards a break with classicism, returned in Iran, during the 4th/10th century, to the classical language of the Arabians but in various new and unprecedented forms which reflected the diversity of the Iranian society in those days, as well as the complexity of its culture.

Hamadhānī, in his evaluation of literatuere, has introduced the general literary values of his milieu, and was honest, indeed, in applying them in his own literary product. He was a reformist but not in the means i.e. Arabic language. He favored complexity, yet not at the expense of delicacy. He encouraged the spread of rhymed prose but not the coarse of it. Arabic literature, in Hamadhānī's taste, can be observed as an 'aristocratic phenomina' in the process of cultural devel-

---

49 Tha'ālibī, *Yatīmat al-dahr*, vol.III, pp.269-276.

50 In the Istanbul edition of the *Maqāmāt* and in Abduh's which adopted the titles of the former, this maqāma is entitled the ' The Maqāma of Ḥamdān'. However, this was a wrong and misleading title. Hamadhānī did not give any titles to his maqāmas but several of them became known by certain titles according to the content and not the sitting. The 30th Maqāma was known as the 'Maqāma of Horse'. (cf. Cambridge University Library MS. Or.1452 (7), fol.69[b]).

opment, because it was not written in the language of the rank and file, and perhaps not even for them since the use of Arabic was becoming less common among the majority of Iranians at the eve of the Buyid age.

The most accurate description of Hamadhānī's literature, which was an image of Arabic literature in Iran during the 4th/10th century, in general, may be that of Muhammad Abduh in his introduction to the *Maqāmāt*. He says:[51]

> What distinguished his utterance was the fact that its staidness and loftiness vies in beauty and elegance the utterance of Bedouins and, at the same time, its tenderness and artificiality is blended by the urbanite's innate disposition. At the time that the listener to his [utterance] imagines himself within the [desert] tents, he conceives himself among [urban] edifices [as well].

51 Abduh, *Maqāmāt*, p.1.

# The Art of Entertainment: Forty Nights with Abū Ḥayyān al-Tawḥīdī

*Lale Behzadi (University of Göttingen)*

Al-Tawḥīdī's *Kitāb al-imtā<sup>c</sup> wal-mu'ānasa* (The Book of pleasure and enjoyment/companionship) is a remarkable example for an artistically nested text with so many layers and ramifications that we can hardly see where the composition begins and where the textual movements end.[1] It displays the skills of the author and the high quality of literature of that time. Above that, it shows the richness literary texts can possess and the turns they take, quite often – we must assume – without being intended by the author.

If we look at al-Tawḥīdī's life we can use his work first as a source of information about the conditions he lived in, the political situation of that period and especially the circumstances of those who wanted to make a living out of writing. Abū Ḥayyān al-Tawḥīdī (*c.*315/927-*c.*411/1023) travelled around to find the right place and mentor for his literary ambitions. He was an admirer of al-Jāḥiẓ (d. *c.*255/868), making an endeavour to reach his unique method of prose writing, a combination of huge knowledge and easiness of style. The tragedy of al-Tawḥīdī's life is that he failed to reconcile the fact that he, as a court writer, had to be at service and was captivated in the usual hive of intrigue with the way he saw himself, an artist of words, and a servant of literature. As readers, we gain a lot from this inconsistency since he permanently had to close the gap, to satisfy his sponsors without betraying his principles. Frustration and restriction, as destructive as they may be for the person, sometimes cause creativity and resourcefulness. This is what one can witness in al-Tawḥīdī's texts, especially those like the one at issue, who give hints about their genesis.

Second, his work provides us (as well as his contemporary readers) with information about several fields of knowledge, especially philosophy, theology, rhetoric and behaviour in general. It shows, above that, how the author tried to present his knowledge in a readable form and artful language, using passages of poetry and rhyming prose, parallels and other forms of rhetoric to shape his writing and amuse the audience. The abundance of knowledge is stunning, leaving the reader as well as the listener in the book (the vizier) somewhat exhausted at the end of each chapter, which induces the vizier regularly to ask for an amusing anecdote before his companion leaves him at the end of the night.

This article focuses on the third facet (which is connected to the first), the narrative strategies the text presents in view of the circumstances under which the au-

---

1 Abū Ḥayyān al-Tawḥīdī, *Kitāb al-imtā<sup>c</sup> wal-mu'ānasa*, eds. Aḥmad Amīn/Aḥmad al-Zayn, vol. 1-3, Dār maktabat al-ḥayāt lil-ṭibā<sup>c</sup>a wal-nashr wal-tawzī<sup>c</sup> (further referred to as IM).

thor has written the book. The aim is not simply to explain the text with its historical background. Instead, al-Tawḥīdī himself gives a complicated introduction in which the reader gets a hint on how to find his way through the labyrinth of frames. This concept of presentation shall be our main focus, for it provides indications and instructions on how to understand the sequence of the chapters. We are told stories within stories, we are lead to paths which end suddenly or go back to an irritating crossroad. Al-Tawḥīdī is so eager to take us by the hand that it should be illuminating to stop, turn around and examine the motifs, dodges and wrappings that are arranged around what is called the "essence" of his book, the philosophical reflections.[2] Step by step analysis of the frame construction will be made to try and find out which paths we are meant to take and which side roads suddenly open up and what connection this has with a narrative structure.

Since the mere sequence of events does not make a story we should ask what al-Tawḥīdī does to make his work attractive. One could argue that the philosophical thoughts in themselves bear enough attraction; that the arrangement and the introductory remarks are merely details without much importance. In the course of this article I will show the immense impact these arrangements have and how they can shape our perception of the whole book. Although this is only one reading version amongst others, this is the nature of reading in general: there is no isolated validity.

## *1. The Genre*

The book *Kitāb al-imtāᶜ wal-muʾānasa* belongs to a genre which, in a broader sense, can be called court literature. Along with the need of the still young Islamic society to collect traditions and knowledge in all conceivable fields, there grew the demand of the higher classes to acquire education, style and awareness. The vehicle of all this was *adab*, a product as well as an attitude, an active process as well as a condition.

At a first glance, Abū Ḥayyān al-Tawḥīdī's work is part of the *majālis* genre, compilations that were written as materials for the entertainer and guests at the courts. The increasing number of governors and wealthy notables opened a market for stories, texts and pieces of news that had to come along educating, exciting and amusing, but not without a certain intellectual standard – to be presented at the soirées and salons. The audience had had certain expectations that

---

2 It should not be denied that we of course can read the whole book as "a mine of information about contemporary intellectual life" and that it "should prove invaluable for a reconstruction of the doctrines of the Baghdad philosophers", as S. M. Stern put it in his Article on al-Tawḥīdī (Encyclopedia of Islam, 2nd Edition, 1960). Though acknowledging this statement and many others which claim al-Tawḥīdī above all as a transmitter of philosophical ideas, the objective of this article is to show that it is quite difficult to extract "pure" information without being influenced by the modes of presentation.

had to be fulfilled or at least stimulated by the professional entertainer (*nadīm*), who thankfully used these works to feed the ever hungry minds.[3]

Compilations of *adab* works in this way could be used as manuals for intellectual court life. They showed also the horizon and education of the author and compiler. Above that, they were the currency in which the writers, authors and scholars paid back the protection and livelihood they enjoyed under the reign of the respective caliph, governor or emir. Al-Tawḥīdī himself classifies his book by stating the exact genesis of the writing, the original idea, the patron, the difficulties of translating the idea into action, and the relations between the participating persons. He has been hired to entertain the vizier Ibn Saᶜdān (i.e. Abū ᶜAbdallāh al-Ḥusayn b. Aḥmad b. Saᶜdān, called al-ᶜĀriḍ being a former army inspector)[4], and he documents these conversations in a book. This book has several functions: it provides evidence for his nights at the court; it is the favour in return for having been chosen as the companion of the vizier; it shows the educated and cultivated state of the author; it can be used by other readers either to amuse and educate themselves or to entertain others and organize a social evening.

The genre of court literature includes different kinds of books: textbooks that teach the bureaucrats how to write (letters, calculations, lists, epistles, for example Qudāma b. Jaᶜfar (d. 337/948)[5]: *Kitāb ṣināᶜat al-kitāba*); books that collect news about different topics in order to insert them into the conversation (Ibn Qutayba (d. 276/889): *ᶜUyūn al-akhbār*); books with instructions for different groups of professions (al-Jāḥiẓ: *Kitāb al-muᶜallimīn*); books that elaborate on certain concepts and principles (by al-Tawḥīdī himself, for example, *al-Sadāqa wal-sadīq*), stressing the positive and negative sides of each phenomenon (the subgenre of *maḥāsin wa-masāwī*, thus showing the eloquence of the author)[6]. Although introductory remarks were quite common, mainly because of thankful remarks to the patron, the main focus laid on the presented material. The author could show his brilliance and advocate himself this way for further orders.

Nevertheless introductions were important to give a foretaste to the coming treasures and explain the motifs of the author.[7] They therefore were composed very carefully by giving examples of the writer's literary skills. What is remark-

---

3 cf. Roger Allen, *The Arabic Literary Heritage. The development of its genres and criticism*, Cambridge University Press 1998, 238.

4 Vizier 373-375, under the reign of Ṣamṣām al-Dawla, executed 375. For historical deductions see Aḥmad Amīn in his introduction, IM I, Z. Kraemer, in his detailed introduction into Buyid court life, gives 374/984 as the year of Ibn Saᶜdān's execution (Joel L. Kraemer, *Humanism in the renaissance of Islam: the cultural revival during the Buyid age*, Leiden: Brill 1992², 191) while Bergé dates his death to 382-3/992-3 (M. Bergé, "Abū Ḥayyān al-Tawḥīdī", in *The Cambridge history of Arabic literature, ᶜAbbasīd belles-lettres*, ed. Julia Ashtiany et al., Cambridge University Press 1990, 112-124, here 122.

5 There are other dates as well, d. 938.

6 An example for this can be found in the ninth night, providing a list of opposites but without further elaborations such as certainty-doubt, knowledge-ignorance etc.

7 See the article by Bilal Orfali in this book on the "Art of the *Muqaddima*."

able here is that al-Tawḥīdī mixes genres: he serves the need to be entertained and to provide intellectual food – which is what is generally expected from *majālis* literature - but at the same time he presents a report on his conversations with the vizier. He goes even further and reveals all the details that led to the book in the first place.

## *2. The Framework*

One of the features that shape this book is its framework or, to be more precise, the encapsulation of frames. These are connected with the announced addressees of the book and the relationships of the persons who play certain (official and unofficial) roles in the setting.

The author, through the choice of his title, already declares that he wishes to entertain and to give pleasure – to whom? There are at least three targets/ addressees:

A. The author claims to be in personae one of the two dialogue partners and the narrator, respectively. As the evening entertainer of the vizier it is his main goal to provide amusement and make conversation. We can assume that he also had the vizier in mind, at least theoretically.
B. The author's friend and mentor Abū l-Wafāʾ al-Muhandis for whom this book has been written and who, as we learn, is eager to know what the vizier and al-Tawḥīdī were talking about.
C. The broader readership (the educated people, the salons), since the book has been officially published and distributed.

We should look closer at these addressees and relationships and ask some questions, for example why al-Tawḥīdī gives us this variety of the auditory, and what effect does it have on the readership? Moreover, what do the multiple embedding of stories and supposed attendant circumstances do with the "main" material?

### *A*

If the book were written for the vizier only (for the record, so to speak), it would have been enough to report the conversation itself with some praise to the vizier at the beginning. It would also have been politer and smarter to give the vizier a more active part or to eliminate the dialogue structure and give the lectures only. Instead, we notice that al-Tawḥīdī speaks the most. With some exceptions the pattern is the same: the vizier poses a question or a demand and al-Tawḥīdī answers, often in a long monologue, sometimes interrupted by comments or further questions. This arrangement offers al-Tawḥīdī a stage to present everything he knows and to prove above all of his rhetoric skills and his sharp mind. It is true that the vizier often initiates the conversation; and, of course, he has to have an educated horizon to ask the questions and to add his remarks.[8] However, in comparison to his guest he makes a rather dull impression. He asks whatever comes to mind and seldom contributes original remarks. Instead, at the end of the evening, he often demands a funny story as though tired of all the intellectual conversation. While al-Tawḥīdī tries to give all he has, the vizier remains on the receiving end of the conversation. On the other hand his questions give the opportunity to explain some thoughts in more detail or to provide the background of theories and theses. It seems as if these questions function as the scaffolding of the conversation building. They justify turns and digressions the author cannot be blamed for (similar to al-Jāḥiẓ whose subject-hopping and unorganized writing became nearly proverbial)[9].

The talks with the vizier are embedded into the most visible frame of the book: the division of the text into forty nights. The narrator, al-Tawḥīdī, has spent approximately forty evenings with the vizier each of which contains discussions about certain themes like philosophy, language, theology etc. (*adab* in the best sense of the word).

This reminiscence of 1001 Nights immediately brings up certain references of structure and storytelling (more so today, since this collection gained a lot of its popularity only after the first translations into French in the 18th century). The figure of the storyteller who night by night tries to entertain his audience has been a well-established institution in Arabic literature for a long time. The forty chapters – with few exceptions – can be read independently from each other. They mostly deal with a certain subject, started by the vizier's question about something followed by al-Tawḥīdī's reply and, sometimes, going on as a dialogue.

As in 1001 Nights the partners of this frame have got different positions in the hierarchy. Although al-Tawḥīdī unlike Shahrazād is not threatened by death, he is in a dependent position and has to please the vizier in order to earn a living and useful recommendation. Al-Tawḥīdī has to manage the difficult balancing act to appear as the educated and self-confident scholar who is worth sitting next to the vizier and impressing him with his knowledge and rhetoric. At the same time he must neither bore nor lecture his partner and he has to be aware of the vizier's power and how fate can change within the court from one minute to the next (even the vizier himself will later become another victim of the court intrigues, although he is still unaware of his fate while talking to al-Tawḥīdī).[10]

---

8 Kraemer describes Ibn Saᶜdān as a rather decent man who established a cordial and cultured soirée, contrary to the scheming atmosphere at court and the difficult economical and political situation (Kraemer, *Humanism*, 191f.).

9 For further reading with respect to the audience see Lale Behzadi, *Sprache und Verstehen.* al-Jāḥiẓ *über die Vollkommenheit des Ausdrucks*, Wiesbaden: Harrassowitz 2008.

10 See the aforementioned execution of Ibn Saᶜdān after his brief intermezzo as vizier; fn. 4.

*B*

Another addressee is al-Tawḥīdī's mentor and friend Abū l-Wafāʾ al-Muhandis (d. 997).[11] This relationship is the primary narrative (and the first frame) into which the other mentioned narratives (and frames) are embedded. As we are told in al-Tawḥīdī's preface, Abū l-Wafāʾ had done him the favour of introducing him to the vizier and (in turn) demanded a detailed report on their conversation. A closer look at this preface will reveal how the introduction influenced the whole book.

After a few introductory remarks on the importance of a friend's guidance, al-Tawḥīdī addresses his benefactor directly: "*Ayyuhā l-shaykh*." He praises him and wishes him well in a delicate manner using rhyme prose and parallelisms.

In his speech he refers to a talk they had the day before (*fahimtu jamīʿa mā qultahu lī bil-ams …*), thus evoking a presence and nearness to the action, i.e. the reader can nearly follow in real time. Abū l-Wafāʾ had apparently given him some advice regarding the expected encounter with the vizier.

Al-Tawḥīdī quotes Abū l-Wafāʾ who reminds him of the circumstances that brought him from Rayy to Baghdād and from Ibn al-ʿAmīd to Ṣāḥib b. ʿAbbād in the first place at the end of the year 370 after hijra. He also reminds him of the encounters they have had and how they have profited from each other. Abū l-Wafāʾ connected his friend to Ibn Saʿdān, vizier of Ṣamṣām al-Dawla b. ʿAḍud al-Dawla in the years 373 to 374/375 after hijra:

> "Yes", Abū l-Wafāʾ says, "I arranged all this and I will not stop doing so in my relationship to you […] for all the reasons I gave, and you owed this to me that you spend successive nights alone with the vizier; you can talk to him whatever you like and choose, and write to him message after message."[12]

What starts as an explanation on how al-Tawḥīdī got the honour to become the vizier's company turns into a severe reproach. Abū l-Wafāʾ continues to dwell on al-Tawḥīdī's lack of experience with court matters and how lucky he can call himself to come into this position missing the manners and necessary skills to do well at court. He then insinuates that his friend claims all the honour and benefit for himself without acknowledging that he would never stand where he is now without his (Abū l-Wafāʾs) help, guidance and conveyance. Al-Tawḥīdī presents all this in direct speech, quoting Abū l-Wafāʾ, who gets really annoyed about al-Tawḥīdī's ingratitude, along several pages. Abū l-Wafāʾs rage culminates in the warning that he will rip the friendship with al-Tawḥīdī off his heart unless "you inform me completely about what you two talked about and shared in good and bad."[13] His condition for maintaining the friendship and forgetting the betrayal

---

11 Famous especially as a mathematician, see the article *Abu l-Wafāʾ al-Būzadjānī* by H. Suter in the Encyclopaedia of Islam, 2nd Edition, and the chapter on Ibn Saʿdāns court and on al-Tawḥīdī in Kraemer, *Humanism*, 191ff, 212-222.

12 IM I, 5.

13 IM I, 7.

is to take part in the experience of the soirées as if he himself had been present: "... as if I were watching you or sitting between you and joining you."[14]

Abū l-Wafā' threatens al-Tawḥīdī to withdraw from their relationship in case he refuses to do what he asked him to do:

> And if you don't do this, wait for the consequence of my estrangement from you and expect to be disregarded by me, as if I am with you and you become thirsty and bewildered; O Abū Ḥayyān, you will eat you finger from regret, and you will swallow your saliva from grief ...[15]

*C*

The general audience is manifold. There is the contemporary audience al-Tawḥīdī must have had in mind. Like any other author, al-Tawḥīdī tried to produce a text that is worth reading. The pleasure he promises is to be found in the amount of knowledge and anecdotes he provides. To gain attention he has to bring more than a mere collection of material worth knowing. He decides to raise the attention by a special presentation of this material. This way the audience gets the impression of being a part of a distinguished company and to witness the results of two interesting relationships (al-Tawḥīdī and the vizier; al-Tawḥīdī and his friend). On the other hand, the contemporary audience was familiar with the situation at the court. To give details about the evolving of a text may also aid in unfolding the practice of patronage and connection in the higher society, a practice with which al-Tawḥīdī was highly unsatisfied.

We should ask what happens with the modern reader who knows nothing about the life at the court in the 10th century and is not familiar with the names that are dropped by al-Tawḥīdī and his conversation partners. Maybe some of the allusions escape his notice, maybe he is not at all interested in sharing the ideas on philosophy and literary theory going back to the 10th century. Still, there is more about the book than compiling ideas and revealing some embarrassing facts of court life.

## 3. *Perspective*

A question which has been discussed with respect to historical texts is the way in which the author has influenced his material and thus manipulates the reader. While historians try to distinguish between facts and fictional elements or stating the creative character of every form of writing,[16] artful literature from the begin-

---

14 IM I, 7.

15 IM I, 7.

16 See Stefan Leder (ed.), *Story-telling in the framework of non-fictional Arabic literature*, Wiesbaden: Harrassowitz 1998, and Eva Orthmann, *Stamm und Macht. Die arabischen Stämme im 2. und 3. Jahrhundert der Hiǧra*, Wiesbaden: Reichert 2002.

ning tries to create something that is beyond the pure report, more than submitting details and events. One may object that every text in itself is a composition and always carries subjective characteristics of the author. Above that, every text changes in the course of its reception; this is common knowledge by now. We also read historical texts and political analyses, religious treatises and manuals from that point of view. What is interesting here are the styles used by the Arab authors who definitely intended to write literary works. They consider themselves professional writers; they claim to create a text which is entertaining, educating and stimulating. It is evident that classical Arabic literature has not been mainly written as fictional literature. Nevertheless it enters realms where readers have to use their imaginative power. Their expectations interact with the linguistic material and with other literary and non-literary discourses, and thus produce what we call *literariness* and lead to the result which we call literature.

The paradox in the case of al-Tawḥīdī is that he uses a conventional pattern for his book, court literature, varying it and breaking through it during the writing process. These acts of approaching a convention and leaving it in the next moment add to the appeal of the text. Another paradox can be found in the double figure author/narrator who claims to be both. It is not the problem of authenticity that is of interest here (for that, see below) but the question of whose point of view the whole story is told from. Only if we answer this question can we make a statement on the reliability of the narrator. Author and narrator carry the same name, al-Tawḥīdī. He has at least three tasks to fulfil: to entertain the vizier, to report on his friend and to prove himself as an author. Since these tasks sometimes contradict each other (for example, the report down to the last detail versus the loyalty to the vizier or the standard of literature) we cannot be sure what to believe. Which of these many conditions is responsible for the rhetoric style? Are we sure that we are told everything and if not, is that the result of confining court secrets or due to something that has to be hidden from Abū l-Wafāʾ, or simply due to the fact that it is too trivial to find a place in a piece of work by someone who claims to be more than a secretary? In the tenth night, for example, al-Tawḥīdī switches his focus, turning from a participating actor to a commenting narrator. The narrator in one of the rare occasions enters the picture (whereas he usually is hidden behind the conversation partner and gives only direct speech), describing the vizier's reactions, giving summaries of the conversation and even adding information that was not part of the evening talks. Here the writer wants to complete a chapter to be satisfied with the arrangement. We learn also that al-Tawḥīdī had read this (previously composed) chapter aloud to the vizier in the course of two nights.[17]

[17] IM I, 195.

## 4. *Authenticity*

The narrator seems to be identical to the author, hence giving the book its authentic form of a report: a report about producing entertaining and artful literature.

Beginning with the preface, the reader is initiated into the art of creating an entertaining text.

The narrator/author gives the impression of retelling everything that happened in a certain period of time and suggests to the reader (the common reader, his friend, and the vizier) that he (the reader) witnessed the disclosure of the author's composition process. Here, the question of "real" authenticity is of secondary importance (i.e. the question of whether these soirées have taken place exactly under the reported circumstances or whether every word was spoken the way al-Tawḥīdī has documented).[18]

The artistic point here is the trick of authenticity which – when properly used – never fails to have the desired effect: to draw the attention of the audience although they surely recognize the construction (this being one of the miracles of good literature: we see through the tricks and yet we are spellbound). We can even assume that al-Tawḥīdī took the job (to entertain the vizier) not only to get access to court, to earn money, and to gain at least some of the respect he was always looking for, but al-Tawḥīdī immediately must have seen the opportunity of processing this experience. This prospect in turn would have inspired him during the talks themselves. The result would be an artistically arranged reality, the boundaries between the so-called reality and our perception of it being blurred. Thus, literature becomes far more than a means to entertain; it creates reality because a certain activity has been undertaken with the prospect of writing about it.

As readers we can take the chance to be part of what has happened and of how the report has been created. We could apply performative speech act qualities to this sort of literature which comes into being only by being ordered and, vice versa, reports on a reality that has been created (only?) by writing about it.[19]

---

[18] This has been doubted, with good reason, before, as for example in Kraemer, *Humanism*, 217-18.

[19] This phenomenon has been discussed recently in modern literature, too, where books with assumed authenticity are presented; they are perceived as literature, not documentaries, see for examples Thomas Glavinic, *Das bin doch ich*, München: Hanser 2007, and Christa Wolf, *Ein Tag im Jahr*, München: Luchterhand 2003. Beside the critical enthusiasm both have also been criticized in the feuilletons for taking it too easy (just writing about their daily life) instead of making an effort and creating a story. However, this "documentary approach" has a special impact on both the reception and the writing which is why one could question Iser's statement of literature as something that mostly remains "without consequences" (Wolfgang Iser, *Das Fiktive und das Imaginäre. Perspektiven literarischer Anthropologie*, Frankfurt/M.: Suhrkamp 1993, 512). On the contrary, not only do these texts leave traces in the reality; the concept itself evokes a certain perception, inside and outside the text.

Again, this arrangement creates a sort of diffusion or uncertainty. How should we perceive the assumption that al-Tawḥīdī was fully aware of the potential processing of the conversation while performing it? How did this influence his role at the soirée? Would his rhetorically refined style and his way of answering the vizier have been different had he been unaware that the whole project would end in a book? And how did the assumed charge to report shape his encounters with the vizier? Or, the other way round, how did the conversation (or the pieces on philosophy, literature etc.) influence the way of reporting?

## *5. The plot*

For a long time, the plot of a story was used as an instrument for measuring literature. There are different definitions to the term; let us just start with a simple old-fashioned test: to summarize a book.[20] There are several ways to do this with al-Tawḥīdī's book, each giving away another purpose and another meaning to his work.

1. The book *Kitab al-imtāʿ wal-muʾānasa* is the written version of evening conversations between the narrator and Ibn Saʿdān that lasted forty nights. We are presented with little stories woven around well-known scholars, ideas on certain subjects, anecdotes. Each chapter is dedicated to one night, as previously mentioned, that generally goes the same way: the vizier asks a question or makes a request and al-Tawḥīdī answers it. The vizier could add this book to the memorabilia of his term.

2. The book is a wonderful source of contemporary philosophical thought. In it we find not only al-Tawḥīdī giving his opinions on matters of life, society and literature, he also quotes a lot of other scholars and thus gives us evidence for statements that otherwise would have been forgotten. That is why this book is often considered as a work on philosophy and not as a literary text, albeit literarily shaped (like the often mentioned title of al-Tawḥīdī as a literary philosopher or a philosophical literary writer)[21].

3. The book is an example of carefully shaped language. Al-Tawḥīdī chose his style very purposefully, using all kinds of well-known rhetorical and poetical refinement, such as parallelisms, *sajʿ*, *tajnīs*, or the art of brevity, giving the shortest

---

20 For inspiration I have to refer to Peter Brooks, *Reading for the plot: design and intention in narrative*, Harvard University Press 1992. Although he gives a far more complex definition of plot he does not rule out the possibility to summarize and look at what we get by that, see for example p. 7.

21 See, for example, Ibrāhīm Zakariyya, *Abū Ḥayyān al-Tawḥīdī: adīb al-falāsifa wa-faylasūf al-udabāʾ*, Cairo: al-Hayʾa al-miṣriyya al-ʿāmma lil-kitāb 1974.

definition of a phenomenon[22]. He also presents a theoretical approach to the field of prose and poetry in Arabic literature.[23]

4. The book is a story about dependence and pride, friendship and misuse of friendship, because it tells us about two men who are related to each other through the process of writing and submitting a book (al-Tawḥīdī and Abū l-Wafāʾ).

5. The book is nothing of the above mentioned or all of it together; at the same time it is mostly and primarily a book about writing under certain historical circumstances as well as the aesthetic setting of the writing process.

As we have seen, we cannot really decide what sort of book we are dealing with when we try to make out its plot. This is one of the specialties of literary analysis, being itself part of the material that it is dealing with.[24]

Purposefully or not, al-Tawḥīdī created a text that no longer (if ever at all) can be divided into the "main message" and the "literary measures" with which this message is transmitted. The transmitting tools themselves carry and create a chain of meanings which overlay and change the "official" meanings. Al-Tawḥīdī comments on the transmitting process at the beginning of part two where he assures Abū l-Wafāʾ that no detail is missing, that he even explains the unclear, but declares at the same time that he also added remarks of important personalities to round off the subject.[25]

## 6. *Mode of presentation*

Court literature is supposed to summarize what has been talked about in the evenings in order to give the potential reader the essence of the sessions and not to bother him with unnecessary details. By choosing the valuable pieces of the conversation the writer proves his ability to abbreviate. He forms a text corpus which no longer is a mere reflection of what happened at the *majlis*; instead he takes the raw material and creates something entertaining for an audience that was not present at court or would reread the shared ideas and discussions in an entertaining way. It is clear that the writer was not supposed to take the minutes; rather he should and would refine what has been discussed and by doing this raise himself as well as the conversation partners.

---

22 As in the 26th night, IM II, 147-153.

23 Which has been translated and commented upon by Klaus Hachmeier, "Rating *adab*: Al-Tawḥīdī on the Merits of Poetry and Prose. The 25th night of *Kitāb al-Imtāʿ wa-l-muʾānasa*, translation and commentary", *Al-Qanṭara* 25 (2004), 357-385.

24 This is the reason why we, according to Paul de Man and others, should be suspicious to all sorts of final statements when it comes to literature. See the introduction by Werner Hamacher to the German edition of Paul de Man, *Allegorien des Lesens [Allegories of Reading, 1979]*, Frankfurt/M.: Suhrkamp 1988, 25.

25 IM II, 1f.

Al-Tawḥīdī, instead of summarizing gives (or appears to give) the whole account of the evening conversation. What the reader is supposed to get, according to the promise to Abū l-Wafāʾ, is a reflection of what happened, al-Tawḥīdī being only the medium that transfers the information from one place to another.

The authenticity of the *majālis* takes up the performative character of Arabic poetry which has to be presented to listeners in order to develop the full impact. The author of *majālis* literature - taking part at the session, witnessing it and writing the record - is situated in the conflict of maintaining the spontaneous character of the conversation and the ambition to shape his material and to slip off the role of the secretary. It is quite difficult to transform this character into a written genre. The writer wants to give an idea of the atmosphere at court; he shows the skills of the host and the guests and especially his own to answer and maintain a conversation while upholding a high standard of language and education. As an author, however, he wants to show his abilities in the written form which survives the moment. It has been mentioned before, that, albeit rarely, al-Tawḥīdī openly adds text that does not have any origin in the conversation; he feels, for example, that the subject of the 13th night (the human soul) would not be treated thoroughly without the ideas of Abū Sulaymān[26]. Al-Tawḥīdī explains this unusual digression ("there is no excuse to withhold them") and even elaborates on the difference between oral and written commentaries.[27]

Al-Tawḥīdī does not restrict himself to reproduce stories, ideas and arguments; the text with at least the same force pronounces the manner in which the soirées have taken place. We learn about the fragile relationship between the author and his patron; we notice that the narrator feels compelled to mark abridgments of the texts and continuously addresses his patron.

This way, the reader is periodically interrupted and torn away from his reading the „philosophy", „anecdote" or else part of the information. Instead, every once in a while these passages point to the crucial constellation (al-Tawḥīdī and Abū l-Wafāʾ).

It is possible to read this phenomenon historiographically with respect to al-Tawḥīdī's notorious dissatisfaction.[28] We can also take al-Tawḥīdīs explanation for granted: he apologizes for the scattered presentation but takes no responsibility for it, Abū l-Wafāʾ being the one who insisted on a reproduction of the court sessions.[29]

---

26 al-Sijistānī al-Manṭiqī (d. *c.*375/985)

27 IM I, 201f.

28 And to point out his need to take revenge, see Allen, 244. De Man expressed his astonishment that literary critics tend to describe structures of meanings mostly in historical terms rather than in semiotic or rhetoric terms; *Allegories*, 118. This is especially the fact when it comes to historical "foreign", in our case Arabic, literature.

29 IM I, 225f.

On the other hand the trialogical character of the text (al-Tawḥīdī, the vizier, Abū l-Wafāʾ) generates suspense not only with respect to the question of how the conversation continues, but also whether al-Tawḥīdī sticks to his promise to retell everything, even the tiniest detail. The story behind the story is thoroughly composed, whether it has taken place exactly that way or not. The book is entertaining even on this completely different level which – we can assume – has been created quite purposefully to achieve a special effect. One can call this a slanderous way of writing and attribute it to al-Tawḥīdī's wounded pride; however, it is a literary strategy which keeps awake the interest, and this is what counts.

Consistently at the beginning and end of a volume the reader gets an insight of the state of things between patron and writer. Again he seemingly takes part in the process of creating a book; again he can have the feeling of being present when literature comes into being. At the beginning of the second part al-Tawḥīdī announces to Abū l-Wafāʾ that this volume will reach him within a week. He asks him to treat it, like the first part, strictly confidential as to protect it from the eyes of all the jealous rivals.[30]

The author presents himself as somebody who has to be careful in two ways – in front of the vizier who represents the political power and wants to be entertained, and in front of Abū l-Wafāʾ who wants the report on every detail. At the end of the book we learn how painfully al-Tawḥīdī was dependent on payment and patronage. He nearly begs Abū l-Wafāʾ for more money, lamenting that he does not get enough for each soirée with the vizier. The category of narrative desire, once introduced to analyse the motor of a text, gets a disturbingly practical meaning.[31]

## *7. The making of the text*

The aesthetic experience this kind of literature provides takes place not only on the level of the collected thoughts and anecdotes. The joy of reading and listening to this mixture of entertaining material is embedded in and interrupted by narrative remarks. In contrast to al-Jāḥiẓ, whom he adored so much and whose style he tried to develop further, al-Tawḥīdī obviously did not only present a repertoire that teaches and informs the reader. His work tells a story and gives insights into human behaviour.

---

30 IM II, 1.

31 See Brooks, *Reading*, 37-38, 60-61, 143. The "desire to tell" interferes with other shades of desire, such as the desire to take part at and influence the cultural life at court, the desire to thank the patron, the desire to raise himself above his patron, the desire to fill the well-earned post of a leading intellectual figure etc. At the same time desire rises from other parts of the narrative construction: the desire to listen, the desire to communicate with the story etc.

We can look at this kind of composition in different ways: as a source of information about the situation at court; as a valuable collection of philosophical ideas of that time; as a game to produce literature.

However we might read the text, it is fascinating to see how many layers of reading it offers. Whenever a reader assumes that they have gotten the right perspective and understand the aim of the text, the next turn crosses their way and overlays the previous point of view.

It is worth asking if this book can today be entertainment, if there is something other than the presentation of a historical constellation. I am convinced that early Arabic literature has more to offer than just answering our cultural curiosity. If we get involved in reading these texts without the attitude of an archaeologist[32] we could let them have their direct impact on us and might get access to another angle of literature, thus becoming aware of the abyss, the labyrinthian qualities every text possesses.

As a conclusion I would like to go back to the starting point of the book. How was literature shaped and by which means did it get characteristic features? Al-Tawḥīdī's style is elaborated in a way that often got him the label of al-Jāḥiẓ's worthy successor. He is a professional in using rhyme prose; he knows a lot of metaphors; he also knows where to stop using rhetorical figures as not to appear too playful (something al-Jāḥiẓ condemned). But at his time all these talents, although still required from any author, were nothing rare, nothing to be distinguished from the growing number of people who wanted to write for a living. Already al-Jāḥiẓ moaned about the many who thought to be experts in language and poetry and heavily criticized *l'art pour l'art* in rhetoric. Everybody who felt a talent in this field should examine himself scrupulously before he decided to publish his works.[33]

As we have seen we can read al-Tawḥīdī's book in a lot of different ways that even contradict each other: a documentary on Arabic Abbasid court life, a philosophical text-book, a double-faced revenge on all his "patrons" (among them the vizier and Abū l-Wafāʾ), a display of his genius in using the Arabic language or in showing his philosophical excellence etc.[34] It also goes without saying that the conventional expectations of the readers vary not only in time but also according to their respective background. For me, the most interesting aspect of this text - and the point where its artful shaping is most clearly visible - is its self-

---

32 By which I do not mean to discredit archaeologists; literary archaeology as a way to reveal forgotten texts and to decipher and understand ancient cultures is, of course, necessary when studying literature.

33 ʿAmr b. Baḥr al-Jāḥiẓ, *Kitāb al-bayān wal-tabyīn*, vol. I-IV, ed. ʿAbdassalām Muḥammad Hārūn, Cairo: Maktabat al-Khānjī bi-Miṣr 1968 vol I, 203.

34 In one of the numerous Arabic studies on al-Tawḥīdī we still find the notion used in classical times that al-Tawḥīdī was "gifted" (*maṭbūʿ*, the opposite to *maṣnūʿ*, a quasi compensation for the lack of this somehow supernatural talent). See Fāʾiz Ṭāha ʿUmar, *al-Nathr al-fannī ʿinda Abī Ḥayyān al-Tawḥīdī*, Baghdad: Dār al-shuʾūn al-thaqāfiyya al-ʿāmma, 130.

referential power that in one moment takes the reader as its accomplice and in the next disposes of this confidentiality. The setting as a report feigns to leave the reader outside, to leave him the part of the spectator. The narrator goes even further and claims neither to be responsible for the conversations (because it is not he who suggests the subject) nor for the presentation (because again it is not he who set the form). But it is impossible to narrate or to read without being involved.[35] The literariness, from this point of view, evolves when al-Tawḥīdī or, to be more precise, the text juggles with the interaction of the narrator and his co-actors on one side, and with the permanent circumvention of expectations and genre characteristics on the other side. The motivation of the plotting is shattered and put together like a kaleidoscope, thus hinting to another meaning of "plot", the scheming. As the reader cannot even be sure who initiated the book in the first place,[36] he step by step is pulled down into the depths and whirls of the text.

The goal of this study is not to expose the author by proving that the text somehow works against his intentions. Rather it should be showed how contradictory and inconsistent textual movements can be, whether the author was aware of this phenomenon or not (it is not up to us to decide it); how the text claims circumstances which he denies on the next level; how very sophisticated Arabic literature in the 10th century meets and evades the expectations. It shows furthermore how even the literary analysis enters the same stage as the text itself and in the course of deciphering creates new meanings and uncertainties.[37]

---

35 The need for an interlocutor is especially visible in framed texts; see Brooks, *Reading*, 216. Roland Barthes stressed the fact that all storytelling is contractual (Roland Barthes, *S/Z*, engl.transl. R. Miller, New York: Hill and Wang 1974, 95-96). It is this indissoluble relationship that we find in al-Tawḥīdī's writing, be it between the narrator and the unknown reader, or between the *nadīm* al-Tawḥīdī and his patron; there are more of these relationships as mentioned above.

36 While in the introduction Abū l-Wafāʾ is quoted to have connected al-Tawḥīdī to the vizier (thus doing him a favour), the reader in the first night gets to know that the vizier himself had asked for al-Tawḥīdī. IM I, 19.

37 It might be useful to remember Paul de Mans remark on Proust where he states that deconstruction is nothing that we add to the text; instead deconstruction forms the text first of all. It is also there that de Man speaks about the double face of every literary text, claiming and at the same time denying the authority of its rhetoric form; see de Man, *Allegories*, 48.

# The Art of the *Muqaddima* in the Works of Abū Manṣūr al-Thaʿālibī (d. 429/1039)[1]

*Bilal Orfali (American University of Beirut)*

By the second half of the 3rd/9th century prose in Arabic literature had begun to supersede poetry as the preeminent form of artistic expression in most literary functions. This development reached its zenith in the 4th/10th century, as seen in the Arabic belles-lettres, the *maqāmāt* genre, and the various *adab* works of the period.[2] The artistic prose of this period is characterized by a number of features that became the norm in *adab* writing in the following centuries, lasting until the advent of the modern period. These features are: (1) adherence to rhyme and rhythmical balance (*al-sajʿ wa-l-muwāzana*), (2) extensive use of figures of speech (*badīʿ*), (3) synonymity and prolixity (*al-tarāduf wa-l-iṭnāb*), (4) adaptation and inclusion (*al-iqtibās wa-l-taḍmīn*), (5) brilliant exordia (*barāʿat al-istihlāl*).[3]

This style of writing dominated *adab* works but was rarely seen in scientific or historical writings, which featured a more serious and terse approach. It is erroneous, however, to assume that the use of artistic prose in the 4th/10th century and onwards was restricted to *adab* works. Frequently, this ornamented prose is encountered in the *muqaddimāt*[4] (sing. *muqaddima*, "introduction, preface, foreword, opening, exordium") of many books, regardless of the subject of the book. The authors of these *muqaddimāt* usually employ an artistic style characterized by verbal fireworks which is not always continued in the works themselves. Moreover, these *muqaddimāt* share a considerable degree of conventionality, featuring common topoi, regardless of the subject of the work they introduce. This justi-

---

1 I would like to thank Professors Beatrice Gruendler, Everett Rowson, Gerhard Bowering, and Dimitri Gutas for reading an earlier draft of this article. Their comments and suggestions saved me from many a mistake and oversight.

2 An examination of the table of contents of five books from this period (namely: the *Ghurar al-balāgha* of Abū Hilāl al-Ṣābī, *al-Fuṣūl al-adabiyya* of al-Ṣāḥib b. ʿAbbād, *al-Iʿjāz wa-l-ījāz* and *Siḥr al-balāgha wa-sirr al-barāʿa* of Abū Manṣūr al-Thaʿālibī), and *al-Durar wa-l-ghurar* of Abū al-Ḥusayn al-Ahwāzī illustrates this new function of Arabic prose. These authors assemble passages of artistic prose arranged according to *aghrāḍ* [thematic intensions/genres], such as boast [*fakhr*], praise [*madīḥ*], admonition [*ʿitāb*], felicitation [*tahniʾa*], lampoon/satire [*hijāʾ*], elegy [*rithāʾ*], condolence [*taʿziya*], hedonism [*lahw*], licentious or impudent attitude [*mujūn*], description [*waṣf*], and various other genres and sub-genres, some of which were traditionally restricted to poetry.

3 These major features of artistic prose did not originate in the 4th/10th century, as one can see precursors in the Umayyad and early ʿAbbāsid prose literature. It is rather the excessive application of these features that determines the style of the 4th/10th century.

4 Synonyms are: *taṣdīr*, *iftitāḥ*, *madkhal*, *tawṭiʾa*, *tamhīd*, *istihlāl*, *dībāja*.

fies the classification of *muqaddimāt* as an independent literary form of Arabic prose from the 4th/10th century onwards.[5]

This paper treats the literary aspects of *muqaddimāt* in the 4th/10th century by concentrating on the works of Abū Manṣūr al-Thaʿālibī (350-429/961-1039). The choice of al-Thaʿālibī serves three main purposes: (1) al-Thaʿālibī composed some ninety books on a range of subjects, almost half of which survived either in print or manuscript, and examining these introductions demonstrates the artistry of *muqaddimāt* in a wide variety of subjects; (2) modern scholarship celebrates al-Thaʿālibī primarily as a compiler and/or anthologist, less frequently as a critic, but only rarely as an author of artistic prose. A close study of his *muqaddimāt* is a first step towards reassessing this perception of him.[6] (3) Al-Thaʿālibī was a celebrated figure in numerous fields of knowledge and prodigious in his output. On the whole, however, he has not received his due in modern scholarship. Therefore, examining his *muqaddimāt* will both shed more light on his method of writing and help in determining the authenticity of some of his unpublished works.

## Muqaddima *in Arabic Literature*

The Qurʾān, the first lengthy written Arabic prose text, starts with an opening [*al-Fātiḥa*]. This set up a convention that Arabic books maintained regardless of their subject, and which developed, from the 3rd/9th century onwards, into an independent literary form. These introductions possess a tripartite structure consisting of initial commendations, a middle section which provides the objectives of the introduction and work itself and closing praises.

The initial commendations almost always adhere to the custom initiated by the Qurʾān in starting with the *basmala*, often followed by the *ḥamdala*.[7] In the

---

5 On the subject of introductions [*muqaddimāt*] in Arabic literature see Peter Freimark, *Das Vorwort als literarische Form in der arabischen Literatur*, Ph.D. thesis, Münster: 1967.

6 Muḥammad ʿAbdallāh al-Jādir was the first to note the activity of al-Thaʿālibī as an *adīb* by examining his prose and poetry. In his relatively short section on al-Thaʿālibī's prose, al-Jādir cites a number of quotations from al-Thaʿālibī's *muqaddimāt*, entries on poets from his anthology *Yatīmat al-dahr*, and various other books. In general, al-Jādir concentrates on al-Thaʿālibī's technique in *ḥall al-naẓm* [prosification, lit: untying the poetic string] in his *Nathr al-naẓm wa-ḥall al-ʿaqd* and his use of *badīʿ* in general, see al-Jādir, *al-Thaʿālibī nāqidan wa-adīban*, Beirut: Dār al-Niḍāl 1991, 301-33. This article concentrates on al-Thaʿālibī's *muqaddimāt* as an independent literary form of Arabic prose but is far from providing a comprehensive study of al-Thaʿālibī's prose. To conduct such a study, however, one needs first to determine the authenticity of some of his works. Most important in this regard is the history on Persian kings attributed to him: the*Ghurar mulūk al-furs*. We are even faced with this problem of authorship within al-Thaʿālibī authentic works, for in several of his books, al-Thaʿālibī does not state whether he is quoting or composing original prose. Indeed, many of his statements in these works can be traced to prominent figures of his time.

7 *Basmala* is coined from the formula *bi-smi-llāhi r-raḥmāni r-raḥīm* [in the name of God, the Merciful, the Compassionate], while *ḥamdala* is coined from the formula *al-ḥamdu li-llāhi*

middle section – which ranges from several sentences to many pages – the author may state the reason/s for writing the book, dedicate it to a patron, present the state of the art of its subject, specify its audience, explicate its method, indicate its sources, and discuss any other technical aspects related to its subject area. To achieve these goals, the author usually resorts to certain topoi, especially in stating the reason for his composing the work, such as, 'I have been requested to write a book on the subject', or 'I shall report briefly and avoid prolixity', 'No one has ever written directly or completely on the subject', etc.[8] The modesty topos, as a *captatio benevolentiae*, is popular in almost all literatures.[9] Also equally admired is the familiar *'querelle des Anciens et des Modernes'*,[10] as well as the praise of the virtues of the patron.[11] A typical distinguishing feature of Arabic introductions in comparison to other literatures is the request for God's help and succor in completing the task of writing.

## *Abū Manṣūr al-Thaᶜālibī and His Works*

Abū Manṣūr ᶜAbd al-Malik b. Muḥammad b. Ismāᶜīl al-Thaᶜālibī (350-429/961-1039) was a prominent critic of Arabic literature, an anthologist, and an author of works on *adab* and lexicography.[12] A prominent figure of his time, he participated in the extraordinary literary efflorescence which, in his generation, made the cities of his region, Khurāsān, serious rivals to Baghdād and its wider cultural sphere. Al-Thaᶜālibī's life was politically unstable due to the continuous conflicts between the Būyid, Sāmānid, Ghaznavid, and Saljūq rulers who had created independent states that served as destinations for itinerant poets and prose writers. Hence, during the course of his life, al-Thaᶜālibī traveled extensively within the eastern part of the Islamic world, visiting centers of learning and meeting other prominent figures of his time. These travels allowed him to collect, directly from various authors or written works, the vast amount of material he deploys in his

---

*rabbi l-ᶜālamīn* [Praise be to God, the Lord of the worlds]. In texts other than the Qurʾān, *basmala* and *ḥamdala* can take different forms, as illustrated below.

8 Freimark points out that many of these topoi have parallels in European literatures of the late classical, medieval, and early modern times. On the other hand, some of the topoi frequently found in antiquity are relatively rare in the Arabic tradition, as when an author asks a friend to judge his work. See: ibid., 35ff. and the references cited there.

9 Ibid., 68-71.

10 Ibid., 53-8.

11 Ibid., 65-8.

12 For a detailed biography of al-Thaᶜālibī see Rowson, "al-Thaᶜālibī", in *The Encyclopaedia of Islam*, 2nd ed., X, Leiden: Brill 2000, 426a-427b; C. Brockelmann, *Geschichte der arabischen Litteratur*, Leiden: Brill 1937-49, I, 284-6, S I, 499-502; C. E. Bosworth (tr.), *The Laṭāʾif al-Maᶜārif of Thaᶜālibī* [*The Book of Curious and Entertaining Information*], Edinburgh: Edinburgh University Press 1968, 1-31; al-Jādir, *al-Thaᶜālibī*, 15-132; Zakī Mubārak, *al-Nathr al-fannī fī l-qarn al-rābiᶜ*, 2nd ed., Cairo: al-Maktaba al-Tijāriyya al-Kubrā [1957], 2: 179-90 and the primary sources provided there.

numerous wide-ranging works, many of which are dedicated to the prominent patrons of his time.

Attempting to compose a bibliography of al-Thaʿālibī's works presents problems of false attribution and duplication. The longest list of his works available from primary sources is provided by al-Ṣafadī[13] and contains titles of seventy works including some duplications and false attributions.[14] Some of these works survive only in manuscript, while more than thirty authentic works have been published. In addition to his authentic published works there are a number of other published works attributed to him that lack scholarly consensus as to their authenticity. The following is a list of al-Thaʿālibī's authentic works that are examined in this article and available either in print or manuscript: [15]

- *Abū-l-Ṭayyib al-Mutanabbī mā la-hu wa-mā ʿalayhi*
- *Ādāb al-mulūk = Sirāj al-mulūk = al-Mulūkī = al-Khwārizmiyyāt*
- *Aḥsan mā samiʿtu = al-Laʾālī wa-l-durar = Aḥsan mā samiʿtu min al-shiʿr wa-l-nathr = Aḥāsin al-Maḥāsin*
- *Ajnās al-tajnīs = al-Mutashābih = al-Mutashābih lafẓan wa-khaṭṭan =Tafṣīl al-siʿr fī tafḍīl al-shiʿr*
- *al-Anīs fī ghurar al-tajnīs*
- *Bard al-akbād fī-l-Aʿdād = al-Aʿdād*
- *Fiqh al-lugha wa-sirr al-ʿarabiyya = Sirr al-adab fī majārī kalam al-ʿArab*[16] *= Shams al-adab = Maʿrifat al-rutab fī-mā warada min kalām al-ʿArab = al-Muntakhab min sunan al-ʿArab*
- *al-Iʿjāz wa-l-ījāz = al-Ījāz wa-l-iʿjāz = K. Ghurar al-balāgha fī-l-naẓm wa-l-nathr = K. Ghurar al-balāgha wa-ṭuraf al-barāʿa*
- *al-Iqtibās min al-Qurʾān*
- *Khāṣṣ al-khāṣṣ*

---

13 Ṣalāh al-Dīn Khalīl b. Aybak al-Ṣafadī (d. 696-764/ 1297-1363), was a philologist, literary critic, litterateur, and biographer, who is famous for his great biographical collection *al-Wāfī bi-l-wafayāt*, see F. Rosenthal, "al-Ṣafadī", in *The Encyclopaedia of Islam*, 2nd ed., VIII, Leiden: Brill 1995, 759a.

14 See al-Ṣafadī, *al-Wāfī bi-l-wafayāt*. Wiesbaden: Franz Steiner Verlag 1988, 21: 194-9.

15 I did not include in my list the works whose attribution to al-Thaʿālibī are still debated, most important of these are *Tuḥfat al-wuzarāʾ* and *Ghurar Mulūk al-Furs*.
The most comprehensive list of al-Thaʿālibī's works with a good discussion of biographical problems is compiled by M. ʿA. al-Jādir, *al-Thaʿālibī*, 58-132. This list, however, is already outdated since more manuscripts of al-Thaʿālibī's works have been published and/or discovered, and the discussion of the biographical problems continued in modern scholarship. A more updated, yet less thorough list, is provided by Y. ʿA. al-Madgharī in his introduction of al-Thaʿālibī, *Mirʾāt al-murūʾāt*, ed. Y. ʿA. Madgharī, Beirut: Dār Lubnān 2003, 30-41. Another important list is that of Q. al-Samarrai, "Some biographical notes on al-Thaʿālibī", *Bibliotheca Orientalis* xxxii (1975), 175-86. For a discussion of the general content of al-Thaʿālibī's works see E. K. Rowson, "al-Thaʿālibī", 426a-427b.

16 Two different books of al-Thaʿālibī are printed under this title: *Fiqh al-lugha* and *Lubāb al-ādāb*.

- *al-Kināya wa-l-taʿrīḍ* = *al-Nihāya fī-l-kināya* = *al-Kunā*
- *Laṭāʾif al-ẓurafāʾ min ṭabaqāt al-fuḍalāʾ* = *Laṭāʾif al-ṣaḥāba* = *Laṭāʾif al-luṭf*
- *Laṭāʾif al-maʿārif*
- *Lubāb al-ādāb* = *Sirr al-adab fī majārī kalām al-ʿarab*
- *al-Luṭf wa-l-laṭāʾif*
- *Man ghāba ʿanhu l-muṭrib* = *Man aʿwazahu l-muṭrib*
- *Mirʾāt al-murūʾāt*
- *al-Mubhij*
- *al-Muntaḥal* = *Kanz al-kuttāb* = *Muntakhab al-Thaʿālibī* = *al-Muntakhab al-Mīkālī*
- *Nasīm al-saḥar* = *Khaṣāʾiṣ al-lugha*
- *Nathr al-naẓm wa-ḥall al-ʿaqd*
- *Risāla fī mā jarā bayn al-Mutanabbī wa-Sayf al-Dawla*
- *Sajʿ al-Manthūr* = *Risālat sajʿiyyāt al-Thaʿālibī* = *Qurāḍat al-dhahab*
- *Siḥr al-balāgha wa-sirr al-barāʿa*
- *Taḥsīn al-qabīḥ wa-taqbīḥ al-ḥasan* = *al-Taḥsīn wa-l-taqbīḥ*
- *al-Tamthīl wa-l-muḥāḍara* = *Ḥilyat al-muḥāḍara* = *al-Maḥāsin wa-l-aḍdād*
- *Tarjamat al-kātib fī adab al-ṣāḥib*
- *Tatimmat Yatīmat al-dahr* = *Tatimmat al-Yatīma*
- *al-Tawfīq li-l-talfīq*
- *Thimār al-qulūb fī-l-muḍāf wa-l-mansūb*
- *Yatīmat al-dahr fī maḥāsin ahl al-ʿaṣr*
- *al-Yawāqīt fī baʿḍ al-mawāqīt* = *Yawāqīt al-mawāqīt* = *Madḥ al-shayʾ wa-dhammih*
- *Zād safar al-mulūk*
- *al-Ẓarāʾif wa-l-laṭāʾif* = *al-Ṭarāʾif wa-l-laṭāʾif* = *al-Maḥāsin wa-l-aḍdād*

## *The Content of al-Thaʿālibī's* Muqaddimāt

### *I- What Makes Thaʿālibī Write?*

Many of al-Thaʿālibī's works are dedicated to prominent patrons of his time and it is clear from al-Thaʿālibī's different dedications and travel route that he, like most contemporary literary figures, survived on patronage. Al-Thaʿālibī considers the act of dedicating books necessary to fulfill his service [*khidma*] to a patron.[17] In several instances al-Thaʿālibī mentions that the subject of the book was sug-

[17] See al-Thaʿālibī, *al-Iʿjāz wa-l-ījāz*, ed. Ibrāhīm Ṣāliḥ, Beirut: Dār al-Bashāʾir 2001, 17; *al-Anīs fī ghurar al-tajnīs*, ed. Hilāl Nājī, Beirut: ʿĀlam al-Kutub 1996, 41; *al-Tawfīq li-l-talfīq*, ed. Ibrāhīm Ṣāliḥ, Beirut: 1990, p. 23; *Taḥsīn al-qabīḥ*, ed. Shākir al-Āshūr, Baghdad: Wizārat al-Awqāf 1981, p. 28; *Mirʾāt*, p. 66; *Thimār al-qulūb*, ed. Muḥammad Abū-l-Faḍl Ibrāhīm, Cairo: Dār al-Maʿārif 1985, 3; *Khāṣṣ al-khāṣṣ*, ed. Ṣādiq al-Naqawī, Ḥaydarābād: Dāʾirat al-Maʿārif al-ʿUthmāniyya, 1984, 2.

gested by a certain patron.[18] In other instances, however, al-Thaʿālibī claims that he is writing to fill a lacuna, especially if no one has ever written on a particular topic. In doing so, he claims originality and innovation [*ṭarāfa, badāʿa, ikhtirāʿ*].[19] In a few instances al-Thaʿālibī compiles a work following a personal experience and with no dedication. Such is the case in his *Tarjamat al-kātib fī ādāb al-ṣāḥib* [On the proper conduct of friends], in which he states that the reason for writing the book towards the end of his life is his appalling experiences in friendship.[20] Finally, in *al-Iqtibās min al-Qurʾān* [Quoting from the Qurʾān] he states that he always had a 'strong intention' [*niyya qawiyya*] to compile a book on this subject.[21]

*II- Choosing a Title*

Al-Thaʿālibī states that he sometimes chooses a title that 'reveals the content' of his work,[22] and this holds true for most of his surviving works. In most cases al-Thaʿālibī mentions the title of the work in his *muqaddima*. In *Ādāb al-mulūk*, however, he seems reluctant to choose one title; he writes:

وكنت أردت أن أترجمه بالنسبة إلى الاسم الشريف فأخبرني أبو عبد الله محمّد بن حامد أنّ بعض المؤلّفين سبقني إليها... فقلت: الآن إن سمّيته الملوكيّ كنتُ صادقًا، وإن لقّبته تحفة المملوك وعدّة الملوك لم أكُ كاذبًا، لكنّي آثرت تفخيمه بالخوارزم شاهي...

> And I desired to entitle it using his noble name [i.e. *al-Maʾmūnī*], but Abū ʿAbdallāh Muḥammad b. Ḥāmid informed me that some authors had preceded me in this... So I said, "Now, if I call it *al-Mulūkī* [The royal book], I would be sincere, and if I called it *Tuḥfat al-mamlūk wa-ʿuddat al-mulūk* [The present of the servant and the provision of the kings], I would not be dishonest. But I prefer to glorify it as *al-Khwārizmshāhī*...[23]

---

18 Such is the case when the Khwārizm Maʾmūn b. Maʾmūn commissioned him to write *Lubāb al-ādāb* as a literary anthology and *Ādāb al-mulūk* on politics. See: *Lubāb al-ādāb*, ed. Q. R. Ṣāliḥ, Baghdad: Dār al-Shuʾūn al-Thaqāfiyya, 1988, 19; *Ādāb al-mulūk*, ed. Jalīl al-ʿAṭiyya, Beirut: Dār al-Gharb al-Islāmī 1990, 31. *Taḥsīn al-qabīḥ* and *Khāṣṣ al-khāṣṣ* were compiled by the order of [*bi-rasm*] Abū al-Ḥasan Muḥammad b. ʿĪsā al-Karajī and Abū al-Ḥasan Musāfir b. al-Ḥasan respectively, see *Taḥsīn*, p. 27; *Khāṣṣ al-khāṣṣ*, 1.

19 See *Yatīmat al-dahr*, Cairo: Maṭbaʿat al-Ṣāwī, 1934, 4-5, MS Laleli 1959 (Istanbul: Süleymaniye), 2v-3r; *Taḥsīn al-qabīḥ*, 28; *Mirʾāt*, 65-66; *al-Luṭf wa-l-laṭāʾif*, M. ʿA. Jādir, Maktabat Dār al-ʿUrūba, Baghdad 1984, 19; *al-Kināya wa-l-taʿrīḍ*, ed. Faraj al-Ḥawwār, Baghdād 2006, 26; *al-Mubhij*, ed. Ibrāhīm Ṣāliḥ, Damascus: Dār al-Bashāʾir 1999, 23; *al-Ẓarāʾif wa-l-laṭāʾif* and *al-Yawāqīt fī baʿḍ al-mawāqīt* (printed together) *in al-Ẓarāʾif wa-l-laṭāʾif wa-l-Yawāqīt fī baʿḍ al-mawāqīt*, compiled by Abū Naṣr al-Maqdisī, ed. N. M. Jād, Cairo: Dār al-Kutub wa-l-Wathāʾiq al-Qawmiyya 2006, 49-50; *Bard al-akbād fī-l-Aʿdād*, in *Khams rasāʾil li-l-Thaʿālibī* [*wa-ghayrih*], Istanbul: Maṭbaʿat al-Jawāʾib 1881, 103.

20 See *Tarjamat al-kātib fī ādāb al-ṣāḥib*, MS Hecimoglu 946-1 (Istanbul: Süleymaniye), 87r.

21 See *al-Iqtibās min al-Qurʾān*, ed. I. M. Al-Ṣaffār and M. M. Bahjat, Baghdad: Dār al-Wafāʾ 1992, 37.

22 See *Lubāb*, 19; *Fiqh al-lugha*, Beirut: Dār wa-Maktabat al-Ḥayāt 1980, 11.

23 *Ādāb al-mulūk*, 32.

The preface provides three titles for the same book. It appears that later scholars, referred to the book using different titles.[24] This is nevertheless not the only instance in which confusion reigns regarding the titles of al-Thaᶜālibī's works. Many of them survive under more than one title, due either to scribal errors or later catalogers relying on phrases – which are not necessarily titles – from his prefaces, conclusions, or other works as definitive titles.[25] In other cases al-Thaᶜālibī himself revised a work several times under different titles, rededicating it to different patrons (as will be discussed in more detail below).

## *III- Opening the* Muqaddima

Al-Thaᶜālibī usually adheres to the tradition of Arabic literature by starting with the *basmala* following it with the *ḥamdala* in ornate form, and then continuing with a prayer for the prophet. In some instances he adapts or includes Qurʾānic phrases in his *ḥamdala*. This is a technique he was very interested in, as evidenced by his devoting an entire chapter to it under the title of '*al-taḥāmīd al-muqtabasa min al-Qurʾān al-karīm*.' [Phrases of praising God adapted from the noble Qurʾān] in his *al-Iqtibās*.[26] The following are few of his openings using this technique:

أمّا على إثر حمد الله الذي هو أوّل كتابه وآخر دعوى ساكني دار ثوابه.

As for what comes after praising God, which opens His book[27] and is the last prayer of the inhabitants of the abode of His reward[28].[29]

الحمد لله {الذي علّم بالقلم، علّم الإنسان ما لم يعلم}، و{الحمد لله الذي هدانا لهذا وما كنّا لنهتدي لولا أن هدانا الله}، و{الحمد لله ربّ العالمين} حمد الشاكرين على نعمه التي لا يبلغ أقصى حمد الحامدين أوائل حدودها، ومنحه التي لا تؤدي نهايات شكر الشاكرين أداني حقوقها.

24 For example al-Ṣafadī, Al-Kutubī and Ibn Qāḍī Shuhba refer to it by al-Khwārizmshāhī or al-Khwārizmiyyāt, see *al-Wāfī*, 21: 197; al-Kutubī, *ᶜUyūn al-tawārīkh*, MS Dār al-Kutub al-Miṣriyya 1487 (Cairo), 457; Ibn Qāḍī Shuhba, *Ṭabaqāt al-nuḥāt wa-l-lughawiyyīn*, MS al-Ẓāhiriyya 438 Tārīkh (Damascus: Maktabat al-Asad), 388.

25 For example in *Thimār al-Qulūb* he quotes from his *al-Kināya wa-l-taᶜrīḍ* referring to it as *al-Kunā*, while in *Mirʾāt al-murūʾāt* he quotes from it as *al-Kināya*. In the preface of the book he refers to the work as *al-Kināya wa-l-taᶜrīḍ*, while in the conclusion he calls it *al-Nihāya fī-l-kināya*. See *Thimār*, 606; *Mirʾāt*, 27, *al-Kināya*, 27, 341.

26 See *al-Iqtibās*, 47ff.

27 A reference to the opening of the *Q.* 1: 1.

28 A reference to *Q.* 10: 10.

دَعْوَاهُمْ فِيهَا سُبْحَانَكَ اللَّهُمَّ وَتَحِيَّتُهُمْ فِيهَا سَلَامٌ وَآخِرُ دَعْوَاهُمْ أَنِ الْحَمْدُ لِلَّهِ رَبِّ الْعَالَمِينَ

29 *Al-Tamthīl wa-l-muḥāḍara*, ed. ᶜAbd al-Fattāḥ al-Ḥulw, Cairo: al-Bābī al-Ḥalabī 1961, 3; a very similar phrase is in *Nasīm al-saḥar*, ed. I. M. al-Ṣaffār, in *al-Mawrid* I (1971), 131.

> Praise be to God who taught by the pen, taught man what he did not know,[30] and praise be to God Who guided us to it, we would never have been guided had not God guided us.[31] And praise be to God, Lord of the worlds, [32]the praise of the thankful, for his blessings whose first boundaries are not touched by the last praises of the thankful, and for His gifts whose lowest recompense is not conveyed even by the ends of gratitude.[33]

In some cases al-Thaᶜālibī stops at the *basmala* and skips the *ḥamdala*.[34] While it can be attributed to al-Thaᶜālibī's favoring other techniques, the absence of *ḥamd* may also result from scribal error, neglect, or a conscious decision on the part of the scribe to omit it. In a few instances al-Thaᶜālibī also embellishes the prayer for the prophet. For example he says:

والصلاة على مصابيح الظلمة وكاشف الغمّة عن الأمّة وآله مفاتيح الرحمة.

> And may peace be upon the [person who acts as] the lamps of the night, who lifts [the shroud of] grief from the nation, and [peace be upon] his family, the keys of mercy.[35]

*IV- Writing and Rewriting the Work*

To justify the continuous re-editing of his *Yatīmat al-dahr* al-Thaᶜālibī quotes the following wise saying in his preface:

إنّ أول ما يبدو من ضعف ابن آدم أنّه لا يكتب كتاباً فيبيت عنده ليلة إلا أحبّ في غدها أن يزيد فيه أو ينقص منه، هذا في ليلة واحدة فكيف في سنين عدّة.

> The first weakness that appears in man is that he does not write a book and sleep over it without desiring on the following day to extend or abridge it; and this is only in one night, so what if it were several years?[36]

The above quotation faithfully describes al-Thaᶜālibī's scholarly attitude. A book for al-Thaᶜālibī is a work in progress and its immediate publication is necessary to satisfy a certain "need" [*ḥāja*].[37] The circulation of the work, however, does not prevent the author from re-editing, re-dedicating, and even re-naming it. In some instances, as in the *Yatīmat al-dahr*, there is a final version, and only this is

---

30 A reference to *Q.* 96: 4-5:

الذي علّم بالقلم علّم الإنسان ما لم يعلم.

31 A reference to *Q.* 7: 43:

وَنَزَعْنَا مَا فِي صُدُورِهِم مِّنْ غِلٍّ تَجْرِي مِن تَحْتِهِمُ الأَنْهَارُ وَقَالُواْ الْحَمْدُ لِلّهِ الَّذِي هَدَانَا لِهَـذَا وَمَا كُنَّا لِنَهْتَدِيَ لَوْلا أَنْ هَدَانَا اللّهُ لَقَدْ جَاءتْ رُسُلُ رَبِّنَا بِالْحَقِّ وَنُودُواْ أَن تِلْكُمُ الْجَنَّةُ أُورِثْتُمُوهَا بِمَا كُنتُمْ تَعْمَلُونَ.

32 *Q.* 1: 2, 10: 75, 40: 65.

33 *Al-Iqtibās*, 37.

34 As is the case in: *Nathr al-naẓm wa-ḥall al-ᶜaqd*, ed. A. ᶜA. Tammām, Beirut: Muʾassasat al-Kutub al-Thaqāfiyya 1990, 7; *Sajᶜ al-Manthūr*, 82; *Ajnās al-tajnīs*, ed. M. ᶜA. al-Jādir, Baghdad: Dār al-Shuʾūn al-Thaqāfiyya 1998, 24; *al-Kināya*, 23; *al-Mubhij*, 23.

35 *Nasīm*, 131.

36 *Yatīma*, 5, MS Laleli 1959, 3r.

37 *Yatīma*, 5, MS Laleli 1959, 2v.

put into circulation, although previous versions had been widely circulated and copied, as al-Thaᶜālibī himself admits. This final version, however, is followed by a continuation, *Tatimmat al-Yatīma*, which adopts the method and regional divisions of the original, but includes new material that had not been available to the author earlier. Al-Thaᶜālibī could have incorporated the new material into the original book, creating a new edition, but it seems he did not want to interfere with the officially published version that had already gone through a long history of editing, which he thus describes:

> وقد كنتُ تصدّيت لعمل ذلك في سنة أربع وثمانين وثلثمائة والعمر في إقباله والشباب بمائه فافتتحته باسم بعض الوزراء مجرياً إيّاه مجرى ما يتقرّب به أهل الأدب إلى ذوي الأخطار والرتب... ورأيتني أحاضر بأخواتٍ كثيرة لما فيه وقعت بأخرة إليّ وزيادات جمّة عليه حصلت من أفواه الرواة لديّ... فجعلتُ أبنيه وأنقضه وأزيده وأنقصه وأمحوه وأثبته وأنتسخه ثم أنسخه وربما أفتتحه ولا أختتمه وأنتصفه فلا أستتمّه والأيام تحجز وتعد ولا تنجز إلى أن أدركتُ عصر السنّ والحنكة... فاختلست لمعة من ظلمة الدهر... واستمررت في تقرير هذه النسخة الأخيرة وتحريرها من بين النسخ الكثيرة بعد أن غيّرت ترتيبها وجدّدت تبويبها وأعدت ترصيفها وأحكمت تأليفها... فهذه النسخة الآن تجمع من بدائع أعيان الفضل ونجوم الأرض من أهل العصر ومن تقدّمهم قليلاً وسبقهم يسيراً... وتتضمّن من طرفهم وملحهم لطائف أمتع من بواكير الرياحين... ما لم تتضمّنه النسخة السائرة الأولى.
>
> I had set out to accomplish this in the year three hundred and eighty four, when [my] age was still in its outset, and youth was still fresh. I opened it with the name of a vizier, following the convention of the people of *adab*, who do this to find favor with the people of prestige and rank... And I recently found myself presented with many similar reports to those in it and plentiful additions that I obtained from the mouths of transmitters... So, I started to build and demolish, enlarge and reduce, erase and confirm, copy then abrogate, and sometimes I start and do not finish, reach the middle and not the end, while days are blocking the way, promising without fulfilling, until I reached the age of maturity and experience... So I snatched a spark from within the darkness of age... so I continued in composing and revising this last version among the many versions after I changed its order, renewed its division into chapters, redid its arrangement and tightened its composition... This version now contains marvels by the prominent people of merit, the contemporary stars of earth, and by those who slightly preceded them in time... It comprises witty, rare coinings and anecdotes, more pleasurable than the early basil and the fresh aromatic flowers... [All of] which the first widely circulating version did not include.[38]

Even this continuation of *al-Yatīma* was revised later after the first dedication to Abū al-Ḥasan Muhammad b. ᶜĪsā al-Karajī.[39] This process of revising takes place in other works of al-Thaᶜālibī as well and is by no means restricted to his celebrated *al-Yatīma*. In fact, the multiple titles of works in his bibliography sometimes result from re-workings or re-dedications, a fact about which al-Thaᶜālibī himself tells us in his prefaces. For example, in the preface of *al-Mubhij* he explains that he re-edited the book after its first dedication to a point that he "re-established and re-formed it once again".[40] He also states in *Siḥr al-balāgha* that

---

38 *Yatīma*, 5- 6, MS Laleli 1959, 2v-3r.
39 *Tatimma al-Yatīma*, 7.
40 *al-Mubhij*, p. 23; *al-Kināya*, 27.

the final version dedicated to ʿUbayd Allāh b. Aḥmad al-Mīkālī[41] is the third (and last?) version after two previous editions "close in method and volume", the first dedicated to Abū Sahl al-Ḥamdūnī[42] and the second to a certain Abū ʿImrān Mūsā b. Hārūn al-Kurdī.[43] The same can be said about his *al-Iʿjāz wa-l-ījāz*, of which three different versions of the book survive in a number of manuscripts with considerable variance, different prefaces and sometimes different titles, all undoubtedly by al-Thaʿālibī himself, given their distinctive style. Thus Al-Thaʿālibī must have re-worked the work three times, dedicating the first version to a certain Abū Saʿd Muḥammad b. Aḥmad b. Ghassān, the second to Manṣūr b. Muḥammad al-Azdī al-Harawī,[44] whereas in the third and final version he omits the dedication altogether, as he did in the final copy of the *Yatīma*.[45]

*V- Presenting the Plan and Method*

In addition to explaining the editorial process, al-Thaʿālibī occasionally spends more time discussing his writing method in composing a certain book. In *al-Iqtibās min al-Qurʾān* he notes that he wrote it over a long period of time, with many breaks ranging from days to years.[46] In *al-Mubhij* he indicates that he relied on his "memory rather than notebooks" and his "mind rather than transmission" [*ʿawwaltu fīhī ʿalā khawāṭirī lā dafātirī, wa-ʿalā maʿqūlī lā manqūlī*].[47]

One of the universal topoi in prefaces is the one of brevity. Al-Thaʿālibī often describes a book as "light in size, heavy in worth, and great in benefit" [*khafīf al-ḥajm, thaqīl al-wazn, kabīr al-ghanm*],[48] accordingly he selects the most important material:

والشرط في هذه الأخرى إيراد لبّ اللبّ، وحبّة القلب، وناظر العين، ونكتة الكلمة، وواسطة العقد، ونقش الفصّ.

And the condition of this last edition is to include the essential core, the innermost heart, the pupil of the eye, the point of the phrase, the central [pearl] of the necklace, the engraving of the gem-stone.[49]

---

41 See his biography in *Yatīma*, 4: 326; Al-Bākharzī, *Dumyat al-qaṣr wa-ʿuṣrat ahl al-ʿaṣr*, ed. Muḥammad al-Tūnjī, Beirut: Dār al-Jīl 1993, 2: 984.

42 For information on him see Ibn al-Athīr, *al-Kāmil fī al-tārīkh*, Beirut: Dār Ṣādir 1966, 9: 379, 381, 428-9, 435-6, 446, 458.

43 See *Siḥr al-balāgha*, Beirut: Dār al-Kutub al-ʿIlmiyya 1984, 4.

44 For information about him see *Yatīma*, 4: 321; *Tatimmat al-Yatīma*, ed. M. M. Qumayḥa, Beirut: Dār al-Kutub al-ʿIlmiyya, 232.

45 See *al-Iʿjāz wa-l-ījāz*, ed. Ibrāhīm Ṣāliḥ, Damascus: Dār al-Bashāʾir 2001, 17-21.

46 See *al-Iqtibās*, p. 37.

47 See *al-Mubhij*, p. 23.

48 See *al-Iʿjāz*, 17, 19, 20; *al-Kināya*, 25; *Ajnās*, 25; *Laṭāʾif al-ẓurafāʾ*, ed. Q. al-Samarrai, Leiden: Brill 1978, 4; *Mirʾāt*, 66. See also *Sajʿ al-manthūr*, Yani Cami 1188 (Istanbul: Süleymaniye), 82.

49 *Yatīma*, 5, MS Laleli 1959, 3v.

وأودعته منها ظرف الظرف وروح الروح وعقود الدر وعُقد السحر.

> I entrusted to this book the very elegancies, the innermost soul, the strings of pearls and the knots of magic.[50]

Al-Thaᶜālibī frequently mentions in his *muqaddimāt* whether he selects his material from ancient or modern sources or both. Moreover, he almost always clearly presents the scope of his books and offers a considerably detailed outline.

### *VI- Dedicating the Work*

A few of al-Thaᶜālibī's books take the form of mementos to friends. The *muqaddima* in these cases acts as a *risāla* or a *qaṣīda ikhwāniyya*; the book, however, can deal with any subject. For example, in *Nasīm al-saḥar*, a book on the peculiarities of the Arabic language, dedicated to a friend who is described as using the same title phrase, the early morning breeze, al-Thaᶜālibī writes:

وحين كاد غراب البين ينعب بين المحبَّيْن وأوعد الدهر كعادته في تفريق متآخيين، أحببت أن تصحبه تذكرة مني تجدّد ذكري بحضرته وتنوب عني في خدمة مودّته، فألّفت له واختصرت هذا الكتاب.

> When the crow of separation cawed between the lovers, and fate threatened, as is his habit, to separate the brothers, I desired that a memento from me accompany him which will renew my recollection in his presence and will replace me in the service of [brotherly] affection. Thus, I composed this book for him and kept it brief.[51]

As in the case of most books dedicated to patrons, al-Thaᶜālibī's dedications usually fall into the end of the *muqaddima*, and follow a conventional format. In this regard, the preface acts like a panegyric poem. Just as the panegyric poem establishes a contract between a poet and a patron, so the preface of a book functions like a contract between the author and his patron. Fulfilling his part of the contract, the author "sells" his book and draws a flattering portrait of the patron, whom he describes with motifs usually encountered in panegyric *qaṣīdas*. There are also cases where panegyric poets rededicated their *qasīdas* to different patrons.[52] Consequently, al-Thaᶜālibī's act of re-dedicating books to other patrons in his prefaces can be compared to the practice of rededicating *qaṣīdas*, although with some differences. A book is different from a *qaṣīda* in that it does not contain the portrait of the patron, but rather it is the *muqaddima* of the book that serves this function. Thus, it was acceptable for al-Thaᶜālibī to re-dedicate his work to another patron without violating the ethics of patronage if he provided every new edition with a new preface, a rule that he observed faithfully.

---

50 *Laṭā'if al-ẓurafā'*, 4. For the same motif see also *Tatimma*, 8; *Nasīm*, 131.

51 *Nasīm*, 131.

52 See for examples, Kilito, *The Author and His Doubles*, tr. Michael Cooperson, Syracuse, N.Y.: Syracuse University Press, 2001, 24ff.

Indeed, al-Thaʿālibī's debt to the *madīḥ* tradition shows in his numerous common motifs and conventions. One of these conventions is praying for the patron. Throughout his *muqaddimāt*, al-Thaʿālibī follows the convention of asking God to prolong the patron's life. He sometimes adds a prayer for the patron's offspring as well, or prays for his patron's life to last until he sees his children become grey headed.[53] Moreover, al-Thaʿālibī often asks God to bestow on the patron as many gifts from His bounty as the number of the letters in the book he is dedicating; he says:

وإلى الله الرغبة في أن يعرّفه من بركاته ما يزيدُ على عدد ما فيه من الحروف بألوف.

My desire is that God make him witness thousands more of His blessings than the number of letters in [the book]. [54]

Borrowing other motifs from the *madīḥ* tradition, al-Thaʿālibī often names his patron as the reason behind "the revival of language, literature, or proper conduct",[55] "the one who encompasses the extreme ends of glory" [*jāmiʿ aṭrāf al-majd*],[56] or the best qualities in general.[57] In other instances al-Thaʿālibī finds no need to name the patron, for the superior qualities he mentions are unique to him.[58] Sometimes he claims that his patron is "the direction of prayer" [*qibla*] and/or a figurative *kaʿba* for supplicants and pilgrims.[59] In other cases, he declares that his praise cannot possibly live up to the deeds of his patron and thus he cannot hope to do justice to his patron by praising him or dedicating a book that matches him.[60] Alternatively, his praise sometimes matches the deeds: in which case he would state that his book and his patron suit one another,[61] or

53 See for example, *al-Yawāqit*, 51; *Taḥsīn*, 29; *Thimār*, 9.

54 *Al-Tawfīq*, 24; see also *al-Iʿjāz*, 21; *Taḥsīn*, 28, *Mirʾāt*, 69; *Zād safar al-mulūk*, MS Chester Beatty Ar. 5067-3 (Dublin), 44a.

55 See *al-Ẓarāʾif*, 48; *Ajnās*, 25; *Fiqh*, 4; *Ādāb al-mulūk*, 30; *Lubāb*, 18.

56 See *Ādāb al-mulūk*, 30; *Laṭāʾif al-maʿārif*, ed. I. al-Ibyārī and Ḥ. K. al-Ṣayrafī, Cairo: Dār Iḥyāʾ al-Kutub al-ʿArabiyya 1960 [?], 3; *Fiqh*, 3.

57 See *Mirʾāt*, 65-66; *al-Kināya*, 24-5.

58 See *al-Tamthīl*, 3; *al-Kināya*, 24.

59 In using the term *kaʿba* al-Thaʿālibī specifies that the patron is the *kaʿba* of sovereignty or majesty [*kaʿbat al-mulk* or *al-suʾdud*], *al-Tamthīl*, 4; *Yawāqīt*, 50; on the other hand, he uses the word *qibla* in common Islamic convention as the direction of prayer, see *Nathr*, 7; *Fiqh*, 9. Al-Thaʿālibī also uses this same motif in his own poetry; see for example *Dīwān al-Thaʿālibī*, collected by M. ʿA al-Jādir, Beirut: ʿĀlam al-Kutub 1988, 102, 111. For instances of this motif in Ibn al-Rumī's poetry see Gruendler, Medieval Arabic Praise Poetry: Ibn al-Rūmī and the Patron's Redemption, New York: Routledge Curzon 2003, 239ff; see also *Dīwān Abī Tammām*, ed. M. Ṣubḥī, Beirut: Dār Ṣādir 1997, 2: 100, 248, 297; *Dīwān ibn Nubāta*, ed. Mahdī Ḥabīb al-Ṭāʾī, Baghdad: Wizārat al-Iʿlām 1977, 1: 409 ; *Kushājim, Dīwān*, ed. N. ʿA. Shaʿlān, Cairo: Maktabat al-Khānjī 1997, 61.

60 See for example *Taḥsīn*, 28, *Bard*, 103; *al-Iʿjāz*, 17, 19; *Laṭāʾif al-Maʿārif*, 3; *al-Tawfīq*, 23; *al-Ẓarāʾif*, 4. *al-Tawfīq*, 23; *Thimār*, 3; for examples of this motif in poetry, see Gruendler, 248ff.

61 See *Taḥsīn*, 28.

that his book compared to other speech is like his patron compared to the nobles of his time.[62]

Another common topos in al-Thaʿālibī's prefaces is apologizing for the delay in dedicating the work to his patron. He usually attributes this delay to his incapability of matching the patron's qualities with a product of his composition. He then moves to comparing his books to the qualities of the patron, resorting to the modesty topos and drawing interesting comparisons that can often be rendered generally as "He who carries owls to Athens or coals to Newcastle"[63]:

وإنّي أخدمه بكتبي كمن يهدي الخضاب إلى الشباب وينقل الفقه إلى الشافعي، والشعر إلى البحتري.

> My service to him with my books is like him who presents hair dye to a youth, like him who transmits jurisprudence to al-Shāfiʿī and poetry to al-Buḥturī.[64]

كمن يهدي إلى الشمس نورًا أو يزيد في البحر نهرًا.

> Like him who offers light to the sun and adds a river to the sea.[65]

ككوز ماء أجاج يحمل إلى بحر فرات عجاج.

> Like a jug of brackish water carried to a raging sweet-watered sea[66]

وكيف تؤلّف الكتب للجاحظ ويُهدى الفقه إلى الشافعي والشعر إلى البحتري والغناء إلى إبراهيم بن المهدي.

> And how can one compose books for al-Jāḥiẓ, dedicate jurisprudence to al-Shāfiʿī, poetry to al-Buḥturī and song to Ibrāhīm b. al-Mahdī?[67]

كمهدي العود إلى الهنود وناقل المسك إلى أرض الترك وجالب العنبر إلى البحر الأخضر.

> Like him who offers incense to the Indians, carries musk to the land of the Turks, and imports ambergris to the Green Sea.[68]

In the passages above we see al-Thaʿālibī lamenting the inferiority of his works to his patron, yet he justifies the act of dedicating a deficient work with two lines by his friend Abū al-Fatḥ al-Bustī:[69]

لا تنكـرنّ إذا أهـديتُ نحـوَك مـن　　　علومـك الغـرّ، أو آدابـك النتفـا
فقـيّمُ البـاغ قـد يهـدي لمالكـه　　　بـرسم خدمتـه مـن باغِـه التحفـا

> Do not condemn [me] when I present to you the choicest from your [own] venerable sciences or bits from your [own] literary arts

62 See *Khāṣṣ al-khāṣṣ*, 1.
63 See D. E. Marvin, *The Antiquity of Proverbs*, New York, London: G.P. Putnam's Sons 1922, 281-2.
64 *Taḥsīn*, 28; *Bard*, 103; *Khāṣṣ al-khāṣṣ*, 2.
65 *Al-Iʿjāz*, 17, 19.
66 *Laṭāʾif*, 3; *al-Tawfīq*, 23; *al-Ẓarāʾif*, 3b.
67 *Al-Tawfīq*, 23.
68 *Thimār*, 3.
69 See his biography in Ibn Khallikān, *Wafayāt al-aʿyān*, ed. Iḥsān ʿAbbās, Beirut: Dār al-Thaqāfa 1968, 3: 376.

> Indeed, the gardener presents to the owner the precious produce from his [own] garden by virtue of his service.[70]

Using this analogy of the gardener, al-Thaʿālibī finds a clever way of justifying the presentation of a supposedly inferior book. Moreover, the analogy is even cleverer in the fact that it suggests that he deserves no credit for what he offers, since it was not his property in the first place. By means of this crafty trick, al-Thaʿālibī makes the patron the virtual author of the book. He states this even more clearly in another instance, claiming that his entire *Mirʾāt al-murūʾāt* is a portrait of his patron's qualities and thus the patron is the real author of the book.[71] In another instance al-Thaʿālibī justifies his gift by claiming that *adab* is his only possession, and he is presenting it to the patron only because he recognizes that knowledge of the subtleties of *adab* are intrinsic to the nature of the patron.[72]

## *The Form of al-Thaʿālibī's* Muqaddimāt

### *I- Rhyme and Rhythmical Balance* (Sajʿ wa-Muwāzana)

*Sajʿ* is rhymed prose while *muwāzana* is the rhythmical and/or syntactical balance in the sentence (traditionally in terms of words).[73] Both *sajʿ* and *muwāzana* are major characteristics of 4th/10th-century artistic prose, although they can be traced back to the soothsayers' prose [*sajʿ al-kuhhān*] of pre-Islamic Arabia. In many cases, however, and especially in the works of later critics, *sajʿ* assumes *muwāzana*.

One of the earliest rhetoricians to discuss *sajʿ* in some detail and in numerical terms was Ḍiyāʾ al-Dīn b. al-Athīr (d. 637/1239).[74] Ibn al-Athīr shows by examples how the length of one rhythmical unit is very close to the length of its part-

---

70 *Bard*, 103; *Thimār*, 3.

71 *Mirʾāt*, 65-6. One can see this motif for example in Ibn al-Rūmī's panegyrics; see for details Gruendler, 227ff and especially 253-255. Such a book, of course, cannot be rededicated to another patron after this claim, since it is the whole book in this case that presents a portrait of the patron and not only the *muqaddima*. Rededication in this case would obviously violate the ethics of patronage.

72 *Khāṣṣ al-khāṣṣ*, 2.

73 *Sajʿ*, according to Régis Blachère's translation, is "rhymed and rhythmic prose", see Régis Blachère, *Histoire de la littérature Arabe des origines à la fin du Xve siècle de J. –C*, Paris: Adrien-Maisonneuve 1964, 189. This definition of *sajʿ* includes *al-muwāzana* as an integral part of *sajʿ*. As *Sajʿ* and *muwāzana* do not always presume each other I take them to be separate in this paper.

74 See his biography in F. Rosenthal, "Ibn al-Athīr", in *The Encyclopaedia of Islam*, 2nd ed., Leiden: Brill 1979, III: 723b-5a. Some other medieval authors who treated the same subject are Abū Hilāl al-ʿAskarī (d. after 395/1005) in his *Kitāb al-Ṣināʿatayn*, and al-Qalqashandī (d. 821/1418) in his *Ṣubḥ al-aʿshā fī ṣināʿat al-inshāʾ*.

ners in terms of words – with no mention of syllables.[75] In this respect the single word [*lafẓa*] in prose corresponds to the poetic foot [*tafʿīla*] in poetry. Ibn al-Athīr proposes two major categories, short *sajʿ* [*sajʿ qaṣīr*] and long *sajʿ* [*sajʿ ṭawīl*]. The former consists of two to ten words in each colon, while the latter counts eleven or more.[76] Modern scholarship, in contrast, discusses the numerical balance of *sajʿ* with regard to the number of words as well as syllables.[77] These recent studies reveal fascinating rhythmical patterns of *sajʿ* some of which one encounters in Thaʿālibī's *muqaddimāt* as well. One example will suffice to demonstrate this aspect of his *muqaddimāt*. Al-Thaʿālibī says:

أيّام مولانا الملك المؤيّد ... مواقيت الشرف والفضل. وأوقاته تواريخ الكرم والمجد. وساعاته مواسم الأدب والعلم. وأنفاسه نِعَم. وأقواله نَعَم. وأفعاله سيَر. وآثاره غرر. وألفاظه درر. ومعاليه تباهي النجوم ارتفاعاً. ومكارمه تضاهي الجوّ اتّساعاً. ومحاسنه تباري الشمسَ ظهوراً. وفضائله تجاري القطرَ وفوراً.

The days of our lord, the supported king, ... are rendezvous for honor and virtue, his periods are times of generosity and glory, his hours are seasons for literature and knowledge, his breaths are blessings and his sayings are always "yes". His deeds become customs, his achievements illustrious, his utterances pearls. His high ambitions rival the stars in height and his noble deeds rival the horizon in width. His good qualities compete with the sun in brilliance and his merits compete with rain in abundance.[78]

In the first three phrases al-Thaʿālibī does not employ rhyme; instead he uses *muwāzana* making the three phrases parallel syntactically and, almost, morphologically. This morphological and syntactical parallelism is maintained to the end of the paragraph and coupled with *sajʿ*. We can also see that al-Thaʿālibī maintains a rather strict parallelism of syllables throughout the paragraph. The following diagram shows parallelisms in al-Thaʿālibī's three groups of cola in this paragraph:

75 See: *al-Mathal al-sāʾir fī adab al-kātib wa-l-shāʿir*, Cairo: Maktabat Nahḍat Miṣr 1959-62, 1: 271-337.

76 Al-Qazwīnī, on the other hand, divides *sajʿ* into three groups: short, medium, and long, but without specifying the borders of each; see *al-Īḍāḥ fī ʿulūm al-balāgha*, ed. Muḥammad ʿAbd al-Munʿim al-Khafājī, Beirut: Dār al-Kitāb al-Lubnānī 1949, 2: 248-9.

77 The most important recent works on *sajʿ* are: Stewart, Devin, "Sajʿ in the Qurʾān: prosody and structure", *Journal of Arabic Literature* XXI-2 (1990), 101-139; Zakī Mubārak, *La Prose Arabe au IVe siècle de l' Hégire*, Paris: Maisonneuve 1931, 78-94; idem, *al-Nathr al-fannī fī l-qarn al-rābiʿ*, Cairo: Dār al-Kātib al-ʿArabī 1934, 1: 75-123, 137-53; Afif Ben Abdesselem, "*sajʿ*", in *The Encyclopaedia of Islam*, 2nd ed., Leiden: Brill 1995, VIII: 734a-8b. Works taking syllables as a basis were initiated by Maḥmūd al-Masʿadī, *al-Īqāʿ fī-l-adab al-ʿarabī*, Tunis: Muʾassasat ʿAbd al-Karīm b. ʿAbdallāh li-l-Nashr wa-l-Tawzīʿ 1986; Yūnis, ʿAlī, *Naẓra jadīda fī mūsīqā l-shiʿr al-ʿarabī*, Cairo: al-Hayʾa al-Miṣriyya al-ʿĀmma li-l-Kitāb 1993; a statistical approach to *sajʿ* is applied in Adrian Gully and John Hinde, "Qābūs ibn Wushmagīr: a study of rhythm patterns in Arabic epistolary prose from the 4th century AH", *Middle Eastern Literatures* vol. 6 no. 2 (July 2003).

78 *Nathr*, 7.

Group One

| | | |
|---|---|---|
| *ʾay/yā/mu/ (maw/lā/na)* | *ma/wā/qī/tush/sha/ra/fi/wal/faḍ/li* | - - v (- - v) v - - - v v v - - v |
| *ʾaw/qā/tu/hū/* | *ta/wā/rī/khul/ka/ra/mi/ wal/maj/di* | - - v - v - - - v v v - - v |
| *sā/ʿā/tu/hū/* | *ma/wā/si/mu-l/ʾa/da/bi/ wal/ʿil/mi* | - - v - v - v - v v v - - v |

Group Two

| | |
|---|---|
| *wa/ʾan/fā/su/hu/ni/ʿam* | v - - v v v - |
| *wa/ʾaq/wā/lu/hu/na/ʿam* | v - - v v v - |
| *wa/ʾaf/ʿā/lu/hu/si/yar* | v - - v v v - |
| *wa/ʾal/fā/ẓu/hu/du/rar* | v - - v v v - |

Group Three

| | |
|---|---|
| *wa/ma/ʿā/lī/hi/tu/bā/hin/nu/jū/mar/ti/fā/ʿan* | v v - - v v - - v - - v - - |
| *wa/ma/kā/ri/mu/hu/tu/ḍā/hil/jaw/wat/ti/sā/ʿan* | v v - v v v v - - - - v - - |
| *wa/ma/ḥā/si/nu/hu/tu/bā/rish/sham/sa/ẓu/hū/ran* | v v - v v v v - - - v v - - |
| *wa/fa/ḍā/ʾi/lu/hu/tu/jā/ril/qaṭ/ra/wu/fū/ran* | v v - v v v v - - - v v - - |

This diagram shows that al-Thaʿālibī does not only maintain an equal number of words in every *sajʿa*, which constitutes the best type of *sajʿ* according to Ibn al-Athīr, but also maintains an equal number of syllables with almost perfect parallelism.

Needless to say, al-Thaʿālibī does not follow a uniform pattern of *sajʿ* in his *muqaddimāt*; rather, he varies his patterns to avoid boredom, as do most authors of artistic prose of the 4th/10th century. One can generalize, however, and say that most of al-Thaʿālibī's *sajʿ* range between two to six words, placing his *sajʿ* in the category of short *sajʿ*, according to the division of Ibn al-Athīr, who stressed his preference for this type of *sajʿ*.[79]

*II- Extensive Use of Figures of Speech* (Badīʿ)

Ibn al-Muʿtazz gathers as many as eighteen figures of speech in his *K. al-Badīʿ*: the initial five, according to the author, are artifices of figures of speech [*badīʿ*], while the rest are artifices for the embellishment of speech [*maḥāsin*]. Later, however, the term *badīʿ* was applied to *badīʿ* figures and *maḥāsin* alike. Even before the 4th/10th century many books dealt with the subject, most importantly the *K. Naqd al-shiʿr* of Qudāma b. Jaʿfar (d. before 337/948),[80] *K. al-Ṣināʿatayn* of Abū Hilāl al-ʿAskarī (d. after 400/1010),[81] and *Iʿjāz al-Qurʾān* of al-Baqillānī

79 See *al-Mathal*, 1: 335-6.

80 See his biography in S.A. Bonebakker, "Ḳudāma b. Djaʿfar", in *The Encyclopaedia of Islam*, 2nd ed., Leiden: Brill 1986, V: 318b-22a.

81 See his biography in J.W. Fück, "al-ʿAskarī", in *The Encyclopaedia of Islam*, 2nd ed., Leiden: Brill 1960, I: 711b-13a; B. Gruendler, "Abū Hilāl al-ʿAskarī", in *The Encyclopaedia of Islam*, 3rd ed. Leiden: Brill (in press).

(d. 403/1013).[82] A total of twenty-nine figures collected from these books and their use became customary requirements of *balāgha* in both prose and poetry. Qābūs b. Wushmgīr, the famous Persian ruler and author of *belles-lettres*,[83] for example, claims to have invented fourteen figures of speech.[84] By the beginning of the 5th/11th century, the number of figures of speech had reached nearly one hundred.[85] Al-Thaʿālibī, however, while not devoting a whole book to a comprehensive discussion of *badīʿ* figures,[86] sets aside whole books for individual common ones. He discusses, for example, *tajnīs* [paronomasia] in his *Ajnās al-tajnīs* and *al-Anīs fī ghurar al-tajnīs*, *kināya* [allusion/metonymy] in *al-Kināya wa-l-taʿrīḍ*, and gives illustrations of *sajʿ* [rhymed and rhythmic prose] in *Sajʿ al-manthūr*. Moreover, al-Thaʿālibī discusses various figures of speech in scattered passages in his books, especially his *Yatīmat al-dahr*. It is natural, then, that al-Thaʿālibī's interest in *badīʿ* finds a place in his own writing; he says, for example, in his *muqaddimāt*:

الشيخ الأمير السيّد تحفةٌ تجمعُ أبكارَ الأفكار وتنظم أسرارَ الأسفار وتسحر القلوبَ بنثار النثر وشِعار الشعر المختار.

The Amīr, Shaykh and Master is a masterpiece that collects the virgin thoughts, strings the secrets of tomes, enchants the hearts with the coins of prose and the signs of select poetry.[87]

فمن الكبائر أن تسيرَ مؤلّفاتي في البلاد مسيرَ الأمثال وتسري مسرى الخيال، إذ هي رياحين الملوك والأمراء وفواكه الفضلاء والرؤساء وليس لي مؤلّف برسم الشيخ...

It is a grave sin that my works circulate in countries like proverbs and travel like phantoms, being the basil flowers of kings and governors and the fruit of the virtuous and leaders, while I have no work by the order of the Shaykh…[88]

...ومحاسن سيرٍ تطرّسها أسنّةُ الأقلام وتدرسها ألسنةُ الليالي والأيّام.

---

82 See his biography in R.J. McCarthy, "al-Bāḳillānī", in *The Encyclopaedia of Islam*, 2nd ed., Leiden: Brill 1960, I: 958b-59a.

83 See his biography in C. E. Bosworth, "Ḳābūs b. Wushmgīr", in *The Encyclopaedia of Islam*, 2nd ed., Leiden: Brill 1978, IV: 357b-358b.

84 See Qābūs b. Wushmgīr, *Kamāl al-balāgha*, ed. ʿA. al-Yazdadī, Baghdād: al-Maktaba al-ʿArabiyya 1922, 19-32.

85 Usāma b. Munqidh's work *al-Badīʿ fī naqd al-shiʿr*, which was composed in the first quarter of the 6th/12th century contains 95 figures of speech, see *al-Badīʿ fī naqd al-shiʿr*, ed. A. A. Badawī et al., Cairo: al-Bābī al-Ḥalabī 1960, 91-92. For more information on figures of speech in Arabic Literature see W. Heinrichs, "Badīʿ", in *Encylopedia of Arabic Literature*, ed. Julie Scott Meisami and Paul Starkey, London: Routledge 1998.

86 The *Rawḍat al-Faṣāḥa* that is falsely attributed to al-Thaʿālibī by M. I. Salīm belongs to a later period. Despite the little evidence in the introduction of the work, mainly the start with *barāʿat al-istihlāl* coined with Qurʾānic quotations and the emphasis on the brevity and the worth of the book, the work includes numerous quotations by later authors, including al-Ḥarīrī (d. 516/1122) and al-Zamakhsharī (d. 538/1144).

87 *al-Anīs*, 41.

88 *Al-Iʿjāz*, 20.

> … And qualities that the spearheads of pens guard and the tongues of days and nights study.[89]

> عونك اللهمّ على شكر نعمتك في مَلِكٍ كَمَلَكٍ وبحر كقصرٍ وبدرٍ في دسْتٍ وغيثٍ يصدر عن ليثٍ وعالَمٍ في ثوب عالِمٍ وسلطانٍ بين حُسنٍ وإحسانٍ.

> O Lord, we seek your assistance to thank your beneficence for a king like an angel, a sea like a castle, a full moon in a seat of honor, rain stemming from a lion, a cosmos in a garment of a scholar, and a ruler [shifting] between beauty [of creation] and good deeds.[90]

## *III- Synonymity and Prolixity* (al-Tarāduf wa-l-Iṭnāb)

Al-Jurjānī (d. 816/ 1413) defines synonymity [*tarāduf*] as "unanimity in meaning" and "the succession of the single phrases that point to the same thing under the same aspect",[91] while Abū Hilāl al-ʿAskarī defines prolixity [*iṭnāb*] as: "expanding speech to increase the benefit".[92] Both *tarāduf* and *iṭnāb* were common practices in the 3rd/9th century, especially with al-Jāḥiẓ. However, these two techniques were developed further in the 4th/10th century to the point that the literary framework became much wider than its content. Al-Thaʿālibī uses both techniques in his prose writing, for example:

> هذا كتاب يشتمل على محاسن الألفاظ الدعجة وبدائع المعاني الأرجة ولطائف الأوصاف التي تحكي أنوارَ الأشجار وأنفاسَ الأسحار وغناءَ الأطيار وأجيادَ الغزلان وأطواقَ الحمام وصدورَ البازات والشهب وأجنحةَ الطواويس الخضر وملحَ الرياض وسحرَ المقل المراض، وتحرّك الخواطرَ الساكنة وتبعث الأشواقَ الكامنة وتُسكر بلا شرابٍ وتُطرب من غير إطرابٍ وتهزّ بأطرابها كما هزّت الغصنَ ريحُ الصبا وكما انتفض العصفورُ بلّله القطرُ من نثرٍ كنثر الورد ونظمٍ كنظم العقد.

> This is a book that includes the best of pretty utterances, the marvelous fragrant meanings, and subtle descriptions, [all of] which imitate the blossoms of trees, the breeze of early mornings, the singing of birds, the necks of gazelles, the collars of doves, the breasts of falcons and buzzards, the green wings of peacocks, beautiful gardens, and the charm of the languid eyes.
> [The content of the book] moves still minds, arouse hidden desires, intoxicate without drink, and delight without music, and cause tremors from this delight (just) as the east winds shakes the bough, (and) as the bird who was splashed by rain shakes off the moisture – all this being prose that is like the scattering of rose water and poetry like the stringing of [pearls] in a necklace.[93]

Al-Thaʿālibī here presents two main points: first, that his book includes excellent utterances, meanings, and descriptions that rival the beauty of nature, and sec-

---

89 *Al-Tamthīl*, 3.
90 *Al-Kināya*, 23.
91 Al-Jurjānī, *K.*, *al-Taʿrīfāt*, Beirut: Maktabat Lubnān 1969, 58.
92 Abū Hilāl al-ʿAskarī, *al-Furūq fī l-lugha*, Beirut: Dār al-Āfāq al-Jadīda 1973, 32.
93 *Man ghāba ʿanhu-l-muṭrib*, ed. N. Shaʿlān, Cairo: Maktabat al-Khānjī 1984, 3.

ond, that it includes both prose and poetry that exert an effect on the human mind. However, in repeating the same concepts in different phrases and listing examples of "subtle descriptions", he provides the text with a considerable verbal effect, though it adds nothing to the content.[94]

*IV- Adaptation and Inclusion* (al-Iqtibās wa-l-Taḍmīn)

Quoting or adapting Qur'ānic verses, *ḥadīth*, or lines of poetry is another major feature of 4th/10th-century prose writing that al-Thaʿālibī employs in his *muqaddimāt*. In the case of poetry, the examples above demonstrate that when al-Thaʿālibī quotes poetry in his *muqaddimāt*, it is usually only a few lines and typically not his own. In some instances the poetry is quoted because it reminds al-Thaʿālibī of some meaning or motif he is expressing in the surrounding prose. In these cases the poetry runs parallel to the prose text, does not add to the meaning, and functions simply to illustrate the original motif. This also shows al-Thaʿālibī's ability in applying *ḥall al-naẓm* [prosification] in this practice.[95] Al-Thaʿālibī in these cases depends on poetic motifs from ancient or contemporary poetry. Indeed, al-Thaʿālibī's general works demonstrate an interest in *ḥall al-naẓm*, in particular a whole book dedicated to this practice, his *Nathr al-naẓm wa-ḥall al-ʿaqd* [Releasing of the Poetic String and Untying of the Knot]. Drawing his reader's attention to this technique, he says:

> أمّا بعد فإنّ هذا الكتاب أخرجت بعضه من غرر نجوم الأرض، ونكت أعيان الفضل من بلغاء العصر في النثر وحللت بعضه من نظم أمراء الشعر الذين أوردت ملح أشعارهم في كتابي المترجم بيتيمة الدهر.
>
> Thereupon, I brought out half of this book from the best [outcome] of the planets [i.e. authors] of the earth and the best eloquent people of the age in prose writing, while I released its [other] half from releasing the poetic string of the princes of poetry, whose good poetry I cited in my book *Yatīmat al-dahr*.[96]

In other instances al-Thaʿālibī quotes poetry as part of the prose text, making use of what al-Qalqashandī considers *fann al-imtizāj* [the art of intermingling] [97]:

---

94 See other examples of both techniques in quotations number 6, 8, 10, 11, 17.

95 On the genre, see Amidu Sanni, *The Arabic Theory of Prosification and Versification*, Beirut-Stuttgart: Franz Steiner Verlag 1998.

96 *Siḥr al-balāgha*, 3.

97 For details see al-Qalqashandī, *Ṣubḥ al-aʿshā fī ṣināʿat al-inshā'*, Cairo: al-Mu'assasa al-Miṣriyya al-ʿĀmma 1964, 1: 280. An extreme case of this art, one from which the term *al-imtizāj* might have originated, is found in the *rasā'il* of Badīʿ al-Zamān al-Hamadhānī, a case that al-Thaʿālibī himself quotes in his *Yatīmat al-dahr*:

إنّا لقرب الأستاذ أطال الله بقاءه **{كما طرب النشوان مالت به الخمر}**، ومن الارتياح للقائه **{كما انتفض العصفور بلّله القطر}**، ومن **الامتزاج** بولائه، **{كما التقت الصهباء والبارد العذب}** ومن الابتهاج بمرآه، **{كما اهتزّ تحت البارح الغصن الرطب}**

هذا كتاب يشتمل على محاسن الألفاظ الدعجة وبدائع المعاني الأرجة ولطائف الأوصاف التي تحكي أنوار الأشجار ... وتحرّك الخواطرَ الساكنة وتبعث الأشواقَ الكامنة وتُسكر بلا شرابٍ وتُطرب من غير إطرابٍ وتهزّ بأطرابها {**كما هزّت الغصن ريح الصبا**} و{**كما انتفض العصفور بلّله القطر**} من نثرٍ كنثر الورد ونظمٍ كنظم العقد.[98]

In this example the phrase "*kamā hazzati-l-ghuṣna rīḥu-ṣ-ṣibā*" is a hemistich in *al-Mutaqārib* meter,[99] while the second "*kamā intafaḍa-l-ʿuṣfūru ballalahu-l-qaṭṭru*" is in *al-Ṭawīl*,[100] and al-Thaʿālibī uses both as part of the prose text with no indication to this fact, except for the hint provided at the end of the sentence explaining that the book includes both prose and poetry.

Al-Thaʿālibī in his *muqaddimāt* applies the same technique of quoting poetry in his quotation of Qurʾānic verses, i.e. the verses are included in the text as a part of the main speech and not as a quotation. Al-Thaʿālibī dedicates a whole book to this technique entitled *al-Iqtibās min al-Qurʾān*, which was discussed earlier.[101] To give an example from another work, comparing the family of al-Mīkālī to the "good tree" [*shajara ṭayyiba*] mentioned in the Qurʾān, al-Thaʿālibī says in the *muqaddima* of *Fiqh al-lugha*:

كانت شجرته الميكالية في قرارة المجد والعلاء و{**أصلها ثابت وفرعها في السماء**}

His Mīkālī tree was situated in the depth of glory and highness, its root is firm while its branches are in the sky[102].[103]

---

My condition [in longing] to approach the Master {is like [the condition of] the intoxicated man who is swayed by wine}, and in my gratification to his encounter [I am like] {the bird who, splashed by rain, shakes off the moisture}, and for attaining his amity , [I hope to be] {like the wine which mixes with cold fresh water}, and in my delight by seeing him, I am {like the damp bough which shakes in the hot wind of summer}.

See *Kashf al-maʿānī wa-l-bayān ʿan rasāʾil Badīʿ al-Zamān*, ed. A. al-Ṭarābulsī, Beirut: al-Maṭbaʿa al-Kāthūlīkiyya 1890, 128-9, and *Yatīma*, 4: 243, MS Laleli 1959, 546v. Other examples by al-Hamadhānī are in *Kashf*, 139, 141, 292, 375.

98 See translation in Quotation number ten above.

99 The full line, by al-Nājim (d. 314/926), is:

تهزّ القريض بألحانها كما هزّت الغصن ريح الصّبا

See al-Ḥuṣrī al-Qayrawānī, *Jamʿ al-Jawāhir*, ed. ʿA. M. Al-Bajāwī, Beirut: Dār al-Jīl 1987; Idem, *Nūr al-ṭarf*, ed. L. ʿA. Abū Ṣāliḥ, Beirut: Muʾassasat al-Risāla 1966, 258, Ibn Abī ʿAwn, *Kitāb al-Tashbīhāt*, ed. M. ʿA. Khān, Cambridge: Cambridge University Press, 122.

100 The hemistich is attributed to many poets; most probably it originated from the line of by Abu Ṣakhr al-Hudhalī [d. 80/700]:

وإنّي لتعروني لذكراكِ هزّةٌ كما انتفض العصفورُ بلّله القطر

See Abū al-Faraj al-Iṣbahānī, *al-Aghānī*, Cairo: Maṭbaʿat Dār al-Kutub al-Miṣriyya 1932, 5: 184.

101 See Quotation two above.

102 A reference to Q. 14: 24.

103 *Fiqh*, 3; see also for another example 10.

*V- Brilliant Exordia* (Barāʿat al-Istihlāl)

Al-Jurjānī defines the term *barāʿat al-istihlāl* as follows: "*barāʿat al-istihlāl* occurs when the author makes a statement at the beginning of his work to indicate the general subject before entering into the details, i.e. when the beginning of speech is suitable to the intended [subject]; it frequently occurs in the exordiums of books."[104] Al-Thaʿālibī often recognizes this convention in writing. For example, in *Ādāb al-mulūk* [On the proper conduct of kings] he says in his *taḥmīd*:

ثمّ الحمد لله الذي استخلف الملوك في أرضه واسترعاهم أمور خلقه وجعلهم المدافعين عن سواد الأمّة وبياض الدعوة والأزمّة على الملّة والحوزة.

Then praise be to God who made kings his successors in land, asked them to look after the matters of His creation, made them the defenders of the common [lit: black] people and the pure [lit. white] call, the keepers of the faith, as well as the owners [of this faith].[105]

Although al-Thaʿālibī usually uses *barāʿat al-istihlāl* immediately at the beginning of his *muqaddima* – often in the *taḥmīd* section – he sometimes leaves this to the middle of his *muqaddima*. For example, he employs *barāʿat al-istihlāl* in *al-Kināya wa-l-taʿrīḍ* [book of hinting and allusion] in praising his patron:

هذه صفة تُغني عن التسمية ولا تحوج إلى التكنية، إذ هي مختصّة بمولانا الأمير السيّد الملك المؤيّد.

This is a description that obviates the necessity of naming and does not need *any hinting* for it is special to our master, the chief prince, and the supported king.

In this quotation the word "hinting" [*takniya*] refers to the title of the book. Sometimes al-Thaʿālibī indicates the subject of his book more subtly by writing the preface in a style that constitutes the subject of the book itself. An example of this is the previously discussed *al-Iqtibās min al-Qurʾān* [Quoting from the *Qurʾān*], in which al-Thaʿālibī starts the *taḥmīd* section with the series of Qurʾānic excerpts quoted above. Another example is his *Thimār al-qulūb* where he writes in its preface:

...وإن كنتُ في ذلك كمهدي العود إلى الهنود وناقل المسك إلى أرض الترك وجالب العنبر إلى البحر الأخضر.

...even if in doing so I am like him who offers incense to the Indians, carries musk to the land of the Turks, and imports ambergris to the Green Sea.[106]

This sentence is part of the modesty topos discussed previously, which occurs frequently in al-Thaʿālibī's *muqaddimāt*. However, the phrases *ʿūd al-hind*, *misk al-*

---

104 *Al-Taʿrīfāt*, 64; see also, *Ṣubḥ al-aʿsha*, 11: 73ff.
105 *Ādāb al-mulūk*, 30.
106 *Thimār al-qulūb*, 3.

*turk*, and *ʿanbar al-baḥr al-akhḍar* [107] are examples of the material of the book that is an alphabetically-arranged lexicon of two-word phrases and clichés.[108]

## *Conclusion*

Using al-Thaʿālibī's scholarship as a point of departure, this article has presented the *muqaddima* as an independent literary form of Arabic artistic prose by drawing attention to both its content and form. With respect to content, the article has illustrated the conventional aspects of al-Thaʿālibī's *muqaddima* by examining its prefatory remarks, presentation of the title work, delineation of the method and plan of the work, and finally the dedication, or rededication, of the work. In terms of the content, the *muqaddima* acts as a panegyric poem – a contract between the author of the work and his patron – by drawing a portrait of the dedicatee to be matched by his acts of generosity. With respect to form, this article has shown that the *muqaddima*, at least in the case of al-Thaʿālibī, enjoys all of the features of artistic prose from the 4th/10th century, thereby expanding the range of artistic prose to genres beyond those of *adab*, *maqāmāt*, and *belles-lettres*. Indeed, biographers and anthologists living shortly after al-Thaʿālibī's death did not hesitate, when selecting from al-Thaʿālibī's literary product, to include his *muqaddimāt* as a proof of his excellent prose.[109] This fact shows that these *muqaddimāt* where considered to be artistic prose at the time. Finally, this article analyzes the artistic techniques employed by the author for the purpose of showing his own literary talents, on the one hand, and attracting and directing the attention of the reader, on the other. In this respect, the effect of these *muqaddimāt* is like that of an overture with which a composer starts an opera.

---

107 For a discussion of the three terms see *Thimār al-qulūb*, 533.

108 For an excellent example of *barāʿat al-istihlāl* in al-Thaʿālibī's works see *Zād safar al-mulūk*, 43b-43a.

109 Ibn Bassām is a prime example in this respect, for in his entry on al-Thaʿālibī in *al-Dhakhīra* includes several of al-Thaʿālibī's *muqaddimāt* filling several pages along with quotations from *Yatīmat al-dahr* and al-Thaʿālibī's poetry; see Ibn Bassām al-Shantarīnī, *al-Dhakhīra fī maḥāsin ahl al-jazīra*, ed. Iḥsān ʿAbbās. Beirut: Dār al-Thaqāfa 1979, 8: 560ff.

# The double entendre (*tawriya*) as a Hermeneutical Stratagem: A 'Forensic *Maqāma*' by Abū Muḥammad al-Qāsim b. ʿAlī al-Ḥarīrī[1]

*Angelika Neuwirth (Free University Berlin)*

> The alexandrine, for instance, has value both as meaning
> of a discourse and as signifier of a new whole,
> which is its poetic signification.
> [Roland Barthes, Mythologies]

## *A Premodern Arabic Dramatic Genre: the* maqāma[2]

The *maqāma*, an Arabic literary genre that, once developed in tenth century Iran, was soon to cross the borders of literary provinces and linguistic traditions to establish itself in such non-Arabic literatures as the Syriac and the Hebrew,[3] is certainly more than just another genre of narrative. Very much like the case claimed by Roland Barthes for classical European poetry, the *maqāma* written in rhymed and rhythmically structured prose is "a strongly mythical system, since it imposes on the meaning one extra 'signified', which is regularity".[4] The classical *maqāma* is replete with rhetorical patterns based on analogy, and by virtue of its regularities enjoys the reputation of stylistically exemplary literature, apt to exemplify grammatical norms, thus occupying a place in the core of traditional Arabic Islamic education. In view of the prevalent patriarchal values in classical Islamic culture, it comes as no surprise, that the presentation of women in these texts relies on the "repetition of recycled clichés" and "reverberates fixated views

---

1 This is an extended and thoroughly revised version of two previous attempts by the present author to explore this particularly complex text, cf. Neuwirth (1999) and Neuwirth (2005).

2 All too often in Western criticism the particularly artistic character of the *maqāma* style consisting of *sajʿ* and poetry, has been taken as merely ornamental and disapproved of as unduly artificial, see for a strikingly sarcastic judgement Charles Pellat: Article *Maqāma* in EI VI: "Al-Ḥariri (...) gave the genre its classic form, freezing it, so to speak and diverting it from its actual function; according only a secondary interest to the content and placing his entire emphasis on the style which often takes on the nature of ponderous obscurity. Al Hariri's ultimate aim is the preserving and teaching of the rarest vocabulary. The success of al-Hariri's *Maqāmāt* (...) appealed to the taste of readers to such an extent that, after the Qurʾān, children were to memorise them (...).

3 Hämeen-Anttila (2002); Kilito (1983).

4 Barthes (1972), 133, n. 10.

about women" not unlike their appearance in the Hebrew *maqāma* described by Tova Rosen in her seminal study *Unveiling Eve. Reading Gender in Medieval Hebrew Literature.*[5] It is not least these fixed traits attributed to the female gender in literature – that can be subsumed under the heading of 'ambiguity' - that easily lend themselves to a mythicization of woman that is to be encountered in the Arabic and the Hebrew *maqāma* alike. In rhetoric terms, this image of the female is related to the figure of the *double entendre*, of *tawriya*[6].

A case will be studied below.[7]

The most prolific and influential writer of Arabic *maqāmāt*, Abū Muḥammad al-Qāsim al-Ḥarīrī (d. 1122), left a collection of fifty *maqāmāt* that for their stylistic artistry early became part of the Arabic literary canon. Al-Ḥarīrī's *maqāmāt* rigidly follow a stereotypical structure: The narrator – *al-rāwī* – named al-Ḥārith ibn Hammām in each single *maqāma* reports an event focusing on one and the same protagonist, Abū Zayd al-Sarūjī, a picaresque person who earns his living by his often treacherous tongue. Abū Zayd is the narrator's admired mentor, a gifted poet and rhetorician, whom he encounters in diverse places, always staging a 'drama'[8] engaging in it a group of persons present on the spot – a kind of anticipation of the so-called 'Invisible Theatre', currently practised in Latin America[9]. Each time in the guise of a new identity, Abū Zayd by his rhetorical artistry captivates his unsuspecting co-actors and ends up extracting gifts from them. Recognized toward the end of the play by al-Ḥārith, the hero has to submit himself to a trial and to render account in front of his disciple for his deceptive play – a task he often fulfils in poetic form. After this sort of 'post-drama', al-Ḥārith departs from the scene, thus marking the end of the *maqāma*. Drama and 'post-drama', then, are the two main structural elements of al-Ḥarīrī's *maqāma* situated around the axis of an *anagnorisis*, the unveiling of the main protagonist's identity. The plot, thus, with striking regularity reiterates the model of crime and rendering account.

Yet, the *maqāma* plots are hardly intended to criminalize Abū Zayd[10]. The narrator functioning as judge is an alter ego of the offender, belonging like Abū Zayd to those intellectuals who take interest not in warranted and established

---

5 Rosen (2003), 8.

6 Bonebakker (1966).

7 The particular category of the forensic *maqāma* has been discussed by Neuwirth (1999).

8 Moreh (1992) regards the *maqāma* as a dramatic genre, 105f.: "All this confirms our assumption that the *maqāma* proper is an act, a written composition for mimetic declamation and used a haranguing style with a prodigious store of sophisticated rhetoric and eloquent turn of phrase. These characteristics endowed the *maqāma* with the seriousness Muslims sought and admired in Arabic literature. It overshadowed all other oral genres."

9 Chenou (1995).

10 I do not share Robert Irwins's view (1999) 187 who holds that Abū Zayd is a "liar and cheat". What is at stake in the *maqāma* is not a moral but a hermeneutical issue: Abū Zayd's staging *adab* is not a real discourse, but a meta-discourse.

knowledge (*ᶜilm*), the ideal human tenet in Islamic culture, but rather in the extraordinary, in miraculous and a-normal phenomena (*ᶜajīb*). He follows the sophisticated, well-versed men in the ways of the world, who choose to rely on their own experience rather than on pious transmission, replacing the religiously meritorious 'journey in search of knowledge' with its subversive counterpart, the journey in search of the strange and unusual:

> *Kuntu akhadhtu ᶜan ūli t-tajārīb / anna s-safara mirʾātu l-aᶜājīb / fa-lam azal ajūbu kulla tanūfah / wa-aqtaḥimu kulla makhūfah / ḥatta jtalabtu kulla uṭrūfah.*
>
> "I had gathered it from men of experiences, that travel is a mirror of marvels, wherefore I ceased not crossing every desert, and braving every danger, so that I might bring into my reach everything wonderful."[11]

It is obvious that such a person posing as judge cannot give a convincing verdict on the offence of Abū Zayd's deceptive play and use of his rhetorical gifts outside the realm conceded by societal norms. Things are different when, instead of al-Ḥārith, the offender's alter ego, a genuine judge, a *qāḍī*, is involved and the play is staged in a court of law. Then the debate of the 'post-drama' is exposed to a kind of microscopic magnification: Once the spokesman of norms himself is implied, it is no longer the individual act of deception that is tried, but rather the legitimacy of Abū Zayd's practice as such, advocating instead of the ideal of norm-abiding traditional behaviour, rather the anti-norm, the ideal of play involving the extraordinary and unusual. As a '*maqāma* about the *maqāma*', i.e. about the legitimacy of play based on fiction, and thus deception and fraud in the categories of the patriarchal norm system, the 'forensic *maqāma*', thus, deserves particular interest within the corpus as a whole.

## Al-maqāma ar-ramlīya: *the argument*

Let us turn to the *maqāma* of Ramleh[12] as an example of such a 'forensic *maqāma*'. There appears before the judge of Ramleh an old man in shabby guise together with a beautiful young woman equally clad in rags. In front of the *qāḍī* they together stage a topsy-turvy world in which woman dominates man verbally, "forbids him to bark". She unveils shamelessly to anticipate his attempt to speak up first with a forceful flow of words of her own. Her speech, consisting of seven poetical verses – making up her great entrance – is not without sophistification: She claims against her husband that he neglects his marital duties. The claim is presented in a much exaggerated and at the same time disguised form, since she projects the offence, the missed intercourse, from her body onto the cosmic centre of the world, the Kaᶜba. It is the rites of the Kaᶜba that her husband has been neglecting for a long time:

---

11 al-Ḥarīrī (1976), V 185; Steingass (1898), II 142.

12 For a more comprehensive presentation of the *maqāma*, see Neuwirth (1999).

> *Yā qāḍiya r-ramlati yā dhā lladhi/ fi yadihi t-tamratu wa-l-jamrah / ilayka ashkū jawra baʿli lladhī/ lam yaḥjuji l-bayta siwa marrah.*
>
> "O *qāḍī* of Ramleh, in whose hands there is for us the date or else the hot cinder-coal / to thee complain I of my mate's cruelty, who pays his pilgrim's duty but once in a while."[13]

Nothing less than a ritual omission that threatens world order itself is at stake. Although her complex metaphor of various pilgrimage performances does allude to sexual acts, yet her speech, over the first four verses, has no explicit mention of the female body thus giving the claim a touch of an enigma. All the more daring is the reference to the authority of the renowned early Islamic jurist Abū Yūsuf, whose recommendations as to the ritual performance of the Islamic pilgrimage, the *ḥajj*, are used frivolously as evidence for the meritoriousness of frequent intercourse:

> *Wa-laythahu lammā qaḍā nuskahu/ wa-khaffa ẓahran idh rama l-jamrah / kāna ʿalā raʾyi Abī Yūsufin/ fī ṣilati l-ḥijjati bi-l-ʿumrah.*
>
> "Would that, when his devotion has come to end, and eased his back is after his pebble-throw / he followed Abū Yūsuf's wise rule and wont to join the lesser with the chief pilgrimage."[14]

The female body thus, is perceived as a cosmically relevant surface on which the juridical rulings of the classical legal scholar are projected, a treatment of the body which deserves to be called 'grotesque' in the Bakhtinian sense. It is only in the second part of her speech, exposing her expired patience, that the woman speaks in her own right as 'I' and threatens – in case of a non-satisfactory solution of the problem – to strip herself of all decency, i.e. to rebel openly against social norms and give herself up to the rival par excellence of her legitimate partner, Satan himself:

> *Famurhu imma ulfatan ḥulwatan / turḍī wa-imma furqatan murrah / min qabli an akhlaʿa thawba l-ḥayā / fi tāʿati sh-shaykhi Abi Murrah.*
>
> "So bid him show me henceforth sweet kindliness, or make him drink the bitter draught of divorce / before I put from me the last shred of shame, obedient to old Abū l-Murra's (i.e. the devil's) hest."[15]

Woman's beauty is charged with ambivalence, she may at any moment threaten order by exercising temptation (*fitna*), which is the very domain of the devil, the Arabic word *fitna* itself being ambiguous, denoting both the female virtue of excessive beauty and the equally female as well as devilish device of beguiling and deceiving[16].

---

13 al-Ḥarīrī (1976), V 186; Steingass (1898), II 142.
14 al-Ḥarīrī (1976), V 186; Steingass (1898), II 142.
15 al-Ḥarīrī (1976), V 186; Steingass (1898), II 142.
16 Saleh (1999).

The old man strikes back with a rhetorically, no less refined reposte. As the woman before, he refers to both juridical and social issues constructing a reality that is diametrically opposed to the normal. His house – he claims – has been turned from a home into a wasteland, the body of his wife has been stripped of the conventional signs of social esteem, i.e. jewellery:

*Fa-manzilī qafrun ka-mā jīduha / ʿuṭlun mina l-jazʿati wa-sh-shadhrah.*

"So my abode is empty, as unadorned her neck you see by shell or gold ornament."[17]

In spite of his legal right "to till his field" guaranteed by an explicit Qurʾanic ruling[18] still he cannot afford progeny:

*Wa-miltu ʿan ḥarthiya lā raghbatan / ʿanhu wa-lākin attaqī badhrah.*

"And not from grudge held I aloof from my field, only from fear to see the seed spring in halm."[19]

His abstinence – he claims – is in glaring contradiction to his personal faith, since in matters of love he is along the same line with the Udhrites, the Banū ʿUdhra, known for their passion. And what is more, the offence – he claims – is not the social shortcoming he is charged with, but a criminal delict: robbery of possessions, stripping of his wife's body and devastation of his house, committed not by him but by a third person, that is *al-dahr*, fate, devastating time:

*Wa-innama d-dahru ʿadā ṣarfuhu / fa-btazzana d-durrata wa-dh-dharrah.*

"But Fortune's fitful freak has come over us, ruthlessly robbing us of both pearl and bead."[20]

The judge, equally alienated by the woman's threat of disclosing her hidden female nature and positively impressed by the man's argument, admonishes the woman and decrees that the man is right. The woman is left speechless, but quickly changes back to fit the patriarchal image of a chaste and modest female showing regret and complaining about having suffered public exposure in vain:

*Wayḥaka [...] wa-mā fīnā illā man sadaq / wa-hataka sawnahu idh nataq / fa-laytanā lāqaynā l-bakam / wa-lam nalqa l-ḥakam.*

"Alas, is there concealment after appeal, and remains to us a seal upon any secret? There is neither of us, but says that which is true and tears the veil of modesty in speaking out. So would God that we had been visited with dumbness and not repaired to the judge."[21]

She then veils herself anew bashfully: *thumma ltafaʿat bi-wishāḥihā/ wa-tabākat li-ftiḍāḥihā.*

---

17 al-Ḥarīrī (1976), V 194; Steingass (1898), II 143.
18 *Qurʾān* 2:227.
19 al-Ḥarīrī (1976), V 195; Steingass (1898), II 143.
20 al-Ḥarīrī (1976), V 194; Steingass (1898), II 143.
21 al-Ḥarīrī (1976), V 196; Steingass (1898), II 144.

"Thereupon she covered herself with her kerchief, and pretended to weep at her exposure".[22] The judge joins in the man's complaint against fate, *al-dahr*, and alleviates their hardships by a generous gift whereupon they part peacefully from the stage. The marital problem seems to be solved and patriarchal order restored.

This point, when Abū Zayd has received his recompense, marks the turning-point, where his recognition is due. Indeed, the judge's admiration soon turns into curiosity; he feels he should know more about the couple, whose eloquence has impressed him:

> *Wa-tafiqa l-qāḍī baʿda masraḥihimā / wa-tanāʾī shabaḥihimā / yuthnī ʿalā adabihimā / wa-yaqūlu hal min ʿārifin bihimā.*
>
> "After they had gone, and their persons were at a distance, the qāḍī began to praise their cultured minds, and to ask: 'Is there anyone who knows them?'"[23]

Thereupon follows the anticipated *anagnorisis*, the revealing of the deception which is brought about by the *qāḍī*'s entourage who have recognized Abū Zayd. The *qāḍī* as the victim feels duped. The fictitious case thus turns into a genuine case, i.e. the 'post-drama' demanded by the *maqāma*'s structure, where now the *qāḍī* has to negotiate the offence of play in the place of seriousness, of deception through the practicing of subversive rhetoric. A messenger is sent out to bring the offenders back to court. But too late: He has found the couple preparing their escape. The old man has, however, left a message to submit to the *qāḍī* presenting his defence in written form. He hands over to the messenger a poem which contains – again – a pleading for play, for fiction. Within the debate which has now widened into a conflict of norms, Abū Zayd in his authentic role as an artist, as the spokesman of the norms of art and play, confronts the *qāḍī* as the spokesman of legal norms. First he pays back the *qāḍī*'s generosity with an advice clad into a gnome, a saying of wisdom, 'Never regret a good deed':

> *Ruwaydaka lā tuʿqib jamīlaka bi-l-adhā*:
>
> "Eh, gently, let not bounty be followed by injury".

Material gain and prestigious praise are not available at the same time: *fa-tuḍḥī wa-shamlu l-māli wa-l-ḥamdi munṣadiʿ*:

> "[F]or else both thy wealth and fame alike will be lost and gone."[24]

But, since the case is – apart from the issue of the particular deceptive play – about the legitimacy of fiction and play in general, he reminds the *qāḍī* that fictitious speech to gain material support, to win someone as a patron, is by no means 'new', i.e. in terms of jurisprudence, suspicious of a heretical innovation:

---

22 al-Ḥarīrī (1976), V 196; Steingass (1898), II 144.
23 al-Ḥarīrī (1976), V 198; Steingass (1898), II 144.
24 al-Ḥarīrī (1976), V 201; Steingass (1898), II 146.

*Wa-lā tataghaḍḍab min tazayyudi sāʾilin / fa-mā huwa fī ṣawghi l-lisāni bi-mubtadiʿ.*

"And fly not into passion if a beggar exaggerates, for he is by no means first to polish and gloss his speech."[25]

The *qāḍī* has simply served as a patron. The most striking argument however that the offender puts forward to support his poetical anti-norm is his playful re-interpretation of the juridical key concept of *taqlīd*, emulation, through which he willfully turns the painful and humiliating experience of deception into something agreeable, even into a meritorious act in religious terms: The *qāḍī*, he argues frivolously, has done well to emulate his great precursor, the jurist Abū Mūsā al-Ashʿarī, whose fame is due not least to his having been fatefully deceived as the spokesman of the fourth caliph, ʿAlī ibn Abī Ṭālib, during the tribunal held to decide about the right to the caliphate disputed between ʿAlī and his rival Muʿāwiya:

*Wa-in taku qad sāʾatka minnī khadīʿatun / fa-qablaka shaykhu l-Ashʿariyyīna qad khudiʿ.*

"And if some deceit of mine is taken by thee amiss, remember, Abū Mūsā before thee has been deceived."[26]

The *qāḍī* is captivated anew and proves again – this time intentionally – a patron by procuring the couple through a riding messenger with a generous gift. He openly declares his confirmation of membership to the world of fictitious play:

*Sir sayra man lā yara l-iltifāt / ilā an tara sh-shaykha wa-l-fatāt / fabulla yadayhimā bi-hādha l-ḥibāʾ / wa-bayyin lahumā nkhidāʿi li-l-udabāʾ.*

"Fare speedily like one who turns neither right nor left, until thou seest the Shaykh and the wench / and moist their hands with this gift, and show to them how fain I am to be beguiled by the literati."[27]

This spontaneously playful abdication of the official spokesman of public norms from his judicial office and thus the elevation of the literarily gifted rogue to the rank of a competent authority, a guarantor of new norms, moves the narrator, al-Ḥārith, to utter a justifiedly superlative judgment:

*Qāla r-rāwī fa-lam ara fī l-ightirāb / ka-hadha l-ʿujāb / wa-la samiʿtu bi-mithlihi mimman jāla wa-jāb.*

"Quoth the narrator: Now in all my wanderings abroad, I never saw a sight as wonderful as this nor heard I the like of it from anyone who roved about and roamed through the lands."[28]

---

25 al-Ḥarīrī (1976), V 201; Steingass (1898), II 146.

26 al-Ḥarīrī (1976), V 201; Steingass (1898), II 146.

27 al-Ḥarīrī (1976), V 202; Steingass (1898), II 146. This confession of a judge will find a counterpart some 600 years later in the similar closure of another famous forensic affair in literature, Friedrich Schiller's balad "The Pledge" (Die Bürgschaft) which also ends up with the judge joining the offenders' ranks: "Ich sei, gewähret mir die Bitte, in eurem Bund der dritte!"

## *Tracing the* ʿajīb*: the hermeneutic impact of* tawriya

What is the magic in Abū Zayd's practicing his art that finally gives it precedence over the norms represented by the qāḍī? The qāḍī's conversion appears to be due to a particular aura emanating from subversively employed literary art, from the staging of fiction. Obviously a carnivalesque situation had been created, dominated by particular aesthetics that in Bakhtin's terms is to be called 'grotesque'.

*The grotesque* – Bakhtin argues – *frees from all the forms of inhumane necessity that the ruling concepts of the world are imbued with. It exposes them as being but relative and limited in nature. The element of laughter, of a carnivalesque perception of the world that underlies the grotesque, annihilates austerity as well as any claim to timeless validity and inalterability of the concepts of necessity. The representation of the grotesque focuses on the body, and particularly on those parts of it where the body transcends its own limits, where it produces a new body […]. The essential event in the life of the 'grotesque body', the acts of the body drama: eating, drinking, sexual intercourse […] – take place at the borders between body and world, at the borders between the old and the new body.*[29]

The play staged in our *maqāma* is marked by its extensive verbal and gestural references to the female body and sexuality conveying a uniquely *carnivalesque* touch. It is certainly grotesque that the woman claims a cosmic analogue to her body to illustrate her complaining about her husband's sexual negligence. She further proves frivolous in exposing this cosmically enlarged body to the ritual rulings of a juridical-political authority. The realms of erotic and jurisprudence thus have been made mutually permeable. But has not the woman already deeply invaded the territory of her juridical adversary by drawing a parallel between the Kaʿba and the female body?

After all she has hidden her erotic claim under a juridical metaphor. Looking closely at her argument it turns out that she has all the time been alluding to a particular juridical issue defined by Abū Yūsuf: the pilgrimage modality known as *mutʿat al-ḥajj*, 'enjoyment of the pilgrimage'. This pilgrimage pattern, which demands a temporary interruption of the rites, is already put in close context to sexual pleasure in an early tradition traced back to a companion of the Prophet saying: *Mutʿatāni kānatā ʿalā ʿahdi rasūli llāh: mutʿatu l-ḥajj wa-mutʿat an-nisāʾ*: "Two enjoyments existed during the time of the messenger of God: the enjoyment of the (interrupted) pilgrimage and the enjoyment of women"[30]. Through this *iunctim* the 'interrupted pilgrimage' preserved its erotic connotation in the Islamic juridical lore where the tradition was long discussed. By alluding to it the woman demonstrates how different discourses, the juridical, the ritual and the socio-traditional, are all closely related to the erotic discourse, indeed end up in it. We

---

28 al-Ḥarīrī (1976), V 202; Steingass (1898), II 146.
29 Bakhtin (1990), 28.
30 The relationship between the two 'enjoyments' has been discussed by Gribetz (1994).

are confronted with a most sophisticated use of the rhetorical figure of double entendre: The woman describes – without explicitly mentioning the crucial word 'enjoyment' (*mutʿa*) – *mutʿat al-ḥajj*: the 'enjoyment of the (interrupted) pilgrimage', intending, however, *mutʿat an-nisāʾ*: the 'enjoyment of women'. Needless to say that this particular application of the figure of speech presupposes intimate juridica knowledge.

Little surprise then, that the speech of the man is committed to the same pronouncedly sensual concept of the body: He focuses on the erotic play with the female body: *fa-mudh nabā d-dahru hajartu d-dumā*: "But since fell fortune fled I left dolls alone",[31] a second metaphor alluding to the act of intercourse is based on the well-known Qurʾānic allegory that pictures women as a field: *wa-miltu ʿan ḥarthiya lā raghbatan / ʿanhu wa-lākin attaqī badhrah*: "And not from grudge held I aloof from my field, only from fear to see the seed spring in halm."[32] Again, frivolously, an authority is brought into the debate on sexuality, this time not a learned but an ideological one, the Banū ʿUdhra: *wa-kuntu min qablu arā fī l-hawā / wa-dīnihi ruʾyā banī ʿUdhrah*: "Erewhile my views on love and his creed and cult were those professed so staunchly by ʿUzrah's tribe"[33] – so as if orthodoxy *in causa Veneris* was to be demonstrated, as if the opening of the juridical discourse toward the erotic had to be proved a second time.

## *The Poet and his Society – a Quarreling Couple?*

Obviously this sophisticatedly *carnivalesque* neutralization of the deceptive play is sufficient for the artist to win his case against the qāḍī in the play – but is it enough as well to make an act of deception committed against a qāḍī, indeed, a jurist's subsequent 'conversion' to the norms of the literati, acceptable to the listeners as well? What is it that gives the protagonist the peculiar authority so as to make his offence against the spokesman of their norms reasonable to them?

Here, when we leave the internal level of the dramatic interaction and turn to the perception of the listeners confronted with al-Ḥarīrī s particular staging the antagonism between the artist's and the jurist's norms – we come across a set of symbols that endow the literary artist's relation to the female with virtually mythical dimensions. Already the analogy drawn by the woman between the Kaʿba and the female body was to arouse suspicion as to the merely private character of the debate. The introduction of the intricate juridical problem of the interrupted pilgrimage into the debate, a topic reaching deeply into the normative system of the collective had further enhanced the impression that a political point is being made, a socially significant message is being conveyed through a

31 al-Ḥarīrī (1976), V 195; Steingass (1898), II 143.
32 al-Ḥarīrī (1976), V 195; Steingass (1898), II 143.
33 al-Ḥarīrī (1976), V 194; Steingass (1898), II 143.

complex allegory. Looking closer at the woman's claim against the deficient partner one finds that the ideas behind both the metaphor 'pilgrim' and its substrate 'husband' converge at a common nucleus crucial for the creation of order, both warranting the continuance of the world: The pilgrim serves to uphold world order by performing the prescribed rites; the husband contributes to guarantee the survival of society by procreation. What is that momentous role entrusted to the *maqāma* hero, the artist, that is hidden behind the doublefold metaphor 'husband-pilgrim'? What is the public relevance of his task?

Here again, the figure of the double entendre is involved. What is actually a political sous-entendu of the play about the quarrelling couple becomes clearer through the speech of the man. He has been the victim of a hostile aggression, of robbery and devastation of the home for which offences he claims the responsibility of a figure, who has been since time immemorial the adversary of him who practices the art of poetry, namely *al-dahr*, fate. It is the courageous rebellion against *al-dahr*, the paralyzing power of the inescapable fate "erasing human works without hope for life beyond death",[34] that in ancient Arabic tradition makes up the heroic profession of the poet, who is bound to ever restore the consciousness of self-assertion to his tribal group. To be sure, what had once been a matter of personal experience has become for the literary artist of the ʿAbbasid era a poetical mimesis in emotion, to quote Andras Hamori: "They remove us into a world that half knows itself to be poetic rather than realistic."[35] Yet, in spite of the poet's political significance actually lost, poetry still constitutes that free space beyond the ruling norms that has been once called Arab humanism. To put it metaphorically: The later poet has saved the ancient aura of the rebel – the icon of which is the fight against *al-dahr*. To suffer defeat by *al-dahr*, therefore, comes equal to his impotence to perform the creative act for his world that he is due: to impregnate his language community with his word, to guarantee her spiritual continuance. Claiming that *al-dahr* has overwhelmed him, devastating his abode and stripping his female companion of her jewellery, the artist-protagonist clads the public disaster into two images taken from the female realm that graphically expose the shapelessness and lack of attraction that society suffers once art and play are banned and absent.

The play staged by the literary artist thus projects into the private sphere what in reality takes place in the public realm. Under the veil of his private companion is hidden – consciously or unconsciously – realizable for the listeners an allegory of society, who takes the case of the defeated and deserted spokesman of artistic freedom to court. Art is neglected – the poet has become virtually impotent, since the patrons supposed to support him in his struggle against destructive fate, viz. loss of meaning, are no longer to be found. Once no construction

---

34 Böwering (1997), 57.

35 Hamori (1974), 65.

of meaning is possible any more, world order and continuance, in spite of the continuing validity of normative values, are endangered. The complaint of the woman is a true plight, only its staging as a private case is deception, or – for him who comprehends – allegorical theatre. For the comprehending listener at this point the woman's enigma put forward in the beginning of the play through her introduction of the enjoyment, as a double entendre, becomes fully soluble in the end. The reference to the 'enjoyment of the (interrupted) pilgrimage' (*mutʿat al-ḥajj*), as a mask for the 'enjoyment of women' (*mutʿat al-nisāʾ*), turns out to be covering still another *mutʿa*: The truly missed enjoyment is that particular pleasure that only the literary artist, follower of the ancient poet's excessive ways transcending the realm of norms, can convey to his language community: the fulfilment of enjoying meaning, of gaining knowledge through unrestrained aesthetic experience, through fiction and creative invention. The artist thus, has won his case: Artistic norms have prevailed over juridical norms.

## *Woman and fictional literature*

The woman in our *maqāma* is presented as extremely witty, able to place her argument into a cosmic context, indeed eclipsing her male companion in poetical invention. Accordingly, the victory over the judge is essentially hers. Yet, on closer look her intrusions into the male discourses, the legal and the ritual, prove ambivalent. The intertext evoked through her male rhetoric, the tradition about the 'two enjoyments', points to a crude form of male exploitation of women as objects of sexual pleasure. Not only is the legal discourse presented in her speech as permeated by sexual associations, sexuality as such is located unambiguously into the context of exclusively male competence. The woman's case is little different from that of her counterparts in Hebrew literature lucidly analysed by Tova Rosen, where "dramatic irony continues when the woman 'stumbles' time and again on talmudic texts, of whose implication she is not supposed to be aware... The community of educated males communicates over the head of the probably illiterate woman who parrots male texts."[36] Furthermore, in view of her companion's profession of a poet, she must be suspected to play a role that he has designed for her, and we hear little of her, once her role in the presence of the qāḍī has been ended.

Should she then be viewed as a mere mouthpiece of the picaro employed to dramatize his case? Or might the author have introduced her for another sake? In addition to her dramatic function in the play she appears to bear a symbolic function in the author's vision of art, as an embodiment of the very gift of poetry and fiction itself. Such a perception though it is not made explicit by al-Ḥarīrī, who more directly introduces her as an allegory of society lamenting ste-

[36] Rosen (2003), 181.

rility in the absence of art, would not be unique in pre-modern oriental literature. Tova Rosen has alerted us to the close "association between the beautiful-but-untruthful poem and the attractive-but-deceitful female" that was "exploited in a variety of modes and resulted in varying attitudes toward poetry and poetic enterprise"[37] in medieval Hebrew literature. The association is not limited to medieval thought. As Rosen shows, an intrinsic connection between a particular norm-subverting thinking and the female gender reappears as a key figure in modern philosophy, where according to Nietzsche "the female's distrust of the truth derives from the fact that she does not ever consider truth; truth does not concern her. And so, for Nietzsche, woman paradoxically becomes the symbol of elusive truth, that same alluring but noncommittal entity, beguiling and seductive, that the male forever tries to attain – but in vain... The scepticism of the woman, for whom the only truth is the realization that there is no truth, coincides with the philosophical view that Nietzsche exemplifies and which underlies his thought."[38]

In the pre-modern Muslim perspective of al-Ḥarīrī's time the woman is, of course, not yet looked upon from psychological perspectives. Still, a number of gender-specific attitudes attributed to her lend themselves to a synopsis of both the female sex and literary art such as presented in al-Ḥarīrī's *maqāmāt.* Since in the *maqāmāt* ambiguity, even untruth, as long as it is presented in adorned speech, is viewed as acceptable, indeed as an empowerment of art that helps to transcend all too sober and uninspired normal reality, the assumption that there is an implicit female gendering of art in the *maqāma* suggests itself. Literature, particularly poetry, is beguiling, it does – like female beauty – constitute a *fitna*, a temptation, for the recipients – in our case the qāḍī himself found himself "beguiled", *inkhidāᶜ*, and thus 'converted' to the adherence to the anti-norm. Art is deceptive and untruthful, it creates *mutᶜa*, enjoyment, by disempowering social constraints – in the Bakhtinian sense of carnival – and replacing the norm-committed reality by a carnivalesque topsy-turvy world where patriarchal rules are out of power. What is most telling, however, is that poetical speech is veiled – through metaphors – like the female body should be veiled, whereas all the other realms of medieval Muslim culture are subjected to permanent processes of intellectual unveiling (*kashf*). Walid Saleh who has investigated "The woman as a locus of apocalyptic anxiety"[39] claims that "medieval Muslim culture was one obsessed with unveiling. Knowledge lies just beneath a veneer, and stripping it is the process by which knowledge was acquired. The female body, the only entity in this culture that should be veiled, presents an epistemological crisis."[40] There is thus a convergence of the female image and of the pre-modern perception of art, par-

---

37 Rosen (2003), 65.
38 Rosen (2003), 65.
39 Saleh (1999).
40 Saleh (1999), 140.

ticularly literary art, viz. poetry, which is conceived as ornament and thus, as Tova Rosen as shown for the case of Hebrew medieval poetry, "a cover of or a subsidiary to truth".[41] If the naked, literal speech constitutes truth, then al-Ḥarīrī's extremely ornate prose certainly comes close to deception. His *maqāmāt* display a high degree of syntactical and structural regularity on the one hand and of semantic extravagance when it comes to poetical embellishments such as images and metaphors, on the other. His dual 'radicalism', his eagerness to meticulously follow accepted rules that on a linguistic level reflect the social norms established in a patriarchal system, but at the same time to subvert them in a fictitious, carnivalesque, deceptive play, may be understood as indicating a rebellion. Viewed from this perspective, al-Ḥarīrī, writing from the very centre of a strong patriarchal norm system, seems to plead for a less 'normal'/norm-oriented and more poetically minded society where play and fiction have their due part – in accordance with a vision of art inspired by a female image.

## *Bibliography*


Bakhtin, Michail M., *Literatur und Karneval. Zur Romantheorie und Lachkultur*, Frankfurt/M.: Fischer 1990.

Barthes, Roland (1972): *Mythologies*, selected and trans.: Annette Lavers. London: Cape 1972. French. Orig.: *Mythologies*, Paris: Editions du Seuil, 1957.

Böwering, Gerhard, "The Concept of Time in Islam". In: *Proceedings of the American Philosophical Society* 141 (1997).1, 57.

Bonebakker, S.A., *Some Early Definitions of the Tawriya and Ṣafadī's Faḍḍ al-xitām ʿan al-tawriya wa-l-istixdām*, The Hague 1966.

Chenou, Marianne, „Dramatische Strukturen in den Maqamen al-Hamadhanis und al-Hariris". In: Christoph Bürgel & Stephan Guth (eds.): *Gesellschaftlicher Umbruch und Historie im zeitgenössischen Drama der islamischen Welt*. Beirut und Stuttgart 1995 (Beiruter Texte und Studien 65) 87-100.

Gribetz, Arthur, *Strange Bedfellows: mutʿat al-nisāʾ and mutʿat al-ḥajj. A Study based on Sunnī and Shīʿī sources of tafsīr, ḥadīṯ and fiqh*. Berlin: Klaus Schwarz 1994.

Hämeen-Anttila, Jaakko, *Maqama. A History of a Genre*. Wiesbaden: Harrassowitz 2002.

Hamori, Andras, *On the Art of Medieval Arabic Literature*. Princeton: Princeton University Press 1974.

al-Ḥarīrī, Abū Muḥammad al-Qāsim b. ʿAlī, *al-Maqāmāt, Sharḥ maqāmāt al-Ḥarīrī li-Abī l-ʿAbbās Aḥmad b. ʿAbd al-Muʾmin al-Qaysī al-Sharīshī*. Ed. Muḥammad Abū l-Faḍl Ibrāhīm, 5 Vols, Cairo: al-Muʾassasa al-ʿarabiyya al-ḥadītha 1976.

Irwin, Robert, *The Penguin Anthology of Classical Arabic Literature*. London 1999.


41 Rosen (2003), 66.

Kilito, Abdelfattah, *Les Séances. Récits et codes culturels chez Hamadhānī et Harīrī*. Paris: Sindbad 1983.

Moreh, Shemuel, *Live Theatre and Dramatic Literature in the Medieval Arab World*. Edinburgh: Edinburgh University Press 1992.

Neuwirth, Angelika, "Adab Standing Trial – Whose Norms Should Rule Society? The Case of al-Ḥarīrī's 'al-Maqāmāh al-Ramlīyah'". In: *Myths, Historical Archetypes and Symbolic Figures in Arabic Literature. Towards a New Hermeneutic Approach*. Eds. Angelika Neuwirth et al., Beirut, Stuttgart: Steiner 1999, 205-224.

Neuwirth, Angelika, "Woman's Wit and Juridical Discourse: A Forensic Maqama by the Classical Arabic Scholar Al-Hariri". In: Barbara Winckler & Angelika Neuwirth (eds.): Figurationen gender literatur kultur 01/05: Arabesken/arabesques. Köln: Böhlau 2005. 23-36.

Pellat (1991): Article: Maḳāma. In: EI VI (New Ed.). Leiden.

Rosen, Tova, *Unveiling Eve. Reading Gender in Medieval Hebrew Literature*. Philadelphia: University of Pennsylvania Press 2003.

Rückert, Friedrich, *Die Verwandlungen des Abu Seid von Serug, oder die Makamen des Hariri*. Trans.: Friedrich Rückert. Reprint of the 1837 edition with an epilogue by Wiebke Walther, Leipzig: Reclam 1989.

Saleh, Walid, "The Woman as a Locus of Apocalyptic Anxiety in Medieval Sunnī Islam". In: *Myths, Historical Archetypes and Symbolic Figures in Arabic Literature. Towards a New Hermeneutic Approach*. Eds. Angelika Neuwirth et al., Beirut, Stuttgart: Steiner 1999, 123-145.

Steingass, F., *The Assemblies of al-Hariri. Translated from the Arabic, with notes, historical and grammatical, by Dr. F. Steingass*. Vol. II containing the last twenty-four assemblies. London: Royal Asiatic Society 1898.

## *Authors*

*Vahid Behmardi*
Assistant Professor of Arabic Literature & Comparative Studies, Department of Humanities, Lebanese American University, Beirut, Lebanon

*Lale Behzadi*
Associate Professor of Arabic and Islamic Studies, University of Göttingen, Germany

*Geert Jan van Gelder*
Professor of Arabic, University of Oxford, United Kingdom

*Beatrice Gruendler*
Professor of Arabic, Department of Near Eastern Languages and Civilizations, Yale University, New Haven, U.S.A.

*Jaakko Hämeen-Anttila*
Professor of Arabic and Islamic Studies, University of Helsinki, Finland

*Philip Frederick Kennedy*
Associate Professor, Department of Middle Eastern & Islamic Studies, New York University, U.S.A.

*Marianne R. Marroum*
Lecturer in Comparative Literature and Cultural Studies, Department of Humanities, Lebanese American University, Beirut, Lebanon

*Angelika Neuwirth*
Chair of Arabic Studies, Free University Berlin, Germany

*Bilal W. Orfali*
Assistant Professor of Arabic Literature, Department of Arabic and Near Eastern Languages, American University of Beirut

*Everett K. Rowson*
Professor of Arabic, New York University, U.S.A.

المعهد الألماني للأبحاث الشرقية

# ORIENT-INSTITUT BEIRUT

## BEIRUTER TEXTE UND STUDIEN

1. MICHEL JIHA: Der arabische Dialekt von Bišmizzīn. Volkstümliche Texte aus einem libanesischen Dorf mit Grundzügen der Laut- und Formenlehre, Beirut 1964, XVII, 185 S.
2. BERNHARD LEWIN: Arabische Texte im Dialekt von Hama. Mit Einleitung und Glossar, Beirut 1966, *48*, 230 S.
3. THOMAS PHILIPP: Ǧurǧī Zaidān. His Life and Thought, Beirut 1979, 249 S.
4. ʿABD AL-ĠANĪ AN-NĀBULUSĪ: At-tuḥfa an-nābulusīya fī r-riḥla aṭ-ṭarābulusīya. Hrsg. u. eingel. von Heribert Busse, Beirut 1971, unveränd. Nachdr. Beirut 2003, XXIV, 10 S. dt., 133 S. arab. Text.
5. BABER JOHANSEN: Muḥammad Ḥusain Haikal. Europa und der Orient im Weltbild eines ägyptischen Liberalen, Beirut 1967, XIX, 259 S.
6. HERIBERT BUSSE: Chalif und Großkönig. Die Buyiden im Iraq (945–1055), Beirut 1969, unveränd. Nachdr. 2004, XIV, 610 S., 6 Taf., 2 Karten.
7. JOSEF VAN ESS: Traditionistische Polemik gegen ʿAmr b. ʿUbaid. Zu einem Text des ʿAlī b. ʿUmar ad-Dāraquṭnī, Beirut 1967, mit Korrekturen versehener Nachdruck 2004, 74 S. dt., 16 S. arab. Text, 2 Taf.
8. WOLFHART HEINRICHS: Arabische Dichtung und griechische Poetik. Ḥāzim al-Qarṭāǧannīs Grundlegung der Poetik mit Hilfe aristotelischer Begriffe, Beirut 1969, 289 S.
9. STEFAN WILD: Libanesische Ortsnamen. Typologie und Deutung, Beirut 1973, unveränd. Nachdr. 2008, XII, 391 S.
10. GERHARD ENDRESS: Proclus Arabus. Zwanzig Abschnitte aus der Institutio Theologica in arabischer Übersetzung, Beirut 1973, XVIII, 348 S. dt., 90 S. arab. Text.
11. JOSEF VAN ESS: Frühe muʿtazilitische Häresiographie. Zwei Werke des Nāšiʾ al-Akbar (gest. 293 H.), Beirut 1971, unveränd. Nachdr. Beirut 2003, XII, 185 S. dt., 134 S. arab. Text.

12.* DOROTHEA DUDA: Innenarchitektur syrischer Stadthäuser des 16.–18. Jahrhunderts. Die Sammlung Henri Pharaon in Beirut, Beirut 1971, VI, 176 S., 88 Taf., 6 Farbtaf., 2 Faltpläne.

13.* WERNER DIEM: Skizzen jemenitischer Dialekte, Beirut 1973, XII, 166 S.

14.* JOSEF VAN ESS: Anfänge muslimischer Theologie. Zwei antiqadaritische Traktate aus dem ersten Jahrhundert der Hiǧra, Beirut 1977, XII, 280 S. dt., 57 S. arab. Text.

15. GREGOR SCHOELER: Arabische Naturdichtung. Die zahrīyāt, rabīʿīyāt und rauḍīyāt von ihren Anfängen bis aṣ-Ṣanaubarī, Beirut 1974, XII, 371 S.
16. HEINZ GAUBE: Ein arabischer Palast in Südsyrien. Ḫirbet el-Baiḍa, Beirut 1974, XIII, 156 S., 14 Taf., 3 Faltpläne, 12 Textabb.
17. HEINZ GAUBE: Arabische Inschriften aus Syrien, Beirut 1978, XXII, 201 S., 19 Taf.

18.* GERNOT ROTTER: Muslimische Inseln vor Ostafrika. Eine arabische Komoren-Chronik des 19. Jahrhunderts, Beirut 1976, XII, 106 S. dt., 116 S. arab. Text, 2 Taf., 2 Karten.

19.* HANS DAIBER: Das theologisch-philosophische System des Muʿammar Ibn ʿAbbād as-Sulamī (gest. 830 n. Chr.), Beirut 1975, XII, 604 S.

20.* WERNER ENDE: Arabische Nation und islamische Geschichte. Die Umayyaden im Urteil arabischer Autoren des 20. Jahrhunderts, Beirut 1977, XIII, 309 S.

21. ṢALĀḤADDĪN AL-MUNAĞĞID, STEFAN WILD, eds.: Zwei Beschreibungen des Libanon. ʿAbdalġanī an-Nābulusīs Reise durch die Biqāʿ und al-ʿUṭaifīs Reise nach Tripolis, Beirut 1979, XVII u. XXVII, 144 S. arab. Text, 1 Karte, 2 Faltkarten.

22. ULRICH HAARMANN, PETER BACHMANN, eds.: Die islamische Welt zwischen Mittelalter und Neuzeit. Festschrift für Hans Robert Roemer zum 65. Geburtstag, Beirut 1979, XVI, 702 S., 11 Taf.

23. ROTRAUD WIELANDT: Das Bild der Europäer in der modernen arabischen Erzähl- und Theaterliteratur, Beirut 1980, XVII, 652 S.

24.* REINHARD WEIPERT, ed.: Der Dīwān des Rāʿī an-Numairī, Beirut 1980, IV dt., 363 S. arab. Text.

25.* ASʿAD E. KHAIRALLAH: Love, Madness and Poetry. An Interpretation of the Mağnūn Legend, Beirut 1980, 163 S.

26. ROTRAUD WIELANDT: Das erzählerische Frühwerk Maḥmūd Taymūrs, Beirut 1983, XII, 434 S.

27.* ANTON HEINEN: Islamic Cosmology. A study of as-Suyūṭī's al-Hayʾa as-sunnīya fī l-hayʾa as-sunnīya with critical edition, translation and commentary, Beirut 1982, VIII, 289 S. engl., 78 S. arab. Text.

28. WILFERD MADELUNG: Arabic Texts concerning the history of the Zaydī Imāms of Ṭabaristān, Daylamān and Gīlān, Beirut 1987, 23 S. engl., 377 S. arab. Text.

29. DONALD P. LITTLE: A Catalogue of the Islamic Documents from al-Ḥaram aš-Šarīf in Jerusalem. 1984, XIII, 480 S. engl., 6 S. arab. Text, 17 Taf.

30. KATALOG DER ARABISCHEN HANDSCHRIFTEN IN MAURETANIEN. Bearb. von Ulrich Rebstock, Rainer Osswald und Ahmad Wuld ʿAbdalqādir, Beirut 1988. XII, 164 S.

31. ULRICH MARZOLPH: Typologie des persischen Volksmärchens, Beirut 1984, XIII, 312 S., 5 Tab., 3 Karten.

32. STEFAN LEDER: Ibn al-Ğauzī und seine Kompilation wider die Leidenschaft, Beirut 1984, XIV, 328 S. dt., 7 S. arab. Text, 1 Falttaf.

33. RAINER OSSWALD: Das Sokoto-Kalifat und seine ethnischen Grundlagen, Beirut 1986, VIII, 177 S.

34. ZUHAIR FATḤALLĀH, ed.: Der Diwān des ʿAbd al-Laṭīf Fatḥallāh, 2 Bde., Beirut 1984, 1196 S. arab. Text.

35. IRENE FELLMANN: Das Aqrābāḏīn al-Qalānisī. Quellenkritische und begriffsanalytische Untersuchungen zur arabisch-pharmazeutischen Literatur, Beirut 1986, VI, 304 S.

36. HÉLÈNE SADER: Les États Araméens de Syrie depuis leur Fondation jusqu'à leur Transformation en Provinces Assyriennes, Beirut 1987, XIII, 306 S. franz. Text.

37. BERND RADTKE: Adab al-Mulūk, Beirut 1991, XII, 34 S. dt., 145 S. arab. Text.

38. ULRICH HAARMANN: Das Pyramidenbuch des Abū Ğaʿfar al-Idrīsī (gest. 649/1251), Beirut 1991, XI u. VI, 94 S. dt., 283 S. arab. Text.

39. TILMAN NAGEL, ed.: Göttinger Vorträge – Asien blickt auf Europa, Begegnungen und Irritationen, Beirut 1990, 192 S.

40. HANS R. ROEMER: Persien auf dem Weg in die Neuzeit. Iranische Geschichte von 1350–1750, Beirut 1989, unveränd. Nachdr. Beirut 2003, X, 525 S.

41. BIRGITTA RYBERG: Yūsuf Idrīs (1927–1991). Identitätskrise und gesellschaftlicher Umbruch, Beirut 1992, 226 S.

42. HARTMUT BOBZIN: Der Koran im Zeitalter der Reformation. Studien zur Frühgeschichte der Arabistik und Islamkunde in Europa, Beirut 1995, XIV, 590 S. dt. Text.

43. BEATRIX OSSENDORF-CONRAD: Das „K. al-Wāḍiḥa" des ʿAbd al-Malik b. Ḥabīb. Edition und Kommentar zu Ms. Qarawiyyīn 809/49 (Abwāb aṭ-ṭahāra), Beirut 1994, 574 S., davon 71 S. arab. Text, 45 S. Faks.

44. MATHIAS VON BREDOW: Der Heilige Krieg (ğihād) aus der Sicht der malikitischen Rechtsschule, Beirut 1994, 547 S. arab., 197 S. dt. Text, Indices.

45. OTFRIED WEINTRITT: Formen spätmittelalterlicher islamischer Geschichtsdarstellung. Untersuchungen zu an-Nuwairī al-Iskandarānīs Kitāb al-Ilmām und verwandten zeitgenössischen Texten, Beirut 1992, X, 226 S.

46. GERHARD CONRAD: Die quḍāt Dimašq und der maḏhab al-Auzā'ī. Materialien zur syrischen Rechtsgeschichte, Beirut 1994, XVIII, 828 S.

47. MICHAEL GLÜNZ: Die panegyrische qaṣīda bei Kamāl ud-dīn Ismā'īl aus Isfahan. Eine Studie zur persischen Lobdichtung um den Beginn des 7./13. Jahrhunderts, Beirut 1993, 290 S.

48. AYMAN FU'ĀD SAYYID: La Capitale de l'Égypte jusqu'à l'Époque Fatimide – Al-Qāhira et Al-Fusṭāṭ– Essai de Reconstitution Topographique, Beirut 1998, XL, 754 S. franz., 26 S. arab. Text, 109 Abb.

49. JEAN MAURICE FIEY: Pour un Oriens Christianus Novus, Beirut 1993, 286 S. franz. Text.

50. IRMGARD FARAH: Die deutsche Pressepolitik und Propagandatätigkeit im Osmanischen Reich von 1908–1918 unter besonderer Berücksichtigung des „Osmanischen Lloyd", Beirut 1993, 347 S.

51. BERND RADTKE: Weltgeschichte und Weltbeschreibung im mittelalterlichen Islam, Beirut 1992, XII, 544 S.

52. LUTZ RICHTER-BERNBURG: Der Syrische Blitz – Saladins Sekretär zwischen Selbstdarstellung und Geschichtsschreibung, Beirut 1998, 452 S. dt., 99 S. arab. Text.

53. FRITZ MEIER: Bausteine I-III. Ausgewählte Aufsätze zur Islamwissenschaft. Hrsg. von Erika Glassen und Gudrun Schubert, Beirut 1992, I und II 1195 S., III (Indices) 166 S.

54. FESTSCHRIFT EWALD WAGNER ZUM 65. GEBURTSTAG: Hrsg. von Wolfhart Heinrichs und Gregor Schoeler, 2 Bde., Beirut 1994, Bd. 1: Semitische Studien unter besonderer Berücksichtigung der Südsemitistik, XV, 284 S.; Bd. 2: Studien zur arabischen Dichtung, XVII, 641 S.

55. SUSANNE ENDERWITZ: Liebe als Beruf. Al-'Abbās Ibn al-Aḥnaf und das Ġazal, Beirut 1995, IX, 246 S.

56. ESTHER PESKES: Muḥammad b. 'Abdalwahhāb (1703–1792) im Widerstreit. Untersuchungen zur Rekonstruktion der Frühgeschichte der Wahhābīya, Beirut 1993, VII, 384 S.

57. FLORIAN SOBIEROJ: Ibn Ḫafīf aš-Šīrāzī und seine Schrift zur Novizenerziehung, Beirut 1998, IX, 442 S. dt., 48 S. arab. Text.

58.* FRITZ MEIER: Zwei Abhandlungen über die Naqšbandiyya. I. Die Herzensbindung an den Meister. II. Kraftakt und Faustrecht des Heiligen, Beirut 1994, 366 S.

59. JÜRGEN PAUL: Herrscher, Gemeinwesen, Vermittler: Ostiran und Transoxanien in vormongolischer Zeit, Beirut 1996, VIII, 310 S.

60. JOHANN CHRISTOPH BÜRGEL, STEPHAN GUTH, eds.: Gesellschaftlicher Umbruch und Historie im zeitgenössischen Drama der islamischen Welt, Beirut 1995, XII, 295 S.

61. BARBARA FINSTER, CHRISTA FRAGNER, HERTA HAFENRICHTER, eds.: Rezeption in der islamischen Kunst, Beirut 1999, 332 S. dt. Text, Abb.

62.* ROBERT B. CAMPBELL, ed.: A'lām al-adab al-'arabī al-mu'āṣir. Siyar wa-siyar ḏātiyya. (Contemporary Arab Writers. Biographies and Autobiographies), 2 Bde., Beirut 1996, 1380 S. arab. Text.

63. MONA TAKIEDDINE AMYUNI: La ville source d'inspiration. Le Caire, Khartoum, Beyrouth, Paola Scala chez quelques écrivains arabes contemporains, Beirut 1998, 230 S. franz. Text.

64. ANGELIKA NEUWIRTH, SEBASTIAN GÜNTHER, BIRGIT EMBALÓ, MAHER JARRAR, eds.: Myths, Historical Archetypes and Symbolic Figures in Arabic Literature. Proceedings of the Symposium held at the Orient-Institut Beirut, June 25th – June 30th, 1996, Beirut 1999, 640 S. engl. Text.

65. Türkische Welten 1. KLAUS KREISER, CHRISTOPH K. NEUMANN, eds.: Das Osmanische Reich in seinen Archivalien und Chroniken. Nejat Göyünç zu Ehren, Istanbul 1997, XXIII, 328 S.

66. Türkische Welten 2. CABBAR, SETTAR: Kurtuluş Yolunda: a work on Central Asian literature in a Turkish-Uzbek mixed language. Ed., transl. and linguistically revisited by A. Sumru Özsoy, Claus Schöning, Esra Karabacak, with contribution from Ingeborg Baldauf, Istanbul 2000, 335 S.

67. Türkische Welten 3. GÜNTER SEUFERT: Politischer Islam in der Türkei. Islamismus als symbolische Repräsentation einer sich modernisierenden muslimischen Gesellschaft, Istanbul 1997, 600 S.

68. EDWARD BADEEN: Zwei mystische Schriften des ʿAmmār al-Bidlīsī, Beirut 1999, VI S., 142 S. dt., 122 arab. Text.

69. THOMAS SCHEFFLER, HÉLÈNE SADER, ANGELIKA NEUWIRTH, eds.: Baalbek: Image and Monument, 1898–1998, Beirut 1998, XIV, 348 S. engl., franz. Text.

70. AMIDU SANNI: The Arabic Theory of Prosification and Versification. On ḥall and naẓm in Arabic Theoretical Discourse, Beirut 1988, XIII, 186 S.

71. ANGELIKA NEUWIRTH, BIRGIT EMBALÓ, FRIEDERIKE PANNEWICK: Kulturelle Selbstbehauptung der Palästinenser: Survey der modernen palästinensischen Dichtung, Beirut 2001, XV, 549 S.

72. STEPHAN GUTH, PRISKA FURRER, J. CHRISTOPH BÜRGEL, eds.: Conscious Voices. Concepts of Writing in the Middle East, Beirut 1999, XXI, 332 S. dt., engl., franz. Text.

73. Türkische Welten 4. SURAYA FAROQHI, CHRISTOPH K. NEUMANN, eds.: The Illuminated Table, the Prosperous House. Food and Shelter in Ottoman Material Culture, Beirut 2003, 352 S., 25 Abb.

74. BERNARD HEYBERGER, CARSTEN WALBINER, eds.: Les Européens vus par les Libanais à l'époque ottomane, Beirut 2002, VIII, 244 S.

75. Türkische Welten 5. TOBIAS HEINZELMANN: Die Balkankrise in der osmanischen Karikatur. Die Satirezeitschriften Karagöz, Kalem und Cem 1908–1914, Beirut 1999, 290 S. Text, 77 Abb., 1 Karte.

76. THOMAS SCHEFFLER, ed.: Religion between Violence and Reconciliation, Beirut 2002, XIV, 578 S. engl. u. franz. Text.

77. ANGELIKA NEUWIRTH, ANDREAS PFLITSCH, eds.: Crisis and Memory in Islamic Societies, Beirut 2001, XII, 540 S.

78. FRITZ STEPPAT: Islam als Partner: Islamkundliche Aufsätze 1944–1996, Beirut 2001, XXX, 424 S., 8 Abb.

79. PATRICK FRANKE: Begegnung mit Khidr. Quellenstudien zum Imaginären im traditionellen Islam, Beirut 2000, XV, 620 S., 23 Abb.

80. LESLIE A. TRAMONTINI: „East is East and West is West"? Talks on Dialogue in Beirut, Beirut 2006, 222 S.

81. THOMAS SCHEFFLER: Der gespaltene Orient: Orientbilder und Orientpolitik der deutschen Sozialdemokratie von 1850 bis 1950. In Vorbereitung.

82. Türkische Welten 6. GÜNTER SEUFERT, JACQUES WAARDENBURG, eds.: Türkischer Islam und Europa, Istanbul 1999, 352 S. dt., engl. Text.

83. JEAN-MAURICE FIEY: Al-Qiddīsūn as-Suryān, Beirut 2005, 358 S., 5 Karten.

84. Türkische Welten 7. ANGELIKA NEUWIRTH, JUDITH PFEIFFER, BÖRTE SAGASTER, eds.: The Ghazal as a Genre of World Literature II: The Ottoman Ghazal in its Historical Context. Würzburg 2006, XLIX, 340 S.

85. Türkische Welten 8. BARBARA PUSCH, ed.: Die neue muslimische Frau: Standpunkte & Analysen, Beirut 2001, 326 S.

86. Türkische Welten 9. ANKE VON KÜGELGEN: Inszenierung einer Dynastie – Geschichtsschreibung unter den frühen Mangiten Bucharas (1747–1826), Beirut 2002, XII, 518 S.

87. OLAF FARSCHID: Islamische Ökonomik und Zakat. In Vorbereitung.

88. JENS HANSSEN, THOMAS PHILIPP, STEFAN WEBER, eds.: The Empire in the City: Arab Provincial Capitals in the Late Ottoman Empire, Beirut 2002, X, 375 S., 71 Abb.

89. THOMAS BAUER, ANGELIKA NEUWIRTH, eds.: Ghazal as World Literature I: Migrations and Transformations of a Literary Genre, Beirut 2005, 447 S.

90. AXEL HAVEMANN: Geschichte und Geschichtsschreibung im Libanon des 19. und 20. Jahrhunderts: Formen und Funktionen des historischen Selbstverständnisses, Beirut 2002, XIV, 341 S.

91. HANNE SCHÖNIG: Schminken, Düfte und Räucherwerk der Jemenitinnen: Lexikon der Substanzen, Utensilien und Techniken, Beirut 2002, XI, 415 S., 130 Abb., 1 Karte.

92. BIRGIT SCHÄBLER: Aufstände im Drusenbergland. Ethnizität und Integration einer ländlichen Gesellschaft Syriens vom Osmanischen Reich bis zur staatlichen Unabhängigkeit 1850-1949, Beirut 2004, 315 S. arab. Text, 2 Karten.

93. AS-SAYYID KĀẒIM B. QĀSIM AL-ḤUSAINĪ AR-RAŠTĪ: Risālat as-sulūk fī l-aḫlāq wa-l-aʿmāl. Hrsg. von Waḥīd Bihmardī, Beirut 2004, 7 S. engl., 120 S. arab. Text.

94. JACQUES AMATEIS SDB: Yūsuf al-Ḫāl wa-Maǧallatuhu „Šiʿr". In Zusammenarbeit mit Dār al-Nahār, Beirut 2004, 313 S. arab. Text.

95. SUSANNE BRÄCKELMANN: „Wir sind die Hälfte der Welt!" Zaynab Fawwāz (1860-1914) und Malak Ḥifnī Nāṣif (1886-1918) – zwei Publizistinnen der frühen ägyptischen Frauenbewegung, Beirut 2004, 295 S. dt., 16 S. arab., 4 S. engl. Text.

96. THOMAS PHILIPP, CHRISTOPH SCHUMANN, eds.: From the Syrian Land to the State of Syria and Lebanon, Beirut 2004, 366 S. engl. Text.

97. HISTORY, SPACE AND SOCIAL CONFLICT IN BEIRUT: THE QUARTER OF ZOKAK EL-BLAT, Beirut 2005, XIV, 348 S. engl. Text, 80 S. farb. Abb., 5 Karten.

98. ABDALLAH KAHIL: The Sultan Ḥasan Complex in Cairo 1357-1364. A Case Study in the Formation of Mamluk Style, Beirut 2008, 398 S., 158 Farbtaf.

99. OLAF FARSCHID, MANFRED KROPP, STEPHAN DÄHNE, eds.: World War One as remembered in the countries of the Eastern Mediterranean, Würzburg 2006, XIII, 452 S. engl. Text, 17 Abb.

100. MANFRED S. KROPP, ed.: Results of contemporary research on the Qurʾān. The question of a historio-critical text of the Qurʾān, Beirut 2007, 198 S, engl., franz. Text.

101. JOHN DONOHUE SJ, LESLIE TRAMONTINI, eds.: Crosshatching in Global Culture: A Dictionary of Modern Arab Writers. An Updated English Version of R. B. Campbell's "Contemporary Arab Writers", 2 Bde., Beirut 2004, XXIV, 1215 S. engl. Text.

102. MAURICE CERASI, et alii, eds.: Multicultural Urban Fabric and Types in the South and Eastern Mediterranean, Beirut 2007, 269 S. engl., franz. Text, zahlr. Abb., Karten.

103. MOHAMMED MARAQTEN: Altsüdarabische Texte auf Holzstäbchen. In Vorbereitung.

104. AXEL HAVEMANN: Geschichte und Geschichtsschreibung (BTS 90). Arab. Übersetzung. In Vorbereitung.

105. SUSANNE BRÄCKELMANN: „Wir sind die Hälfte der Welt" (BTS 95). Arab. Übersetzung. In Vorbereitung.

106. MATTHIAS VOGT: Figures de califes entre histoire et fiction – al-Walīd b. Yazīd et al-Amīn dans la représentation de l'historiographie arabe de l'époque abbaside, Beirut 2006, 362 S.

107. HUBERT KAUFHOLD, ed.: Georg Graf: Christlicher Orient und schwäbische Heimat. Kleine Schriften, 2 Bde., Beirut 2005, XLVIII, 823 S.

108. LESLIE TRAMONTINI, CHIBLI MALLAT, eds.: From Baghdad to Beirut... Arab and Islamic Studies in honor of John J. Donohue sj., Beirut 2007, 502 S. engl., franz., arab. Text.

109. RICHARD BLACKBURN, ed.: Journey to the Sublime Porte. The Arabic Memoir of a Sharifian Agent's Diplomatic Mission to the Ottoman Imperial Court in the era of Suleyman the Magnificent, Beirut 2005, 366 S.

110. STEFAN REICHMUTH, FLORIAN SCHWARZ, eds.: Zwischen Alltag und Schriftkultur: Horizonte des Individuellen in der arabischen Literatur des 17. und 18. Jahrhunderts, Beirut 2008, 204 S., Abb.

111. JUDITH PFEIFFER, MANFRED KROPP, eds.: Theoretical Approaches to the Transmission and Edition of Oriental Manuscripts, Würzburg 2006, 335 S., 43 Abb.

112. LALE BEHZADI, VAHID BEHMARDI, eds.: The Evolution of Artistic Classical Arabic Prose. Im Druck.

113. SOUAD SLIM: The Greek Orthodox Waqf in Lebanon during the Ottoman Period, Beirut 2007, 265 S., maps, plates.
114. HELEN SADER, MANFRED KROPP, MOHAMMED MARAQTEN, eds.: Proceedings of the Conference on Economic and Social History of Pre-Islamic Arabia. In Vorbereitung.
115. DENIS HERMANN, SABRINA MERVIN, eds.: Courants et dynamiques chiites à l'époque moderne (1800-1925). In Vorbereitung.
116. LUTZ GREISIGER, CLAUDIA RAMMELT, JÜRGEN TUBACH, eds.: Edessa in hellenistisch-römischer Zeit: Religion, Kultur und Politik zwischen Ost und West. Im Druck.
117. MARTIN TAMCKE, ed.: Christians and Muslims in Dialogue in the Islamic Orient of the Middle Ages, Beirut 2007, 210 S. dt., engl. Text.
118. MAHMOUD HADDAD, et alii, eds.: Towards a Cultural History of Bilad al-Sham in the Mamluk Era. Prosperity or Decline, Tolerance or Persecution? Im Druck.
119. TARIF KHALIDI, et alii, eds.: Al-Jahiz: A Muslim Humanist for our time. Im Druck.
120. FĀRŪQ ḤUBLUṢ: Abḥāṯ fī tārīḫ wilāyat Ṭarābulus ibbān al-ḥukm al-Uṯmānī, Bairūt 2007, 252 S.
121. STEFAN KNOST: Die Organisation des religiösen Raums in Aleppo. Die Rolle der islamischen Stiftungen in der Gesellschaft einer Provinzhauptstadt des Osmanischen Reiches. In Vorbereitung.
122. RALPH BODENSTEIN, STEFAN WEBER: Ottoman Sidon. The Changing Fate of a Mediterranean Port City. In Vorbereitung.
123. JOHN DONOHUE: Robert Campbells Aᶜlām al-adab al-ᶜarabī (Arbeitstitel). In Vorbereitung.
124. ANNE MOLLENHAUER: Mittelhallenhäuser im Bilād aš-Šām des 19. Jahrhunderts (Arbeitstitel). In Vorbereitung.
126. MARTIN TAMCKE, ed.: Christliche Gotteslehre im Orient seit dem Aufkommen des Islams bis zur Gegenwart, Beirut 2008, 224 S. dt. u. engl. Text.

* Vergriffen

Die Unterreihe „Türkische Welten" geht in die unabhängige Publikationsreihe des Orient-Instituts Istanbul „Istanbuler Texte und Studien" über.


Orient-Institut Beirut
Rue Hussein Beyhum, Zokak el-Blat,
P.O.B. 11-2988, Beirut - Lebanon
Tel.: 01-359424, Fax: 01-359176
e-mail: oib-bib@oidmg.org
homepage: www.oidmg.org

Vertrieb in Deutschland:
ERGON Verlag GmbH
Keesburgstr. 11
D-97074 Würzburg
Tel: 0049-931-280084, Fax: 0049-931-282872
e-mail: service@ergon-verlag.de
homepage: www.ergon-verlag.de

Vertrieb im Libanon:
al-Furat
Hamra Street
Rasamny Building
P.O.Box: 113-6435 Beirut
Tel: 00961-1-750054, Fax: 00961-1-750053
e-mail: info@alfurat.com

Stand: November 2008